✦ Scrolls of Testimony ✦

Samuel Bak, *The Family*, 1974

SCROLLS OF TESTIMONY

✣ ABBA KOVNER ✣

Translated by Eddie Levenston
Illustrations by Samuel Bak

THE JEWISH PUBLICATION SOCIETY
PHILADELPHIA
2001 ✣ 5761

The Jewish Publication Society
2100 Arch Street, 2nd floor
Philadelphia, PA 19103
www.jewishpub.org

Design and composition by Scott-Martin Kosofsky
at The Philidor Company, Cambridge, Massachusetts.
Text set in Philidor Schmidt, Metro, and Koch Antiqua.
Printed in Canada.

Photo, page 22, reprinted by permission of Institute of Contemporary History and Wiener Library Limited. The following publishers have generously given permission to excerpt from copyrighted works: From "Hachnisini Tachat Knafeich," by Chaim Nachman Bialik, ©DVIR Publishing, reprinted by permission of DVIR Publishing House and The Institute for the Translation of Hebrew Literature. "Babii Yar," by Yevgenyi Yevtushenko, reprinted by permission of Marion Boyars, Publishers, Ltd. From "My Little Sister," by Abba Kovner, translated by Shirley Kaufman, from *My Little Sister and Selected Poems*, © 1986 Oberlin College Press, reprinted by permission of Oberlin College Press. From *Survival in Auschwitz*, by Primo Levi, translated by Stuart Woolf, translation copyright © 1959 by Orion Press, Inc., © 1958 by Giulio Einaudi editore S.P.A., reprinted by permission of Viking Penguin, a division of Penguin Putnam, Inc. From "Glost Zikh Mir Tsav Tan A Tfila," by Avraham Sutzkover, © Avraham Sutzkover; "Shir Hapartizanim," by Hirsh Glick, © Hirsh Glick; and "Lifnei Shaar Haafel," by David Fogel, © David Fogel; reprinted by permission of Acum House. From the diaries of Zelig Kalmanovitch and Hermann Kruk, reprinted by permission of YIVO Institute for Jewish Research.

01 02 03 04 05 06 07 08 09 10 10 9 8 7 6 5 4 3 2 1

Library of Congress Cataloging-in-Publication Data
Kovner, Abba. 1918-1987
 [Megilot ha-'edut. English]
 Scrolls of testimony / Abba Kovner; translated by Eddie Levenston.
  p.cm.
 ISBN: 0-8276-0710-5
    0-8276-0723-7 (gift edition)
  1. Holocaust, Jewish (1939-1945)—Fiction. 2. Holocaust, Jewish (1939-1945)—Literary collections. I. Levenston, Edward A. II. Title
 PJ5054.K6 M4413 2001
 892.4'36—dc21

                                        00-059250

The publication of this book is made possible through major gifts from

The Memorial Foundation for Jewish Culture,

who initially supported this project

Judy and Michael Steinhardt, Jewish Life Network

Conference on Jewish Material Claims Against Germany

The Lucius N. Littauer Foundation

as well as contributions by

Beverly Franzblau Baker, in memory of Morris D. Baker

Dr. and Mrs. Sylvan Gross

Sam Halpern and Ari Halpern

✦ Contents ✦

✤ Foreword ✤

The appearance of an English translation of Abba Kovner's already classic *Megillot Ha-Edut* (Scrolls of Testimony) is a moment of joy and liturgical triumph for world Jewry. Thanks to a fine English translation by Dr. Eddie Levenston, English-speaking Jewry can experience firsthand this stirring retelling of the Shoah, the Holocaust. This is also an opportunity to take a measure of the man, Abba Kovner—partisan, poet, prophet, public intellectual, essayist, educator, moral gadfly, and secular rebbe par excellence.

Says the Talmud: "Each generation [has] its own [distinctive] wise ones . . . each generation [has] its own [distinctive] interpreters. . . ." Abba Kovner was one of those rare historic wise men of the generations. We should note that it takes exceptional greatness of wisdom to attain understanding sufficient to guide a generation filled with events of such historic magnitude as the Shoah and the rebirth of the State of Israel that will shape the millennia to come. Kovner's sagacity, combined with his pedagogic genius, enabled him to play a seminal role in the creation of Beit Hatefutsot (the Museum of the Diaspora), a path-breaking institution of historical memory and a pioneering museum in that it uses narrative (rather than historical artifacts) to communicate the essence of Jewish history. Kovner understood that education should be experienced not only in the universities or in the *yeshivot*, but through informal channels as well. An effective educational message and method had to reach every kind of Jew—adults and children alike—and bring them together. This wisdom and educational insight led him to write the book that lies before you.

Kovner applied his profundity to an astonishing range of topics in every area of life. Whence came Abba's philosopher's stone that gave him insight everywhere?

He once said, "Millions stood on the mouth of the abyss. Hundreds saw it, the abyss. And only tens understood it." He was one of those few who understood it. During the Shoah, his early insight that everyone was going to die freed him to envision the possibility of military resistance at a time when senior leadership and people with far more experience than he still believed that such resistance could only bring catastrophe. That moment when one saw the failure not only of life, but of the friends and of the comrades-in-arms, and of the other philosophies that could not absorb so dissonant a truth gave him a wisdom that never left him. The yawning gulf of the Shoah did not drive him to give up; rather, it gave him very deep understanding.

His wisdom was that of a person without illusions. He had stood on the brink of the abyss, and the force of that moment stripped away so many of the social constructions of reality that buffer people's lives but skew their perceptions. That moment—that eternity—permanently liberated Kovner from many of the ideological and personal self-deceptions that cloud most people's judgment.

Few faiths were able to guide people adequately during the Holocaust. This realization gave Kovner the strength not to give up his faith but to accept it, often with eyes that saw all its limitations. Henceforth, he was able to see what was good, as well as what was bad, in every political group and ideological position. He was a man of Ha-Shomer Ha-Tza'ir (a secular, socialist Zionist movement), which never weakened or backed away from its position. Yet because of his lack of illusions about Ha-Shomer Ha-Tza'ir and about the anticlerical, political-social Left in Jewish life, he could simultaneously value the role of faith, tradition, observance, and religion in Jewish history. Everywhere, his vision was binocular. As one can see in the narrative of the Beit Hatefutsot exhibition (most dramatically in the culminating section on the new Jewish state), Kovner was convinced that the State of Israel was the climax of Jewish history and the place that every Jew had to be. Yet he did not fall into simplistic *shlilat ha-golah* (the negation of the Diaspora) or into illusions about American Jewry disappearing in accordance with Zionist stereotypes about the future of the Diaspora.

He said in his essay "Shliḥut Am," "To realize our historic duty, we must unify all of the creative building forces in the Jewish nation. By understanding the catastrophe and the danger, we must attain a unity of soul, *aḥdut neshamah*, of the Jewish people, as a primary condition of national self-defense." That unifying quality led him to embrace the whole Jewish tradition while simultaneously following a nonreligious lifestyle and a political orientation that was completely different from that of most of the people who seemingly embodied Judaism itself. (The ability to transcend ideologic lines guided him and made him a penetrating critic *and* an instructive supporter of many different types of projects to build Jewish life.)

He embraced that totality, of left and right, without self-deception and without anger. He was able to see the delusions that others had about non-Jews and about Arabs without turning anti-gentile or anti-Arab. On the contrary, he remained committed to humanitarian goals all his life. He had no illusions about religious extremism, yet he saw the purity of the lives of the ultrareligious and the strength of traditional observance and its role in Jewish culture and Jewish history. That is why he could reach out across religious and secular lines simultaneously.

Kovner had the courage of those in the Shoah who, like him, fought for the sake of memory, not out of bravado or a feeling of superiority to those who did not fight. He said in "Shliḥut Am," describing what it meant to arise and organize armed resistance: "We only wanted to die. But to die in order to live on in your [the Jewish people's] memory." He deeply regretted that he had ever written the phrase "as sheep to the slaughter." The aphorism was written to goad the ghetto fighters and the ghetto residents to give up their illusions. Used for that purpose, it was appropriate. But when taken out of context decades later to judge and "condemn" those victims who did not take up arms against the Nazis, it came across as critical of those who did not fight, implying that they were inferior or weak. That was a total misreading of the phrase; those who used it only proved that they did not begin to understand the spiritual greatness of the people who simply lived and died during that time.

One night in 1977, I heard Kovner speak at a seminar at Zachor, the Holocaust memorial project of CLAL—the National Jewish Center for Learning and Leadership. David Roskies asked him about the passage in Zelig Kalmanovitch's diary of the Vilna ghetto that denounced him. Kovner dropped his guard and he spoke of what it meant to him and his young friends (Kovner was twenty-three then) to realize that by undertaking armed resistance you were endangering the whole ghetto, that the only excuse for such action was that all the Jews were going to die anyway—but how difficult it was to live with that kind of a truth! I often reflect on his comment that, postwar, every time he was introduced as a hero of the Jewish people, what went through his mind was the thought: "Am I this Abba Kovner, the hero? Or am I Abba Kovner, the man who betrayed his mother, who left her behind to go to the forests to fight?" What incredible courage it took to live with that memory and not betray one's own heroic insight, nor compromise one's actions and criticize the resistance, as Kalmanovitch did! Kovner knew that he had made the right decision, but he also knew the moral cost of that decision. One should not be allowed to talk about the Holocaust or about resistance and "sheep to slaughter" without in some way sharing and living that kind of a life. This remarkable understanding of every *sitz im leben* (original context) enabled Kovner to enter into the experience of the *Judenrat* (the Jewish councils that organized Jewish life under the Nazis and their leaders) and to offer a compassionate embrace and forgiving judgment, as he does in *Scrolls of Testimony*.

Abba Kovner understood that after the Shoah there had to be a fundamental change. In "Shliḥut Am" he wrote: "To change ways of thinking, to change ways of understanding, not just a policy here, or a policy there." He came to Israel determined to carry out that fundamental change. With other survivors he tried to organize a political approach to transform the State of Israel and the Jewish people. But he did not succeed. He was not political enough to carry out his vision, and the truth is that hardly anybody was ready for the kind of basic transformation that the event of the Shoah really demanded.

But when he gave up his political agenda, he did not turn bitter. He could accept defeat and disappointment because he had an extraordinary lack of ego. I cannot think of a person equal to Kovner in accomplishments who worried so little about getting recognition; I cannot imagine anyone else who had the strength to testify about the Holocaust—after what he had gone through—and not be concerned about whether or not he would get the attention he deserved. Nor have I ever met anyone who was so little marked by regret for missing or being denied opportunities to educate and guide us all.

If Kovner did not accomplish his goal as a politician, then he would work at it as a poet, then as a writer, and finally as an educator. He wrote in "Shlihut Am": "Did they understand, that with a standard philosopher's education, no matter how beautiful or good, we cannot fulfill the mission of the generation?" He understood that. And because he was a man of extraordinary creativity, when one path was closed to him, he responded with the creation of new institutions and educational methods, with poetic force and fresh thinking.

He watched with concern as Israel began to evolve toward what today is called post-Zionism, a dismissal of special expectations or any claimed national unity based on a sense of mission for the Jewish state, on the grounds that Israel is now an established, "normal" nation. He regretted and fought the growing polarization of Left and Right, of religious and secular, of Zionist and post-Zionist. He felt that the Shoah, properly understood, could be an ongoing source of education for life, for unity, for humanistic morality, for dealing with the necessities and temptations of power. He concluded that the Shoah was not yet incorporated sufficiently into the mainstream of Jewish culture, religion, and memory. He knew that a cornerstone of the Shoah memory was missing. With his profound grasp of Jewish history and tradition, he understood that there was a need for a liturgy and a narrative that would make Shoah remembrance the internalized possession of an entire people. In 2000 years of exile, the combination of annual commemoration dates and *megillah* (scroll) readings had made both the catastrophe of the First and Second Temples' destruction and the redemption from the genocide of Purim permanent elements in Jewish historical memory. The holiday of Purim and the fast of Tishah be-Av, the rescue from Haman and the victimization of Rome had been woven into the warp and woof of Jewish culture and thus indelibly impressed in Jewish identity. The same must be done for the Shoah, lest its memory be lost when the survivor generation passes away.

Kovner turned this way and that way and saw there was no person who had successfully undertaken this liturgical task. So, at the end of his life, he set about to write a narrative of the Holocaust that could serve as a liturgy. To strengthen its impact, he decided to incorporate learning into the experience by writing narrative, notes, and source citations that would ring the text much as a page of Talmud is surrounded by its commentaries and other notes. When he started the project, he did not know that throat cancer was to strike him down. But when he learned of his fate, he raced to complete the work. While there are some incomplete sections and the full narrative was not realized, important elements were completed. He left us with a liturgical masterpiece.

Kovner did not explain how he planned to use *Scrolls of Testimony;* all he wrote was that it is "... a reader ... for the individual, the family, the community." Kovner was so suffused with the texts, language, and models of the tradition that he was able to evoke past paradigms of liturgy and memory while writing a chronicle of the greatest tragedy in Jewish history. Yet the anthology is too long to be read in its entirety in any normal service. Possibly he intended that sections be read aloud during Yom ha-Shoah (Holocaust Memorial Day) services, and that the entire text be studied over the course of the year or read during extended study sessions such as *layl shimurim* (all-night seminars) that he developed as a medium for intensive adult learning of Jewish tradition.

Scrolls of Testimony brilliantly solves a number of conundrums that tax our capacity to commemorate the Holocaust appropriately. As Gershom Scholem has pointed out: "In the past, historical events in themselves have not shaped Jewish values (and the liturgy) as much as the midrashic or folk representation of these events." One of the great moments of the classic Yom Kippur liturgy—the Ten Martyrs, which makes up the martyrology section of the service—is a legendary account of the death of ten of the greatest Rabbis of the Mishnah. The killings are telescoped, interwoven with legend, and brought together for dramatic unity—as if all the Rabbis were executed at the same time and by a coherent plan. (Another version of the Ten Martyrs story, with significant differences in the telling, is a highlight of the Tishah be-Av Kinot service.) Yet anti-Semites, unrepentant Nazis, and revisionists driven by hatred wait in the wings to deny the factual truth of the most demonically planned and most heavily documented crime in history. Any imaginative addition to the facts, even if well intentioned, could be "refuted" and then used to undercut the credibility of the actual record.

Moreover, in dealing with the Holocaust, embellishment is offensive. To try to make the burning of children into the stuff of edifying drama would be morally repugnant;

to accomplish it, the writer would have to achieve a clinical detachment more appropriate for the cold-blooded, indifferent bystanders. Any attempt to turn the nakedness of defenseless mothers into emotional currency would more likely end up in exploitation and sleaze than in transfiguration. Imaginary scenes from the Holocaust have already been used for purposes of pornography or to give pseudo-depth to standard literature.

On the other hand, it is almost impossible to maintain objectivity when dealing with the Holocaust. The testimony of survivors is normally the most reliable source of information, but in this circumstance such testimony is not only limited by their partial view of what happened, but it is also biased, colored by their own perceived guilt. These innocent victims feel guilty for having survived, whereas many murderers and indifferent bystanders are filled with a sense of their own innocence. This paradoxical fact colors all accounts of the Shoah. Since most of the records and the pictures of the Holocaust were kept by the Nazis and their allies, anybody who presents their documentation only may be giving over the Nazi-approved version. What the Nazis left out may be part of their total war on the Jews. Thus, Raul Hilberg's masterwork volumes on the killing process, *The Destruction of the European Jews,* which are based on the Nazi records, understate the level of Jewish resistance and dignity during those terrible years. Furthermore, some historical treatments convert these events—events so powerful that to touch them is to risk moral or emotional electrocution—into a routine recounting that mitigates the cruelty and betrays the actual suffering.

Kovner's response to the challenge of capturing the reality of the Holocaust was to tell its story from within that world, from the vantage point of many who were there, so that it rises above the limits of any one person. Told from the perspective and with the voices of a *minyan* (prayer quorum) who lived through all or most of the Holocaust, the account is at once devastating in its realism and healing in its understanding. While the events have been shaped as narrative, they are the unembroidered truth. Kovner's account was selected and condensed from the total record; every detail is accurate, documented by firsthand evidence and often derived from eyewitness testimony. In sum: The art is artless; the elements of narrative are elemental. The effect is overwhelming.

The decision to write five *megillot,* or scrolls, clearly reflects the fact that there are five *megillot* in the Hebrew Bible. Of the biblical scrolls, only one, Lamentations, is focused on destruction; namely, the destruction of the First Temple. By choosing to write five scrolls, Kovner's implicit message is that the Holocaust goes beyond the destruction of the Temple in its vastness, intensity, and implications. Unlike Albert H. Friedlander's *Megillat Ha-Shoah* (Scrolls of the Holocaust), whose five-chapter structure imitates Lamentations, Kovner's account parallels all five scrolls in extent but none of them in

structure. (Note also that Kovner's title *Scrolls of Testimony* is more modest than Friedlander's; less is more.) Just as the Holocaust is at once overwhelmingly continuous and
totally distinctive from past tragedies, so is *Scrolls of Testimony* in relation to the ages-
old historical narratives that make up Jewish sacred literature. In literary sophistication
and narrative technique, in their portraits of individuals, in their unrelenting impact,
the *megillot* are inescapably modern. In their unadorned account, in fablelike simplicity,
in the elements of witness and testimony, they come right out of the ancient world of
saga in whose midst the Bible record emerged and in whose nimbus it speaks. The
megillot beg to be read aloud, to be chanted, to be encountered, to have *midrashim*
written about them.

One cannot plunge in medias res into the world of Auschwitz any more than one can
stand before the soaring flames of Divine Revelation on Mount Sinai again without
being gradually ushered in. Therefore, Kovner's first scroll begins with an invocation
poem to be spoken silently before reading the scroll:

The Author speaks

This scroll is different from all other scrolls. In all other scrolls, we recount
   what happened to our fathers and forefathers in ancient days.
In this scroll we tell what happened to our fathers and to us in the generation
   of Auschwitz.
The slaughtered Jewish people speaks, in silence and in words, to the living
   Jewish people:
You who were unable to save us, listen now with all your heart to our testi-
   mony; it is all that remains of our lives.
Try to understand the meaning of destruction and what words would have
   strengthened our spirit at the moment of parting.

The Scroll speaks to the Reader:

Do not regard this testimony as an inspiration for hatred. By the rivers of
   Europe we sat down and wept when our turn came to be murdered. By the
   chimneys of the crematorium
                         even there
                                        we preserved scraps of incinerated
   time and we pondered the future as we thought of you. . . .
Do you have a spare moment to think of us
   innocent of crime and unashamed?

The prologue that follows asserts that in every generation, humanity's evil urges burst forth. History is full of mass murders, from ancient tribal enmities to the Mongol massacres, from medieval holy wars to the extermination of the Indians and the Armenian genocide. All the rivers of blood run to the sea, and the sea of death flows around the whole world and flows back again. Yet the Holocaust was an organized annihilation whose equal the human race has not seen. This was neither the rampage of rabble nor the desperate revenge of the oppressed; this was no atrocity driven by religious frenzy or revolutionary fervor that would stop at nothing. This was total extermination of a people undertaken by government decision, pursued day and night without pause for holy day and with no exception for age or gender or health or location. This was carried out as a policy overriding all other considerations in the high noon of the twentieth century.

The introduction is written and laid out in a style that evokes the Bible. Its enumeration of the hunting groups: "The SS and the SA and the SD and the Gestapo; the Einsatzgruppen and the Hitlerjugend, the Wehrmacht . . . and the "Blue" Police of Poland . . . and the Ypatingas from Lithuania and . . . the men of Vichy in France; and the Nazis in Austria and Mussolini's Fascists in Italy . . . the Iron Guard in Romania and the party of the Arrow-Cross in Hungary; the Ustashi in Yugoslavia . . ." at once summons up the ten sons of Haman and the list of unclean birds of prey in Leviticus.

The prologue tells the story of the Holocaust in highly condensed form as a historical chronicle: from the beginning of Hitler's reign through segregation and exclusion; from mass shootings to ghettoization and roundups; from forced labor and gassings to pulling the gold teeth and burning the bodies; from mass transports in cattle cars to death marches. Jewish response is portrayed from the self-deceptive patriotism of German and Italian Jews to the reality denials of Hungarian and East European Jews arriving before the gates of Auschwitz; from the persistence of teachers who continued to teach children in the face of death to the tenacity of those who collected and wrote down accounts of life in the face of oblivion.

Then *Scrolls of Testimony* turns to the telling of the tale. The first scroll focuses on Jews of Germany and the Baltic states on the fringe of that culture. A German father writes to his son who is abroad (significantly this chapter is titled "The Man with His Head on the Block Continues to Hope"). In a series of letters, the father, who runs the Jewish orphans' home in Dinslaken, describes the deterioration of the Jewish condition, culminating in the Kristallnacht pogrom. The burning of the synagogue and a roundup of Jews being shipped to Dachau climaxes in a stunning, humiliating beating of one Hugo Cohen, a distinguished veteran of World War I. Before the Nazi era, Cohen was given a place of honor at all patriotic public occasions since he was the only possessor of the Iron Cross, First Class, in Dinslakhen. "Jewish swine, where did you steal that medal?" swears the S.S. man who sets upon him for daring to wear this cross when the Jews are paraded through the streets on the way to the train to the camps.

The second and third scrolls, called "By the Waters of the Four Countries," capture the experience of Jews in Poland and Lithuania. These scrolls include two unforgettable portraits. One *parashah* (narrative potion), "The Travels of Dvora from Kalisz and Letters to Nowhere," tells of a young woman whose wanderings take her from refugee flight to love, relationship, and life in Warsaw and participation in the Vilna ghetto resistance. The character has in her not a little of Vitka Kovner, Abba's wife, colleague in resistance and lifelong partner. The other portrait, of Sha'ul, has in it not a little of Kovner's own experiences. Sha'ul recalls many happenings: recollections of childhood in a living Jewish community, memories of everyday life suffused with the glow of holiness, panicky days and devastating roundups in the ghetto, mass shootings and frantic hiding, and nostalgia of near-miss escapes from Nazis and service with partisans. His reveries are full of searing images: months of living hidden in a convent; narrow escapes accompanied by death on all sides; survival in the merciless forest, first amid hostile anti-Semitic partisans and then among fellow Jewish fighters.

In the fourth scroll, *"Ash of the Heavens,"* the opening *Does Birkenau Exist?* includes a cluster of personal accounts by a group of prisoners in the seventh block at Auschwitz. Block Seven was the last step before the gas chambers, yet these inmates retained their humanity and dignity as Jews. They include Raphael Habib, rabbi of Salonika, Greece, who survived the original selection by passing as a stevedore; Gonda Redlich, a Czechoslovakian *ḥalutz* (Zionist pioneer-in-training) who set up children's schools in Theresienstadt; and Nathan Cassuto, a member of the traditionalist branch of an aristocratic, assimilating Italian Jewish family. He was an ophthalmologist who turned to serving as a rabbi after he was expelled from the government clinic in which he worked. Each life portrait is indelibly etched. They exemplify the entire Jewish experience, yet they have the rawness and textured quality of life rather than of literary artifice. One gets a sense of the overflowing tide of evil and the infinite sands of suffering, the countless daily acts of love and heroism, and the inescapable abandonments and despair that made up the mosaic of existence in the Holocaust.

The scrolls tackle incredibly difficult themes with feeling and dignity; for example, a portrait of *Judenrat* and how they worked is etched in unsparing detail and with compassionate understanding. One major section of the fifth scroll, "The Death March," was planned, but Kovner's hand was stilled by death before he could write it. The final chapter captures the postwar *briḥah* (illegal immigration) to Palestine and the cruel British war against the survivors and their deportation to Cyprus. The chapter is interspersed with the survivors' memories of their Shoah experiences and an account of life with the Jewish partisans that is stirring without romanticizing.

Three remarkable characteristics of these scrolls must be understood. The first is the use of words as recurrent narrative themes. Studded through the verses are hundreds of motif words that summon up biblical or other classic texts. Each association refracts the light and mirrors meanings back and forth between the present text and the classic source. This word method is used in the Hebrew Bible to give multiple meanings and textual interactions among many different narratives in it. It is also found in rabbinic midrash and modern Hebrew literature. In *Scrolls of Testimony,* such words give depth to the field of vision in each scene and add layers of historical meaning to every event. The language depicts the uniqueness of the moment and simultaneously reveals it to be the enactment of a repetitive scene from Jewish history.

Because only the Hebrew language carries these overtones, it is almost impossible to capture the full extent of this effect in translation, despite the fine work of Dr. Levenston. A few examples give an inkling, as in a reverie by a partisan on Jewish isolation: "Scholars will investigate and thinkers wise after the event will find it difficult to know how the people sat solitary between the walls, shouting in blood with no one to hear." (Compare this to Lamentations 1:1.) And in describing a party guided by a youthful Italian informer about to seize Nathan Cassuto: "The Italian officer, Mario Gazzini, who had shot Anna Maria, a German SS man and a Fascist youth [little child] guiding them . . . ." (Compare this to the classic messianic scene in Isaiah 14:6.)

In a scene depicting the life-endangering lashing of a prisoner for the "crime" of wearing tefillin (prayer boxes) in Auschwitz, the beating count is represented as follows: ". . . One and two. One and three. One and four. . . ."–evoking the classic liturgical retelling of the High Priest's repeated sprinklings during the Yom Kippur purification rite in the Holy of Holies. A Jewish woman reflecting on the unceasing evils visited on the head of Lithuanian Jewry recites a reverse *Dayenu* (the seder prayer that recounts God's overflowing miracles): "If our daughter had been captured by the Lithuanians and there had been no war–*Dayenu* (it would have been sufficient). If there had been a war and the wicked kingdom of Poland had fallen, and there had been no Soviet regime–*Dayenu.* If there had been a Soviet regime and the lovely big house had not burnt down–*Dayenu.*" Hundreds of such passages in the five scrolls are woven into a seamless web with the classic sources of the past.

The second characteristic is the scrolls' incorporation of a torrent of unforgettable vignettes so overwhelming in their repeated impact as to suddenly make real the classic Jewish outcry in extremis: "The waters have risen to [the point of drowning] the soul!" In every aspect of the Holocaust, Kovner has found the telling detail that releases the flood of our emotions. For example, there is Leo der Grosse, a defiant Jewish orphan in Dinslaken. When a Nazi teacher enters for the first time, he introduces himself: "My name is Levine, but I am not of the tribe of Moses." Leo der Grosse (in a stage whisper): "Thank God, until now we've never had a donkey in the class." The teacher calls him up and slaps his face. Without hesitation, Leo der Grosse returns the teacher's slap forcefully. (After Kristallnacht, Big Leo is sent to the camps.) Describing the constant search for the right personal category to protect one from selection, and the constant German shifts and reversals, Kovner writes: "Every personal detail seemed fateful—age, sex, occupation, refugee or citizen of the Reich—but no one knew which detail would seal his fate when the day arrived."

The text continually reveals the shattering event that breaks down all routine, smashes defenses, and breaks the heart. A thousand scenes haunt the mind:

The blood of a Jewish woman whose throat has been cut mixing with the trickle of rain that flows beneath the body and gradually staining the water red; the Italian Jews facing a roundup who know that "it can't happen here"; the Jewish children, accepted and hidden in a convent on condition that they not make trouble, who refuse to eat pork and to deny their name; Berele Lopatin, the *Judenrat* head who refuses to send one hundred Jews to an unknown—but really known—fate . . . and the Nazis back down; a devoted Jewish father, suddenly destroyed by the announcement that 200 able-minded men including him will be spared but the other 6000 ghetto Jews will be selected, ignores the permission to go home and walks over the line of those whose lives were spared, without going to say goodbye to his wife and family; a starving young girl who hides the body of her four-year-old brother who died of hunger under her bed for a week so she can use his ration card—until she is felled by the smell of decay; a father who pulls out his own gold-crowned teeth to barter for life-giving medicine for his son; the Germans who save the lives of a couple who have slashed their own wrists—and then send them to the shooting pits to establish the principle that it is the Germans who decide when Jews live and when they die; the inebriated feeling of the Vilna ghetto group that has just decided to organize and fight; the feelings of guilt and betrayal that assail those who must leave their parents behind to go to the forest to fight; the boy, sentenced to a few lashings for religious behavior, who refuses to cry out, so the blows are heaped on, up to fifty lashes, and afterward, close to death, he wearily says: "It was worth it"; a prisoner in Block Seven who sings an *El Male Raḥamim* (prayer for the dead) that at once defies humans and God; two brothers working as a team caught smuggling, each vies to convince the sadistic SS supervisor that *he* is the one who did it (the officer scornfully kills them both for daring to have courage at such a moment).

If divine inspiration is proven by power rather than by sponsorship, then this is holy writ.

Finally, an authentic scroll for the Holocaust should capture the experience of every kind of Jew with integrity. Only then can it speak to and for *Clal Yisrael,* for the unity and totality of the Jewish people. *Scrolls of Testimony* is marked by a deep understanding of the existential unity of the Jews, a oneness rooted in their common fate. Just such awareness is a thread that runs through all the portions of the scrolls. These strands guide us through the labyrinth of death that European Jewry wandered in from 1933 to 1945, and they manage to bring us out, shattered in spirit but whole in heart.

From the prologue:

"One and all they were marched through the streets, bareheaded or wearing *shtreimels,* those whose tunics were fastened with three buttons, and those who worried lest–God forbid–they lose the fourth button required by a different Hasidic court. And when they looked at the most recent arrivals, wearing stiff hats from Amsterdam and some deported from Budapest actually flaunting real top hats, they did not laugh or show surprise, for they saw the common heap where all the caps, bowlers, and *papachas* would end up."

Scenes:

An observant family takes four young road-weary, dirty, bloodstained secular *ḥalutzim* (pioneers) into their Sabbath meal without asking any questions.

Shmuel, a *ḥalutz* on the way to Palestine, walks from Warsaw to Kovel, where he faints from exhaustion. The religious family that rescues him finds that he has wrapped a Zionist flag around himself under his shirt in order to save it from the Nazis. "Some men wear a fringed garment [*tzitzit,* ritual fringes] close to their body, and some wear a flag," says the father. "Both kinds of men are serving God," whispers the mother.

The orphanage was one institution, perhaps unfortunately, the only one, where both Jewish languages, Hebrew and Yiddish, had equal status as languages of instruction; children sang both "Kinneret, Kinneret" and "Oyfn Pripetshik" and emerged unscathed.

Dolek, a Zionist underground movement leader, "organizes" and trades for wax to provide Sabbath candles for a group of his erstwhile women comrades who hold an *Oneg Shabbat* (Sabbath celebration ceremony) every Friday night in Auschwitz. But then Dolek is taken to his death, and for weeks, Eli, a young fair-haired assimilated boy from Paris whom Dolek has befriended, trades his own bread to provide the candles for these women he has never met, until his own death.

Two children of a deported Italian rabbi are placed in a convent and absorbed into its life. During the battle for liberation of the area, one of the boys, nine years old, is sent to get water; dodging bullets, he bumps into Eliahu Klatzkin, a member of Ha-Shomer Ha-Tza'ir and a hardcore secularist serving in the British army. The boy sees the Star of David on Eliahu's dog tag and whispers, "*Shema Yisra'el.*" Eliahu recovers the two orphans and returns them to their family.

There is an incredible level of empathy in the scrolls that enables Kovner, in the wisdom of old age, to present every experience with an understanding that surpasses understanding. Time and time again the scrolls pass up the easy victory of hindsight to see the deeper dignity of those who lived in the reality of the "planet Holocaust." How easy it would have been to mock the patriotism of Hugo Cohen, who marches to the train for Dachau wearing his Iron Cross. But even as he describes the rain of blows on Cohen's head, Kovner captures the majesty of the man: "But he continued to march with dignity, as though on parade for the last time." Kovner, who in his youth authored the famous stinging critique, "Do not go as sheep to the slaughter," now can present those *Judenrat,* who accommodated and temporized, yet tell their tale with absolute accuracy and compassionate understanding:

"It is not one of the easy tasks to be the leader of the Jews at such a time. A person awakens in the morning and finds that he is the representative of the Jews before Nazis and representative of the Nazis before his brothers, his people." In these pages, thousands go on death marches, thousands walk to the gas chambers. We are so deeply within their world that we live it and understand it and embrace it; we are not able to step outside of that world and (falsely) judge it. There are no easy escapes into blaming it all on modernity; nor is there any explaining away the Holocaust as an atavistic reversion to barbarism: "Explain it to me, how could it happen. In enlightened Europe, in the middle of the twentieth century, how could it happen?" asks one person. "It happened because we didn't believe it could happen!" answers his friend.

The account of the scrolls ends with the Israeli captain of an illegal immigration ship lecturing the passengers about the dangers of the forthcoming journey into a hostile sea, filled with blockading enemy ships. He offers the passengers a last chance to debark and seek asylum in another land. Do we not read here Kovner's prophetic call to the Jewish people who have now embarked on a historic voyage to freedom and power over the stormy seas of history? Sailing in waters as uncharted and unknown as the oceans were to the pioneering discoverers of new worlds in the fifteenth and sixteenth centuries, facing trackless seas filled with monsters more dangerous than the feverish imaginations of medieval superstition could have conjured up, can this people successfully pursue the goal of creating life overflowing? Can it build a just society without being crushed by evil or warped by hatred and arrogance along the way? The last words are those of Leo der Grosse, a survivor of Germany and Eastern Europe and the forest and the camps. He turns to Sha'ul and says: "Tell your friend he doesn't have to frighten us. We're Jews who are not afraid anymore. Tell him."

The inscription of the fifth scroll offers the true conclusion:

> The finish but not the end
> of the Scrolls of Testimony.

> "And more than I have told you is written here." (Mishnayot Yoma 7:1)

No words can ever contain the world of the Holocaust. But here, in verses that will be read as long as Jews live, is a passageway into that world. Whoever goes in will not return unchanged.

—IRVING GREENBERG

Irving Greenberg is president of Jewish Life Network, a Judy and Michael Steinhardt Foundation. He also serves as chairman of the United States Holocaust Memorial Council. Dr. Greenberg has written extensively on Jewish thought and religion and on American Jewish history. His books include *Theodore Roosevelt and Labor, 1900-1918* (Garland Publications, 1988), *The Jewish Way* (Summit Books, 1988), and *Living in the Image of God: Jewish Teachings to Perfect the World* (Jason Aronson, 1998).

Elements of this foreword are derived from the review of *Megillot Ha-Edut (*Scrolls of Testimony) in *The Jewish Way: Living the Holidays* (Summit Books, 1988).

❖ Acknowledgments ❖

W E ALL OWE A DEBT OF GRATITUDE to Vitka Kovner and her family, who persisted in their mission to make *Scrolls of Testimony* available first in Hebrew and now in English; to Dr. Eddie Levenston, who succeeded in translating them from the Hebrew; to Dr. Ellen Frankel, CEO and editor-in-chief of The Jewish Publication Society, and her staff, for undertaking the difficult and costly task of publishing so complex a book; and to Debra Tenzer, without whose indefatigable enthusiasm and ardent stewardship this English edition would not have been possible.

Thanks to Rabbi Doug Kahn, head of the San Francisco Jewish Community Relations Council, for his valuable insight; Aaron Breitbart, Senior Researcher at the Simon Wiesenthal Center, who helped with fact verification; Shirley Kaufman, award-winning poet, who translated Kovner's poetry, and Professor Hillel Daleski, Israel Prize winner for Literature—both dear friends of the Kovner family who helped find the translator for this edition. And to Rachel Levine, assistant to Rabbi Irving "Yitz" Greenberg, who was instrumental in obtaining funding; Aviva Kempner, producer of the award-winning film *Partisans of Vilna*, for her enthusiastic support; Rich Cohen, whose book *The Avengers: A Jewish War Story* describes Kovner's heroism and many of the events in *Scrolls of Testimony*; Jacob Snir, a close friend of the Kovner family and a great source of information about Kovner's life and the book; Dr. Irving D. Goldfein, head of Infomedia Judaica, an early enthusiastic supporter of the book who helped obtain funding for this project; Dr. Jerry Hochbaum, head of the Memorial Foundation for Jewish Culture and Abba Kovner's friend, who initiated this project almost twenty years ago.

Thanks also to Dr. Michael Berenbaum for his guidance; Dr. Shalom Luria, longtime Kovner family friend, who with great devotion put together all of Kovner's notes and edited the Hebrew edition (he is also the son of Zelig Kalmanovitch, whose diary is quoted in the book); Bernie and Sue Pucker of the Pucker Gallery in Boston, for bringing Sam Bak into the project; and to Sam Bak, a child of Vilna like Abba Kovner, whose artwork graces the cover and pages of the book.

And to the many donors, whose generous support made publication possible. Jewish history and Jewish tradition are in their debt.

May the rewards of all who gave of themselves so willingly to this project come in the form of thousands and tens of thousands of readers of these scrolls of testimony.

❖ Translator's Preface ❖

O F ALL THE MANY BOOKS written about the Holocaust, Abba Kovner's *Scrolls of Testimony* is unique both in form and content. Typographically, it dares to resemble the Talmud: each page of the book has a central body of text, surrounded by relevant accompanying documents of various kinds—statistical, biographical, historical, poetic. The central narrative tells the story of individuals caught up in the maelstrom of events that convulsed the world. Using a variety of fictional devices—from conventional third-person storytelling to the personal diary of a teenage orphan to letters from a father to his son—it exploits the power of fiction to grip those readers who would not trouble to consult what they would think of as a dry historical record or encyclopedia. The accompanying side notes provide the factual information required for a deeper understanding of the central story and strengthen the emotional impact with further eyewitness accounts of life in the death camps and poetic responses to personal bereavement.

In translating a work of such stylistic variety, I found it important to find and maintain appropriate styles for each of the different genres that contribute to the total impact of this remarkable work. The biographical accounts of Jewish writers and thinkers that shaped the worldview of pre–World War II Eastern European Jewry, the historical details in the various centers of Jewish settlement, the explanations of the various Yiddish, German, and Russian words without which the story would lose much of its vitality—all these additions to the central text constitute a mini-encyclopedia, and should read like one. It is there to be consulted, not read straight through from beginning to end. But the third-person narrative that forms the bulk of the central text from the beginning of the Second Scroll must grip the reader like a vise or it will fail in its purpose. Here, Kovner wrote in a rich Hebrew that draws on vocabulary from all the periods of historical development of the language: biblical, mishnaic, medieval, and modern. Even the syntax occasionally shifts. It moves from biblical tense sequences for the ongoing account of the wanderings of refugees across war-stricken Poland, reeling from the ferocity of the initial German attack, to a more modern, impressionistic string of present tenses that bring to life the daily routine of a Jewish village on a peaceful pre-war market day. I have aimed throughout for readability, for a story whose suspense will hold the reader's attention, however inevitable its tragic outcome may appear to be. I have done so even at the expense of occasionally failing to provide any English equivalent of the richness of vocabulary that characterizes the Hebrew.

I have also not hesitated to adjust the contents of the side notes, adding and subtracting according to the needs of the English-speaking reader, who does not need to be told that Macy's is a large department store in Manhattan, but who may not grasp the significance of a bedtime injunction to "not forget to say the *Shema.*" Moreover, all Hebrew literature is saturated with references to the Bible, and many poets and writers exploit the overtones that such references can give to their texts. Kovner is no exception. I have not identified every such reference, but I have felt it appropriate, in many instances, to supply more than Kovner gives the Hebrew reader. One example is the story of how Sonia Soltanek, despite the need to put in a full day's work outside the ghetto at the airfield, struggles to get her three sons ready for the train journey that will inevitably lead to their deaths. The narrator notes laconically: ". . . the work was hard but the mother of sons rejoices." Kovner takes it for granted that his Hebrew-speaking reader will hear the words of Psalm 113, the first psalm in the liturgical sequence known as *Hallel:* "He sets the childless woman among her household as a happy mother of children. Hallelujah." The irony is heartrending.

It had always been Abba Kovner's hope that *Scrolls of Testimony* would become the one book on the Holocaust that would have a place on the bookshelf of every Jewish household, whatever the language of the family. As he said in the lecture included in his introduction, it is an "educational imperative for the remnant of the generation that survived Auschwitz . . . to try to inscribe on the memory of coming generations" the memory of what happened. Perhaps others would have used the words "sacred duty" rather that "educational imperative"; it is not by chance that in form the book emulates the Talmud, or that there are five "scrolls," corresponding to the five *megillot* in the Bible (Song of Songs, Ruth, Lamentations, Ecclesiastes, and Esther). Much of the success of *Scrolls of Testimony* derives from the appropriateness of the talmudic layout to the author's unique purpose. The suspense of the ostensibly fictional narrative ensures that it will be read. The attested facts of his own life and heroic leadership of the revolt in the Vilna ghetto give the narrative the stamp of authenticity: it comes as no surprise to learn that the experiences of Sha'ul and Dvora in the book are based to some extent on the personal lives of Abba and Vitka Kempner Kovner. And the wealth of accurate information in the side notes is an adequate alternative for most of us to the library of works needed by the specialist in Holocaust studies.

Kovner's hope has not yet been realized. He did not live to see the book's publication in Hebrew and died before any progress had been made toward ensuring its publication in English or any other widely spoken language. I first became acquainted with *Scrolls of Testimony* several years ago when I was commissioned by the Memorial Foundation for Jewish Culture to translate one of the scrolls. I was so moved and impressed by its power and scope that I decided to begin translating the rest of the scrolls in advance of any specific commitment to publish them in English. I am pleased to have played a part in moving Abba Kovner's hope and dream closer to fulfillment.

—Eddie Levenston
March 2000

⁑ Designer's Note ⁑

THE TALMUD, in the printed form we know it today, with central text surrounded by commentaries, is a flower of the Renaissance in Europe, made possible by the advent of moveable type. In its original handwritten form, the three main strands of the Talmud were separate. To combine them on the same page would have required more preparatory work than was practicable. Moveable type made it possible to take an accurate measure of each segment, then juggle and justify the type on the pages—not unlike the way we designers and typesetters work today on computers.

The interlocking layout of the printed Talmud is unique, most likely an æsthetic choice rather than one of technical necessity. The tight weaving of its strands creates lines of odd length and paragraphs of unusual shape that require the reader to slow down and digest the words slowly. Abba Kovner's masterpiece, a series of liturgical narratives accompanied by notes and excerpts from poetry and prose, is an idea so unusual and open-ended that he could have chosen any form he desired. The allusion to Talmud perfectly suited his purpose, especially since it demanded contemplative reading. Although reminiscent of the Talmud, *Scrolls of Testimony* is not the Talmud. The material that complements the central text does not follow the regularity of the Talmud's commentaries. Kovner's annotations are marginalia, sometimes extensive and sometimes spare, and their great variation calls for flexibility and variety in the layout of each page.

The text is set in Philidor Schmidt, a typeface family (roman, italic, small caps) I made for this book, based on the mid-eighteenth-century types in the possession of the Bundesdruckerei in Berlin, which are themselves heavy-handed interpretations of the then-fashionable French style of Pierre-Simon Fournier. They are *kartoffelschriften*, "potato types" that are highly readable yet somewhat homely. The bold sans serif type that begins each piece of marginalia is William A. Dwiggins's always vigorous Metro, first issued in 1929; the type used for the running heads and folios is Koch-Antiqua, which made its first appearance in 1922. Rudolf Koch (1876-1940) was the most humanistic and humane of German designers, a twentieth-century original. Among his disciples, to whom he was beloved, were the distinguished Jewish designers Berthold Wolpe and Imre Reiner.

✦

This English edition of *Scrolls of Testimony* is illustrated by the paintings of Samuel Bak, who, like Kovner, is a son and survivor of Vilna and a great observer of human behavior under terrible duress. Bak has recorded what few have ever seen: The whole world, indiscernibly animate or inanimate, limping along prosthetically in order to survive. While literature and movies have terrorized us with tales of the undead, Bak and Kovner have shown us the far more terrifying—and all too real—world of the unliving.

Eight paintings of Samuel Bak's are shown in this book. One, a vast canvas (160 x 200 cm) entitled *The Family,* dominates in number and in tone. It is shown in its entirety on the dustjacket and as the frontispiece, and throughout the rest of the book in a number of its harrowing details. On the following page are the uncropped images of each of the seven other paintings.

−Scott-Martin Kosofsky
The Philidor Company
Cambridge, Massachusetts

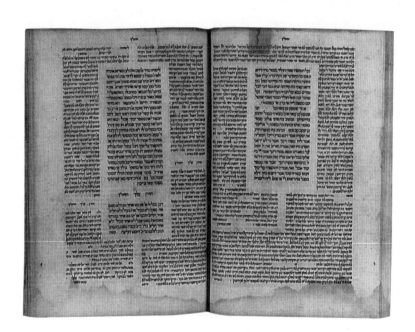

The tractate *Yebamot* from the Talmud printed in Pesaro, Italy, in 1508 by Gershom Soncino. In the center of each page is the Mishnah text followed by its Gemara. Rashi's commentary can be found at the inner margins and the commentaries of the Tosaphists at the outer margins.

Alone III, 1994. Oil on canvas, 92 x 122 cm.

Journey, 1991. Oil on canvas, 200 x 160 cm.

Trains, 1991. Oil on canvas, 122 x 160 cm.

Stone Age, 1968. Oil on canvas, 65 x 46 cm.

Waiting in Line, 1981. Oil on canvas, 116 x 89 cm.

Entire City, 1977. Oil on canvas, 163 x 122 cm.

Smoke, 1997. Oil on canvas, 200 x 160 cm.
National Gallery of Canada.

Paintings by
SAMUEL BAK
b. Vilna, 1933

xxxi

❖ Author's Introduction ❖

On the Possibility of Transmitting Our Experience
to Future Generations

WHILE THERE IS STILL TIME, we must come to the realization that the Holocaust is not just an obsession of those who survived. A sense of communion with the six million victims and the aura of the period is not just the private concern of those who personally witnessed the horrors; it is part of the long collective memory of the Jewish people. The Holocaust has a place in the historic consciousness of every Jewish generation, wherever it may be.

This realization is one of the central principles of Jewish identity in our time. Without it, it is doubtful whether one can achieve identification with a creative, living, positive Judaism. More than ever the future of the Jewish people depends on the way Jews relate to themselves and to their past, to their magnificent heritage and to the awesome tragedy, and to the spiritual accounting that this historic consciousness demands of them.

But how does one cultivate such an awareness? How does one bring about a personal and national spiritual accounting? In the notebooks of the writer Shmuel Yosef Agnon we find an old Hasidic story: Whenever the Baal Shem Tov felt that some great trouble was about to befall the Jewish people, and it was time for a moral stocktaking, he would take his stick, put on his coarse sheepskin coat, and go to the forest. There, in a secret place, he would light a fire at the foot of an ancient oak and stand a long while in the silence of the forest, with his eyes closed, concentrating his heart on a special prayer, and the plea of the Baal Shem Tov would open the gates of heaven, the gates of mercy.

One generation after the Baal Shem Tov, another pious Jew was called upon to act in a matter of life and death. This was in the days of the *Maggid* from Mezricz. He put on his black cloak and turned to the same forest; he found the same ancient oak, and stood and said, "We are no longer capable of lighting a fire like the Baal Shem Tov, but it is within our power to say the same prayer." He said the prayer and his plea too was answered.

Another generation passed and this time it was the Rabbi of Sasov who was asked to act in a great matter of life and death. Moshe Leib of Sasov rose and put on his ceremonial silk gown, went to the forest, and as he stood there he said, "We cannot light the fire and we have forgotten the special meanings of that holy prayer, but we still remember where it took place—and perhaps that will suffice." And this too was sufficient, and the evil decree was averted.

Yet another generation passed, and Rabbi Yisrael from Rozhin was asked to act to prevent a great calamity. The Rabbi of Rozhin is known to have been a great leader who knew his own worth, and behaved in his court like a king. He heard the request and understood that the time had come for a spiritual accounting. He sat down in his gilded chair in the middle of his splendid mansion, closed his eyes, and said, "Because of our many sins, we can no longer go to the forest and light the fire, we have forgotten the prayer, and we don't even know where the events took place. But we can still tell the story of what happened!" And the writer S. Y. Agnon adds: "And the story told by the last generation was no less effective than the deeds of the pious in earlier times." (See S. Y. Agnon, *Sipur shel Yeshu'a* [A Story of Salvation] in *Sefer, Sofer ve-Sipur* [Book, Writer, and Story], published by Schocken, Tel Aviv and Jerusalem, 1978, p. 439.)

This story hints at everything I had in mind in presenting these lectures, but I cannot discharge my debt with mere hints. I must take time, therefore, to explain a little.

At a conference of Holocaust survivors and their children in Jerusalem, people met who had not seen each other for twenty years. Television viewers in Israel, including youngsters who at the time of the Eichmann Trial were still babies, or had not yet been born, were able for the first time in their lives to witness human encounters of a kind they had never known before, reunions between people who had not known which of them would remain alive and which would be killed. One sight was especially moving, and not only for the young Israelis: It was when one of the guest survivors was visiting Yad Vashem and recognized in one of the exhibits hanging on the wall the prisoner's uniform of his dead comrade. In the background you could see the huge photograph of the hut at Auschwitz and the tortured figures peering from their three tiers of bunks. For a moment the visitor stood silent in front of the exhibit, his gaze fixed on the number written on the hanging uniform, and a silent dialog ensued between the survivor and the empty garment. Suddenly the man rolled up his sleeve and on the television screen we could see the two numbers, the one on the empty coat and the one on the living man's arm, and they were almost the same, differing only in the last digit.

The television reporter who immortalized this encounter was unable to restrain himself and asked, "Did you know him, sir?"

"Yes. We lay on the same bunk."

"And what happened to your friend who bore that number?"

"He was sent to the gas chamber. His number completed the quota for that day. And that was the last day the crematorium functioned. My number was the one after his, and that's how I survived."

"And what do you feel when you stand here now in front of this picture?"

The man tried to respond but only his lips moved. A long, stifled stammer was heard and then the transmission was interrupted—the transmission, but not the effect on the hearts and minds of the viewers who witnessed the encounter. Each one felt that at that moment a transfer had taken place, which could not have worked in any other way, cognitively or pedagogically. That moment of living confrontation with his comrade's empty garment, and the simple, dreadful story is the kind of thing that cannot be forgotten.

But the number of people who can take part in such a meeting, roll up their sleeves, and match number with number, is growing smaller and smaller. And for those who are left, their memories grow dim. In another generation there will be none among us who know the way to the forest, who remember the place where it happened, and it is doubtful whether there will be anyone who can testify to the true meaning of the prayer.

Even for those survivors still living among us, it can be difficult to share with their children what happened to them during the Holocaust, even when the children display a desire to know.

One day my son, who was born at the time of the establishment of the State of Israel, said to me, "Dad, I'd like to go with you some day to your town of Vilna, and you can show me the place where the events occurred."

My son was somewhat surprised when I said to him: "There's no longer any such place. Strangers live in my house; it's not recognizable. The school where I learned Hebrew is a timber yard. The ghetto has been plowed under. There's no trace of the house of study of the Vilna Gaon. The streets of the Jews have become playing fields and a public park."

In the old market you can no longer hear a fishwife tell a stingy customer, who prods a fish but doesn't buy it, "Lady, the church on the hill should only collapse, with you sitting on the point of the spire!"—a curse uttered in Yiddish, of course. At the same time the woman's free hand would be stroking her tiny grandson's curly head as she says to him in quite a different voice, "Darling! You have such wise eyes, just like Rabbi Akiba!" And you would be almost convinced that the woman had personally seen Rabbi Akiba, of mishnaic fame, only yesterday in the fish market. But she is there no more, and neither are her customers.

In the Strashun Library the lights no longer burn. By their glow, on wooden benches polished from so much wear, rich and poor, young and old, used to sit crowded together, concentrating on their studies. We read subjects that were denied to us in the regular school, from treasured books revealed to us as a source of living water of wisdom, that banished from our minds the hoof beats of the evil culture that was already lurking at the gate. And since none of them exist any more, the place no longer has meaning. For a place where the memory of the dead, their very identity, has been whitewashed away is not a place that you and I can revisit. I too had a forest and a private path in it. On the edge of the great swamp in the partisans' forest, I knew an old tree in whose shade I sometimes used to sit, summer and winter. I would come there secretly and sit for a while in solitude, cut off from the camp of fighters, shut my eyes and say a silent prayer.

I am no longer able to take that path to the old tree, nor can I remember the private meaning of my prayers in the winter of 1943. If I could remember, I fear I would not have the courage today to let them cross my lips. Even our own personal prayers acquire a new interpretation in the course of time! We are no longer capable of lighting the fires we lit there, of standing in that special place. But before the ancient prayers fade completely from our memories, let us tell our children simply what occurred. That is something my generation can do.

This story, as distinct from historical research, is not required to answer the crucial questions: How did it happen, how could it happen in the heart of Europe, in the center of western civilization, in the middle of the twentieth century? This story has no need to seek out what to emphasize and how to judge, to pass judgment on the question of collective guilt—nor to take a stand on the most burning issue of our time: Does man—every man—bear responsibility for his actions?

Before we become involved in historical, philosophical, or theological aspects of the issue and draw simplistic, facile, distorted conclusions, using concepts from the world of the ghetto and the death camps to present arguments of topical relevance in rhetoric, politics, and economics, we should not forget or allow to be forgotten *what happened*—the story, which will enable another generation to look through a window onto that "other planet," which was none other than our own!

Since I was no longer able to take my son physically to the place, I opened a window for him onto a place that was—one unique location—an empty apartment. A flight of wooden stairs. Broken windows. Near a stove of ceramic bricks you can still see the secret entrance that led to a hideaway between the walls. In due course, the Jews of the ghetto became skillful in digging *malines*—hiding places—in cellars and secret places underground, but in the early days, when they were still very confused, people were sure they could find shelter in any improvised hiding place—until the storm had passed. On that day, September 20, 1941, at dawn, or what passed for dawn in the ghetto sky, the residents of the house woke to the sound of yelling Germans. The commands, bidding everybody assemble in the street, sounded nearer and nearer. With incredible speed and dexterity, in which young and old were already well practiced, people managed to hide in a tiny closet behind a concealed entrance and hold their breath. There were seventeen men and women and three children, including a baby two months old. It was cramped and stifling in the closet, but no one complained or uttered a sound as the steps of the Gestapo drew nearer. As they heard through the partition the repeated commands of the Germans, warning the Jews that anyone found in hiding would be shot, the baby started crying. The mother gave her the breast and rocked her in her arms. But for some reason the baby refused to be comforted, and the sound of her sobs filled the room with terror and frayed everyone's nerves.

"Shhhhhhh!" whispered the mother, and the others echoed her, hissing like snakes caught in a fire.

"Do something!" muttered somebody, "or we shall all be lost!"

Everybody's gaze focused on the mother's pale face, but she only held the child more tightly against her breast, either suffocating her or protecting her, and nobody moved an inch. The footsteps of the soldiers could be heard on the stairs and close at hand there was a burst of rifle fire.

The father, who was sitting curled up at some distance from his wife, jumped up with a pillow in his hand. He seemed about to take the pillow and lean over the baby in order to suffocate her, when suddenly he collapsed and lost consciousness. At that moment an old gray-haired woman rose to her feet, thrust with all her strength against the concealed entrance to the hideaway and burst through. She managed to stand in front of the entrance as the Gestapo broke into the apartment. She raised her voice in a hysterical shout, which became a moan. The soldiers saw a crazy woman in front of them making faces and with some repugnance seized her by the hair. She shouted at them, "Why are you late, sirs? I've been waiting for you! Hurry up and take me where you took my children, and my grandchildren and all my family. Hurry! Hurry! Do you realize who will judge you for what you are doing?"

The men of the Gestapo burst out laughing and dragged her downstairs. When the murderers had left the house and disappeared from the street, the people emerged from their hiding place, and the terrifying feigned laughter of the grandmother still seemed to be echoing in the air.

"Mamma! Mamma!" sobbed her son, the father, and covered his eyes with his hands. The others stood a long while huddled together in silence, and each one felt as though his own flesh had been seared.

Is it easy to overcome such a searing fire and simply return to one's daily routine, since "we are commanded to continue living"? Is it easy after that to talk in high tones about the sanctity of life, as something to be taken for granted?

It seems to me that anyone who looked behind that wall and heard the sounds from that *maline* would feel as I do—in that place our feet stand on the border between affirmation of life and life as a curse!

And perhaps this is the educational imperative for the remnant of the generation that survived Auschwitz, to try to inscribe on the memory of coming generations the message—a hard one but sincere and true—of ours: For a Jew who knew the Holocaust, his life is in perpetual tension between the blessed and the accursed, between affirmation and denial of life. A knowledge of the abyss on the brink of which we stood is from now on an inseparable part of our historic consciousness and our Jewish identity.

A lecture in Yiddish before the plenary meeting of the
Memorial Foundation for Jewish Culture,
Geneva, June 11, 1981.

❖ The Scrolls ❖

✤ The First Scroll ✤

Preludes to Darkness

✣ INVOCATION ✣

Spoken in a whisper

before reading

the scroll

The Author speaks:

This scroll is different from all other scrolls. In all other
  scrolls, we recount what happened to our fathers and
  forefathers in ancient days.

In this scroll we tell what happened to our fathers and to
  us in the generation of Auschwitz.

The slaughtered Jewish people speak, in silence and in
  words, to the living Jewish people:

You who were unable to save us, listen now with all your
  heart to our testimony; it is all that remains of our
  lives.

Try to understand the meaning of destruction and what
  words would have strengthened our spirit at the
  moment of parting.

The Scroll speaks to the Reader:

Do not regard this testimony as an inspiration for hatred.
  By the rivers of Europe we sat down and wept when
  our turn came to be murdered. By the chimneys of the
  crematorium

> > *even there*

> > > > we preserved scraps of
  incinerated time and we pondered the future as we
  thought of you. . . .

Do you have a spare moment to think of us
  innocent of crime and unashamed?

⊹ PROLOGUE ⊹

Countdown or

the Corridor

of Lost

Alternatives

HITLER AND HIS NAZI PARTY'S RISE TO POWER

JANUARY 30, 1933: Hitler was appointed head of the German government. His official title was *Reichskanzler*. The appointment was made by the president, Field Marshal Paul von Hindenburg, following the elections to the Reichstag (the Parliament) in November 1932. Although the National Socialist Party lost the election, having obtained 2,000,000 votes and 34 seats, it remained the largest party, with over a third of the delegates to the Reichstag. But in order to form a government it needed the support of the German National Party, headed by Alfred Hugenberg. **FEBRUARY 27, 1933**: The burning of the Reichstag building in Berlin, which was followed by a wave of arrests and Nazi terror throughout Germany. **APRIL 26, 1933**: Establishment of the Gestapo, the Nazi secret police. **MAY 10, 1933**: Jewish books and books by opponents of the Nazis are publicly burned throughout Germany. **JULY 14, 1933**: All political parties but the Nazi Party are prohibited in Germany. **APRIL 1, 1934**: Heinrich Himmler is appointed head of the SS in Germany. **JUNE 30–JULY 2, 1934**: "Night of the Long Knives," a murderous outbreak of terror perpetuated by members of the SA against men considered undesirable by Hitler, including Röhm and his associates. **AUGUST 2, 1934**: Field Marshal von Hindenburg, the German president, dies. Hitler takes over as head of state.

"In appointing Hitler Chancellor of the Reich, you have placed our holy German nation in the hands of one of the greatest demagogues of all time. I prophesy that this evil man will lead our country to the abyss and cause our nation incalculable hardship. Future generations will curse you in your grave for this act." –From a telegram sent by General Ludendorf to his comrade Field Marshal von Hindenburg, February 1, 1933.

ADOLF HITLER (1889–1945): Born in Austria, Hitler lived for a time in Linz and Vienna. In 1913, Hitler came to Munich, and at the outbreak of World War I volunteered for the army. He reached the rank of corporal, and was wounded by poison gas. The defeat of Germany drove him into political activity. In 1919, he joined the small German Worker's Party in Munich, which numbered 55 members. The platform of this party was based on racism, hatred of the Jews, and opposition to socialism and liberal democracy. This was the nucleus of the Nazi Party, which was officially founded in 1920. In 1923, Hitler tried to take over power in Bavaria by revolution. The attempt failed and Hitler was imprisoned. In prison he wrote his book *Mein Kampf* (My Struggle). After his release he set

5 minutes to 12

4 minutes to 12

3 minutes to 12

2 minutes to 12

1 minute to 12

12 o'clock. Berlin, January 30, 1933.✣

A black Mercedes passes through the gate of the Kaiserhof Hotel and turns toward the residence of Field Marshal von Hindenburg,✣ the aged president of the German Republic. In the back seat sits Adolf Hitler,✣ leader of the National Socialist German Workers' Party, a frustrated painter from the gutters, a Bohemian corporal when he enters the building and the new ruler of Germany when he leaves; in extensive articles accompanied by front-page photographs the most important journalists in the capital have reported the annual press ball, held last night in Berlin. In close-up photographs the high society of the great metropolis can be seen joyfully celebrating in evening dress and resplendent gowns, glasses of champagne in their hands.

In private soundproof drawing rooms, Berliners leafed through their favorite newspapers without a word, while close at hand, beyond the walls, legions of Hitler's supporters paraded through the streets of the capital. They wore caps, flaunted swastikas of various sizes, and waved party flags. They streamed toward the Brandenburg Gate,✣ and the dark winter night was broken by the vast light of flaming torches as hands were raised in a mass salute.

In one of the splendid marble buildings an emergency meeting of the Prussian State Council has been called. Before the chairman can open the meeting, the mayor of Altona, the last stronghold of the short-lived Weimar Republic,✣ rises in his seat, and, with an effort at self-

---

✣ *This symbol denotes corresponding sidenote(s). However, some sidenotes are meant to provide additional information on the text in general and do not correspond to a specific symbol.*

about organizing all the malcontents, and his movement gained strength after the economic crisis of 1929. By 1932, the Nazi Party was the largest political force in Germany. With his ascent to power he became known as the *Führer* (Leader), established a dictatorship, and dragged Germany into a maelstrom of war, conquest, mass murder, and crushing defeat. Hitler committed suicide on April 29, 1945, a week before the fall of Berlin.

BRANDENBURG GATE: Brandenburg was one of the outlying principalities in Germany, ruled by princes of the House of Hohenzollern. At the end of the fifteenth century, the rulers of Brandenburg established their capital in Berlin, where they built palaces. The Brandenburg Gate, famous in our time as the main gateway in the wall that divided East Berlin from West Berlin until the reunification of Germany, is a remnant of one of these palaces.

THE WEIMAR REPUBLIC: In 1919, at the end of World War I, which brought about the defeat of Germany and the abdication of the kaiser, the German National Assembly met in the East German town of Weimar and confirmed the democratic Weimar Constitution. The Democratic Republic of Germany, known as the Weimar Republic, held power in Germany until Hitler took over on January 30, 1933.

A notice in the March 21, 1933 newspaper Völkische Beobachter *(People's Observer), the Nazi Party daily, announcing that on March 22, 1933, the first concentration camp for political prisoners will be set up near Dachau.*

THE COMMUNIST PARTY (KPD): The German Communist Party had considerable influence among the workers, the trade unions, and in the Reichstag. At the head of the party stood Ernst Tellmann (1886-1944). The leader of the KPD party in the Reichstag was an experienced, well-respected party worker, Ernst Torgler. The philosophy of the Communist Party was based on Marxist-Leninist theory and the principles of revolution. According to this view, the revolutionary proletariat had no interest in the continued existence of the Weimar Republic or indeed of any other organized, legal regime. Consequently, it was difficult for other movements to form alliances or even cooperate with the Communists. The Social Democrats (SPD) were the main faction supporting the stable continuance of the Weimar Republic. Any coalition with the Communists was therefore out of the question. Moreover, the Communist Party was convinced that its true enemies were the Social Democrats. At a party congress June 8-15, 1929, the Communists coined the term "Social Fascists" and in their fanaticism used it as a label for the Social Democrats. They offered no strenuous opposition to the rise of the Nazis, on the assumption that "after Hitler, we'll take over."

THE MONGOLS: The tribes of Mongolia were united in 1206 under their leader Temuchin, better known as Genghis Khan (1167-1227). He established the Mongolian Empire and is considered one of the greatest conquerors in history. The Mongolian Empire stretched from China in the east to Hungary in the west. Genghis Khan ruled over central Asia and he came westward as far as Kiev, the capital of the Ukraine. The Mongols also invaded Persia and Iraq. Their cruelty toward the people they conquered is notorious. The united Mongol kingdoms held on until the end of the

control, moves behind the chair of the leader of the Communist Party.✣ Bending over the ear of his colleague and rival, he murmurs discreetly, "Comrade Torgler! This is zero hour and you can see what is happening. Perhaps finally you will behave logically and cooperate with us, with the Socialists, to avert the imminent danger."

Torgler, an intelligent man, a brilliant speaker, a seasoned politician, leader of the largest of the parties, leans slightly backward and without blinking an eyelid answers the mayor of Altona. "That is quite out of the question, Comrade Brauer. The Nazis must win and take over the government. Then—it won't take more than three or four weeks—the whole of the working class will fall in behind us."

And in the darkness of their ignorance
> at zero hour
> at zero hour
> at zero hour
> fear and darkness covered the land;

fear and darkness covered the land, and the Holocaust that befell the Jewish people was the greatest atrocity that human history has ever known; in every generation the human impulse for evil breaks out, the forces of destruction rampage, and the history of mankind is full to overflowing with bloodshed:

the blood of conquered tribes

> in ancient times;

the blood of whole populations slaughtered

> by the Mongols,✣

which flowed like rivers for a thousand years

> between the old and the new;

that was spilled in the appalling religious wars

> in the name of God and His prophet;

the blood of the innocents who died

> when the peasants and Cossacks rebelled;

the flow of blood from American Indians

> who were wiped off the land of their fathers by

weapons in the hands of enlightened nations: Spain, France, England, and America. And the Turks who slaughtered the Armenian people;✣

> and all these rivers of blood flowed down

to the sea, and the sea ebbed and flowed around the Old World and the New

> World and the Third World;

and there is no diminution
of civil wars, and revolutions, and counterrevolutions, world wars and local conflicts between nations,

> both then and now.

fourteenth century, though the process of dissolution began with the death of Kublai Khan (1294).

SLAUGHTERED THE ARMENIAN PEOPLE: After the conquest of Armenia by its neighbors the Turks in 1473, the Armenians began to spread throughout the Ottoman Empire. They fulfilled important roles in the bureaucracy, in handicrafts, and in commerce. From time to time there were Armenian uprisings against Turkish rule, which were put down with the utmost cruelty. Well-known, for instance, is the Slaughter of the Armenians that took place after the uprising of 1895. And one year later, the Turks slaughtered en masse the Armenians who were living in Constantinople. In 1915, during World War I, the Turks murdered at least 800,000 Armenians, at the express command of the government, which was in the hands of the party of "Young Turks."

EXTERMINATING THE JEWS

MARCH 22, 1933: The establishment of Dachau, the first Nazi concentration camp in Germany. The watchword of the camp command was "Tolerance means weakness." Dachau was the original camp, and it continued to exist for 12 more years. **1936**: Establishment of the camp at Sachsenhausen, in the suburb of Oranienburg near Berlin. After Kristallnacht, 10,000 Jews from Berlin, Hamburg, Mecklenburg, and Pomerania were imprisoned there. The total number of victims at Sachsenhausen equaled 100,000. **AUGUST 1937**: Establishment of the concentration camp at Buchenwald. **JULY–AUGUST 1938**: Establishment of the concentration camp (Grade III, for handling severe punishment) at Mauthausen near Linz. **MAY 1939**: Establishment of the concentration camp for women at Ravensbrück in northern Germany. **MAY 20, 1940**: Establishment of the concentration camp at Auschwitz. The slogan "Work Sets You Free" was blazoned above the gate. **JUNE 1940**: Establishment of the concentration camp at Neuengamme near Hamburg, Gross-Rosen in Silesia. **FEBRUARY 22, 1941**: Deportation of the Jews of Amsterdam to Buchenwald. **JULY 1941**: Jews are murdered en masse at Ponar, near Vilna. By July 1944, about 100,000 Jews had been murdered at this place. **JULY 31, 1941**: Göring makes Heydrich responsible for implementing the Final Solution. **LATE AUGUST 1941**: 23,000 Jews are shot at Kamenetz-Podolsk. **SEPTEMBER 29–30, 1941**: 34,000 Jews from Kiev are murdered in the valley at Babii Yar. **OCTOBER 2, 1941**: Opening of the death camp at Yasnowech in

Nevertheless
    the Holocaust
was a project of annihilation, the like of which mankind has never seen, different from the pogroms and evil decrees that the persecuted Jewish people have known throughout the ages;
For
        this was not the rioting of an incited rabble.
    Nor an outbreak of vengeance by the
        poor and hungry.
    Nor the hysterical outcome of religious fanaticism.
    Nor a revolution whose ends justified the means.
    The ghetto was not a prisoner-of-war camp.
    It was not attacks from the air that caused Auschwitz
        to burn with a fire that consumed human beings
        for four whole years.
For the first time
    a whole nation was consigned to destruction by order of a government, which organized, planned to the last detail, practiced, and carried out a giant safari, and the hunt was maintained summer and winter, from the Atlantic coast to the foothills of the Caucasus, from the frozen North sea to the shores of the Mediterranean, everywhere, with no pause for holidays, day and night, in
    the high noon of the twentieth century;
    and assistants of every tongue took part, in every land, by agreement and on one condition, that the hunted be members of the Jewish people, men and women, young and old, pregnant, sick, disabled, and healthy, with no exceptions, and to this one purpose were allotted all the financial resources, the transport and the communication services required;
    and the hunt for Jews continued as planned for almost a hundred thousand hours, which is twelve years, three months, and fifty days without end;✢

and the Jewish people had no shield or savior.
No asylum, no escape.

Germany reaches Auschwitz. **MID-JANUARY 1943**: Further consignments of Jews from the Theresienstadt ghetto reach Auschwitz. **JANUARY 21, 1943**: Victims of the second mass *Aktion* in the Warsaw ghetto reach Treblinka. **FEBRUARY 12, 1943**: About 10,000 Jews from the Bialystok ghetto reach Treblinka. **MARCH 15, 1943**: Jews from Greece reach Auschwitz. **APRIL 1943**: The remaining Jews of Warsaw are sent to Auschwitz and Treblinka. **MAY 1943**: Convoys of Jews from Amsterdam reach Auschwitz and Sobibor. **LATE AUGUST 1943**: The number of Jews killed at Treblinka reaches 800,000. **OCTOBER 10, 1943**: 1,000 Jews from Rome are deported to Auschwitz. **NOVEMBER 3, 1943**: 10,000 Jews are murdered at Majdanek. **APRIL 28, 1944**: The first trainload of Jews from Hungary reaches Auschwitz. **MAY 15, 1944**: The systematic deportation of the Jews of Hungary to their death at Auschwitz begins. **SEPTEMBER 23, 1944**: Jews from the Vilna ghetto and Riga are murdered in the camp of Kaluga, in Estonia. **OCTOBER 31, 1944**: 14,000 Jews from Salonika are brought to Auschwitz. **END OF OCTOBER 1944**: The last 20,000 Jews from the Theresienstadt ghetto reach Auschwitz. **NOVEMBER 8, 1944**: 37,000 Jews from Budapest begin the death march to the Austrian border. **JANUARY 17, 1945**: The death march of the prisoners of Auschwitz. **JANUARY 25, 1945**: The death march of the prisoners of Stutthof. **APRIL 10, 1945**: The death march of the prisoners of Buchenwald.

SS: The strike force of the Nazi Party, under the leadership of Himmler. Members wore black uniforms and the insignia of a skull.

SA: The elite unit of the Nazi Party. Organized by Ernst Röhm, it became an instrument of terror dreaded by all, individuals and communities.

Croatia. **OCTOBER 13, 1941**: Establishment of the death camp complex at Auschwitz-Birkenau. **OCTOBER 23, 1941**: 19,000 Jews are murdered at Odessa. **MARCH 26, 1942**: The first convoys of Jews from Slovakia reach Majdanek and Auschwitz. By September nearly 60,000 Jews had been deported. **MARCH 28, 1942**: The first deportation of French Jews to Auschwitz. **JUNE 1, 1942**: Opening of the death camp at Treblinka. **JULY 17, 1942**: The second dispatch of Dutch Jews is sent to Auschwitz. **JULY 22, 1942**: The first convoy of deportees from the Warsaw ghetto is sent to Treblinka. **AUGUST 28, 1942**: Part of the Jewish population of Antwerp reaches the death camps. **SEPTEMBER 14, 1942**: More than a quarter million Jews from Warsaw are murdered at Treblinka. **SEPTEMBER 30, 1942**: The first wave of Croatian Jews reaches Auschwitz. **OCTOBER 28, 1942**: The first consignment of Jews from Theresienstadt reaches Auschwitz. **NOVEMBER 25, 1942**: Jews from Norway reach Auschwitz. **DECEMBER 10, 1942**: A consignment of Jews from

SD: The security arm of the SS.

GESTAPO: Political secret police. The Gestapo was established on April 26, 1933, within the framework of the SS. It was the principal executive arm of the dictatorship and the symbol of torture and murder.

EINSATZGRUPPEN: Operational units. An improvisation of 1938, these operational units cast dread over Poland at the time of the conquest in 1939. Reestablished on the eve of the invasion of the Soviet Union, the Einsatzgruppen accompanied the regular army forces as they advanced into Russia. They systematically killed Jews in the conquered territories, even before the establishment of the death camps.

HITLERJUGEND: The organization of Hitler youth, led by Baldur von Schirach.

THE WEHRMACHT: The regular German army.

THE "BLUE" POLICE: The Polish police, which cooperated with the Nazi conqueror. It excelled in persecuting Jews and extorting money from its victims.

VLASOVITES: Andrei Vlasov, a captured Soviet general, cooperated with the Germans. A "Liberation Army" under his name numbered two divisions and was composed of Soviet deserters and prisoners of war. The Germans took about 5 million Soviet prisoners of war, officers and men, of whom about 2.5 million died in the P.O.W. camps of hunger or disease; about 150,000 were killed outright by the Germans.

YPATINGAS: Lithuanian auxiliary units, which acted in the service of the Germans and helped them carry out the murders.

VICHY: A town in France where in 1940 a government of collaborators with the German conqueror was set up under the leadership of General Henri-Philippe Pétain.

IRON GUARD: A Romanian Fascist organization (established in

From the moment Hitler was made ruler of Germany, he began his war against the Jews. He hated the Czechs, the French, and the English; he detested the Russians and abominated the Poles; he despised the Belgians, the Dutch, and the Italians; he looked down on the Americans. But mortal hatred he bore the Jews. And in Czechoslovakia the Jews behaved like Czechs, in Hungary like Hungarians, in Poland like Poles, and even in Russia they tried to behave like Russians. And in Germany the Jews regarded themselves as German in every respect. And Hitler was hostile to the working class; he legislated against the Socialists and made war on the Communists. He loathed the Liberals. He looked down on writers and was repelled by modern art and by democracy. But more than anything he hated the Jews. For there were many Jews in the ranks of the working class. There were many Jews among the Socialists and the greatest of the Communists were Jewish in origin, and among the important bankers there were men of the Mosaic persuasion, as there were among the leaders of the Liberals, the believers in the Republic, the supporters of the young democracy. In the community of intellectuals, writers, artists, and thinkers, there were very many famous figures descended from Abraham, Isaac, and Jacob. It was they who in those days fashioned German culture, its language and literature, and earned its worldwide reputation.

Hitler despised the weak, and the Western democracies whose power had faded, and those small nations who pinned their hopes on a paper tiger or a dead lion. Most of all he despised the Jews, who had no army and no state and not even a true ally anywhere in the world.

And the net that he spread before them took a thousand forms: the SS⁺ and the SA⁺ and the SD⁺ and the Gestapo;⁺ the Einsatzgruppen⁺ and the Hitlerjugend;⁺ the Wehrmacht.⁺ And there were those countries who sent their own auxiliary police forces against the Jews: the "Blue" Police⁺ of Poland and the Vlasovites⁺ of the Soviet Union; the Ypatingas⁺ from Lithuania and their counterparts from Latvia and Estonia; the men of Vichy⁺ in France; and the Nazis in Austria and Mussolini's Fascists in Italy; the gangs who called themselves the Iron Guard⁺ in Romania and the party of the Arrow-Cross⁺ in Hungary; the Ustashi⁺ in Yugoslavia and the traitors to their country in Greece. In Belgium Degrel's⁺ men moved against the Jews; Quisling's⁺ lay in wait for them in Scandinavia; and

1927) whose members were already carrying out mass pogroms against the Jews in 1941 (in Bucharest and Jassy). After Romania joined the war against the Soviet Union, extremist anti-Semites were responsible for the slaughter of 150,000 Jews in Serbia and Bukovina and the 60,000 Jews of Odessa.

ARROW-CROSS: The militant Nazi Party in Hungary.

USTASHI: Military police units in the puppet state of Croatia during the time of German rule. The Ustashi carried out expulsions and killed tens of thousands of Jews and Gypsies, and hundreds of thousands of Serbs.

DEGREL (1906-1950): Leon Degrel was a Belgian Fascist, who, in the 1930s, with the support of Mussolini, set up a royalist party that preached Fascism and extreme Catholicism. On the whole, the Belgian population did not support it and was not influenced by its anti-Semitism. After the German conquest, Degrel organized brigades of Flemish and Walloons, who fought alongside the Germans on the Russian front. Degrel's party took control of civic institutions and the means of communication. With the liberation of Belgium in September 1944, Degrel fled to Spain, where he was supported by Franco and granted Spanish citizenship.

QUISLING (1887-1945): Vidkun Quisling served as an officer in the Norwegian army and later as military attaché in Petrograd (1918-1919) and Helsinki (1919-1921). As the Norwegian minister of defense (1931-1933), Quisling resigned to form a Fascist organization, National Sammlung. He supported the suppression of the trade unions and the elimination of the Communists. In 1939, Quisling met Hitler and from then on supported the German conquest of Norway. After the German invasion, Quisling proclaimed himself prime minister of Norway and assisted the conquerors, actually serving as the

German commissioner's deputy. Quisling was personally responsible for sending a thousand Jews to the death camps. After the liberation of Norway in May 1945, he was arrested, tried for treason, and executed. His name became a synonym for "traitor" throughout the countries conquered by the Germans.

THE MUFTI (1897-1974): Amin el-Husseini was appointed by the British as grand mufti of Jerusalem and permanent president of the supreme Arab council, the ruling religious body in the Moslem community of Palestine. El-Husseini was engaged in perpetual conflict with Zionism, Jewish immigration, and the sale of land to Jewish settlers. However, he was also in unending internal conflict with the Nashashibi family, who also sought prestige and authority. In 1936, a compromise was reached and the Supreme Arab Committee was set up, which declared a general strike and a state of rebellion against the Mandatory government. The British dismissed el-Husseini from office as head of the council and declared the Committee to be illegal. In the wake of these decrees there was an outbreak of bloody riots from 1936 to 1939. In October 1937, el-Husseini fled to Lebanon, where he reestablished the Arab Committee under his own command. During World War II, he was an ally of Hitler, lived in Germany, and broadcast to the Arab world over German radio. At the end of the war he escaped from Germany to Egypt and from there to Lebanon.

SHTREIMELS: Circular, black fur hats worn by Hasidim.

PAPACHAS: Round fur hats worn by men in Russia.

followers of the Mufti* from Jerusalem briefed the Gestapo in North Africa, assigning places of destruction for the Jews of the Maghreb; Jews from Tunis had already been sent to concentration camps.

In every place Jews were loaded onto waiting trains, and of the condemned none knew who was to live and who was to die. At first they only arrested Communists, and settled the fate of Communists alone. Then they took the various kinds of Socialists, and distinguished their fate from the rest. And when they took those thought to be liberal and loyal to the democracy, the others still considered themselves outside the ring of terror. Then they took statesmen, one third Jewish and one quarter Jewish and veterans of the Kaiser's War who were of Jewish origin, nor did they hesitate to take men of learning and international reputation, and they took writers and journalists and artists who had not already left the country or committed suicide. In the end they also seized those who had succeeded in fleeing Germany but had not gone far enough away from the European continent.

And before the Nazis put them behind walls and watchtowers, they declared the Jews outside the law. In every single state that the Nazi Germans reached, the Jews of that country were deprived of their rights as citizens and forbidden to do business with their Christian neighbors; all services and every kind of human contact were denied them, for they were not Aryan. At that time they stripped the Jews of all their workshops, businesses, and industries, which they and their fathers had built over the years. Their gold and silver were confiscated. And their furs. The carpets were removed from their drawing rooms, and the works of art, which the more senior officials took into their own possession. Quilts and pillowcases embroidered with the monograms of their lawful owners were unhesitatingly commandeered by neighbors. The Jews were then driven from their homes, rich and poor alike.

One and all they were marched through the streets, bareheaded or wearing *shtreimels,** those whose tunics were fastened with three buttons, and those who worried lest—God forbid—they lose the fourth button required by a different Hasidic court. And when they looked at the most recent arrivals, wearing stiff hats from Amsterdam and some deported from Budapest actually flaunting real top hats, they did not laugh or show surprise, for they saw the common heap where all the caps, bowlers, and *papachas** would end up.

When the manhunt began in Paris, the Germans had trouble at first distinguishing a French-Jewish face from a French-Aryan face. But in no time there were enough Frenchmen, in town and country, who were eager to help their conquerors, to be their eyes and show the SS and the Gestapo how to tell a pure French beret from a base beret on the head of one of France's stepsons.

And they seized Jews in coarse working boots, who had never been separated from the tilling of the soil, in the villages of Thrace and the borders of Lithuania, in the Crimea and the small farms of the Carpathians.

They had walked in these places from sunrise to sunset in the shade of broad trees, and had had permission since time immemorial to clear forests and cut up trees and float the logs down the Danube on a vast fleet of barges; and once these men were taken, a tribe of Jewish farmers was wiped off the face of the map of Europe as though they had never existed.

And then came the turn of the speakers of pure German, the intellectuals of Prague and Vienna. You could tell them by their dress, by their jackets with padded shoulders and velvet lapels. Many left their homes in shoes of kidskin, in skirts of suede or patent leather, shining and immaculate.

Even the Bohemians were not disheveled; they wore hats of soft felt with wide brims, tilted slightly to one side. When they climbed up into the railway cars designed for cattle, their faces wore an expression more of surprise than fear; and the country was full of such trucks. Though Germany was at war with Russia in the east and the Allied Forces in the west and needed all forms of transport for moving troops, all railway engines necessary for the movement of Jews were made available and the tracks kept clear. And they traveled with armed guards. And day and night the trains did not stop running.

When they took the Jews from their ancient homes in the towns of Italy, most members of the community still held to the belief that this was just a small cloud, which would in the end pass over. Only a few sensed that their Italian homeland was betraying them in their time of greatest need. Many seemed to be hovering between heaven and earth; a train from the southwest passed a train from the southeast and the Jews deported from Florence did not know that at this unknown junction they were meeting Jews from Zagreb, and Jews on a train from Hungary caught signs of Jews deported from Holland and Belgium and when one of the trains was shunted onto a siding outside town, the few railway workers around seemed to be posing them riddles:

"Westerbroek?"✦ "Drancy?"✦ "Romanesti?"✦

All the trains were bound for Poland, for the unknown. And once the Jews had been uprooted from their homes and deprived of all their property, they were set to work in sweatshops, whether in ghettos or forced labor camps, for a mere pittance. In the end the Nazis and their collaborators took the Jews' suitcases and their shoes and the rest of the clothes they had brought with them from home, and from the women they took their flowing hair; and then they took their souls.

And finally they burned their bodies. They carefully extracted the gold teeth and crowns from the mouths of the dead. They packed them in sealed boxes marked in code plus net weight plus consignment number plus destination, also in code. And the condemned went with hope in their hearts. Day after day they said, "Blessed be the Lord," and hour after hour they waited for a miracle. And hope saved them from utter desolation, and also stifled the spirit of rebellion.

All this time they looked for help—from where? Their longtime neighbors, their natural allies, were against them, most of them with equanimity. In the places where they had been born and raised, in their own towns they drowned in a sea of hostility. Gradually they came to realize the fact that a billion, two billion human beings were looking on and the world had forgotten them while they still breathed. No bomber took off from its base on their behalf; no company of soldiers went ahead and broke through one day in order to release them from the death camps, neither in Estonia in the north, nor at the gates of Budapest, nor to save the survivors of the ghetto of Lodz. Thousands of daring actions were carried out on the soil of Europe against targets of greater and lesser importance, as deemed appropriate by the commanders of the armies of the free world. Only targets of benefit to the Jews failed to inspire acts of daring and imagination, or to figure in the counsels of the leaders.

Youngsters tried to escape. The daring took up arms. More than can be estimated, they made their way, heedless of risk, to the woods and joined the partisans. "*Stoj! Kto jidjot?*" (Halt! Who goes there?) "*Svaj!*" (Friend!)—they tried to explain. Some were accepted and some were rejected. Many who fled the burning ghetto lost their lives on the forest paths, some dying of hunger, some from German bullets, and some even shot in ambushes by those who were meant to be their comrades in arms. Indigent farmers who had not managed to acquire rifles killed them with axes and pitchforks when the hunted sought a night's refuge on their threshing floors. The manhunt continued in the virgin forests.

Thus they went to their deaths devoid of all forms of communal defense. Distinguished among themselves by their dress, their behavior, and their languages, they moved through urban streets humming with life, among friends and acquaintances from the same alley, workmates, classmates, fellow students from the university, speakers of the same language—only one thing they did not have in common with them: their ethnic origin.

Even a Jewish memory, which finds it convenient to forget, could not easily obliterate the effect of finding the ground cut from beneath their feet, not because of any doubt of their citizenship, or disloyalty to their country,

WESTERBROEK: A concentration camp set up by the Germans in the north of Holland. It served as a transit camp for those destined for the death camps.

DRANCY: A French concentration camp whose prisoners were later sent to Auschwitz.

ROMANESTI: Those expelled from Romania.

THERESIENSTADT: Another name for the small Czech town of Terezin, which the Germans turned into a Jewish ghetto on October 16, 1941. Actually, this ghetto was nothing but a transit camp for the gas chambers at Auschwitz. To outward appearances it presented a false image of a model ghetto, with a high standard of living and a rich cultural life. The Germans even immortalized this fake image of the good life in a propaganda film called *The Führer Grants the Jews a Town,* which showed young Jews in a swimming race across the river, well-dressed women sitting in a cafe in Theresienstadt, and a football match in progress. Delegations from the Red Cross and from Denmark were invited to visit the place. They came and saw, and were taken in.

THE END OF THERESIENSTADT: The Allied armies had liberated Paris, Brussels, and Antwerp and had crossed the German border. The Soviet army had liberated Belgrade and was pushing into East Prussia. At that time there remained only one ghetto in Europe, Theresienstadt. The Nazi film studios had successfully completed a bogus documentary film about Theresienstadt in October 1944, the month that saw the beginning of the destruction of what was left of the Jews. The Jews of Bohemia and Moravia numbered 118,000 before the outbreak of hostilities. Thirty

or opinions, or even this time because of their faith and religion. Only their birth determined their fate. Long before they were transported in trains their fate had already been sealed beyond any possibility of appeal, to live a life of endless humiliation and to die powerless. Was this a certainty that could have been foreseen? A disaster that could have been prepared for?

There were some from whom even the certain knowledge of the general disaster was withheld. Even at the gates of Auschwitz they found it hard to grasp the message of a common Jewish fate. After all, they had cut themselves off from their common origin and of their own free will, or that of their parents, had dissociated themselves from the Jewish people. Few of them remembered the shape of the letter *yud.* When the knock came at the door, they could not believe it—descendants of court Jews who by exemplary effort worthy of the highest praise had created a quite unprecedented harmony between their self-negating Jewishness and their utter Germanism, were they too to be deported? One old lady was taken to Theresienstadt.✝ In a trainload of notables she was transported along with the other assimilated Berliners of Jewish origin.

The Germans joked with her with exaggerated politeness, since she was a great granddaughter of the composer Liszt, and a cousin of Gerhart Hauptmann,✝ one of Germany's greatest writers. Though they treated her with special respect, she suffered greatly. Sitting in her cell, the old lady sobbed and mumbled, "If Gerhart knew what they were doing to me, oh Gerhart!" And the prisoners of Theresienstadt looked on the old lady with pity, for it is hard to live in the shadow of death, and even harder to stand in the presence of living shadows.✝

"Such is Jewish fate. Professor Aron has died here (in the ghetto of Theresienstadt) at the age of 86. After the Great War (World War I), the French imprisoned him at Strasbourg, on the grounds that he sympathized with the Germans. He remained some time in prison and then the French deported him to Germany. Until 1936, he was a university professor. One of his sons was an officer on the Eastern front. One of his daughters emigrated to Israel, the second was sent with him to Theresienstadt. Jewish destiny: one son fought the Bolsheviks, one daughter came to Israel."

—GONDA REDLICH,
Life as If (a diary)

THE FINAL SOLUTION: The German plan for the destruction of the Jewish people. According to Hitler's fundamental belief, it was necessary to find a "revolutionary" solution for the Jewish problem. Either Reinhard Heydrich or Adolf Eichmann coined the label "the Final Solution." When, in the summer of 1941, it was decided that the Jews should be murdered and the exterminations were already at their height, a conference was convened at Wannsee, a suburb of Berlin, in a building that served as the German branch of Interpol. Its aim was interdepartmental coordination for the continuation and expansion of the policy of murder. Responsibility for carrying out the Final Solution was placed on the leader of the SS (the *Reichsführer* SS). It was at the Wannsee Conference that the decision was made about the means of carrying out the annihilation, and authority for its implementation was placed in the hands of Eichmann and his command.

thousand remained in the Theresienstadt ghetto, including thousands of youngsters yearning to follow the example of their brothers in Slovakia, who had rebelled and fled to the hills. The Germans decided to destroy them by bombing the ghetto from the air. Dr. Epstein, the last of the puppet leaders, was told to report to the German broadcasting studio in Dresden and protest to the world about the cruel bombings being carried out by Allied warplanes, so it seemed, against the ghetto. Dr. Epstein refused and was the first to be killed that day. On explicit orders from Berlin, all leaders of the Zionist and communal organizations and community executives were transferred from Theresienstadt to Auschwitz, together with the leaders of Czech Jewry, its writers, actors, musicians, sportsmen, singers, youth leaders, children, and their parents. Heroes of World War I, Jews from Denmark and Holland, and members of mixed marriages were included in this last transport, and were killed in the gas chambers of Birkenau on the night of October 28, 1944, a day of national celebration for the Czech parliament of Masaryk. After that, the gas chambers of Auschwitz ceased to function.

GERHART HAUPTMANN (1862-1946): Writer, poet, and playwright, Hauptmann was one of the greatest modern German writers. Unlike other German writers and thinkers, he did not leave Germany when the Nazis came to power, expressed no reservations about the Hitler regime, and did not utter a word of protest.

THE FINAL SOLUTION:

Q: Wasn't the Final Solution the realization of the racist theories that the Nazis had advocated from the very beginning?

A: The germ of the plan for the destruction of European Jewry is to be found in Hitler's Mein Kampf *and in his speeches in the Reichstag, but the intent went through various stages before it was put into effect. Until the beginning of 1939 at least, Hitler said nothing, neither in print nor in speech, about what he wanted to do with the Jews. If a plan for murder had taken shape in his mind, he did not share it with those around him.*

Q: In other words?

A: In order to carry out such an appalling, murderous plan, widespread favorable conditions were required, which were hard to imagine.

Q: Such as?

A: Firstly, the denial of all rights of the Jews, the repeal of Emancipation. This meant the cooperation of jurists, lawyers' offices, the ministries of justice and the interior. Secondly, the removal of Jews from the economic system, the theft of the property of millions of Jews, the confiscation of their homes and businesses. So businessmen also took part, industrialists, bankers, manufacturers, trade unions, civil authorities, as well as the police and their ancillary units, clerks at every level, and janitors—for whom personal profit was no small motive in the process of confiscation. Thirdly, social and physical isolation.

Perhaps even before all this, there was total elimination of Jews from all fields of culture, art, science, and education. This involved the cooperation of professors, managers of theaters and orchestras, writers, and poets. And their removal from affiliations they had had.

Q: How many railway workers, engineers, linesmen, transport

The Nazis strove to carry out the Final Solution✢ without compromise, to destroy the Jewish people in its entirety, to wipe it off the face of the earth. And if their plan failed, by a little or a lot, it is not their fault. A stiff-necked people is not easily destroyed. . . .

The Nazis were not content with the death of the Jews, with suffering and humiliation. They wanted the victims to believe that they were rightly despised, that their deaths had no meaning just as their lives were not sacred.✢

But among the Jews there were teachers and educators, a fact which escaped the notice of their murderers; from the days when the Temple still stood, Jewish sages had declared the right and obligation of every Jew to an education. In so doing they had preceded most of the nations of the world by fifteen hundred years. Since that time every Jewish boy at the age of three was already studying with his rabbi and no ideal was more binding upon a Jewish family than the education of its children. Even within the ghetto walls instruction did not cease.✢ The teachers were

L a n d	Zahl
A. Altreich	131.000
Ostmark	43.700
Ostgebiete	420.000
Generalgouvernement	2.284.000
Bialystok	400.000
Protektorat Böhmen und Mähren	74.200
Estland - Judenfrei -	
Lettland	3.500
Litauen	34.000
Belgien	43.000
Dänemark	5.600
Frankreich / Besetztes Gebiet	165.000
Unbesetztes Gebiet	700.000
Griechenland	69.600
Niederlande	160.000
Norwegen	1.300
B. Bulgarien	48.000
England	330.000
Finnland	2.300
Irland	4.000
Italien einschl. Sardinien	58.000
Albanien	200
Kroatien	40.000
Portugal	3.000
Rumänien einschl. Bessarabien	342.000
Schweden	8.000
Schweiz	18.000
Serbien	10.000
Slowakei	88.000
Spanien	6.000
Türkei (europ., Teil)	55.500
Ungarn	742.000
UdSSR	5.000.000
Ukraine 2.994.684	
Weißrußland aus- schl. Bialystok 446.484	
Zusammen: über	11.000.000

A page from the minutes of the Wannsee Conference: the decision to destroy 11 million Jews.

officials, squads of escorts, and such were required for the elimination of the Jews?

A: We haven't yet mentioned the builders of the camps, the manufacturers of the gas, the suppliers of machinery for forced labor, the furnace engineers, and finally the direct perpetrators of murder.

Q: And what about the neighbors, who closed their eyes whether in consent or out of impotence and the convenience of nonintervention?

A: Yes, they too. In other words, throughout this whole terrible process of carrying out a plan with no precedent in human history, a part was played, active or passive, by the broadest sectors of the German people.

Q: And other peoples?

A: And other peoples.

"In a submerged room within the walls of the 'Cavalier' barracks there is a faint light, a smell of urine and physical and spiritual pollution. But the seed of artistic inspiration does not perish, not even in the mud and the mire. There too it sprouts and gives forth blossom, like stars shining in the darkness."
　　—PETER GINZ (age 13), in the ghetto of Theresienstadt

PETER GINZ: A promising young artist who was killed in the gas chambers of Auschwitz. Ginz was 11 years old when World War II broke out. In the Theresienstadt ghetto he edited a children's newspaper for which he wrote and drew illustrations. When he reached the age of Bar Mitzvah, he wrote a novel based on the events of the time. (The manuscript is held in the museum at Terezin. Drawings and etchings from his prolific writing have survived and are on exhibition at Yad Vashem in Jerusalem.)

BUCHENWALD: A concentration camp, situated in central Germany, near Weimar. It was established in the summer of 1937. At first only political prisoners were sent there. In 1938, it began to receive Jews, who were brought en masse after Kristallnacht. In all 238,989 prisoners reached Buchenwald. Most of them were forced to work in the German armaments industry or in the mines. The SS men at Buchenwald displayed a particular measure of cruelty and bloodthirstiness.

YITZHAK KATZNELSON (1886-1944): Katznelson was born in White Russia, in the district of Minsk. From his youth, Katznelson wrote poetry in Hebrew and Yiddish. He also wrote plays and poems, some of them on biblical topics. Katznelson was very active in education and wrote books for children. At the outbreak of the war, he and his family moved to Warsaw, and in the ghetto there he ran a drama group, taught in the underground high school, and helped with the newspaper. His biblical drama, *Job,* was published by the underground press. Together with his son Tzvi, he took part in the first armed clash between the Jewish Fighting Organization and the German conquerors in the Warsaw ghetto, in January 1943. On the previous evening he had given an inspiring speech to his comrades. He wrote of this in his great poem, "The Song of the Murdered Jewish People." After the uprising he was arrested and imprisoned. He tried to maintain contact with his friends, but was sent to some unknown destination and all trace of him was lost.

precisely those who had taught in the schools that had been destroyed, and the youth leaders were those youngsters who had been the pride of the pioneer youth movements. It was they who improvised an organized framework, who set up classes within the walls, finding chalk and notebooks, and candles for lighting. Only their mission was different. They no longer saw their role as imparting knowledge or preparing their pupils thoroughly for the matriculation examinations . . . but to give them something vital for their very existence. They did not declare from their raised dais that the main thing was "to stand firm." Quietly and consistently they tried only to insist on the principle of sustaining the terrified spirit with a life of meaningfulness, the meaning of being a Jew, even on the brink of extinction. They had no time to convene conferences. They received no authorization of credentials or circular letters from any government ministries of education. As if with one common purpose, illegal educational institutions were established within the walls of the Vilna ghetto and the death camp of Buchenwald.✣ In due course they were set up in the displaced persons camps in Germany and in the internment camps on Cyprus. No matter how scattered and isolated, teachers answered the call of their consciences: Yitzhak Katznelson,✣ Emmanuel Ringelblum,✣ and Josef Kaplan✣ and dozens of their comrades in the Warsaw ghetto; Gonda Redlich✣ in There-

centration camp at Travniki (a village near Lublin). With the help of the Pole, Theodor Fayevski, the underground rescued him from there. He secretly returned to Warsaw and continued to work on the collection of invaluable material documenting the destruction of Polish Jewry during the war. When the Germans discovered the shelter where he, his wife, and his son were hiding, they arrested him and 35 other Jews, and tortured and then murdered them in the notorious Pawiak prison.

YIVO: Initial letters of Yidisher Visenshaftlicher Organizatsye, the principal world organization for the preservation of Yiddish culture and research in Yiddish language and literature. It was founded in Vilna in 1925, and has been in New York since 1940.

THE "JOINT": The Joint Distribution Committee—in full, the "Joint Distribution Committee of American Funds for the Relief of Jewish War Sufferers," the leading American Jewish relief organization, founded on November 17, 1914, during World War I.

JOSEF KAPLAN (1913-1942): Kaplan was born in Kalisz and studied at a ḥeder, a yeshiva, and a Hebrew high school. He joined Ha-Shomer Ha-Tza'ir and became an active youth leader and member of the group's directorate. He traveled the length and breadth of Poland organizing seminars, summer camps, and kibbutz training camps. He waived his right to immigration out of devotion to the movement and its activities. A humble man with simple ways, Kaplan spoke little and did much, and knew how to work under conditions of hunger and penury. He became very active in the underground, maintained contact with Jewish institutions and distant branches of the movement, and saw that there was material assistance for those in need. He became a father figure to the Zionist movement in its most difficult days. Kaplan wrote many letters, which were smuggled out through Switzerland, and published the movement newspaper *Neged Ha-Zerem* (Against the Stream). Despite his Jewish appearance, he took the risk of traveling all over occupied Poland in order to keep constant contact with movement members and encourage them. Kaplan was a central figure in the leadership of the Jewish Fighting Organization in Warsaw from its establishment in July 1942. Part of his work involved the forging of documents, and his role in this was discovered when one of the holders of these documents, captured by the Germans, broke down under torture. Kaplan

was arrested in September 1942, and despite attempts to free him, he was executed in the Pawiak prison.

EMMANUEL RINGELBLUM (1900-1944): Born in Buczacz, Ringelblum went to Warsaw in 1920 and studied history at the university, devoting his leisure time to cultural activities for youth. He wrote for the press and taught evening classes for workers. He received his doctorate in 1927. Ringelblum maintained contact with YIVO in Vilna and worked as a high school teacher. There he worked for the "Joint" and was very active in finding productive employment for poor Jews. He also wrote and published many works of scholarship. From the outbreak of the war, he was one of the active leaders of the "Joint" in Warsaw, representing them at the head of social work projects, especially ghetto housing committees, and joining the Jewish Fighting Organization. It was his energy and devotion that led to the establishment in the ghetto of the underground archives, which collected all the documents concerned with the martyrdom of Polish Jewry. After the crushing of the Warsaw ghetto uprising, the Nazis deported him to a con-

sienstadt. And when one was taken off to his death, others took his place. The Hebrew teachers taught in Hebrew and the Yiddish teachers taught in Yiddish and the average teachers, who came from private schools where Jews were taught in the language of the state, taught Jews in the ghetto, men and women, in Polish. And the Germans took the teacher Morgenstern, not because he had a teaching certificate but because he lacked his yellow certificate. They took Morgenstern and his daughter Cherna on the same day. An autumn breeze was blowing outside, and they stood arm in arm, father and daughter. Morgenstern means "morning star" and Cherna was his only daughter—until they were separated at the gate by a gesture from a finger in a leather glove.

GONDA REDLICH (1916–1944): Born in Ullmitz (Olomaicz), Moravia, Egon (Gonda) Redlich studied law and believed in Zionism and self-realization. In the autumn of 1940, at the time of the German occupation, he was vice principal of the Youth Aliyah school in Prague. He was sent to Theresienstadt, where he was very active in youth education. While at Theresienstadt, he kept a diary in Hebrew from 1942 to 1944. The diary was published in Hebrew under the title *Ḥayyim Ke'ilu* (Life as If, Ha-Kibbutz Hame'uḥad, 1984). In 1944, Redlich was deported to Auschwitz. Czech building workers found the diary in its hiding place in 1967.

✣ CHAPTER ONE ✣

*The Man
with His Head
on the Block
Continues to Hope*

"THE INTERROGATION":
From a poem by Erich Mühsam.

The title of this chapter, "The Man with His Head on the Block Continues to Hope," is taken from the writings of the German-Jewish writer and critic Walter Benjamin.

WALTER BENJAMIN (1892-1940): German philosopher and literary critic. During World War I Benjamin made no secret of his pacifist views. He studied philosophy at several universities in Germany and Switzerland. On finishing his studies in 1920, he settled in Germany, where he lived until 1933.

Benjamin is considered one of the great philosophic commentators on German literature. From 1929, he was closely associated with Bertolt Brecht and the Communists, and interpreted the theories of Karl Marx. With the rise of the Nazis, he fled to Paris. There he was arrested as a German citizen and held under supervision until 1939. Before the German occupation of France, he fled south to Nice with a group of refugees, intending to cross the frontier into Spain. When the Spanish Border Police threatened to send them back the way they had come, Benjamin took his own life.

Name? asked the interrogator.*

I told him my name.

Born?

I said: yes.

I mean when!

I gave the date.

Religion?

That's not your concern.

So, a Jew!

ERICH MÜHSAM (1878-1934): A writer and politician who was a German Socialist with Communist-anarchist views. Mühsam, along with other Jewish intellectuals Gustav Landauer and Ernst Toller, was a participant in the revolutionary government of Bavaria under the leadership of Kurt Eisner, which was set up at the end of World War I. Mühsam was murdered by the Nazis after being tortured in the camp of Oranienburg.

KURT EISNER (1867-1919): German writer and political leader who was the son of a Jewish industrialist from Berlin. In 1917, he took part in the founding of the Independent Socialist Party (USPD). With the collapse of the imperial regime, he became head of the revolutionary movement, and was then elected prime minister of the Revolutionary Government of Bavaria by the council of workers, farmers, and soldiers on November 8, 1918. Eisner strove for Bavarian autonomy and fought against German nationalism. His opinions, his actions, and his Jewishness caused a furor in Germany. In the wake of anti-Semitic and nationalist incitement, his party was roundly defeated in the elections and he was murdered on February 21, 1919, by Graf Arco-Valley of the Freikorps, a forerunner of Hitler's storm troops.

GUSTAV LANDAUER (1870-1919): German-Jewish writer and thinker and holder of anarchist views. In 1919, he was appointed minister of culture in the revolutionary government of Kurt Eisner in Bavaria. After a short time he resigned in protest against the violent methods of the new regime, which were carried out by the Communists. When the regime was suppressed, he was murdered by the soldiers who took him prisoner.

ERNST TOLLER (1893-1939): German writer and revolutionary born to a Jewish family. When World War I broke out, Toller volunteered for the army, fought, and was wounded and released as a disabled veteran in 1915. The war had a traumatic effect upon him and turned his views upside down. In 1919 he joined the leadership of the Socialist Republic of Bavaria. After the suppression of the revolution, he was arrested and sentenced to five years imprisonment.

He fought for the Republicans in Spain (1936-1939) and never gave up his war against Nazism and Fascism. His disappointment with the Communist movement and dismay at the victory of Franco in Spain cast him into a profound depression. He took his own life in New York.

REPRESSION SWELLS

MARCH 9, 1933: The beginning of anti-Jewish riots in Germany by storm troopers (SA) and the Stahlhelm organization. **APRIL 1, 1933:** Anti-Jewish boycott in Germany. **APRIL 7, 1933:** Jews in Germany are forbidden to work in government offices. **APRIL 21, 1933:** Jews in Germany are forbidden to practice ritual slaughter. **OCTOBER 17, 1933:** Jews in Germany are forbidden to work for newspapers. **MAY 31, 1935:** Jews are forbidden to enlist in the German army. **JUNE 1935:** Anti-Jewish riots occur in Poland. **DECEMBER 1935:** Riots against the Jews take place at Polish universities; Jewish students are allocated special benches. **MARCH 3, 1936:** Jewish doctors (3,152 in number) are forbidden to work in public health institutions in Germany. **MARCH 9, 1936:** Anti-Jewish riots occur in the Polish town of Paszitik. **DECEMBER 3, 1938:** Jews are excluded from the German economy. **JANUARY 1939:** A law is proposed in the Polish parliament to deprive Jews of citizenship. **JANUARY 30, 1939:** In the Reichstag, Hitler threatens to destroy the Jews of Europe. **FEBRUARY 9, 1939:** A law in Italy reduces the economic activity of the Jews. **APRIL 18, 1939:** Anti-Jewish racist legislation is enacted in Slovakia. **MAY 3, 1939:** A law is passed in Hungary instituting a *numerus clausus,* a quota, restricting the participation of Jews in the free professions.

Dinslaken, August 18, 1935

My dear son,

You're lucky you're not in Germany at this time. But you're not exempt from knowing what is going on in our native land. Our neighbor, Oscar Hermann, has been dismissed from his job. For thirty years we have seen the man working hard in the interests of the city as headmaster of the Wilhelm High School and as the organizer of professional courses, which were famous throughout the land. He has educated thousands of young people, Jews and non-Jews, to a life of productivity, to what should be a life of happiness. This fine scholar who despite his origin—from Russian Galicia—quickly became editor of our splendid scientific encyclopedia, thanks to his elevated German style and his many books on botany and mathematics, which are a credit to our scientific establishment, has been fired. I knew, of course, that Dr. Hermann held socialist views, but he was totally nonpolitical, a pure intellectual, with a fine mind, a man of integrity who sought justice.

As you know, he was our neighbor for many years before you went to study in France, and his wooden leg is a souvenir of his patriotic service in World War I; if I'm not mistaken, he lost his leg at the Battle of Tannenberg.

One of our hooligans yelled at him one day on the trolley car, "Dirty Jew! Disabled or not, you should get up for a German!" and kicked the good doctor off the trolley car (fortunately the car was slowing down before a stop); it was Oscar Hermann who was ashamed to admit to his wife what had happened, and explained away the mud smeared on his coat as just a fall. My God! What kind of mud are they pushing us into?

With much love,
Father

JEWISH RESPONSES

JANUARY 30, 1933: Establishment of the Association for Aid to Jewish Youth in Berlin. **MARCH 27, 1933:** The American Jewish Congress holds a mass demonstration in New York in protest against Nazi terror in Germany. **APRIL 4, 1933:** "Wear Your Yellow Patch with Pride," an article by Robert Waltsch is published in *Jüdische Rundschau,* the German-Jewish Zionist newspaper. It is the first in a series titled "Affirm Your Jewishness." These titles became rallying cries for the Jews of Germany. **APRIL 26, 1933:** Decision by the National Committee of Jews in Palestine to set up a project for absorbing immigrants from Germany. **MID-MAY 1933:** Members of Jewish delegations to the League of Nations present a petition concerning discrimination against Jews in Germany (the Franz Bernheim Petition). **MAY 20, 1933:** Jews of Paris meet in a mass rally to protest against the anti-Jewish campaign in Germany. **JUNE 27, 1933:** The Jews of London hold a mass anti-Nazi protest rally. **AUGUST 10, 1933:** The American Jewish Congress declares a boycott of Nazi Germany. **FEBRUARY 1934:** Kibbutz Ein Harod absorbs the first group of Jewish boys, refugees from Germany. **FEBRUARY 4, 1936:** David Frankfurter attempts to kill Wilhelm Gustlof, the leader of the Swiss Nazi Party, in revenge for the persecution of Jews in Germany. **MARCH 17, 1936:** Jews in Poland, with the participation of Poles from liberal and left-wing circles, conduct mass demonstrations in protest against the riots in Poland. **JUNE 30, 1936:** Jews of Poland conduct a general strike in protest against anti-Semitism. **DECEMBER 1938:** *Aliyah Bet* (organized illegal immigration) is established in Palestine. **JANUARY 1939:** German Jews begin immigrating illegally to Palestine. By the end of 1940, 27,000 immigrants had reached Palestine from greater Germany.

Once the Nazis rose to power, they immediately began to implement their racist theories. Henceforth, blood and race were the criteria for German citizenship, and the expulsion of Jews from public life became a top level priority. This is the sequence of decrees enacted against the Jews of Germany up to the outbreak of World War II: expulsion of Jewish judges from the courts in Frankfurt and Breslau; expulsion of Jewish doctors from public service; riots in Berlin and provincial cities; a *numerus clausus* (quota) for Jewish students at the universities; economic boycott; expulsion of Jewish artists from national associations; and the Nuremberg Laws.

NUREMBERG LAWS: From September 8–14, 1935, the Freedom Convention of the Nazi Party met in Nuremberg. At this convention two laws were ratified whose main purpose was to harm the Jews: a Citizenship of the Reich Law and a Law for the Protection of German Blood and German Honor. The first law revoked civil equality, which had been granted to the Jews during the period of the Emancipation; the second law gave official authority to racism and on grounds of principle separated the Jews from the rest of the population.

GERMANY'S ANNEXATIONS
AND ALLIANCES

OCTOBER 14, 1933: Germany walks out of the disarmament talks at the League of Nations, and five days later leaves the League. **JANUARY 26, 1934**: Germany and Poland sign a pact of nonaggression. **JULY 25, 1934**: The Nazis attempt a coup in Austria; Dolfuss, the Austrian prime minister, is murdered. **JANUARY 7, 1935**: The Franco-Italian Treaty is signed in Rome. The signatories are Mussolini and Laval. **JANUARY 13, 1935**: The Saar region is annexed to Germany. **MARCH 6, 1935**: Compulsory military service is renewed in Germany, in flagrant violation of the Treaty of Versailles, signed at the end of World War I in 1919. **OCTOBER 3, 1935**: Italy invades Abyssinia. **MAY 2, 1936**: The Italian army occupies Addis Ababa, the capital of Abyssinia; three days later Abyssinia surrenders. **JULY 26, 1936**: Germany and Italy begin their military intervention in the Spanish Civil War. **AUGUST 25, 1936**: The Italian-German Treaty, which established the Rome-Berlin Axis, is signed. **JULY 7, 1937**: Japan invades China. **NOVEMBER 25, 1937**: Germany and Japan sign a political and military treaty. **MARCH 13, 1938**: The German Reich annexes Austria. Vienna gives Hitler an enthusiastic welcome. **APRIL 26, 1938**: Regulations are put into effect concerning the confiscation of Jewish property in Germany. **AUGUST 1, 1938**: The Bureau for Jewish Emigration is established under the command of Adolf Eichmann. **SEPTEMBER 27, 1938**: Jewish lawyers in Germany (1,753 in number) are forbidden from appearing in the courts. **SEPTEMBER 29–30, 1938**: The Munich agreement is reached, with the participation of British Prime Minister Chamberlain, French Premier Daladier, Hitler, and Mussolini. England agrees to let Germany annex the part of Czechoslovakia known as the Sudetenland. **OCTOBER 1, 1938**: Germany annexes the Sudeten-

Dinslaken, Tuesday, November 9, 1938

My dear son,

The stranger slipped into my office like a cat. I could see from his face at once that he was a Jew. He said, "I'm the head of the congregation at Dusseldorf. I spent the night in the railway station waiting room at Gelsenkirchen. Please, let me into the orphanage. Just for a little while. Maybe I'll find a way out. They're arresting Jews everywhere. The synagogues are going up in flames."

I listened with growing fear. Before I could get up and say something, the man stepped back and cried in a broken voice, "No! I won't come in! There's no safety here either. We're all lost!"

I saw him vanish in the heavy mist that covered the road, and he never came back.

There's someone at the door. More tomorrow.

Father

My dear Heinz,

You'll be surprised, no doubt, when I tell you that I managed by great effort to show no sign of emotion. This was the only way I could prevent panic from breaking out among the children and the staff. At the same time, I decided I could not leave the children without some preparation for what is going to happen.

That evening I assembled in the dining hall our forty-six staff members and two-thirds of the students. It was 7:30 and I told them briefly, in dry tones:

"Yesterday, as you know, a member of the German Embassy in Paris by the name of vom Rath was murdered. Responsibility for the murder has been placed upon the Jews. All the great political tension is being vented on the Jews alone, and it will no doubt reach a peak in the next few hours. My feeling is," I said, "that the Jews of Germany are in for hard times, worse than anything they have known since the Middle Ages. Be strong hearted, and trust in God."

As I was finishing a squad of marchers passed by outside and their raucous singing was heard within. I heard our teacher's assistant, a young lad who had only recently been taken on, join in singing, humming to himself—in my presence—the "Horst Wessel Lied."✢

"What is this?" I asked in shock.

I ordered everybody to go to the upper rooms, and no one but me was to open the front door, "and from now on, obey my instructions alone!" At 9:30 in the morning there was a ring of the bell at the entrance gate to the Dinslaken Orphanage. I opened the gate; no less than fifty men, most of them in high-necked tunics, burst in. Pushing me to one side, they ran to the dining hall, which was empty, and began their systematic work of destruction. From upstairs could be heard the scared voices of the children. I called out to them, "Boys! Outside immediately! Everyone! Into the street!"

I did this in violation of the orders of the Gestapo. I hoped that in the street, in a public place, we would be in less danger. The children followed my instructions with exemplary dispatch. They streamed down the winding staircase to the back of the building.

land. **OCTOBER 5, 1938**: The passports of German Jews are cancelled. **OCTOBER 28, 1938**: More than 17,000 Jews of Polish nationality are deported from Germany to Zbaszyn on the Polish frontier. **NOVEMBER 6, 1938**: Herschel Grinspan assaults Ernst vom Rath, the secretary of the German embassy in France. **NOVEMBER 9–11, 1938**: The Kristallnacht riots occur in Germany and Austria.

"HORST WESSEL LIED": A German song, which became the anthem of the Nazi storm troopers and was heard constantly throughout Germany and occupied Europe. The song includes the following lines, "When Jewish blood is spilled from the blade of the knife / we feel twice as good."

UNTERMENSCHEN (German): Sub-humans. The Nazis used the term with reference to Jews, Gypsies, Poles, and at a later period also for Soviet soldiers with Mongolian or Tartar features.

The prayer below, composed by Rabbi Leo Baeck for the Eve of the Day of Atonement 5696 (1935), was banned by order of the Gestapo. Dr. Baeck and Otto Hirsch, the leaders of German Jewry, were imprisoned. Here is the prayer:

"At this hour the whole House of Israel stands before God. With the courage with which we stand before Him to confess our sins, as individuals and as a community, with that same courage we express our disgust at the lies that are raised against us, at the accusation that bears false witness against our faith; we have a history of spiritual greatness, a history of pride and glory of the spirit, upon which we take our stand when enemies and detractors would do us harm. God, who guided our ancestors from generation to generation, will guide us and our children at this hour; at this time the whole House of Israel stands before God—grief and suffering in our hearts. By our silence, by this total silence we express before God what is in our hearts. May our silence cry out more than anything we say."

OTTO HIRSCH (1885-1941): Jewish leader and chairman of the Central Association for German Citizens of the Mosaic Faith during the Nazi period. Hirsch stood up to the Nazi authorities with courage and dignity. He was arrested and perished in the camp of Mauthausen.

TROTSKY (1870-1940): A Russian revolutionary born to a Jewish family, Lev Trotsky's original name was Lev Davidovitch Bronstein. Because of his activity on behalf of the Russian Social Democratic Party, Trotsky was imprisoned, exiled, and ultimately fled abroad before the revolution. Trotsky held Marxist views; he was at first a Menshevik, but then joined with Lenin. Trotsky was one of the leaders of the Civil War, which broke out after the October Revolution; he founded and organized the Red Army (1918-1920). After the death of Lenin (1924), Trotsky opposed Stalin, who worked to have him removed from the Communist Party (1927) and expelled from the Soviet Union (1929). In exile Trotsky set up the Fourth Internationale (known by its nickname, the "Trotskisti"). He was murdered in exile in Mexico by an assassin sent by Stalin. To this day there are groups of Trotskyites in the world who preach his ideas of ongoing revolution.

Most of them were bareheaded and had not even taken their coats, though it was cold and wet. I joined them and tried to lead them to a busy junction, near the town hall.

About a dozen policemen were standing in front of us. I ran toward them, intending to ask their help. Captain Freihahn, whom I knew well, quieted the crowd and called out to me, "Don't expect protection! Jews will get no protection from us! Get away from here, you and your vermin!"

And the policemen barred our way and thrust us back.

"Better to kill me, and the children, and the nightmare will be over!" I shouted at him.

"Take it easy!" replied Freihahn, a cynical smile on his lips. He pushed the children onto a wet lawn in the grounds of the orphanage and told us not to leave the place: "That's an order!" We could see how the Gestapo were destroying the building, systematically, under police supervision. Through the breaches in the wall, which hitherto had been doors and windows, they were throwing out beds, tables, cupboards, pieces of piano, books. I saw my gramophone flying through the air.

In the meantime hundreds of people were gathering around the building. Among them were familiar faces, suppliers, craftsmen, friends.

They gazed at the spectacle with total indifference.

At 10:15 the sound of sirens split the air. Immediately, thick smoke could be seen above the roofs: the great synagogue was on fire.

When huge tongues of fire and smoke were already billowing upward, the firemen came in a hurry and worked hard to save from the fire . . . the houses of Christians in the vicinity.

Without my noticing when or how it happened, Jewish refugees from other streets in the area of the burning synagogue had been assembling in our school yard. Most were poorly dressed women, but there were also men who up till now had somehow escaped arrest. Now they were ordered to abandon their homes and assemble in the school yard.

"What are you staring at these *Untermenschen*⁺ for?" screamed the man in uniform as he dispersed the crowd of curious spectators.

Our "family" had grown by ninety souls. We were packed indoors now, in one of the small halls of the school. We were forbidden to go out.

We were soon informed that all Jewish males under the age of sixty were being transported to Dachau. The children's turn would come later.

My son,

Do you remember, perhaps, a boy with a long face and a remarkably high forehead? His name was Leo and I used to call him Leo der Junge, young Leo; I believed he was destined for great things. . . .

Of course, I wasn't thinking of Trotsky⁺ but Leon Blum⁺ . . . they took young Leo with the first group.

It was Herr Hugo Cohen—I'm sure you remember how he was always given a place at the

LEON BLUM (1872-1950): Franco-Jewish statesman and writer who stood at the head of the French Socialist Party. Blum was the first Jew to be elected premier of France, at the head of the Popular Front (1936-1937). As premier, Blum passed numerous amendments to the law for the benefit of the workers. During the German occupation he was arrested by the Vichy government (1940) and handed over to the Germans. Blum was imprisoned in Dachau (1942-1945) because of his opposition to the Petain government, which cooperated with the Germans.

COUNT FONTANA: "Pardon me, Your Holiness. In Berlin I was eyewitness to the loading of Jewish children onto trucks by the Nazis."

The Pope (in anger): "Eyewitness! Count, a diplomat must look, see—and keep quiet!"

Before they could recover from the riots, the Third Reich condemned the Jews to isolation and exclusion by stamping the letter "J" in their passports and personal documents, at the suggestion of Dr. Heinrich Rothmund, the chief of the Swiss police, Aliens Division.

president's table at any important celebration, being the only man in the town who had been awarded the Iron Cross, First Class, for bravery in the War for the Fatherland—who led the men marching off to Dachau, wearing his decoration with pride. "Jewish swine, where did you steal that medal?" With a single blow the SS man sent the medal and its ribbon flying. The Iron Cross, worse luck, hit the patently non-Aryan snout of the *Sturmbannführer,*✢ who shouted, "Mutiny! The Jewish vermin are rebelling!"

A hail of blows from whips and truncheons fell on their heads. The brow and face of old Hugo Cohen streamed with blood. But he continued to march with dignity, as though on parade for the last time. The day grew dark. *Everyone had been savagely beaten.* That evening I tried, for the first time in my life, to get drunk. I covered the windows. *The sound of the siren splashed against our window.* And all this, my son, is no nightmare. It really is happening, here and now, *on the soil of Germany, the warm and generous. . . .*✢

> With much love,
> Father

STURMBANNFÜHRER: An SS officer, equivalent in rank to a major.

The sentences italicized at the end of the letter are lines of poetry by Alfred Mombert and Gertrud Kolmar, German-Jewish poets of the period.

ALFRED MOMBERT (1872-1942): Poet, philosopher, and naturalist who lived in the town of Heidelberg. In 1933, with the rise of the Nazis to power, Mombert was removed from the German Academy for Language and Poetry because of his Jewish origin. Arrested and transferred from camp to camp, Mombert finally reached a detention camp in the south of France. There he fell sick, and his friends in Switzerland succeeded in obtaining his release.

GERTRUD KOLMAR (1894-1943): A Jewish poet from Berlin who is considered one of the greatest women poets in modern German literature. Even though the Nazis were rising in power, Gertrud Kolmar remained in Berlin in order to support her sick father—until she was taken to Theresienstadt. She was arrested along with the last Jews of Berlin, on August 27, 1943, and sent to Auschwitz, where she perished.

✦ CHAPTER TWO ✦

The Diary of Leo der Junge

and a Single Letter

to Cherna Morgenstern

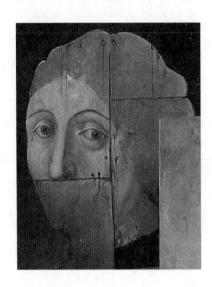

My name is Leo der Junge, and I was an errand boy for the firm Klein und Krever, and I am leaving this notebook here in the cellar as a memorial. Whoever finds it is requested to send it to the following address: Cherna Morgenstern, 3 Chopin Street, Vilna, Poland. Or else to Erik Bader, Somewhere in Palestine. Thank you, whoever you are.

Vienna, March 3, 1938.

Page 1.

I, Leo der Junge, was a boy in the orphanage at Dinslaken in Germany. I had never thought of writing a diary. When I came across this thick notebook, with its copper fastener and clasp, I remembered my cousin's diary. When she was staying with us, I used to see her all by herself by the window, writing down what had happened to her. I didn't understand what happens to a girl of nine, and I asked Cherna whether she wanted to be a writer. Cherna smiled at me and said, "I already am." Cherna had a diary bound in blue velvet, with a gilt clasp. I was five years old. That was my last summer in Berlin. Then my father told me we would have to move to a small town, "small but nice." I cried. Now I have a strong desire to write down what is happening to me and I don't know where to begin.

Page 2.

They call me Leo der Junge, but my real name is Leo Arieh Morgenstern. But from the time I arrived in Dinslaken I have answered to the name of Leo der Junge. For there are three boys named Leo in the orphanage. One of them is Leo Shtik,⁺ a sharp-featured, wily boy almost my age, although he immediately started bullying me as though he were bigger and an old timer. He had been in the orphanage longer than me, and knew lots of mischievous pranks, which is why they called him Leo Shtik. The king of the place was Leo der Grosse. No one knew where he was from. He was a head and shoulders taller than the other boys in the class and already had a golden tuft growing on his upper lip, and anything he said was a sacred command. No one disputed his leadership. Once I helped him solve some problems in mathematics for an exam, which aroused his admiration, and he awarded me the title Professor Einstein⁺ and gave me his protection. There was no one happier than me in the whole of Dinslaken. But our class teacher came and strictly forbade anyone to call me Professor Einstein since,

as he put it, it was not good in those days for a Jewish boy to put on airs. But all I wanted to do when I grew up was excel like Leo der Grosse, who was a champion runner.

Page 3.

The Stahlhelm⁺ hooligans have been rampaging in the neighborhood, and our teachers have been trying to create an atmosphere of peace and security within the walls of the orphanage. Particularly the principal, Dr. Marten. He puts himself now in the front on all our trips. Many people used to raise their caps in greeting to our principal, with his old-fashioned monocle, striding proudly with neck outstretched, like a goose at the head of her goslings. Dr. Marten was concerned to place me near him, and did not conceal his affection for me. It was he who recommended to Professor Hermann that I transfer next year to his Wilhelm High School, and on the last visit of the district inspector I happened to hear Dr. Marten tell him, pointing at me, "and that boy with the high forehead, sir, is a genius." That's why he urged me, after the visit of the men from Kripo,⁺ to go and live in Vienna until the danger passed. He himself was trembling with fury after the visit of the two men from Kripo.

Page 4.

I was six years old when the Nazi Party came to power. I saw their magnificent parades from my window. I loved the evening torchlight processions and the flags waving in the breeze. I couldn't understand why I wasn't allowed like the rest of the pupils to wear the uniform of a shirt and leather belt. I knew of course that I was Jewish and that I and the other four Jewish boys in the school were excused from writing on the Sabbath. I used to visit a lot at the homes of my Christian friends, and I never heard any anti-Semitic

SHTIK (Yiddish): Prank.

PROFESSOR EINSTEIN: The reference is to the great Jewish scientist, Albert Einstein (1879-1955), most well known for his theory of relativity. Einstein was awarded the Nobel Prize in physics in 1921.

STAHLHELM: An organization that began as an association of soldiers released after service at the front in World War I. It was founded in 1918. The organization grew stronger and in the course of time was opened up to ex-soldiers who had not fought at the front. From 1929, the organization drew close to the Nazi Party, and by 1933, large sections of it merged with Hitler's storm troopers.

KRIPO: Abbreviation for Kriminalpolizei, the criminal police in Germany.

KRISTALLNACHT: When the Nazis saw that legal methods would not suffice to compel all the Jews of Germany to leave the country, they arranged the greatest pogrom of the period, known as Kristallnacht (the night of broken glass—when fragments of glass from the windows in Jewish enterprises and synagogues littered the streets). On November 9, 1938, and the two days following, the Nazis and their supporters burned down 250 synagogues, looted and destroyed a tremendous amount of Jewish property, killed many Jews openly in the towns, and sent about 30,000 more to the concentration camps.

KADDISH: The Jewish memorial prayer for the dead, recited during the eleven-month period of bereavement and on the anniversary of the death.

curses or insults—until the night when cries were heard from the end of town where the poor Jewish tanners lived. The next day Otto Reicher turned up in school with his head wrapped in a bloody bandage. He was very pale, but our class teacher, Herr Gaier, calmed us by saying that the rioters were hooligans from out of town and the police would know how to deal with them. On that same occasion our beloved class teacher informed us that he was leaving us, since his new post would take up "all his time and energy." I asked him what this new post was, and Herr Gaier replied that he had been appointed head of the Nazi Party in our town. On Kristallnacht⁺ it was he who presided over the destruction of the orphanage building, that's what Otto wrote me. From him too I learned what happened with Leo der Grosse.

A new teacher came to the institution and immediately introduced himself to the class, "My name is Levine, but I am not of the tribe of Moses."

From a bench at the back a voice was heard, "Thank God, until now we've never had a donkey in the class." It was the voice of Leo der Grosse. He was ordered to approach the dais. The teacher gave him a slap in the face. Without hesitation Leo hit the teacher back, a stinging blow. (A later addition, in pencil.) From the same source: after Kristallnacht, Leo der Grosse disappeared.

Page 5.

I don't like Uncle Arthur, may God forgive me for my ingratitude. It was he who got me into the orphanage at Dinslaken after my father died, and saw to all my needs. Uncle Arthur, who lives in Vienna, is from an old Altona family. Aunt Rita is my father's sister and it was from her that I learned that my father was born in Russia and it was while on his way to Germany that he received the citizenship of the young state of Poland. He was a pharmacist's assistant in a small town, and anyone who didn't know him from the pharmacy knew him as the number one volunteer fireman. My father died in the great fire on Blumenplatz, going to the aid of an old woman and her cat. It was the mayor himself who delivered the funeral eulogy for my father and described him as a perfect example of true German citizenship. Uncle Arthur said it was idiotic on the part of Dr. Marten to start a panic on account of "two Kripo." Of my mother's origin I have learned nothing to this day. Only once did my father take me to visit her grave at Weissensee in Berlin. My father said *Kaddish*⁺ and told me that soon we would be going to live away from Berlin, and that was

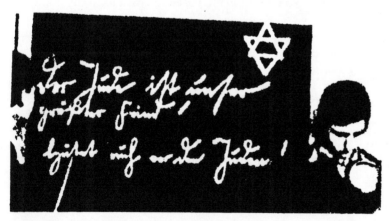

The writing on the blackboard: "The Jew is our greatest enemy. Beware of the Jews."
—Written by a teacher in a German school in 1935.

why we had come to say goodbye to Mother. I asked, "Father, why can't I remember Mother?" and he said to me, "Because she died when you were born." I didn't understand and he explained. For many days and nights terrible pictures haunted me, in my dream I saw my arms clutching my mother's neck like the arms of an octopus. By my father's grave my Aunt Rita held me in her arms and said, "Now, my poor thing, you're a proper orphan." I asked her what a "proper orphan" was and she said, "Somebody who has nobody in the world." I couldn't understand why I was a proper orphan if I still had them, Aunt Rita and Uncle Arthur.

Page 6. April 8, 1938.

This is the story of what they did to a Jewish member of the town council and the rabbi of Vienna. I saw the councilman and his wife crossing Tempelgasse. They were wearing their best clothes, though it was not Shabbat. There were armed guards standing by the community center. They ordered the councilman to go in before his wife could tug at his sleeve. They pushed her back to the other side of the gate. Some minutes later the councilman emerged holding a bucket and a cloth. They ordered him to scrub the tiles of the square. When he hesitated they hit him on the back and he sprawled on the ground. At once he started crawling on all fours and scrubbing as commanded. A crowd gathered by the gate. Some hurried away, turning their faces aside in disgust. Others shouted encouragement to the SS men. Then an old man of seventy or more was brought out of the building. He was wrapped in a prayer shawl and he too was carrying a bucket and cloth. He got down on all fours next to the councilman.

He said, "Good morning, Herr Councilman."

"Good morning, Rabbi," replied the latter.

The Nazi separated them, treading on the end of the trailing prayer shawl. The rabbi's silver hair was revealed, with the tefillin[+] on his forehead. The old man's body crawling forward and being divested of the prayer shawl looked for a moment like some creature shedding its skin. All around me there were chuckles and sounds of astonishment. I couldn't breathe.

The Nazi stooped slightly and said to the rabbi, "Nu, Rabbi, how do you like it?"

The rabbi stared at the young Nazi and said, "If it pleases our Father in Heaven, I am His servant." He continued vigorously scrubbing the tiles.

I found the councilman's wife around the corner, leaning against a tree as though paralyzed. She had a handkerchief gripped between her teeth, and was trembling all over.

"Madame," I whispered to her, "your husband is alive. He is not bleeding."

"He is not bleeding?" she repeated in amazement, and burst into sobs, pressing me to her breast.

Page 7. April 10, 1938.

In Cafe Rapoport they secretly distribute aid to refugees. I went there, but I didn't have the courage to take anything. I very much wanted to find a place of my own

and get away from my uncle's house. It annoyed me that he didn't believe what I had seen in the square of the community center. Uncle Arthur reproached me for spreading false rumors "just like those refugees." How did I know it was a councilman and the rabbi, and not "just ordinary Jews"? I had heard it explicitly from their own lips, but all my precise description of their appearance was of no avail. At work everybody was talking about what had happened. And this annoyed Uncle Arthur even more. He is the chief accountant for Klein und Krever, where I am also working now as an errand boy. I meet Erik on the back stairs and we talk about everything. Erik Bader is my new friend, and he is getting ready to go to Amsterdam to join a pioneer youth training camp. Yesterday I went with him to 42 Kaiserstrasse; maybe I'd manage to get myself on the list. But the Palestine office is very fussy and I'm still a minor in the eyes of the office clerks. Erik's father holds a Dutch passport and Erik is trying to persuade his father they should all go to Amsterdam while it is still possible.[+] Erik's family calls him a "troublemaker" and forbids him to mention the existence of the Dutch passport. A postcard has arrived from Uncle Morgenstern in Vilna. He asks about me. But not a word about Cherna. There's no Hitler but there is fanatical anti-Semitism in Poland.[+] He asks if I would like to join him. The company of Klein und Krever

TEFILLIN: Two small leather cases containing texts from the Pentateuch worn by Jews during morning prayers, one on the head and one on the right arm. For the origin of the practice, see Deuteronomy 6:8: "Bind them [these words] as a sign on your hand and let them serve as a symbol on your forehead."

THE PICTURE BEHIND THE SMILE: A Jew goes to see a friend, the manager of a travel agency in Berlin, to seek his advice about where he could or should flee. America? Not permitted. Argentina? Makes difficulties. He goes through the list of all the other countries; either they place restrictions on immigration or else they have shut the gates completely. In the end, the friend puts a globe in front of him and says, "Here they all are. Choose for yourself!" The Jew examines the globe for a while, first one side then the other, and asks, "Do you have another globe?"

FANATICAL ANTI-SEMITISM IN POLAND: The main anti-Semitic party in Poland was the National Democratic Party (ND), whose members were known as *Andeks*. It was first organized under the name of the National League (LN) by Roman Demovsky in 1893. During the time of Marshal Pilsudski's regime between the two world wars, it formed the right-wing opposition. It had deep roots in Polish society and was very influential. Among student and nationalist circles, more extreme anti-Semitic groups formed, of a more active and militant nature, which advocated in their newspaper "the elimination of the parasitic Jewish community in Poland" and the deliverance of Poland from "the worm that is corrupting everything good in it."

is listed now under the name of a Christian partner but the Kleins are the real owners. Erik and I meet several times a day by the back entrance. We are forbidden to use the front entrance for security reasons.

Erik says grownups are afraid to listen to the truth and sometimes they're even more helpless than children.

Page 8. May 18, 1938.

Herr Klein has been arrested and imprisoned in Dachau. Uncle Arthur was very pale when he got home from work. I heard him telling Aunt Rita the news. He kept on asking, as though talking to himself, "But what was he arrested for? Herr Klein is a very honest man." I'm surprised at Uncle Arthur asking such questions. The owner of the spice shop next door has also been imprisoned in Dachau, and many more. For some days now I've noticed Aunt Rita dressing rather strangely. Before she leaves the house she wraps herself in an enormous sweater that smells of mothballs and looks in all directions in case anyone is watching. I wanted to go with her but she refused point-blank. She forbade me to tell anyone, not even Uncle Arthur, about her going out. Yesterday it happened that something fell out of her sweater. It was a silver candlestick. Aunt Rita swore me to secrecy and hurried out. I followed her as far as the square and saw her enter a house where all the residents are Christian. Aunt Rita has never done anything without Uncle Arthur knowing about it, that's why I was surprised at her behavior. She didn't even protest when Uncle Arthur said, at first in hints and then explicitly, that I should go back to the orphanage at Dinslaken, that it would be better for me. Economically my presence was certainly no burden to them; I earned my keep and they were not yet without means. Something else was worrying my uncle. I never realized that this house too was beset by fear.

Page 9. May 20, 1938.

Uncle Arthur had lived in Vienna for twenty years. Aunt Rita was my father's sister but my uncle came from an old Altona family. He used to tell with pride the story of one of his ancestors, who was a supplier to the crown prince. He saw himself as a believer in the great German culture, and the members of his family in Altona and Berlin felt a

responsibility for the spiritual welfare of a nation that denied their right to be counted among its citizens. I saw him pass the neighborhood notice board with downcast eyes, sneaking a look at the list of ordinances, which was constantly being renewed. Whenever there was talk of foreigners, Uncle Arthur would wave his arm as though driving off wasps and silence the speaker with suppressed anger. He would even glower at his wife, accusing her of supporting the refugees who spread wicked rumors. Among the "refugees" he would include the Jews from Galicia, who had been living here since the end of World War I, some of them his own relatives, who lived in the poor quarter by Grenadierstrasse—I never saw any of them cross his threshold. All these edicts, Uncle Arthur declared with conviction, were meant only for *Ostjuden.*[*] By chance I pulled an old newspaper out of the paper basket and read an editorial that demanded the purification of German civilization from Jewish parasites. I asked my uncle if this also referred to *Ostjuden.* He scolded me for rooting around in garbage. A feeling of shame and a deep-rooted sense of dignity prevented him from spending time like everyone else, men and women, clustered nowadays around the notice board, and only in the evening would he slip out and, as though just passing by, find out what were the latest ordinances.

Page 10. May 22, 1938.

With the rest of the employees of the firm, I was summoned to the large hall to drink a toast on the occasion of the impending release of Herr Klein from Dachau. The deputy inspector of police came in person to tell Frau Klein the good news, that his manifold efforts had borne fruit and within the week her husband would be back home. As everyone pressed around her to shake her hand, there were tears in the eyes of Frau Klein, who had not ceased walking the town and knocking on the doors of influential people, Jews and non-Jews. Erik and I were given the task of taking the deputy inspector's wife a mink coat, packed in a fancy box, as a modest gift . . . for the coming season. On our way back we saw that a crowd had gathered on the corner of Mariahilferstrasse. A Jew of about forty was bandaging his head, which was streaming with blood. He had been thrown off a moving trolley car. I decided not to say anything about it in Uncle's house. I had rented a small room in the Seventh District in Erik's name. At last.

OSTJUDEN (German): Jews from the east. The phrase refers to Jews who reached Germany from Poland and Galicia during the second half of the nineteenth century, and to their offspring; in other words, Jews whose fathers and grandfathers had not been German citizens.

Page 11. May 26, 1938.

House to house searches in the district where I am living. While I was out. Beatings in the street. Jewelry and anything else of value taken. They took the keys from the best apartments. Frau Klein received a notice from the post office to come and collect a small urn containing the ashes of her husband, who had died at Dachau of a heart attack. She had to pay ten marks for the urn. Frau Klein fainted and work stopped at the company. There was general shock. The day before, the wife of the owner of the spice shop had received a similar notice. Someone was wringing his hands and saying, "Terrible! It couldn't be worse!"

May 27.

Erik has gone to Amsterdam! There were about thirty pioneer youths. It was late at night. Many people came to see them off. Erik's father did not come. I was at their house. His family wept as though he was going off to the front. Herr Bader prevented any other members of the family from going to the railway station. "We mustn't rouse *rishes*,"* he insisted. I asked what it meant "to rouse *rishes*" and he replied that you mustn't draw the attention of wicked people to what you were doing. Erik promised to do what he could for me. In the meantime I stood at the railway station and cried.

June 1938.

The lawyer G. managed to get released from Dachau by bribing one of the officials. He saw how Herr Klein was stabbed to death on a punishment march, under searchlights. Uncle Arthur received a deportation order. His friends from other districts also received them, including well-known businessmen. Uncle Arthur believes that in his case there has been a mistake.

July 1938.

Uncle Arthur went into the hospital for a hernia operation before the deportation. I visited him in the hospital and was surprised to meet respectable Jews like Dr. Oscar Greenboim, who wanted to undergo an operation for a hernia before deportation. That day were brought in many wounded Jews, who had been thrown from trolley cars or beaten up in the street.

Page 12. November 10, 1938.

I went to the house of Erik's parents to get the letter he sent me. They were surprised I came on such a day and wouldn't let me go back to the Seventh District. The telephone there was ringing all the time. Friends wanting to know what was happening to them. There had been riots in Wasegasse. There was also a call from Nolingasse and an appeal for help. Herr Bader tried without success to contact the community center and the Palestine Office. In the end he got their operator. He managed only to ask whether anything had happened. The operator said yes and slammed down the receiver. I knew her; her name was Kitty and she had been on the list of pioneer youth to go to Amsterdam. Erik's sister Anna came and told us with bated breath that all over the city synagogues were on fire.

Zbaszyn,* December 18, 1938.

Dear Cherna,

You must already know from the newspapers what happened here on the night of November 9th. Let me describe to you what my fate was. I intended to go back to the orphanage at Dinslaken, but I never made it. I was arrested at a friend's house in the Third District. Everyone was taken outside at six. All the way to the police station on Jochgasse young people, and not so young, ran behind us shouting "*Hep! Hep! Jude Verrehke!*,"* throwing garbage and stones at us. In the police station courtyard many Jews from the Third District were assembled. What happened there is beyond description. Blows and screams of women and children. Then we were loaded on trucks. They beat us as they packed us in. A gang ran all the way behind the truck, violently cursing and abusing us. The Viennese had suddenly turned into wild animals. Wet and crowded together we stood there most of the night. Before dawn I managed to escape. I hid in all kinds of places. I reached the warehouse where I used to work for Klein und Krever and hid the diary I had started keeping. Uncle

RISHES (Yiddish): Wickedness (from the Hebrew *rish'ut*).

ZBASZYN: A border town near Poznan. About 3,500 Jewish refugees were transported there and set down in no-man's-land between Germany and Poland. Among the first of the deportees were the parents of Herschel Grinspan.

"JUDE VERREHKE!": A German curse—literally, "Drop dead, Jew!"

Arthur has been taken for deportation. Aunt Rita drowned herself in the Danube. I was told she was seen jumping into the river and no one tried to stop her. Such sights can be seen every day. On November 27th at ten in the evening the SS came to my apartment and arrested me for the second time. I was by myself with them, and I shall never forget that moment. My words stuck in my throat. I could hardly get dressed. Outside a cold wind was blowing. At the railway station to which they took me there were hordes of Jews rounded up from all the districts. Again we were loaded into wagons, this time on a freight train. Sounds of weeping from children and adults. With heart-rending cries, children sought their parents. I looked for no one and I didn't cry. I acted like an automaton and did nothing except keep close to the wall of the wagon where there was a barred window. The next morning, on the Sabbath, we reached the frontier. For two whole days we stopped at some junction. Trains came from all parts of Germany. I heard the names: Leipzig, Cologne, Berlin. Even Dinslaken. My heart is on fire. I met the famous Professor Hermann. They were searched at the frontier and all their money and valuables were taken. Each one was left with just ten marks. They were told, "You had no more when you arrived in Germany and you won't take any more out." The jest of fate. Professor Hermann's father was one of the greatest builders of railways in Germany.

When we arrived here in Zbaszyn, or Zbonshin, there were many dead bodies in the wagons and even more people who were lying unconscious. I too must have lost consciousness since I found myself lying in a hut with a sister of mercy taking care of me, a Jewish woman from Warsaw. The Polish government will not allow us to enter Poland; there are tens of thousands of us here in terrible conditions. I have joined a class to learn Yiddish. The teacher, a volunteer from Warsaw, knows your father and I am sending this letter with him. His name is Ringelblum. In class they hand out meat soup, and it's not so cold as outside. Every day fresh trains arrive with deportees from Germany and Austria. They write down who has relatives in Poland. I gave your address. Maybe we'll meet soon. Yesterday it was my birthday. How they found out I don't know. Mr. Ringelblum gave me a present, a book by Sholom Aleichem, with illustrations. It's still hard for me to read the language. I'm twelve years old. I'm afraid you won't recognize me. Must stop now. Sudden shouts. Went

to look. A new transport has arrived. A woman paralyzed in both legs. They took her from her home in pajamas, and brought her like that to Zbaszyn. She was howling from cold like an animal.

Leo Morgenstern

The letter was finished, and apparently folded and placed in an envelope that the teacher from Warsaw had provided, but Leo couldn't sleep. Curled up in a rough blanket, he sat by the window and added the following:

Dear Cherna, heavy snow has started falling and covers the ground in no-man's-land. The wind is howling outside and all my bones are shivering with cold. I got out of bed in order to finish the letter with some lines of verse, since I hear that you yourself write poetry. A student from Berlin whose bunk is near mine brought with him a book of verse, and I read two or three poems by an anonymous woman poet.

> The murderers go about in the world all night long
> O my God, all night long!*

These lines fret away at my brain and give me no peace. In another poem I found this sentence: "I have loved thee, my people, dressed in rags." I'm not sure if I have fully understood the poet. The truth is that until now I didn't know exactly who my people were. And here I am among them and they are so frightened, humiliated, lost. My God, if only I could say as she does: "I have loved thee, my people, dressed in rags."

I've just remembered. The name of the poem is "The Cry Falls into the Eternal Abyss."

Yours,
Leo

The words "The murderers go about in the world all night long/ O my God, all night long!" were written by the poet Gertrud Kolmar.

✢ CHAPTER THREE ✢

The Third Tear

"I was told this by a woman named Sarah Menkes, who survived the pit. She told me of the execution of a group of women in October 1941. She told me after some weeks. The group included a student of mine. I had taught her for several months in high school; she was the daughter of a teacher at the Epstein High School in Vilna. Her name was Cherna Morgenstern. I'll keep it short: They were taken to Ponar. After waiting there, a group of them were taken and lined up in a row. They were told to undress. They stripped down to their underclothes. A line of members of the Einsatzgruppen stood opposite them. . . ."

—ABBA KOVNER,
"In the Witness Box, at the Eichmann Trial," From *Al Ha-Gesher Ha-Tzar* (On the Narrow Bridge), Sifriat Ha-Po'alim, 1981, pp. 94–95.

Hush, hush, let us be silent,
There are graves here growing.
Planted by the men who
  hate us…
The roads lead to Ponar,
But none of them lead back.
Your father took the road
  of sorrow,
And with him all our joy.

—SHMERL KACHERGINSKI

Cherna was eighteen years and three days old when the truck stopped by the woods at the top of the hill. She had just managed to gather up her black hair and braid it into a single plait, the way she liked, when the tarpaulin that covered the back of the truck was lifted and flung back. When she was told to take off all her clothes, she did it without thinking, as though it were not her hands that were doing it. She held on to her brassiere and her underwear, until they fell.[+]

And Cherna sat together with the others. One hundred nineteen women crowded together, naked as the day they were born, on the edge of an embankment, waiting their turn.

An early morning sun cast its rays behind the clump of gum trees. Cherna's body suddenly shivered at the sound of gunfire. The shots came in bursts and from near at hand. But the command to get up she heard dimly, as from an immense distance. And she rose and went with the rest of the women into the darkness of the woods.

One hundred nineteen women: They stand in a long row on the edge of an embankment of freshly turned earth. The rays of the sun graze gently on their astonishing nakedness, like an avenue of trees struck by lightning, and the German issues a command, "Hey, you with the braid, step forward!"

And Cherna is freezing and does not understand.

The German yells again, "Don't you want to live, Jewess?"

Her neighbor in the row gives her a nudge. Cherna pulls herself together. "Yes," she mumbles, crossing her arms to hold her breasts, ". . . want . . . to live." She sees the two machine guns on their tripods and the four Lithuanians behind the guns. And the face of the German officer. "How old are you, I asked!" Cherna wants to stop crying. "Eighteen, sir." He seems a good man. "You're pretty, Jewess. You know your worth, you Jew-girls. Soon the moon will rise, and it will be a lovely evening. So leave the row and go. Go, I said—and don't look back!" She hears but does not move. Her good neighbor nudges her in the ribs again. Perhaps the touch of an elbow against her naked body detaches her from the row and she begins to walk; 118 pairs of eyes follow her in fear and envy. Already she has passed half the row. Cherna is near the last tree at the end of the embankment when the first bullet strikes her back. The women in the row see her fall before they hear the sound of the guns. Or the laughter of the Germans. With a wave of his smoking Mauser, the Gestapo man gives the sign to the machine gunners behind the tripods.[+]

When they murdered Cherna, the market at the end of Ponarska Street was still thronged with people. Two young boys were playing near a haberdashery stall. A countrywoman in a coat too big for her spent some time trying on necklaces of artificial coral. First she tried the white one, then she tried the red. The man standing next to her lifted his sack onto his back and said, "I'm going, woman!" The piglet squeaked inside the sack. At that moment, 34,000 Jews were being shot at Babii Yar.[+] In Pressburg,[+] as in Vilna, it was market day. The wagons stood tightly packed and peasants from near and far checked each other's livestock, then spread out their wares. Ukrainians were whispering more than usual, for some reason lowering their voices as they asked where and how the wagons were being taken in these terrible days. Some grumbled

JEWS WERE BEING SHOT AT BABII YAR (Ukrainian): Literally, the Valley of the Young Women. Babii Yar is the name of a beautiful valley on the outskirts of Kiev, the capital of the Ukraine. Units of Operational Brigade C, commanded by officers of the SS, reached Kiev between the 19th and 25th of September 1941. At that time Russian saboteurs had blown up the German headquarters and a large part of the center of the city. In reprisal the Germans demanded a "transfer of population" (deportation) for Jews and ordered them to report on September 29, 1941, for the purpose of transfer. The Germans took the thousands of Jews to the valley known as Babii Yar and shot them nonstop for two whole days—34,000 Jews were massacred there. A detailed account is given by the Russian writer Anatoly Kuznetsov in his book *Babii Yar: A Documentary Novel.* Also well known is the moving response of the poet Yevgenyi Yevtushenko, in his poem *Babii Yar.*

PRESSBURG: A town in western Slovakia, near the border between Austria and the Czech Republic, currently known as Bratislava.

The first acts of extermination by the Germans against the Jews outside the borders of the Soviet Union were actually carried out in Yugoslavia. This was before the notorious Wannsee Conference. The Jews of Serbia were packed into gas trucks and exterminated as they were transported out of town. By March 1942, there was not a single Jew left alive in the capital of Yugoslavia. The annihilation of the Jews of Serbia passed without a word of protest from any state or political organization whatsoever. Afterward, the destruction of Jews spread to Croatia, Bosnia, Herzegovina, Slovenia, and Montenegro. Over 6,000 Jews succeeded in joining the ranks of the partisans. There were also Jews who fled to areas under Italian control and were active there.

"Father, why did the Jews of Yugoslavia become the first target?"

"I'm not sure; it seems they were meant to be the guinea pigs in the great Nazi plan for the extermination of the Jews."

"You mean, the Nazis wanted to see the world's reaction?"

"Yes, maybe."

"And what was the world's reaction?"

"There wasn't any. The extermination of the Jews of Belgrade was passed over without any protest or reaction whatsoever. So the Nazis continued. To this day the world has not heard the names of the death camps inside Yugoslavia, where 60,000 men, women, and children were put to death."

"What about the Jews who fought in the ranks of Tito's partisans?"

"Their story will be told elsewhere, in a later chapter."

about the lack of pity for the poor animals that pulled the carts. Really, the load was inhuman, twenty Jews to one pack animal! And Bondarchik, from the lonely farmstead by the three crosses, sprayed spittle under his mustache as he described how his new, laddered hay cart had come back fouled with excrement and so much blood. Bearded men made the sign of the cross, briefly wiped the sweat from their horses' brows, and hastened to unharness them.

In Odessa, nineteen thousand were shot. In the Crimea, twenty-five thousand in all. How many had already been shot in Dvinsk and Belgrade?* In Kamenetz-Podolsk, transports were seen on their way to the valley of slaughter—carrying Jews from Hungary. Who saw all this, who heard it? Who combined all the numbers into one grand total? The birds of the air? A girl who looks about twelve but is not more than seven or eight is nibbling the end of a cucumber. It has been a good year for cucumbers, and all the carts are loaded to capacity with green and yellow cucumbers. Sellers with bunches of garlic and parsley fill Ponarska Street from beginning to end with an overpowering aroma. There is concern about the price. The girl with the cucumber in her mouth hears her father hum a risqué song, for his female customers burst out laughing when he tosses the fresh vegetables into the lap of their aprons. It is old Vasil Dovina from the other side of the river who asks her father, "What have you done, brother, with Zelig the furrier's new stoves?" Abba-Stakh turns toward the questioner and when he recognizes his friend from across the river, smiles and says, "Nu, it's the good Lord's wish that from now on they should warm the bones of simple folk!"

At that time the fifty thousand Jews of Vilna were being shot in the woods on the hill called Ponar. In the Ninth Fort,* on the deserted site of the old castle at the entrance to Kovno,* forty thousand were shot.*

When they murdered Cherna, lanterns were lit on the road to the railway station. As ever, there was a medley of tongues in the market, Yiddish and Polish chiming together in a single blend: in praise of the merchandise, in

slaughter of the Jews of Kovno. The great massacre began in the middle of September 1941, and continued until the end of October. Thousands and thousands were brought to the fort in small groups and shot.

KOVNO: The capital of Lithuania from 1918 to 1941. Kovno is situated at the conflux of two rivers, the Nemunas and the Vilia. It contained one of the most ancient Jewish communities in Eastern Europe, about a quarter of the total Jewish population of Lithuania (38,000). Most of the Jews of the city were shot at the Ninth Fort, near Kovno. The underground succeeded in smuggling many youngsters out of the ghetto, who then joined the ranks of the partisans.

LITHUANIA: Between the two world wars, 150,000 Jews out of a total population of 2 million maintained 30 primary schools, where the languages of instruction were Hebrew and Yiddish; 14 high schools, Hebrew classes and yeshivas, the most famous of which were those at Telz and Slobodka; and a chair in Semitic studies at the University of Kovno. Ninety percent of Jewish children studied at the various levels of the Jewish educational system. There was also a large-scale Jewish press in Lithuania publishing in Yiddish and Hebrew, and the pioneer youth movements had thousands of members.

The slaughter of the Jews of Lithuania began in the first weeks after the German occupation with the active support of the Lithuanians—nationalists, intellectuals, soldiers, and Fascist "partisans." Of all the Jews of Lithuania, only 5,000 survived, including a few thousand who were left from the "Lithuanian Division," which fought under the Soviet army, and about 1,000 partisans.

A telegram sent on September 12, 1941, 1300 hours, by the German Foreign Office: What's to be done with the Jews of Belgrade? From Adolf Eichmann to the Foreign Office, by telephone: "Shoot them."

THE NINTH FORT: Czarist Russia once erected nine forts around the city of Kovno. Their function was to serve as focal units in the system of fortifications set up to defend the western frontier against attack by the Germans. There were gun emplacements, cellars for the storing of weapons, and more. During the period of Lithuanian independence the forts were used as prisons. The Ninth Fort was chosen as a suitable place for the systematic

oaths, in reproaches. When negotiations came to an end, there were some who sealed the deal with a handshake, in plain peasant terms, but with the traditional Yiddish intonation: May the Lord be blessed! No written contract carried more weight. Vasil Dovina seemed to hear the voice of Zelig singing beyond the steam. But this time the bath house, where the farmer went after market day, was empty of Jews. What a strange tune he had heard from their synagogues, he thought to himself, almost as if the tune could foresee the future. Vasil felt years younger when his feet touched the upper step, wrapped in swirls of thick steam. For a moment he listened to the sound of twigs beating wet bodies, and then saw his son hesitating to step up. "When I was your age," Vasil said, pulling him up, "my father, God rest his soul, used to lift me up to the top step. That's how he taught me wisdom: 'Keep quiet and listen, son, no man who stands on this step will ever fear the fire of Hell!'" The boy looked at his father. "Why should I fear the fire of Hell?" he asked, stiffening with suspicion. They were standing close together in their nakedness on the damp wooden step. The old man said to his son, "Because of the fine things you and your rotten friends have been doing, so I hear, near the ghetto gate!" And the thick steam rose from below and covered their nakedness.

When they murdered Cherna, the gates of the Riga ghetto were opened at an unusual hour and a long line was approaching. The newcomers did not shout or raise their voices. Their wealth was apparent from their dress, but they moved humbly and their faces were lowered. Many carried heavy suitcases and their coattails were muddy. The people of Riga clustered around them in amazement. "Where are you Jews from?" they asked.

Some said "Berlin."

Others added "Stuttgart."

"Breslau."

The people of Riga continued to ask, "So why have they brought you from Germany to Latvia?"

Not all of them had known that this country was called Latvia. They said, "To settle."

"To settle in the East, they told us," others added with greater precision.

Someone in the crowd could not control his laughter, but he was quickly hushed. One of the young men, whose heart shuddered when he heard the word "settle," went up to the newcomers and drawing so close that his face almost touched their lips, stood before the first in line, a man wearing a stiff hat and carrying a leather suitcase, and said, "You poor things. Twenty-seven thousand of our Jews have already been sent to the same place to 'settle.'" He stretched the last word out to the limit. "Do you understand me?" They did not understand.

Did they understand in Jerusalem, in London? In New York, preparations were being completed for the giant Thanksgiving Day parade. In the windows of Macy's, lifesize dolls in the likeness of basketball champions were displayed. The day before, the Harvard Giants had beaten Yale in front of fifty-five thousand spectators. A fashion parade, shown for the first time on television, was going to put New York in the forefront of world fashion; a line two blocks long had stretched from the box office of Radio City Music Hall for a gala performance by Fred Astaire and Rita Hayworth; in the opinion of the *Post,* South America was likely to prove an alternative tourist attraction for citizens of the United States; professional critics and intellectuals continued to debate whether there was such a thing as American art; the *New York Times* was convinced that after the war the main problem in the world would be education; when they murdered Cherna in the woods at Ponar, the year nineteen hundred and forty-one of the Christian Era was nearing its end.

❖ The Second Scroll ❖

By the Waters of Four Countries — 1

The title of this scroll alludes to the lament of the exiles in Babylon ("By the waters of Babylon we sat down and wept, when we remembered Zion" [Psalms 137:1]) and also to the "Four Countries Committee," the umbrella organization of independent Jewish leadership in Poland, Russia, and Lithuania. By about 1580, the "Four Countries Committee" had achieved a solid position as the center for Jewish autonomy.

When Lithuania left the association and set itself up independently in 1623, the Polish Jewish Committee acquired the permanent title, the "Four Nations Committee." This refers to Poland, the Baltic states, the Ukraine, and European Russia. To people at the time the "Four Nations Committee" seemed the peak of Jewish autonomy in the Diaspora.

✢ CHAPTER FOUR ✢

Sha'ul Goes Away

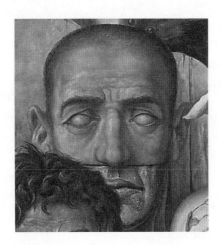

History

In recent generations the largest concentration of the Jewish population has been between the rivers Vistula and Nemunas on one side and the rivers Bug and Prypet on the other. Jewish settlement in Eastern Europe seemed like a continuous forest that grew denser as it moved eastward. About a thousand years ago, in the days when there was not yet a king in Poland, there came to this region a Jewish traveler–itinerant merchant and talmudic scholar.

In that period the gospel of Christianity was only beginning to reach the Slavic countries, and hatred of the Jews had not yet followed in its wake. The story is told of how the inhabitants of the land went forth to greet the wandering Jew, carrying bread and salt. They said to him, "You will reign over us!" The Jew was king of Poland for one day–the next day he was thrown to the dogs.

The story of the Jewish king may be a legend or it may be a true chronicle, but the settlement of Poland by hundreds of thousands, by millions of Jews has a history of close to a thousand years.

The Story of Sha'ul after He Left Home

Sha'ul said, "I don't remember who told us that anyone who gets lost in a forest should go back on his tracks a little, in order to find the parting of the ways where he went astray." To himself he said, "Let's begin from a long way back."

1. A man on the threshold of his house. He sees:

A light burning in the window of Shabbetai the shoemaker. As usual he is the first to get up for work, though he picks up a book before he picks up his awl. Soon the metalworkers and barbers will open their doors in the market street. Wheelbarrows are already creaking up to the market square. A column has been rising from the chimney of Reb Kalman's inn since before dawn. A soup of groats in the smoke. Everyone will make short work of morning prayers today, for this is market day. From beyond the river the west wind brings the scent of orchards full of ripe fruit. It is mixed with the vapors of the swamp. Strongest of all is the stench from the artificial ponds where the tanners dip their skins. A good aroma from the fresh droppings of cows and horses fills the man's nose; all along the path that leads down to the market square are smells that went with him wherever he went in his childhood memories of home. The white church above the clouds. The silent bell tower.

Will there be war?

2. He sees:

Before it is fully light, the market square is already bustling with life. Settlers from the ends of the Pale and farmers from the neighborhood bring in their laddered wagons, unhitch their sweating horses, jostle at the well to draw buckets of water. Two-wheeled carts loaded with merchandise from firms in the nearby town make their way from the new railway station into the village. The Jewish shops in the market square are set up, as though on parade. Respected shopkeepers stand under their signs–Malkovitch with his clothing materials, the widow Tsipel, queen of the shoes, Kramer and Gorfein, and the brothers Kantorovitch. When the farmers have sold their produce, they will spread out among these shops and get all they need for home and farm. Anything a man could need is to be found here: kerchiefs, cloth, sweaters, good quality felt boots and leather boots, furs, hides, accessories for garments–upper and lower, frying pans, pickled herring, cooking oil, lubricating oil, sickles, plows, scythes, hammers, and nails–new and secondhand. Mother also used to sell on credit, from one market day to the next, and give a reduction to anyone who paid cash. A unique miscellany was to be found in Reb Shlomo Gottlieb's shop, things you could only find there! From exercise books with double rows for writing in Cyrillic[*] to pencils and paints, from building materials to even a hay-cutting machine. Reb Shlomo is a merchant by day, a teacher by night, and a cantor during the summer vacation. He is the one who read Dr. Herzl's *Altneuland*[*] and gave his judgment: Utopia!

Since that time there has not been a single self-respecting individual in the village who does not make frequent use in public, or when arguing with his wife, of the word "Utopia." That's what happened with the first moving picture, when it was due to visit from the nearby town. When the elders of the community heard of this technological marvel, they cried aloud, "Utopia! Utopia," "*un fartik!*"[*]

CYRILLIC: The alphabet used for the Russian, Ukrainian, Byelorussian, Serbian, and Bulgarian languages.

ALTNEULAND: A novel in German by Theodor (Benjamin Zeev) Herzl (1860–1904) in which he describes his vision of the future of the Land of Israel.

"UN FARTIK!" (Yiddish): Ready and willing. Here it means "That's it!"

Similarly they cried in the matter of the czar's rubles, though in an opposite sense. The rubles had been hoarded at the end of World War I, in hundreds of thousands of drawers, sacks, and attics, and the House of Romanov[+] had come to an end and no responsible citizen had yet found the courage to burn these *asher-yatzrim*[+] in the stove, lest one day they prove a blessing. And youngsters mocked their elders and said, "Utopia, gentlemen, Utopia." And angry citizens would shake their fists at them and cry, "Shut up, you Bolsheviks. Are you in such a hurry to get yourself killed?"

3. And he sees:

A thoroughfare full of Jewish property owners. Anyone who did not perish in the troubles of the time came back and restored his house and property. And there were other more recent arrivals. They too had acquired plots of land and opened businesses: coopers, tailors, and also Father's brother, Uncle Kalman, who opened the inn by the eastern wall of the market. At the bottom of the street the dealers in *alte zakhen*[+] had taken up position and anyone without a shop had some kind of storeroom in the rear courtyard. Even the small-time peddlers, who had collapsible stalls, seemed content with their lot, for after all there were creatures on God's earth even more wretched than they were: those with neither shop nor stall, only rights to a small patch of ground, who laid out all their merchandise on the naked earth. A few of these peddlers were men like Yukel, the shofar blower. He would sit on an upturned half barrel, wearing a pointed leather skullcap and a caftan tied up with string. His eyes, shaded by thick eyebrows, looked down at the *Ein Yaakov*[+] resting in his lap and he looked neither at customers nor at his neighbors to right and left. These were lively women whose eyes were fixed permanently on the knees of the passersby, if not on their faces, chanting monotonously, "Buy-buy-buy, everything-you-need, buy-buy-buy." Everything from buttons and shoelaces to cheap pies all the year round, and wine bottles. There were frozen apples, in winter, a great favorite with young and old in this part of the world. Though there were very few visitors to the market at the height of winter, these women peddlers never left their stands throughout the period from Hanukkah to Purim. They had a patent device of their own against the cold—saucepans full of glowing embers. Some would hold their tough hands spread out, hovering above the flickering blue flames, others would push the oblong pot under their dresses, right between their knees, and you could smell them from far away. Anyone who fancied a sweet apple would bend down, very respectfully, in front of these "charcoal burners" and not turn up his nose, since everybody knows that poverty has its own special smell. The bells of the Pravoslavic Church[+] ring out.

Will there be war?

4. Life is returning

also to the fish market, stall after stall. On wooden trestles known as "goats," long unplaned boards are laid. These are loaded with flat boxes full of fish of all kinds, arranged according to species, sparkling with sprinkled ice. The female fishmongers here are a race apart. Hard-working women, their hands roughened by ice and scales, with a smell they cannot rid themselves of, neither in bed nor—if you'll pardon the comparison—in synagogue, and God preserve us from the edge of their tongues! As everybody knows, fish were the only survivors of the Flood because they had the sense to keep quiet at the time, and to this day you can't hold a conversation with a fish, so what else can an embittered Jewish woman confined to the company of a fish do but talk for the two of them. And that's what they do, here and now, in a fashion likely to provide a living for several generations of experts on folklore long after these mistresses of repartee have passed away. Here, listen to a dialogue with Manitchka.

THE HOUSE OF ROMANOV: The Romanov Czarist dynasty began with the coronation of Michael Romanov in 1613. Michael was the grandson of the Russian Czar Ivan IV ("the Terrible"), who reigned in the sixteenth century. The Romanov dynasty ruled Russia until the October Revolution in 1917. The last czar, Nicholas II, was put to death by order of the revolutionary authorities.

ASHER-YATZRIM (Yiddish): The term for worthless bits of paper, documents no longer valid, fit only for toilet paper. Here it means Russian bank notes that became worthless because of inflation. The origin of the expression is the prayer—"Blessed art Thou who has created (*'asher yatzar'*) man with wisdom"—that an observant Jew recites after going to the toilet.

ALTE ZAKHEN (Yiddish): Old things, junk. The secondhand merchants sold mainly old clothes, shoes, and various used household objects.

EIN YAAKOV (Jacob's Spring): A collection of legends, fables, and homilies selected from the Babylonian and Jerusalem Talmuds, with a commentary by Rashi, compiled by Rabbi Yaakov-Shlomo Habib at the beginning of the sixteenth century, in Salonika.

THE PRAVOSLAVIC CHURCH: The Russian (also Ukrainian and Byelorussian) branch of the Eastern Orthodox Church. It was cut off from the authority of the Pope (Leo X) and his spiritual leadership in 1054. Almost all the Christians among the Russian Slavs are Pravoslavs. There is a center for the Pravoslavic Church in Jerusalem.

Manitchka, the Old Maid until she married Reb Lazar Gorodnik, the widower, is now referred to as Madame. Reb Lazar is the treasurer of the Choralic synagogue, known to the scholars in the market as the Choleric synagogue, and hence his wife is Mrs. Cholera. Some say it suits her. When she wants to buy a carp, there's nothing suitable in the whole market. Three or four times she'll roam the stalls, prodding here and fingering there, holding fish up to her nose, bold and undeterred. Finally she throws back her head and says, "*Nyet.*"[+] Zelda, at the end of the line, with ten mouths to feed, tries to detain her next to her stock, cajoling Manitchka with quotations from the Bible and the Sages on charity and mercy and fresh fish whose eyes saw the hidden light in the days of Noah, flattering her with "Madame, Madame." But Madame shakes off Zelda the fishmonger with a double excuse. "The fish," she says, "are not so good today, and secondly, I really must go." Zelda replies, "If you're in such a hurry, Madame, be on your way . . . the way of all flesh." And as the woman goes off with a red face, Zelda yells after her, "May the church collapse one fine day when your ladyship is sitting on the tip of the spire!"

The bells of the white church, the Catholic church, ring out in support of the Russian Orthodox bells. Day has dawned.

Will there be war?

5. He sees how

everything goes back to what it was. The wooden porch is turquoise again. The oak arches, the high windows, the three well-trodden steps: this is home. Mother stands behind the counter. The shop is full of vital smells. Farmers are stepping down from the wagons parked outside. They come up in their heavy boots. The hems of their cloaks move like muddy waves. They let fall fragments of speech, deep, gruff, sounding like snorts. Interspersed among them are words from Mother, clear, sweetened sometimes by her high-pitched laughter. When she cries "*Oy vey!*" they laugh around her.

6. Suddenly he feels like laughing:

the legs that pass in front of him are headless. After all, he grew acquainted with the world from the inner curve of a tub that served as his cradle. The tub was placed between the boards that partitioned off the shop counter and his mother's legs; from knee to ankle—that was the limit of his

"NYET" (Russian): No.

vision upward in one direction, and in the other—the whole world seen through a crack. Lots of legs went by and only one head. It was a huge, fearful head and so near! The horse had collapsed in front of the house with a broken leg, its other legs caught up in the harness and flailing the air, its head lying on the ground. Worst of all was the expression in its upturned eyes. Breadcrumbs and pieces of cheese or sausage fell off the counter and onto his eyes. And he cried. Mother, who had no time to bend down, quickly extended a practiced foot and rocked the tub until he calmed down. He calmed down quickly and just as quickly started crying again. For it was nice to be rocked in his cradle, even if it was only by one of his mother's feet. In later years he was wont to say: she was like a pianist using the pedal. Mother's other leg was bandaged and gave off a strong, persistent smell.

When the pale sun penetrates the cracks in the boards, the market breaks up. He hears the wagons, loaded with equipment, begin to move off with a jingling of metal, and through the dancing sunbeams it seems to the child that the whole world is broken into fragments.

7. He sees

the monastery wall. Behind it is the fish pond and then the dusty fields that stretch to the border of the village, the border of the country, and beyond. His feet had taken him everywhere. From the time he first saw the light of day, in every sense, he had crawled out of the tub and almost immediately, to everyone's surprise, stood up—and started walking. The birds had seen him lying sprawled on the embankment above the dam, or perched fearlessly above the raging waters during the thaw. One day he would send his first, heartfelt song sailing on those waves to unknown correspondents, beyond the rivers, beyond the ocean. Why do the church bells to this day sound so threatening? As a child he used to run home as fast as he could to seek shelter from them.

8. Everything

in the house had its place. The furniture seemed to have been created with the walls. The walls were adjusted to the tenants. The curtains filtered a soft light on the people, who absorbed the light and behaved with modesty; the table was laid.

As a lad he had served a four-year apprenticeship, and whenever he and his elder brother returned home from Wolf's carpentry shop, his mother's table was always laid.

In good days and bad it would gleam and glisten and the smell of the food it bore would greet them as they crossed the threshold. As they opened the door, Velvele, his brother Chaim-Ozer's only son, would come rushing toward them. The child would lift up the latest drawing he had done "for Daddy," and wait for praise. But Daddy was sparing in praise, saying only with fatigue, or for some other private reason, "Yes, dear, very nice!" Then Kreine would purse her lovely lips in a grimace of offense, not to say anger. Kreine had come from the regional capital, and had spent the first year of her life, so they say, at her mother's breast, or the breast of a wet nurse, in distant Vienna. When she stood under the bridal canopy, she came as a princess and left as a prisoner in the hands of provincials. From the day her son, her eldest child whom she called Vubik, first held a colored pencil and scribbled whatever it is a normal, healthy child scribbles on a blank sheet of paper, she had had a dream. She embroidered the dream and soon there was no boundary between dream and vision, between vision and reality. Whatever else she was unsure of, she knew with incontrovertible certainty that before many years had passed her son Velvele would be famous worldwide as a great artist and thanks to him she too would be able to escape from "this God-forsaken hole, where life smells of death."

9. Suddenly he saw

that he had strayed from the path that took him out of the village to the main road. Either he wanted to lengthen the moment of departure, or had been lost in thought. The *alte schul,*⁺ a synagogue, which had burned down seventy years ago, had been modestly restored, with its walls sunken into the ground almost up to the window ledges. The courtyard was deserted. Beyond it one could see the gleaming dome of the Choralic synagogue! One day the old Hebrew teacher had kept them behind at *ḥeder* for some unremembered sin; by the time they had broken free it was already evening. A winter's evening, with long shadows. Jumping for joy, with insolent faces, they drew near to the *alte schul.* Everyone knew that this was a shorter route, but the shadows were already long and dark. All the boys in the gang came to a halt together and pricked up their ears: was that the rustle of wings under the roof, or the sound of broomsticks on which the horned spirits rode? He wanted to appear brave but his knees failed him: would he go first? The truth was that he had never met any devils or ghosts,

neither in the deserted courtyard nor anywhere else. But there were bats, fluttering and spraying their disgusting spittle. Their droppings were yellowish-brown and where they splashed against the wall of the old synagogue it looked like the sign of the Evil One, the *Samech-Mem.*⁺ For years, until low-flying Messerschmitts⁺ passed over his head, hunting down and firing at anything alive that moved in the area, till then, perhaps even to this day, the memory of the bats flying in the courtyard of the old synagogue and wrapping themselves round his hair would remain the epitome of terror.

10. What does he see?

He remains standing, his hands protecting his head, now bare. His hat has fallen, his legs have turned to stone, the rest of the boys surround him and he hears not a sound from any of them. At that moment he is not even capable of uttering a cry, his throat is choked as in the nightmares he will know, night after night, when he grows up.

"Don't worry, Mother, the Polish army is ready to take on those arrogant Germans. They won't break our ranks. Really, what is there to worry about? Do you think there'll be a war?"

Since the day his father had been wounded in the disaster at the mill, Mother had been terrified of everything, real or imaginary, as though under an obligation to the living and the dead.

Leaving the center of the village, he moved slowly toward the river sands. By the time the cross at the road junction had come in sight, he could smell the hides. Without meaning to, he stood and identified the tanners by the smell of the hides soaking in their yards. From one end he could distinguish crude shoe leather for soles. From the other direction came the smell of Reb Kalmanke's pools with the finest *chevrette.*⁺ And then there were the Gordons, four or five brothers, all tanners, all fine upstanding men.

The hill on which the sculptured cross stood was strewn with sand, excellent for making sand castles

ALTE SCHUL (Yiddish): The old synagogue. The usual term for an existing synagogue in places where a new one is erected or where each synagogue has its own name.

SAMECH-MEM: A term derived from the two initial letters of the name "Samael," ruler of the spirit world. It derives from a dread of pronouncing the name explicitly.

MESSERSCHMITTS: German fighter planes during World War II.

POOLS WITH . . . CHEVRETTE: Pools for dipping goatskins during the tanning process.

and tunnels. He may have been the one and only Jewish boy who played there with Paszibosz and the Yatskis, building wonderful sand castles on the hill of the cross, on weekends and holidays, gaining a reputation as a budding architect. Until the day when Paszibosz, after several embarrassed hesitations, said, "Dad says . . . My dad says that the Jews are to blame for the sufferings of Lord Jesus. You crucified him and you have to pay for it." That's what Paszibosz said, with his thousand freckles, as he took a step back from the edge of the tunnel that Shaulik had constructed. And the boy Sha'ul came storming back to his father and asked him, "Is it true that we murdered their Lord Jesus?" His father told him, "It's a blood libel, my son, centuries old. And you're not to play on that hill any more."

And will there be war?

11. *He saw*

his mother sitting in the armchair, her neck resting against the high back. Beneath her abundant braided hair gleamed a piece of her embroidery. He did not immediately notice that her knees were covered with a woolen blanket, even though the air was warm. Her face, still flushed with the glow of distant youth, seemed transparent and frail. Her

prayer book, with its brown leather binding, lay open before her and the light from the window flickered on her knuckles. Her fingers lay motionless on the pages of the book. His father had brought the prayer book back with him from Aunt Rita's funeral; it had passed down from grandmother to mother to daughter-in-law. Aunt Rita had been married to the head of the community in Düsseldorf, Germany, and in the prayer book he brought back with him as a memento he found places marked with blue pencil, "*Hier weint man*," which means "Cry here." One of their forefathers had marked for his wife the places where tears were appropriate. But his mother had no need of such markings, and didn't like the German prayer book anyway—so why today was she holding it open in front of her?

12. *And she said to him:*

"Listen, Salinka. When the Great War broke out, it was as though the whole world was plunged into an interminable ritual of celebration. Rita's husband was among the first to go off to the front in the name of the Kaiser, and my brother, your Uncle Mark went off to fight him in the name of Czar Nicholas.* Till the war was over we lived with your father. Day and night we spent collecting food for the poor and clothing for the needy, for the town was full of refugees called *Bjezenczi*. They came knocking at our door and the famine was severe. For no recompense or profit, we distributed flour from what we had in store. When the flour ran out we gave out grits. And when they were gone, we shared our bread with others, equally, with no distinction between Jew and non-Jew, Pole or Ukrainian. For every man, your father—God rest his soul—would say, was created in the image of God. That's why people came from far and wide to accompany him to his last resting place. Remember, Salinka, how you didn't shed a tear over his grave? Everyone was amazed but you didn't shed a tear."

"Afterward I cried by myself in the attic for three days."

A faint sweetness rose in his nostrils. Purim honey cakes. Spices, various pickles, with a smell of paraffin and candle grease. Farmers in hooded cloaks, reeking of cheap vodka, checking the blades of sickles and scythes with the concentration of connoisseurs—did their shop really have all those things?

"To this day I meet those farmers who used to be our customers and they refer with great respect to Pan Isaak who did not discriminate between Jew and Christian, neither in business nor in charity. I believe that this time too—

"...IN THE NAME OF THE KAISER... IN THE NAME OF CZAR NICHOLAS": The Great War, now known as World War I, broke out in 1914. Initially, five nations were involved, in two alliances: Germany and Austria on the one side; France, Russia, and England on the other. Wilhelm II was then kaiser of Germany and king of Prussia (1859-1941). He dismissed Bismarck and dragged his kingdom into the war, and when Germany fell, he was obliged to abdicate (1918). Nicholas II, czar of Russia (1868-1918), was embroiled in an unfortunate war with Japan (1904-1905) and had to rule under pressure from growing revolutionary elements at home. He joined the Allies during World War I, abdicated under pressure from the revolutionaries, was arrested, and finally executed. About a million and a half Jewish soldiers fought on all fronts during World War I.

THE FOLLOWERS OF PETLURA: Semion Petlura (1880-1926) was head of the Ukrainian Directorate, the government of independent Ukraine that was formed when the Germans departed the region at the end of 1918. This government waged war against the Bolshevik regime based in Moscow and against Trotsky's Red Army. The Kiev government and its supporters, called Petlurans, organized brigades of Ukrainian *hetmen,* who were given a free hand to slaughter the Jews. The pretext most often used for the pogroms was that the Jews supported the Bolsheviks. In these pogroms about 16,000 Jews were murdered, entire communities were destroyed, much property looted, and blood spilled like water. Any shortcomings in the slaughter were made up for by the Cossacks and the soldiers of the Volunteer Army of White Russian rightist forces, led by General Anton Ivanovich Denikin. The

if, God forbid, we should need their help—the Christians will remember us for good and the good Lord will come to our aid."

13. Since she had fallen silent, she must have been thinking of other, different things. Their journey in burning trains during the time of the Civil War. The pogroms committed by the followers of Petlura[+] and the trail of fire and blood left behind by the armies as they advanced and retreated. When he leaned over to kiss her she was quite startled. She clasped his head firmly, breathing in the smell of his damp battle dress.

"Salinka, be careful."

His mother's eyes scrutinized him. "Do you really think, my son, that there will be no war?"

"Whatever happens, you have nothing to worry about. We shall be there in thousands, Polish and Jewish soldiers together."

Her gaze fell on the bayonet strapped to his hip. She stared at the crosspiece, black above the scabbard, and said without a smile, "My son, do evil to no one."

He asked not to be accompanied to the railway station, and left the town alone, without fuss. Vubik, his nephew, now a lad of sixteen, shook his hand in adult fashion and like all members of Ha-Shomer made a point of pronouncing his uncle's name in Hebrew, "*ḥazak ve-Ematz*,[+] Sha'ul." Somehow he felt an ache in his heart. The last time he had heard the words "*ḥazak ve-Ematz*" had been in synagogue at the end of the Torah reading, in his father's pleasant voice. On Shabbat, after the service, like all the members of the Jewish community, he would walk with his father along the main street of the village, side by side, leaving behind them a trail of intimacies: a Jewish street; Jewish houses; Jewish peace; a Jewish sky.

As he passed the riverbank, where the white rock was hidden somewhere, he remembered the summer when his father taught him to fish. Father had been thinking of moving to Odessa,[+] and the echoes of the arguments between his father and mother had threatened the peace of the household. He had heard there was a sea at Odessa and his boy's heart went out to a real sea with real sand, not like the sand he and Paszibosz used to make castles, and it grieved him that his mother was frustrating his father.

"Your father has an uncle in Odessa and I don't want us to be hanging around the necks of rich uncles," she

explained to him once, and his heart was torn in two. He yearned to see the sea but he did not like his relatives from Odessa, who had once visited the village and been laughed at by the Jews there because of the way they pronounced *Tote* and *Mome*.[+]

"In Odessa," he later heard his father saying wistfully, "you only have to stretch out your hand and you can touch the land of Israel." His father spoke as though sharing a secret and said no more.

At the foot of the white rock there was a small inlet where swans paddled in the clear water for most of the year until it was covered over with ice (where did swans go in the winter?). Rain was beginning to fall and time was pressing—could he cross the embankment and see whether the swans were still paddling at the foot of the white rock?

When he heard the whistle of the train from the direction of the station, he looked back again for a moment. He could still see the long shadows gradually spreading across the solitary street, the Russian Orthodox church on one side and the white Catholic church on the other, and the Jewish village in between.

---

number of Jewish victims rose to 60,000. After the collapse of his government, Petlura was exiled to Paris, where he tried to continue his Ukrainian activities. In May 1926, he was shot to death by Shalom Schwartzbard while leaving a Paris coffee shop. Schwartzbard was a watchmaker and a volunteer in the French army who had visited the Ukraine, the land of his birth, during the pogroms. He could not bear the idea that Petlura, the head of the hooligans, was moving about freely in Paris. Schwartzbard was held in custody for a year, tried, and acquitted by the jury after a speech in which he described to them the horrors of what had happened in the Ukraine.

"ḤAZAK VE-EMATZ": The customary farewell among members of Ha-Shomer Ha-Tza'ir (The Young Watchman) movement. At the end of the annual cycle of weekly readings from the Pentateuch in the synagogue, on the Sabbath

when the last portion of one of the Five Books of Moses is read, the reader and the congregation call out together at the completion of the reading: "Be strong, be strong and may we be strengthened!" The source of "Be strong and of good courage" is to be found in the Bible: Deuteronomy 31: 6, 7, and 23; Joshua 1:6-9 and 18; Psalms 31:25; 1 Chronicles 28:20.

ODESSA: The southwest port of the former Soviet Union, on the shores of the Black Sea in the southern Ukraine. It was a large Jewish center and port of exit for immigrants to the Land of Israel.

TOTE AND MOME: The version of Yiddish, for father and mother, heard among the Jews of Bessarabia (in Kishinev, for example). In this pronunciation, almost every "a" becomes "o," so "tate-mame" sounds like "tote-mome."

✦ CHAPTER FIVE ✦

The Travels of Dvora

from Kalisz

and Letters to Nowhere

WORLD WAR II began on September 1, 1939. The Germans rapidly overran most of Poland, except for the eastern borders, which passed into the hands of the Soviet Union in accordance with the Ribbentrop-Molotov Agreement. The Germans were now in control of the greatest concentration of Jews in Europe, and according to Nazi ideologists, not only the center of Jewish thought and national creativity, but also the main biological resource base for the Jewish people. This was the beginning of the period of persecution and murder, which was to culminate in the policy of genocide.

AUGUST 13, 1939: The Soviet Union and Germany sign a pact known as the Ribbentrop-Molotov Agreement.

SEPTEMBER 1, 1939: The German Army invades Poland.

SEPTEMBER 3, 1939: England and France declare war on Germany.

SEPTEMBER 17, 1939: The Red Army invades the eastern part of Poland.

SEPTEMBER 27, 1939: The Polish Army surrenders in Warsaw.

OCTOBER 10, 1939: Establishment of the General Government in the central part of Poland. Annexation of western Poland by the Third Reich.

✢ Chapter Five: The Travels of Dvora from Kalisz and Letters to Nowhere ✢

After much effort, Dvora Kretchmer's father had obtained a wagon in which to evacuate his family to the countryside. By the end of August 1939, Kalisz[*] was seized with a fever of departure. The Polish authorities encouraged the evacuation. According to the instructions, which were heard from loudspeakers like a divine pronouncement, though confused and changing daily, the arrangements were intended for women and children only. Judging from the appearance of the courtyards and the streets leading out of the city, the fleeing hordes included everyone with a measure of resourcefulness and common sense. The war had not yet broken out and the highways of Poland overflowed with a lava of humanity and harnessed horses thrusting forward in mounting waves. Israel, the eldest son, had been drafted into the army and Dvora and her younger brother, a boy of twelve, rode on top of packages wrapped up in sheets and blankets and straw matting. Father and Mother sat on the driver's bench, hunched up in a double layer of overcoats, and the uncles and aunts and all available descendants were crammed between the side ladders of the farm wagon. The face of the toddler crying because he was squashed between a box and the side of the wagon, and the appearance of all those packed in among the parcels would have been dismal and wretched had it not been for the sparkle in the eyes of the adults, who were happy that the wagon had moved off and was gradually entering and going up Pilsudski Avenue. On all sides people moved on foot, carrying their belongings on their heads and backs, necks weighed down and steps faltering already at the beginning of the trek. Anyone with horse and cart today was king.

And thou shalt look after thy horse as thyself! Before long most of the men, including Father, were compelled to get down from the wagon. They were twenty-five in all and only five remained with the baggage. It was Shabbat morning when they entered the village. But many people from Kalisz had got there first, and since there was no more room in the village they turned toward Turek.[*]

Turek was a medium-sized town and even though its population trebled overnight, no one said there was a shortage of space in Turek. Close to Turek, Dvora jumped for joy at the sight of the Prosna River.

Israel's abrupt mobilization and his mother's grief at the loss of a son had caused Dvora to give up her trip to the movement summer camp, held that year in the fabulous countryside of the Carpathian foothills. Now she could try out her daring new bathing suit in the waters of the Prosna.

It was a glorious, clear day on the sandy banks of the river and Dvora was eighteen, tall and slender. As she emerged from her dip, a troop of horsemen came riding along the bank. They were Polish cavalrymen, Uhlans, riding at ease and singing:

> Gray swans were paddling
> In the river;
> The country has a shield,
> But love is strange forever!
> *Hai du! Hai du!*
> Who comes from the river,
> Breasts like fountains?
> Long live the squadron,
> The land and the mountains!
> *Hai du! Hai du!*

The cavalrymen were scanning the area for somewhere to water the horses; scarlet and black pennants fluttered at the end of long staffs. One of them suddenly stayed his mount from drinking and the horse pawed the ground in obedience. Dvora could hardly believe her ears—the horseman was addressing her by name.

She thought he might do it again. But the song of the troopers grew louder:

> Gray swans paddling
> Where the waters narrow,
> The squadron rides to war,
> Swift as an arrow.

Sha'ul too was unable to explain how he could identify the young woman—those were his words—as his cousin. On their last visit to his home, Dvora had still been a fussy

KALISZ: A town in Poland on the banks of the Prosna River near the German border and west of Lodz. It contained the oldest Jewish community in Poland (established in the twelfth century). On September 4, 1939, on the fourth day of the war, the Germans captured Lodz without a shot being fired. The Jewish community, 30,000 strong, was cast into a hell of torture and oppression. The synagogue became a prison, the Torah scrolls were torn and thrown on the fire, and the Jews were forced to jump over the fire. Within two to three months the last Jews had been eliminated from Kalisz.

TUREK: A small town northeast of Kalisz.

42

young girl, and plain. He recalled—he reminded her now—how she had insisted that her father return immediately to Kalisz, since the apartment had neither lavatory nor bathroom nor even running water. . . .

"And what about now?" she asked and laughed, not knowing how to hide her naked back and shoulders as Sha'ul's eyes roamed up and down, encompassing her dripping body in manifest admiration. He promised to find them in the village and to sit with them that evening and report in detail how he had been drafted and, before finishing his training, transferred to the cavalry here, "where we will stabilize the front and destroy the enemy."

There was much confusion among the refugees in the village. A Polish army unit had entered the village and the major in charge had ordered them to leave the place. They left all their belongings behind with acquaintances and went off, all twenty-five of them in one wagon, including two sick children. Dvora did not meet with Sha'ul, but one troop of horsemen galloped past her on its way to Klo-dowa. At that moment planes appeared from the south, from the direction of the sun. "They're ours! They're ours!" the troopers called out to calm the panic-stricken refugees. But the horses' senses were more attuned. Suddenly they lurched and bolted and almost tore their harnesses.

The planes turned and dived.

The first bombing attack ended and the second began. By the end of two raids, dozens of bodies and burned-out wagons covered the road. Their wagon was undamaged, but Aunt Minna was killed by a single bullet fired from the Messerschmitt's machine gun. They gave Aunt Minna a Jewish burial, and then the first of the Germans caught up with them. The horse and wagon were promptly confiscated, and they were ordered to leave the village.

There were now twenty-four of them and on the fifth day of their wanderings the strength of two of the women gave out and Uncle Lazar had a heart attack. They left him with the miller, also a relative, whose mill and general affluence deterred him from becoming a refugee. They sent Uncle Lazar's wife and their two daughters to the village of Beldzan, sixty kilometers from Kalisz. Infested with lice, starving, and exhausted, Dvora Kretchmer's family returned to Kalisz.

It was the eve of Rosh Hashanah, and there was a heat wave. As they approached Firemen's Square, they saw Jews doing exercises. Young men and old were jumping up and down in pools of water sprayed from firemen's hoses and German soldiers were beating them unmercifully with whips and truncheons. It was too late to turn back.

Mother fainted. Father and his two remaining brothers-in-law lifted her in their arms. Before they could stop her or even understand what she was planning to do, Dvora had broken away from where her mother had fallen and was running straight toward the group of officers standing on the edge of the square, some of them carrying box cameras.

Her family could see her pleading with an officer and pointing toward her unconscious mother, carried in the arms of her men folk. Dvora was not crying, just shouting something.

"You're Jewish?" asked the officer.

"Yes," she replied.

"Ah," said the officer, without another word. He drew the whip from under his arm and gestured to the guard with it to let them through. Then he turned back immediately to the Jews who were jumping up and down, and ordered them to continue jumping.

That same evening a wagon happened to be leaving for Beldzan, and Zvi Kretchmer sent his wife and young son to stay in the village till the storm clouds passed. Dvora packed a few of her possessions that remained in their looted apartment and set off the next morning alone for the railway station.

Monday

The brigade has been surrounded. The CO (commanding officer) has been killed and the staff officers have disappeared. The second-in-command, a courageous *sheygetz*✝ from the countryside, told us to break through the enemy lines under cover of night. "As for you," he rested his hand in friendly fashion on my shoulder, "you've got nothing to lose." We were three Jews in the company and we knew full well what our fate would be if we fell into German hands.

S.

SHEYGETZ (Yiddish): A non-Jewish boy or young man. It is derived from *sheketz,* the Hebrew word for unclean creature.

VOLKSDEUTSCH (German): A member of the German people. One of Hitler's aims was to bring under the protection of the Third Reich all those Germans who were living outside the borders of Germany in Austria, Sudetenland (Czechoslovakia), Poland, Hungary, Romania, Yugoslavia, and the Baltic countries.

On the eve of World War II the population of Lodz, the second largest city in Poland, was 672,000, of whom 250,000 were Jews. Forty-three percent of the Jews of Lodz worked in the textile industry and played a major part in the development of the town's main productive activity. Though tens of thousands of Jews and non-Jews worked together, all attempts to set up joint trade unions failed, apart from the doctors' association. With the growth of anti-Semitism in the 1930s, Jews fell victim to attacks organized by the anti-Semitic parties, which gained a majority in the municipal elections. Two Jewish theaters were active in Lodz, as were the Ha-Zamir choir and a symphony orchestra. There were four daily papers and four high schools (three of which taught in Hebrew), dozens of primary schools, ḥeders and yeshivas, and ORT trade schools. Zionist parties, the Bund, Communists, Agudat Israel, He-Ḥalutz, and youth movements were also present. The activity of all these organizations, along with the social and welfare institutions organized by the Jewish community, made Lodz one of the most vibrant centers of Judaism in Poland and Europe.

On November 9, 1939, Lodz was annexed by the Reich (Germany) and the town and its surroundings were thereby separated from the rest of occupied Poland, which came under the

Wednesday

Thank God! We did it. But maybe we've fallen out of the frying pan into the fire. On the fifth day of the war the Germans conquered Lodz. The following day the town's *Volksdeutsch*✦ emerged. The Poles were amazed at how many of their neighbors declared themselves to be *Volksdeutsch*. They immediately pinned swastikas on their sleeves and set upon any soldiers who had been cut off from their units, and had no mercy on the wounded.✦

S.

Friday

I never expected we would have to be afraid of meeting anyone except Germans. I found shelter with a local family, Sirakoviak, poor people from Balut!✦ Tonight, for the first time in a long while, I shall sit at a Sabbath table.

S.

Sunday

Many refugees who fled the town are coming back; the Germans moved ahead of them and barred their way. What their pursuers fail to achieve on the ground, the Messerschmitts complete from the air. Their cruelty is beyond measure. With their machine guns they hunt down everything moving on the roads, people and cattle. Day by day more and more people are crowding into Lodz. Famine threatens the masses. And Melk Sirakoviak says, "There's no suffering without cause."✦

S.

Monday

They've burnt down the Great Synagogue, the pride of the community. I happened to be walking down Kosciusko Avenue when the blaze was at its height. Polish police and firemen dispersed the crowds of sightseers and made sure no one would try to put out the fire. Soldiers took photographs and laughed. When I got back to the Sirakoviaks, they knew already about the rest of the fires. In every corner of Lodz they had burned down the synagogues.

S.

were arrested and some were executed. For months before the ghetto was established Jews lived in fear of being kidnapped for work camps, which led to mass flight, but once the ghetto was enclosed, most attempts at flight ended in death. One hundred sixty thousand Jews from Lodz and the surrounding area were forced into the narrow confines of the ghetto, and soon they were joined by Jews from Germany, Vienna, Slovakia, and Luxembourg. Forty-two thousand people were packed together in each square kilometer. Ninety-five percent of the living quarters in the Lodz ghetto lacked basic sanitation; 60 percent of them were one-room apartments. In the four years of its existence many died from hunger; many others were deported to the death camps daily from the end of 1941. In 1944, when the destruction of the Jews of greater Poland came to an end, there were still 69,000 people left in the ghetto. These were deported to Auschwitz in August of that year. When the Soviet army entered the town in January 1945, it found less than 900 Jews there; they had been left by the Germans to collect the remains of Jewish property.

BALUT: The poor quarter in Lodz.

"When everything else is forgotten, please inscribe this in your memory: Martha Rein, the first lady of the community of Jewish educators in Lodz, died of hunger in the ghetto when she refused to accept a special ration of food from Romkovsky, the head of the *Judenrat;* she wanted no privileged status at a time when the rest of the people in the ghetto were starving. You did not know our beautiful, always elegant, headmistress. Now she has nothing but rags and wooden clogs. Tomorrow she will be only a memory of perfection."

—SARA FLACHSER-ZISKIND

General Government. Lodz was renamed Litzmannstadt and then began a process of settling masses of Germans, former citizens of Poland. Many Jews and Poles fled the city for the interior of the country. In February 1940, the first ghettos of the twentieth century in Europe were set up in the old city and in the poor quarter, Balut. They were meant to serve as models for the Nazi organization of ghettos. The Germans appointed the businessman Mordechai Chaim Romkovsky to be head of the *Judenrat.* The members of the first council set up by Romkovsky

Tuesday

David, the son of the Sirakoviaks, saw German soldiers tormenting elderly Jews in the streets. Among them was the caretaker from the tailors' synagogue. They made him spread out a Torah scroll in the roadway and forced the Jews to urinate on its pages. Anyone who hesitated was hit across the head with a rifle butt.

S.

Thursday

There was a rumor yesterday that the name of the town has been changed from Lodz to Litzmannstadt, and the town annexed to the Reich. Is this good or bad for the Jews?

Reb Melk Sirakoviak says it's after the German General Litzmann who conquered Lodz during World War I. This same general, so say the elders of the congregation, was a friend of the Jews and helped the needy. "Again we are in great need," says Reb Melk, "and the good deeds of a righteous gentile will surely come to our aid." David saw another atrocity. Soldiers seized the baker's son on the street, whose fringes provoked their curiosity. One of them set fire to them and burned the boy's eyelashes with them. Passersby stood and watched.

S.

Tuesday

The pharmacist's son, who was taken off with other young volunteers to defend Warsaw, has come back from the conquered capital on crutches. All the Jews from Balut stand around as he tells his story: The Germans seized him and put him to work, and when they saw he was inefficient the German guard beat him and broke his leg with a rifle butt. They also seized along with him the rabbi of Praga,* Reb Yaakov Zilberstein, who was on his way to prayer carrying his prayer shawl under his arm. They made him wear it while he was working and tormented him cruelly. Among the Jews who were rounded up was Avigdor Friedman from 30 Brokova Street, one of the Zionist activists, who came to the help of the rabbi, who was stumbling in the mud. At once they pulled him out of the ranks. Ten days later his wife received the body of her husband, bruised all over and tortured.

S.

Wednesday

More men are coming back from the front. A nephew of the Sirakoviaks, also from Warsaw, has turned up sick. He has been hospitalized; his condition is cause for concern. But Reb Melk says, "The main thing is we're all together, *un Got iz a fater*."* No news of my family.

S.

Friday

"He's killing him! He's killing my son!" This terrible cry made me spring to the window, or more precisely to the cracks in the planks that boarded up the window of the little room in which I was hiding, like the rest of the Jewish men in those days. It was the owner of the grocery, who was waving her hands wildly through the open window of the second floor opposite. "My Yankele! Save my Yankele, my darling!"

Yankele, a child of seven, freckle-faced with fair hair and blue eyes, had apparently just doffed his hat, as required of any Jew who meets a German. His hat still in his hand, he was looking up pleadingly at the German sergeant, who was holding the child by the chin. Some people, Jewish women and children, were cowering in the distance, keeping well away. Another German soldier came up to the sergeant, neither of them young. It seemed the sergeant meant no harm, he just wanted to know why a blonde child with blue eyes, looking in all respects just like a Christian Pole, should doff his hat to him.

He held him by the ear to get a better look. "Who are you, son?" he asked with amusement. And then he heard the mother's cry. And looking strangely from the tiny head to the face of the mother crying bitterly at the window, he shook his head in incredulity, and breathed, "*So klein—und schon Jude!*" "So small—and already a Jew!" There were those who swore they saw the German's right hand creeping quietly toward the holster of his Mauser.* But he only pinched the child's earlobe hard, in anger or compassion, and yelled at the grocer's son, whose eyes were streaming with tears, "Scram, you little pig, scram!"

And all the unseen onlookers in Balut breathed a sigh of relief.

S.

PRAGA: A suburb of Warsaw, the capital of Poland.

"… GOT IZ A FATER" (Yiddish): "God is a father," that is, a merciful father, loving and supportive.

MAUSER: The reference here is to the Mauser pistol, which was carried by German army commanders, police, SS, and others as their personal weapons.

In accordance with the Ribbentrop-Molotov Agreement, the Red Army entered Vilna on September 19, 1939. At the end of October, Vilna became the capital of Lithuania and its name was changed to Vilnius. Together with Lithuania, Latvia, and Estonia, it was annexed by the Soviet Union in the middle of June 1940. The stream of refugees flowing east from Nazi-occupied Poland and from the areas conquered by the Red Army included hundreds of members of youth movements. About 14,000 Jewish refugees were concentrated in Vilna, along with the leaders of the Zionist movement and other movements from the large cities of Poland. Rabbis and heads of talmudic academies arrived there, with and without students. The concentration of Zionist pioneer youth, more than 2,000 in number, was an important component in the mass of Jewish refugees in the city.

"I reached Vilna from western Poland, from Kalisz, after the German Occupation, crossing first the German-Russian border and then the Lithuanian-Russian border. There was a large concentration of pioneer youth in Vilna. Later they split into groups with more specific movement identification, such as He-Ḥalutz, Ha-Shomer Ha-Tzaʻir, and Akiva. As members of Rikuz, we were refugees and the "Joint" supported us. But we had no desire to subsist on "Joint" support and went out to work in order to preserve our values, not in order to maintain our existence, since that was guaranteed, though on a small scale. The hostel in which the Rikuz was housed held 40 to 50 of us. We slept two to a bed; there were no blankets and no heating and it was terribly cold. The overcrowding made for intimacy. When the Russians enered, they dispersed the Rikuz."

—VITKA KEMPNER KOVNER

ALEXANDER: A small German town of weavers, 10 kilometers from Lodz, Alexander was first settled in the nineteenth century. It was famous in the Jewish world as the place of residence of the *tzaddik* Rabbi Hanoch-Henekh Levin.

Wednesday

On the round concrete pillar that stands in the square outside the district, new notices appear every morning. Like other Jews, who would be better off keeping well away from the place, I find myself drawn as though hypnotized to the pillar: Each day has its new decrees. All Jews must hand over their radios to the authorities, at once and in toto; anyone failing to do so will be shot. And hand over their furs; anyone failing to do so will be shot. No Jew may enter a cinema. No Jew may walk on the pavements, which are meant for human beings. Worst of all, the town is running short of food. In the long queue for bread, Manka, the concierge, who has been working in Jewish houses for forty years and speaks a fluent Yiddish, is heard to say, "It's the dirty Jews, my friend, who are responsible for all this," and she says this in Polish with a Ukrainian accent, without having to explain why.

S.

Saturday night

There are rumors of the establishment of a ghetto. Everyone asks when it will be set up and where. Some are sure it will be here in Balut. How is that possible?

Dvora, my cousin from Kalisz, has apparently fled to Vilna. Thousands of pioneer youth are stealing across the frontier into Lithuania, which is still independent, the gateway of hope for all those striving to get to Palestine and the free world. It's incredible that such a frail girl as Dvora should display such courage, leave home, and take the dangerous road to Vilna. I hope my sickness will not delay me for long from following her and getting out of hell.✝

S.

Tuesday

In Alexander,✝ the day after they entered the town, the Germans burned down the synagogue and the study house. They threw out the Torah scrolls and made a bonfire of them in the market square. An officer called on one of the inhabitants, who had not yet managed to go into hiding, to tear up the parchment before throwing it into the fire. It was Mottel Hochman whose fate it was to be this victim. Mottel begged to be excused, turning his head this way and that, saying, "I can't, I mustn't, no. No."

The officer drew his pistol, and Mottel Hochman had just caught a glimpse of the long barrel of the Mauser when he was ordered to stand against the wall.

The Jew stood with his back to the wall and closed his eyes.

"*Shema Yisra'el*," he said aloud, with his eyes closed. Before he could see what was happening he was thrown to the ground, strong hands turned him face downward, and he was whipped fiercely across the back. Mottel never heard the officer give orders for him to be whipped, never saw him replace his revolver in its holster, never understood who dragged his aching body away or where to—his senses were dulled. But when he recovered consciousness and found himself in a Jewish house, his first question was, "I didn't tear the parchment, did I?"

S.

Tuesday

And I'm inside. Three months in the ghetto already. Sometimes it seems I can't stand it any longer. Seeing other people who are outside. It's not that the Poles, who have forfeited their independence and lost the war, still feel free. That's simple enough to take. But just the feeling, impossible to explain to anyone who's not here, of what it means to be inside, within, in the ghetto. I see them and know that for them, for the Pasziboszs and the Yatskis, some of whom come up occasionally and peep through, wave a hand in greeting, or worse, there are paths and lanes and streets to walk along, to escape by. I know that they too are not all that free. But we are inside, that's the whole difference.

Hunger. Stench. Disease. I don't know why but I feel a physical sense of shame.✦

        S.

Thursday

It's strange, but all the time I think of Ruschka. Ruschka has green eyes, blazing with a strange fire. I'm afraid she has caught TB from her young brother. Her young brother is seven and sick with galloping consumption. Ruschka is not working, and the slice of bread I bring her she puts aside, wrapped in a kerchief. Sometimes she can't resist and covertly breaks off a crumb. Her young brother cries from hunger all the time. Ruschka is nineteen and looks twice as old. Her father went off to the countryside to make arrangements for them and hasn't come back yet. Her mother is dead and Daniel, her twin brother, is with the pioneer youth in Vilna. That's how I found out that Dvora, my cousin, is not there; she must be still on her way.

        S.

Shabbat

On the other side of the partition, in what was once the pantry in this poor apartment, S. is living with her four-year-old brother. They are refugees from Warsaw. The parents were killed in an air raid on the first day of the war. Danko, her brother, is not back from the front. At the beginning she was among those who were contented, since she cleaned the floors in the house of a German. Since the day she was sacked because she broke a vase, she and her brother have been starving to death.

        S.

Wednesday

The little boy died of hunger and S. hid him in the little room without telling Ruschka, her flatmate. She concealed the body under the bed and pretended she had given her brother for adoption to a Polish woman, and in order to hide the smell of the corpse she drenched it in Lysol. That way she had a ration card for a further week, but on the seventh day she collapsed.

        S.

Shabbat

Ruschka and I went to visit S. in the ghetto hospital. She said, "I'm happy. I'm not hungry here."

        S.

"I went further along the street and saw a body covered with newspaper. I thought it was the body of a child. But when the wind blew the newspaper I discovered it was an old man, dried up and shrunken. Here and there in front of gates you see faded rags and newspapers, their sides held down by stones. These are dead who have been put out by their families without informing the authorities in order to continue using their ration cards."

—HELENA SHARSHEVSKA

47

❖ CHAPTER SIX ❖

The Trail of Fire
and Jewish Brotherhood

GEMILUT ḤESED and **BIKKUR ḤOLIM:** Mutual assistance and charitable activities were highly developed in Jewish communities. Nathan-Neta Hanover pointed out in his book *Yeven Metzulah* (Deep Mire, 1653, see Psalms 69:2), "There were no limits to the extent of charitable activity among the Jews in the state of Poland." Jews regarded charity not as an act of mercy but as a holy obligation of national solidarity. Bikkur Ḥolim and Gemilut Ḥesed were two institutions concerned chiefly with the plight of Jews. Bikkur Ḥolim gave medical assistance, financial support in times of affliction due to illness or want, and visits and encouragement to the sick. Gemilut Ḥesed provided proper burial for the dead who had no family, or lacked the means to arrange a funeral. It was also concerned with comforting the bereaved and providing social and material support for families in need due to the death of the family breadwinner.

YITZHAK GREENBOIM (1879–1970): An eminent Zionist leader in Poland between the two world wars. A public figure in Warsaw, Greenboim supported the idea of Jewish autonomy in the Diaspora. Between 1919 and 1930, he was a member of the Polish parliament and established a block of national minorities. A regular delegate to the Zionist Congresses, Greenboim immigrated to Palestine in 1933. He was appointed first minister of the interior in the new State of Israel.

TERRITORIALISTS: The reference is to an organization that called itself Frayland (Free Country), whose aim was to organize Jewish immigration to a country other than Palestine. The territorialists denied the validity of the Diaspora and did not believe that the Jewish people and their culture could enjoy an untroubled existence in the countries of the dispersion. They also claimed that territorial concentration would facilitate the preservation

I.

Dvora had not yet reached safety and was still roaming the highways. She left Warsaw quite suddenly, just the way she had abandoned home. In years to come she would remember the holes in the clouds that covered the sky over Kalisz that morning, and the scanty blue visible through them. Against this clear blue background could be seen the first planes to emerge through the cracks in the clouds, almost like a hallucination—until the sound of the air raid siren sliced through the air, to be followed by silence, the silence of death before the thunder.

Her relatives in Warsaw were not in the least surprised when, between one air raid and the next, Dvora turned up disheveled at their apartment in the suburb of Praga. "Where are your parents?" they asked.

"They'll come later," she said. And then she told them, "The railway linesmen say the Germans are thirty kilometers from Warsaw."

Her uncle paled and clutched his throat, as though he could feel a noose around it. "Impossible!" he gasped.

There were six of them in the family and he supported them comfortably from the local grocer's shop. Uncle Gershoni had a long day, for he was also secretary of the Gemilut Ḥesed organization and a member of the Bikkur Ḥolim[+] committee. Gershoni was a follower of Yitzhak Greenboim,[+] though his wife, Sarah, sang in the choir of the territorialists.[+] At that time she was going from door to door, along with other members of the choir, collecting copper as a contribution to Poland's war effort. On the sixth of September, before dawn, her uncle—ever prudent and thoughtful—was planning to summon his two older children, Mitek and Toussia, and tell them to be on their way immediately out of Warsaw. The man, who had never in his life allowed his five children to leave the town unsupervised, for whom year after year every departure to a youth movement summer camp was a fresh, wearisome ordeal, was now urging them to get going and not spend even an hour on unnecessary goodbyes. He gave Mitek three notes, one to the family in Bialystok, one to a distant relative in Vilna, and a third to his father's brother, whom he hadn't seen for twenty years, and who was now "some kind of a commissar" in Minsk, the capital of White Russia.

"Move as quickly as you can. The main thing is—keep going east!" he told them, and they didn't recognize their father in this man of decision. "We'll follow later," he promised.

He was referring to his three remaining children, two sons, pupils at the Tarbut[+] High School, and Sarinka, who had only just finished primary school. The following day he sent his wife to Otvotsk with an offer to a man named Koviatkovski, that he should take over the shop for a nominal rent, and to start packing already, "just the essentials," when he was

and development of a Jewish culture in Yiddish. They rejected the Zionist solution, for they did not believe that Palestine could absorb the Jewish masses in their millions, and they had reservations about conflict with the Arabs. Although the Frayland movement had fairly wide support in Warsaw, Vilna, and Paris, it did not have mass appeal. Its search for a country that was open to Jewish immigration gave rise to a number of proposals, all of which came to nothing.

TARBUT: In April 1917, the conference of Ḥovevei Sfat Ever (Lovers of the Hebrew Language) in Russia resolved to set up an institution whose main goal was to establish kindergartens, primary schools, technical schools, high schools, colleges, teacher training colleges, and yeshivas. The language of instruction in all these institutions was to be Hebrew and the name of the central organization was to be Tarbut. In 1917, 200 Hebrew language educational institutions were established in Russia, including 60 kindergartens and 3 high schools. After the October Revolution in 1917, all this effort went to waste: Hebrew language schools were shut down and a campaign was initiated against the revival of Hebrew. Tarbut then transferred its activities to Poland. In 1921, the Zionist Association gave Tarbut the responsibility of organizing a system of Hebrew language education there. In 1919, there were 51 institutions with 2,575 pupils and 233 teachers, and by 1939, there were 269 institutions with 37,000 pupils and 1,300 teachers. Tarbut established 425 Hebrew libraries and published children's magazines and educational materials.

SHIKSA (Yiddish): A non-Jewish girl or woman.

HAKHSHARAH (pl. HAKHSHAROT): One of the *kibbutzim* that were organized in various cities in Poland to bring together those pioneer youths who were ready to immigrate to Palestine and set up their kibbutz there. The members of the *hakhsharot* supported themselves by manual labor under difficult conditions, but the system served as a melting pot for the best of the pioneer youth from all the Zionist youth movements.

KIBITZERS (Yiddish): A jocular term for spectators at a game of chess or cards. It originated from the German word *kiebitz,* which referred to onlookers who give advice to players at the card tables. Actually, the word refers to a bird that takes over the nest of another as if it were its own. In Yiddish the word has connotations of indolence, idle chatter, and gossiping layabouts.

JOSEF HAYYIM BRENNER (1881–1921): A great Hebrew writer, thinker, editor, and translator. Brenner served in the Russian army and during the Russo-Japanese War (1904) he deserted; with the help of members of the Bund he arrived in London, where he founded the journal *Ha-Me'orer* (1906). In 1906, Brenner immigrated to Palestine and there he began publishing stories and essays. He was murdered during the disturbances in Jaffa in 1921. His main works are *Ba-Ḥoref* (In Winter, 1904), *Misaviv La-Nekuda* (Around the Point, 1904), *Mi-Kan U-Mi-Kan* (From Here and There, 1911), and *Shekhol U-Kishalon* (Bereavement and Failure, 1920).

CHAIM NACHMAN BIALIK (1873–1934): One of the greatest Hebrew poets since the revival of the language. Bialik wrote poems in Hebrew and Yiddish. For 20 years Bialik lived in Odessa, where he wrote the best of his poems. The

taken sick with kidney trouble. Toussia, who looked like a *shiksa*✝ in every way, had already left that very morning. Mitek delayed for twenty-four hours in order to organize a group of youngsters from his youth movement. He was caught up in the last-minute preparations and never went back home. He never imagined that he would never see any member of his family again.

Dvora reached Rimarska 12, looking for Yashiu. Her second brother had been staying for a year at the *hakhsharah*✝ camp, and was waiting for his turn for an immigration certificate. The previous Passover he had visited home and, feeling good, had revealed to her his secret, that he had a girlfriend named Mira and that together they would be in Palestine "before the end of winter." Dvora was expecting to find him at the movement house. It took four hours to get from Praga to Rimarska. There were three air raid warnings and before her eyes she saw the streets and houses turn into heaps of rubble. Everyone seemed confused and helpless, you could see the wild look in the eyes of the passersby as they ran, trampling an ocean of fragments of broken glass.

A large signboard from a bookshop, in Hebrew lettering, lay abandoned on its side, the doors of the shop off their hinges. To Dvora's amazement, she found people inside the ruined shop. In those days, at the beginning of the war, there were those who believed that "bombs never fall twice in the same spot." A group of men was playing cards by candlelight. She stepped over the piles of scattered books and the card players were so absorbed in their game they failed to notice her approach.

"Ha-Shomer Ha-Tza'ir?" One of the *kibitzers,*✝ his hat pushed back from his forehead, answered her question, "They're on the other side of the square; they haven't been bombed yet."

The movement house was deserted. Charred papers lay among the ashes of an extinguished bonfire. Streamers of colored crepe paper and other decorations were strewn upon the floor. Only the portraits of Brenner,✝ Bialik,✝ Herzl,✝ and Borochov✝ still hung on the wall, two on either side with a view of the Sea of Galilee in the middle. In the next room someone was standing in front of an open cupboard.

Kishinev pogrom of 1903 roused him to write his two famous poems *Al Ha-Sheḥita* (About the Slaughter) and *Ba-'Ir Ha-Harega* (In the City of Killing), which had a tremendous impact on the Jewish world. Bialik wrote many poems, stories, articles, and essays. In 1924, he immigrated and settled in Palestine. He died in Vienna in 1934.

THEODOR (BENJAMIN ZEEV) HERZL (1860–1904): A writer and journalist born in Budapest to an assimilated family. At the age of eighteen he moved to Vienna, studied law, and embarked on a literary career. There he wrote stories, articles, and plays and worked for the great Viennese daily newspaper *Neue Freie Presse.* Between 1891 and 1895, Herzl worked for a newspaper in Paris. There he encountered the wave of anti-Semitism that swept France at the time of the Dreyfus trial (1895). And there he formulated the idea of the establishment of a Jewish state, which would absorb the millions of Jews who sought to emigrate from the east. In 1897 he convened the First Zionist Congress in Basel and founded the Zionist movement. Five congresses met under his leadership. He had many meetings with wealthy Jews, kings, princes, ministers, even with the Pope, with the aim of winning their support for his idea. Herzl accepted the suggestion of Uganda as a refuge for the Jews, once it became clear to him that the opposition to settling Jews in Palestine was too great. At the Sixth Zionist Congress (1903) the Zionist organization almost split over this issue. Herzl died of a heart attack in 1904.

The father of political Zionism, Herzl created the image of the Jewish state in his book *The Jewish State,* and in greater detail in his Utopian novel *Altneuland.*

DOV BER BOROCHOV (1881–1921): Born in Russia, Borochov was one of the founders of Socialist Zionism and the movement

The man was picking books out of the cupboard and throwing them into a sack at his feet. He opened every one and examined it, cursorily or with attention. One he would throw into the sack, the next return to the shelf. It was clear he was having a hard time, like someone forced to part forever from his dearest friends. Dvora asked about Yashiu.

Apparently her brother had already left, in all probability for Brisk. All the seniors had decided to leave Warsaw. First they would try to cross the frontier into Romania, or make their way eastward to the area in Soviet hands.

The man was about twenty, short in stature, with an intelligent face, and he did not favor her with even a glance.

In Leshno, he said, there was still a group from the Kalisz branch; they were supposed to be leaving immediately for Rovno. It was worth a try. There was a good chance she would find Yashiu among them.

Suddenly he left his post and stared at her with suspicion.

"Are you really Yashiu's sister?"

She smiled, showing her white teeth.

"My name is Dvora."

"Shmuel," he replied.

"And that thing you're holding," she couldn't restrain her curiosity, "isn't that the flag?"

"The movement flag."

"And why have you wrapped it around you like a prayer shawl?" she asked in amusement.

"I'm trying to keep it close to my body. We're taking it with us. Perhaps by virtue of the flag we shall reach our chosen destination."✣

2.

It was a glorious Polish winter and the edge of the woods was bathed in purple radiance. Whenever she found herself pushed to the side of the road, swept along like a log on the stream, Dvora would feast her eyes on the open landscape. Giant chestnut trees stood naked, their fallen copper leaves rustling at her feet.

Other trees were still green and there was no shortage of wild flowers in the meadows. Behind the hedgerows, late flowering sunflowers, not yet cut down, swayed their heads. Nature seemed to take care that not everything should die at once.

Old men and women sat leaning on their suitcases, taking a respite, wheezing and out of breath. They tried to protect themselves from the wave of trampling feet, but anyone who was not quick enough to stand his ground was bound to be pushed down the slope.

Flood waters were flowing at the foot of the embankment, and from time to time a shout of terror would rend the air as someone found himself stumbling and falling into the turbulent sewage. The true river, the river of humanity, flowed along the road above, filling its length and breadth from Warsaw to Lvov and beyond. Everyone was there! Farmers with their families and a bundle of property and a cow pulled along on a rope. Prosperous merchants in well-protected carts, with pieces of fur to cover the feet of the passengers. Householders in wagons with tarpaulins over them, the wagoners sitting up front in their drivers' caps. Country gentry riding

Po'alei Tzion (Workers of Zion). During the pogroms of 1905, he was active in organizing an independent Jewish defense. Borochov was a great scholar and published his works in Yiddish, Russian, and German. In his research he paid particular attention to Yiddish, and he is regarded by many as the founder of philological study of the Yiddish language. His political theory "Borochovism" was based on Marxism. He believed the Jewish workers' movement would be compelled to leave the countries of the Diaspora and immigrate to the Land of Israel, where a Jewish socialist society would be established.

The focal symbol of Ha-Shomer Ha-Tza'ir, a Zionist-Socialist youth movement in Poland devoted to preparing youth for life on an Israeli kibbutz, was a flag that incorporated the symbol of the Scout movement (a fleur-de-lis) and Zionism (a Shield of David); it was light blue at the top and white at the bottom. It was called "the movement flag" and kept at the organization's headquarters in Warsaw. In September 1939, when the Germans occupied Poland, the flag was lowered at a dramatic ceremonial parade conducted by Shmuel Breslau, a leading member of the Warsaw branch, and the movement went underground. Breslau, who made his way eastward with the rest of the group's male members, wrapped the flag around his body and took it with him. He underwent many trials until he reached Rovno, the site of the *hakhsharah* kibbutz of Ha-Shomer Ha-Tza'ir. Breslau had been arrested by Polish soldiers and it was only his personal charm and fluent command of Polish that enabled him to persuade the commanding officer to release him. Hungry, sick, and wounded, he finally reached Rovno after a long journey of 500 kilometers. At that time Rovno was within the area controlled by the former Soviet Union. The flag remained buried in the ground the whole time Breslau was in the hospital. Afterward it was taken by Josef Kaplan, who brought it to Vilna, where it was flown again at Ha-Shomer headquarters during ceremonial parades. The flag was brought to Israel by Zelig Neher and transferred to the archives of Ha-Shomer Ha-Tza'ir at Givat Ḥavivah, where it is now kept.

LEKH-LEKHA: The Lord said to Abram, "Go forth from your native land and from your father's house to the land that I will show you."—GENESIS 12:1

horses, town intellectuals conspicuous in their spectacles, priests, sportsmen on bicycles, lorries creaking under their loads, cars with baskets tied to their roofs and motorcycles hooting to pick a way laboriously through the crowd, for the roads were crammed with thousands of feet.

But soon there was a change in the direction of the flow. While many were still pressing out of Warsaw and the bombed cities of the west, the first of the returnees could be seen making their way back to the banks of the Vistula. Poland had been conquered and the Messerschmitts had stopped harassing the refugees; now the migrants were moving in two directions. More and more the ones moving east were Jews.

Jews from the small towns traveled in wagons. Property was loaded in the front of the wagon, suitcases and eiderdowns. An abundance of eiderdowns. Mostly it was old people, children, and pregnant women who sat in the wagons. The men and youths walked alongside. There were some who had gotten up from their sickbeds, from surgery, some half paralyzed, others holding their hands to their hearts, heads drooping, straining with effort. They came from all directions. At every crossroads more refugees joined them, the column of Jews continued to swell. The majority trudged in silence. The road between Bedzin and Pinczow was strewn with corpses, most of them charred, the skeletons of burned out buses, motorcycles, and suitcases, their contents scattered unheeded. Here a devastating bombing attack had caught them, one of those strafing raids the German pilots took such purposeless pleasure in. The columns passed the charred remnants without stopping, with a mask of indifference. Only the sight of baby carriages lying on their sides stirred them. Some went up and stood the carriages back on their wheels, looking all around in case there were any babies in the vicinity, then lined up the carriages along the side of the road, as though on parade, eleven of them, and burst into tears. The weeping was infectious and became an uninterrupted wail. Suddenly and all together the sobbing ceased and the dense column began to move. At that moment they realized that what they had seen on the road belonged to the past, to the bombings, to the conflagrations of war visited upon Poland; they were all party to her

sacrifices, but from now on the Jews would meet their own fate. "The people of Israel have once again taken up the staff of wandering," said the lawyer Rubinczik. "*Lekh-lekha*–go forth,"* a man from Pinczow said in support. And after a short pause: "Suddenly, about three nights ago, my grandfather came to me in a dream and said, 'go forth from your native land, and from your father's house!' . . . and I didn't understand what on earth he was talking about. I'm not Abraham! But it seems Abraham too didn't understand at the time, and that's where all the trouble started." He stopped talking, with no explanation; the sky overhead grew dark with billowing smoke.

3.

There were four of them and they did not allow the throng to separate them by day, nor the cold to discriminate between them by night. Dvora and her cousin Toussia from Warsaw, Zerah from Kalisz, and David, the man from Pinczow; and Dvora loved David.

"Pinczow is burning," said David from afar.

They could all see that their destination was wrapped in smoke and flames.

"They got there before us," added David.

And they all understood that this time too the Germans had got there first.

And yet in their hearts they refused to believe it. Was it for this that they had suffered for two weeks, passing through the whole region of Kielce just to come up against a wall of fire!

But the nearer they got, the clearer were the flames, leaving no doubt as to their origin. The Germans had started their work there, and it would be suicide to enter the city.

Before Bedzin they were caught in one of the heavy bombardments. Some way Dvora had managed to carry her suitcase next to her chest, but as she stumbled across the plowed field she threw down the suitcase and ran for the woods. She saw David go back on his tracks and lift the suitcase on to his shoulder, next to his own. When they rose to go on, he persisted with his gallant act of carrying both suitcases. The escape route from the road to the forest was strewn with bodies. The wounded groaned. Dvora said, "David, throw away the suitcase. I'm not worried about those rags!"

52

"They're the clothes you got ready to take with you on *aliyah*,[*] if I'm not mistaken." He tied the two suitcases together with a rope now, with a large knot in the middle, put his head through the knot and let the cases hang down over his shoulders like a pair of sacks, one on either side. "Isn't it too early to give up?" he smiled. They were approaching a bridge; it was toward evening and they felt sure they had had their quota of air attacks for the day, when a small German plane suddenly emerged from behind the hill, dived, and machine-gunned the column of refugees who were pressing toward the bridge. It was just a solitary fighter, but behind it came heavy bombers whose target was the bridge. Dvora fell and buried her face in the clods of plowed earth, covering her ears and neck with her two hands. The palm of her hand muffled somewhat the screams of the people and the bellowing of the cattle that were hit, but it couldn't silence the crack of the bullets that were chipping the earth near her and coming nearer and nearer to her head. And then something happened that in days to come would be a cause for laughter and jest, but at that instant of eternity had a feeling of doom. A large heavy mass fell across her, covering her back, her neck, and her head. Her eyes closed and for an instant or two she held her breath: was this the touch of death?

"David, are you crazy?" she shouted when she recovered and realized it was his body that was shielding her from the shower of bullets. "David, get off!"

David blushed, as though he had been dipped in the light of the sunset, and hurried to remove himself from her.

Now that they were standing at the gates of his city, Pinczow, going up in flames, she understood what was in his mind.

"David," she rested her hand on his shoulder. "They may not be there. Maybe they got away?"

"There's no point in going in," she added. He said nothing.

Other refugees had already moved to a path that bypassed them. Suddenly an ambulance came from the direction of the burning town.

Its whiteness as it drove up out of the fire and the blackness was like a hallucination.

The cabin window opened and the Polish driver called out, "Don't go on!"

As though he were standing behind her, Dvora heard her father's voice. He was holding her shoulders and her feet were standing on the lower step of the threshold to the house. "Dorinka, can't you wait a moment to say goodbye to your mother?"

"It's not easy, Father. I shall miss the train with my comrades on it. We'll meet again, won't we?"

But it was David's hands that now rested heavily on her shoulders. And David said, "I shall never forgive myself if I pass by my parents' house and don't go in to see what has happened to them."

"Leave me alone." She pushed his hands away and burst into tears.

Near the orchard beside the river, a tethered goat was circling. It bleated and struck the fence with its hooves. Only when they drew near could they see the wooden hut and its entry gate. Not a single ray of light filtered through from within. When they knocked on the door, there was no reply, but Dvora sensed that someone was looking at them through a crack in the window shutter. Then the door opened and a woman in a kerchief of white lace asked them in Polish, "Are you . . . looking for somebody?"

The table was covered with a white cloth, Sabbath candles glowed from copper candlesticks, and the members of the family, five or six in number, were all dipping slices of ḥallah in fish sauce.

"Can't you see, *Mamele*,"[*] came a male voice from within, "they're *yiddishe kinder!*"[*]

The woman was instructed forthwith to reduce the family's portions, setting some aside for the guests. There were not enough plates or chairs so they had to eat in shifts. They sang the Sabbath hymns together, but they did so quietly. They took pity on Dvora and bandaged her sore feet and would not let them leave till the next morning. It may have been due to their remoteness from town, or perhaps the spirit of the Sabbath, which lent them tranquility. Within the walls of this wooden hut on the edge of the village there seemed no awareness that Hitler and the war were raging outside.

"Were there German tanks here?"

No, they hadn't seen any German tanks.

"Who is in control of the village?"

"As always, the *soltis*."[*]

ALIYAH: Ascent. Here it means immigration to Israel.

MAMELE (Yiddish): Mommy.

YIDDISHE KINDER (Yiddish): Jewish children.

SOLTIS: The term for the head of a village in Poland.

TOCHTER (Yiddish): Daughter.

MONEK (MOSHE) MARIN: The head of the *Judenrat,* the council appointed by the Germans to govern a Jewish community, in Sosnowiec, Marin was also placed in charge of the head office of the Committee of Jewish Councils in Upper Silesia (Zaglebie). From 1940 onward, Marin was in control of 32 communities, including Bedzin and Sosnowiec. For a considerable time the Jews of Zaglebie lived in better conditions than most of the communities of Poland. This fact enabled Marin to claim that the area under his control was not in danger of deportation to the death camps, and many Jews were happy to adopt this attitude. At the beginning of 1942, Mordechai Anielewicz from Warsaw tried to persuade Marin not to place obstacles in the way of the underground movement, to no avail. Marin tried to explain the good intentions behind the activities of his *Judenrat,* but Anielewicz informed him plainly that Jewish youth would offer armed resistance to any deportation of Jews to the camps.

This is what is told of the way Marin rose to power: After the occupation, the Germans imprisoned a group of Jews in Sosnowiec. They were held in custody in a public bathhouse, beaten, ill-treated, and tortured. A German officer interrogated them, insisting on knowing which of them had been members of the community council. Lazarowicz, who had been the council's head, did not dare to speak up and admit it and neither did the rest of the Jews. But Marin stood up and declared himself a member. And that was the beginning—with treachery and tale bearing—of his career as an activist. His work against the underground and frustration of their plans led them to the decision to eliminate him (in November 1942). The task was assigned to Tzvi Donsky and two of his

"And what do you intend to do, stay here?"

Dvora had hardly posed the question when she regretted asking. In a strange house, with unfamiliar people, who had welcomed them so warmly without even asking their names: Why was she interrogating them! Suddenly she felt an electric current pass through the room. The eldest, married daughter tightened her grip on the sleeve of her husband, who was standing next to her chair. A lad of seventeen blinked nervously and his lips parted in astonishment. It was quite obvious that there had been a bitter argument on this very topic. The father of the family, in his mid-fifties, with stubby, callused fingers, a sunburned neck crisscrossed with wrinkles, but a delicate face and a thoughtful brow, was serenely radiant in his skullcap. Suddenly Dvora noticed the ritual tear of mourning on the lapel of his jacket, shifted her gaze from one to another and saw they all bore fresh rents of mourning—could it have been a grandfather? she asked herself, or one of the sons who had fallen at the front?

The man screwed up his eyes in the light of the candle flames in front of his face—they had burned halfway down—raised his black eyebrows, and gave Dvora a long, measured, introspective gaze, seeing and not seeing. "And where do you think, *tochter,*✱ Jews can go?"

Dull thuds could be heard from outside. Dvora shivered.

It was the goat, banging his hooves again on the fence.

In Bedzin David's comrades had burned the movement stamps and membership lists. They packed the books, albums, and instruction pamphlets in boxes and hid them in secret caches. In Zarki, near Bedzin, the Jews were accused of signaling to Polish planes, which were nonexistent; the synagogue was burned down and, according to rumor, three hundred men were carried off to Germany. David's comrades decided to save the senior class of boys from the German conquest, but some of the girls would stay to teach the younger ones. In a few days' time a Jewish council was due to be set up, headed by a gambler named Monek Marin.✱ Everyone was in such a panic that it was difficult for people to tell good from evil.

But Tzvi✱ would say, "Marin is a symbol of evil."

The feeling that something terrible was about to happen had been troubling Tzvi's spirit since the height of the summer of 1939. One of the chief movement leaders in Zaglebie, he had cut short the mountain summer camps and gone on a tour of the *hakhsharah* groups in Kalisz and throughout Zaglebie. Everywhere he urged immigration to Palestine, and whenever possible he pleaded with the higher institutions not to let complacency and bureaucratic inefficiency delay the main effort. And the main effort, Jews, was *aliyah, aliyah.*

comrades. They laid an ambush, but failed, for Marin was always surrounded by Jewish police. In the middle of June 1943, Marin was summoned, along with four other members of the *Judenrat,* to the SS headquarters in Sosnowiec. They were never seen again. Later it was reported that all five were transported to Birkenau and sent to the gas chambers. Within a month and a half the same fate befell the rest of the Jews of Sosnowiec.

TZVI BRANDES (1917-1943): Brandes was born in the village of Zarki, to the northeast of Bedzin. In adolescence he became one of the most active Zionist youth leaders. In 1937, he joined the *hakhsharah* in Kalisz. He returned home just before the outbreak of war and during the war devoted himself entirely to movement affairs. In 1941, under the German occupation, Brandes set up a *hakhsharah* farm at Zarki, which he headed. The farm was broken up in October 1942, and Brandes was sent to Bedzin, where he obtained all kinds of weapons. In August 1943, the Germans began the total annihilation of the ghettos in the towns of Zaglebie. Members of the underground and Jews took up positions in bunkers, but all the bunkers were discovered. Brandes and his comrades opened fire on the Germans from the bunkers but the return fire of the Germans was murderous. Brandes was captured, and shot and killed while trying to escape.

On August 23, 1939, when people were raising their eyebrows at the news on the radio of the agreement signed between the foreign ministers of Bolshevik Russia and Nazi Germany, that same morning a messenger from the movement center in Warsaw got off the train. He had brought with him eleven certificates for eleven fortunate members on *hakhsharah*. Tzvi was not on the list.

Zarki, his birthplace, was a medium-sized to small town, between Czestochowa and Bedzin. Of the five thousand inhabitants, more than three thousand were Jews. When he finished *heder* with Reb Pinchas, Tzvi—like many youngsters in Zarki—had been obliged to choose one of the Hasidic courts that ruled in the area, from Gur to Alexander, from Skierniewice to Radomsk. Small as it was, the town came under the influence of a great Jewish rabbi, Rabbi Abraham Ben-Mordechai, the Admor from Trisk.✢

Yet who can know the ways of the spirit! Even in such a small town, there was room for a different kind of Jewish spirit. In due course a *hakhsharah* group of pioneers in Zarki would keep the flame of hope blazing, even in the midst of the maelstrom of Hitlerism. Tzvi became a free thinker. Not one totally free from the obligation to keep the commandments, for he was one of the leading educators of Ha-Shomer Ha-Tza'ir, a movement whose members took upon themselves the yoke of many commandments, both written and not written in the Torah. When he stood in front of a row of his charges, arranged scout✢ fashion according to height, Tzvi was a whole head shorter than they were. But before many days passed, he would be their acknowledged leader, by virtue of his inner strength. He could not subject his parents to a double burden of grief; he asked for his joining a *hakhsharah* group to be delayed for a year or two, until he had worked and provided some support for his aged parents. In the meantime, he devoted himself heart and soul to the task of education in that workshop known as a *ken* or "nest."

But now, when the long awaited certificates arrived, his years in education did not count, for he lacked the two years of *hakhsharah*.

The town of Zarki was situated at an ancient crossroads known in Polish as the Way of the Thirteen Eagles, and above it towered the castle of Graf Potowski,✢ surrounded by a stout wall. Tzvi and his friend David were strolling around the wall. It was a warm evening. Tzvi was trying to overcome the storm in his heart, both at the news he had heard on the radio and the news brought by the messenger from Warsaw. He said, "It's funny, if Stiebel✢ had not set up the public library and opened a window for me into the wide world, I might have become by now a wandering preacher for the Hasidim of Gur or Alexander."

David laughed and said, "And even beyond!"✢

From the fish pond of the Graf came the raucous croaking of frogs. They both listened to the enigmatic message and Tzvi said, "I shall never get to Palestine."

Now David stood at the entrance to his birthplace and watched Pinczow going up in flames. His mind wavered like a pendulum: Should he go in and see what had become of his family, or should he comfort Dvora in her sorrow? If Tzvi were here, he suddenly thought, he would know what to do!

RABBI ABRAHAM BEN-MORDECHAI, THE ADMOR FROM TRISK (1806–1889): Ben-Mordechai was also known as the "*Maggid* from Chernobyl" or the "*Maggid* from Trisk" because he was born in the former and died in the latter. Most of his followers were learned scholars and rabbis. Hasidim came to him in thousands. His sermons were a mixture of Hasidism and Kabbalah, interspersed with numerology and acronyms. His book *Magen Avraham* (Shield of Abraham) on the Torah and the festivals was published in Lublin in 1887, two years before his death. During the reign of Nicholas I he was arrested for challenging the authority of the government. His three sons—Rabbi Nachum, Rabbi Mordechai, and Rabbi Yaakov—carried on the Trisk dynasty.

SCOUTS: The Boy Scouts was founded in England by Robert Baden-Powell (1857–1941), who conceived the idea of "scouting" as a system of military training incorporating an education in moral values.

THE CASTLE OF GRAF POTOWSKI: The Potowskis, a family of Polish nobility, established themselves in the thirteenth century in the village of Potok in the south of Poland. They won fame as generals in the wars against the Turks and acquired large estates in the lands that they conquered.

AVRAHAM JOSEF STIEBEL (1884–1946): Stiebel founded the first Hebrew publishing house in Moscow during the period of World War I; he published hundreds of books and the periodical *Ha-Tekufah*. After the Russian Revolution, when the government began to suppress the use of the Hebrew language in the Soviet Union, Stiebel moved his publishing house to Warsaw, and from there to Lublin, and finally, during World War II, to New York.

"AND EVEN BEYOND": This is the title of the most famous of Y. L. Peretz's stories, about the attempt of a suspicious "Litvak" (Lithuanian) opponent of Hasidism to examine the strange deeds of the rabbi of Nemirov. He discovers that in the rabbi's secret performance of the commandments, he rises to the greatest heights a man can reach in the fulfillment of God's will. And when he is told that the rabbi secretly visits heaven and prostrates himself before the Throne of Glory, he replies, "And even beyond."

4.

Beyond the Bug.✝

These are the names of those who crossed the Bug in their flight from the Nazis: David, Toussia and Shmuel, Mitek and Dvora. And Dvora met three boys from Krakow, Steffy and Poldek and Shimon, survivors of the train that was bombed. They were joined by Tamara, Shalom, and Fred. There were eleven of them and they crossed the river twice, in a small boat, before the river froze. Once they were near the river and the frontier when a German patrol blocked their path.

"Bloody Jews!" the lieutenant cursed them, "what are you looking for with the Russians? Come back home at once!"

In his confusion David said, "We're from Zamosc,"✝ never imagining that they would actually be transported as prisoners to the town of Zamosc, which he didn't know. It was the lunch break when they were taken off the truck and there was no one in the guard post at Zamosc except one old soldier, a man of about fifty. He asked them, "Why are you running away?"

"We're afraid," Dvora was bold enough to reply. "We want to live."

The German gave her a strange look, and Dvora thought to herself that he must be even older than he appeared.

"You want to live," the soldier repeated, nodding his head. "*Yah, yah . . .* so do we."

Then they were taken to a city square to clear away the ruins. They worked till dark without receiving anything to eat. One fat man, no longer young, was carrying in his arms a huge stone, groaning and gasping as he went. A baby-faced young officer was passing; he flashed his truncheon at the Jew's head. The man's hat fell off, revealing a bald pate gleaming with sweat. For some reason, the sight of the bald head amused the young German, who went back, brandished his lead truncheon, and started beating

him on the head, as though trying to hit the center of the skull, and seemed to be chuckling when the fountain of blood spurted. The stone fell from the hands of the victim, who fell on the stone.

That same night, when the opportunity occurred, they ran away from their prison. They were still running when David suddenly stopped and said in a strange voice, "So this is the place?"

He gazed at the moon hanging over the market square and at the shadows of his comrades moving quickly between the empty stalls.

"*Bay nakht oifen alten markt,*"✝ he said, without explaining.

And Dvora, who was close by, could have sworn she heard him laughing, like someone who has either lost his wits or had a sudden insight.

In Lvov they met Mitek Gross, the first man to establish the escape route (to Vilna). Mitek had a fiancée named Hedva. In those days a fiancée was simply called a "girl-friend."

Hedva had told her parents, "I want to go to Vilna."

Her father said, "What is there in Vilna that is lacking in Lvov?"

She told him, "There's a Lithuanian government, and the hope of *aliyah*. Anyway, everybody's going to Vilna."

"Who is everybody?"

"The pioneer youth."

Her father said, "You mean the refugees, young men and women without family ties. You have a father and a sick mother."

When he mentioned her mother, who was still in bed after an operation, the mother said, "Surely you won't leave us to our suffering and take the dangerous route to Palestine by yourself, alone?"

Hedva said, "Isn't that what you raised me for, in a home inspired by the founders of Zionism?"

The father, whose large store in Janowska Avenue had been confiscated by the Soviets, who had three married sons and just one daughter, Hedva, still in his eyes a child, looked through the window and saw Red Army soldiers singing as they marched, with white bundles under their arms. He remembered their entry into Lvov on Yom Kippur. Before the *Musaf* service the rumor had passed among the congregation, who left their prayer shawls on the synagogue seats and one by one stole out to the street to see for themselves.

BUG: A large river in Poland, 770 kilometers in length. It flows north and is the main tributary of the Vistula River, northwest of Warsaw.

ZAMOSC: A small town in the Lublin region, southeast of Lublin and west of Rovno. The Bug River flows between Rovno and Zamosc. The Jewish writer Y. L. Peretz was born here in 1852.

BAY NAKHT OIFEN ALTEN MARKT (Yiddish): *By Night in the Old Market*, a famous play by Y. L. Peretz, mystic in character, with a profound spiritual self-examination. It is considered one of the author's greatest artistic achievements. The action takes place in the old market, which may be the old market in Zamosc, the birthplace of the author.

They saw them marching with sacks tied on their backs instead of military haversacks. They were short in stature and many of the soldiers were slant-eyed. Among the worshipers was a refugee from Prague. He said, "No matter how wretched they look, Bolsheviks are better than Hitlerites."

They said nothing but in their hearts they all agreed. They went back into the synagogue and began the memorial service for the dead, but did not say the prayer for the government of the state, for the Jews had no government to pray for, and they said *Yizkor,* the prayer to remember the dead, with much weeping. It was the refugees from Vienna and Prague who wept most bitterly, who had been swept along in the stream to Lvov and now the flood had caught up with them.

"Who will be with you, daughter?" he asked.

Hedva said, "Mitek."

The father said, "God be with you."

They met Shmuel⁺ in Kovel.⁺ Shmuel had arrived in Brisk from Warsaw, and found the town in flames. He left for Kovel. He couldn't find a place in a car or a wagon. He went on foot until his strength gave out. He saw a faint light stealing out of a darkened window. He knocked on the shutter but there was no reply. He went back and knocked three times on the door and it opened a crack.

He could see the edge of a black skullcap and arms covered with flour up to the elbows. A smell of fresh baking assailed his nostrils and he collapsed on the threshold. Shmuel woke up on a white bed, surrounded by men and women. Before they spoke, they gave him warm milk to drink. He could see they were looking at him strangely.

"What is this thing we found on your body?" asked the baker.

"What it looks like. A flag."

"It has Warsaw written on it. Are you really from Warsaw?"

He nodded. He saw a man and a woman, three fully grown youths, and a girl of about seventeen; later he noticed that she was lame.

"On foot?" she asked.

"Almost," he said.

"Some men wear a fringed garment close to their body, and some wear a flag," said the baker.

"And where do you think you are taking the flag?" asked the young girl.

"To the Land of Israel," said Shmuel.

Suddenly there was total silence in the room, and they could hear a fly buzzing round the sticky three-sided fly trap hanging from the ceiling. The baker's wife very carefully rolled up the flag and placed it at the head of the bed.

"Both kinds of men," she whispered, "are serving God."

And the baker spoke firmly, "Now wash and eat and go to sleep. And don't forget, son, to say the *Shema.*"⁺

"I made my way on foot 500 kilometers under constant bombardment, past burning cities, the hungry and wounded. Several times en route I was robbed of everything I possessed; a bayonet has been held against my throat–in Rovno I lay in the hospital and underwent surgery on my legs. After all that, leaving the comparative security of the U.S.S.R. demanded of me considerable mental effort and great spiritual self-discipline. I managed–I felt assured I would reach Palestine whatever happened, whatever my personal fate. This belief enabled me to preserve my balance and not to lament what I had left behind in Warsaw."

–From a letter by

SHMUEL BRESLAU OF WILKOMIR (in Lithuania)

SHMUEL BRESLAU (1920-1942): Breslau was born in Moscow to an educated Zionist family. In 1925 the family moved to Poland. In 1938, Breslau became a Zionist youth movement leader and a member of the editorial board of the Polish newspaper for scouts, *Mlodi Czin* (Young Action). At the outbreak of war, Breslau wandered eastward, mostly on foot, with the stream of refugees and suffered every possible form of misfortune, including bombardment and strafing by German planes. He visited branches of the Zionist movement and devoted himself particularly to the branch at Radom. When he returned to the ghetto he began to organize defense units which had begun training with weapons. On September 3, 1942, he was arrested by members of the Gestapo on Nagsza Street and killed.

THE SHEMA: The central prayer of the Jewish liturgy, consisting of three passages from the Torah, repeated three times a day by all observant Jews. The name comes from the first word–*shema,* that is, "hear"–of the first sentence: "Hear O Israel, the Lord our God, the Lord is One."

✧ The Third Scroll ✧

By the Waters of Four Countries—2

Why is your clothing red,
your garments like those of one who treads the winepress?

—ISAIAH 63:2

⁜ CHAPTER SEVEN ⁜

Sha'ul Returns

"Fyodor Gregoryevitch, that's my home over there! On the other side of the river, in front of the woods, you can clearly see the line of the dirt road. Seven hours steady walking, no more."

In a woolen sweater, soaked with the night's rain, with a weather-beaten face, like that of a boatman from the lower reaches of the Volga,[*] Major Fyodor Gregoryevitch was smoothing a piece of German newspaper between two fingers. He pressed the shreds of dried leaves with his two thumbs, making sure that they fitted snugly in place, passed his tongue across the smooth paper, first one way then the other, and already the miserable substitute for a cigarette was stuck between his yellow teeth. And all this time his mind was preoccupied, as he searched for his lighter. "My home is over there," persisted the man with him, afraid he had not been heard, the heavy binoculars he had captured from a German tank commander pressed to his eyes.

With a grubby, gnawed thumbnail the Russian squeezed the wick of the lighter, which refused to light. His face darkened a little, as if singed by shadow. His anger was visibly increasing, whether because of the refusal of his dumb instrument to function or in reaction to the obstinacy of this Jew, behaving like a blind man.

"Permission to leave, sir!" Sha'ul turned, stood at attention, and clicked his heels in the usual fashion.

Finally the Russian succeeded in getting a flame from his smoky lighter and at once the shadow was wiped from his face. He carefully rubbed his back against the trunk of a fir tree, taking care not to let the raindrops fall from the dense foliage directly onto the back of his neck.

"Idiot! Stand at ease," he teased him affectionately.

"Permission to leave, Fyodor Gregoryevitch," Sha'ul repeated less formally but with no change of inflection. He did not move from the rise in the ground he had chosen, or had chanced upon as an observation point. He continued to study the plain, which stretched before him, and what was beyond, with the naked eye, through narrowed lids. Of average height, he seemed taller on the mound of earth. Against the background of the wintry morning sky, whose ashen grayness was beginning to glow in the sunrise, Sha'ul's head with its mass of curly hair and its sharp-featured profile formed an unforgettable picture. His partisan's leather cape, drenched in water, wrapped his shoulders with a tinge of dull bronze.

"Pushkin," murmured Fyodor in surprise.

He looked at Sha'ul as though meeting him for the first time. He felt a sudden twinge of compassion. "There are Germans there."

Sha'ul felt stomach acid in his throat.

"There are Germans, if you don't mind my saying so, everywhere. But there's only one place, over there, where I can find the woman who gave me life."

He regretted his tone of voice, which might have sounded defiant. It was more than two years since he had left home without knowing whether his father had come back from his journey alive. There had been letters at first, but then they too had ceased.

"Understand, I went off to war and left her by herself, sick and lonely."

The major said, "You mean, you don't know what has happened in the meantime to the Jews of the district?"

Sha'ul swallowed his question. He fell silent, his lips twisted.

The Russian pushed his fur cap back on his head as though he needed to scratch. Unwittingly, his language turned prophetic, "Before the winter is out our tiny squad of men will have become a proper regiment. One more winter for this great Fascist army and every healthy lad between the Dnieper[*] and the Dvina[*] will get off his back and join our forces. In a year's time you'll see for yourself, there'll be at least ten thousand Fyodorovchiks.[*] But I'll never forget how twelve of us walked through the marshes. And only two of us remained behind of that gallant band. And you were the first to stick with me, without hesitating, and followed me behind the enemy lines when I was alone and hunted like a wolf. On the great Day of the October Revolution,

VOLGA: A large river in the former Soviet Union and the longest river in Europe. The Volga flows from the north southward and drains into the Caspian Sea. The Volga is linked to the Don by means of a canal that creates a direct connection by water with the northern Baltic.

DNIEPER: A large river in the Ukraine, the Dnieper passes through large towns (Kiev, Dniepopetrovsk, Cherson) and flows into the Black Sea. A main waterway, it is linked by canals to other rivers. The great dam known as the Danyeprostroi was built in 1932, destroyed during the German occupation, and rebuilt.

DVINA: A river in the southwest of the former Soviet Union. It is also known as the western Dvina (to distinguish it from the northern Dvina, which flows into the White Sea at Archangel). The Dvina flows through the north of White Russia and Latvia, and as a wide-flowing stream reaches the Gulf of Riga on the Baltic.

you will be awarded the Order of the Red Flag,✢ First Class."

Deeply moved, Sha'ul took a step, with outstretched arms. "Fyodor Gregoryevitch, I had no idea you had recommended . . ." he said, and drew near to embrace him.

"And now you mean to desert and betray us?"

"You insult me, Fyodor Gregoryevitch." Sha'ul flinched as though bitten by a snake. "All I ask is permission to greet my family and return. And perhaps I will bring my young brother with me."

A sturdy body. A broad frame. From the neck down the form of a bull and in his face the laughing blue eyes of a child. His short legs gave him a rather choppy walk, like a sailor. Gregoryevitch had been a cavalry officer with Budenny✢ until the division had been wiped out. Until the brigade had been surrounded during the panic-stricken retreat and the second-in-command, once the brigade commander had fallen, had led thousands straight into captivity. Harder than the escape from captivity was the encounter with the hostility of his fellow countrymen, who were dismayed by him and his ideas of making for the woods and hitting the Germans from the rear. Here and there a peasant would open his or her door and even offer a piece of bread and a cup of borscht, but most of them, only recently Soviet citizens, had already become turncoats, some out of fear and some out of fear and calculation.

"And I say you will betray us." His voice was low and incisive. Sha'ul's face paled. But the Russian stopped his mouth. "That tongue of yours, before the Gestapo pull it out with white-hot pliers, will betray everything it knows. Me, and the base, and the unit. Yes, and your mother who gave you life."

Sha'ul covered his face with his hands. Stricken, he sat down on a tree stump.

"Don't start with tears. I've never yet seen a partisan cry. And even if you cry buckets, you will not be granted permission."

Sha'ul did not cry. He had made up his mind to leave without delay. There was only one possibility open to him that did not involve disobeying a command: to request a transfer to another unit and in the interim period to run off to the village.

But how could he do such a thing to a man who was like a brother to him. . . .

"Fyodor Gregoryevitch, what would you do if it were your mother, a stone's throw away, and you didn't take the risk in order to do what little you could of your duty as a son; could you bear having this on your conscience for the rest of your life?"

"And what good will you do her, I'd like to know?"

"I don't know. Enough that her eyes should see and her hands should touch her lost son," he said with a brief smile. And did not know what his heart had foreseen.

"You know, you'll get no escort."

"I don't need one, Fyodor Gregoryevitch," he said quickly, with emotion.

"What do you mean, you don't need one! Yoske and Andrei will accompany you to the river, to the ford. After that, you're on your own. To meet your fate."

Sha'ul jumped to his feet. He shook the major's hand, saluted, shook both hands again. And the major said, "And to hell with you if you give up your life to those killers. Remember that, *chelovek!*"✢

And Sha'ul went home and found it empty. And he went to the big city, for the Jews of the villages and the small towns had been gathered together in the big city. And the Jewish population of the city numbered seven hundred thousand. And in all the streets and avenues and markets, which had once been full with the hubbub of Jewish commerce and trade and craftsmanship, no Jewish foot any longer trod. And Sha'ul came to the bank of the river, where most of the ordinary people lived. The houses there were small with sloping roofs that projected like the peak of a carter's cap who has fallen asleep at his stall. Sunlight played on the river where Jewish boys and gangs of local children had filled the shore with the shouts and laughter of children's

THE ORDER OF THE RED FLAG: Beginning in 1918, the award of the Order of the Red Flag was given for heroic bravery in battle for the revolution and the homeland. Later it was awarded also for outstanding effort in work and production. At first it was given only to individuals, but in the course of time the honor was also awarded to factories.

BUDENNY (1883-1973): Commander of the Red Army, Soviet Union marshal. Semyon Mikhailovich Budenny was the son of peasants in the Don region and served as a private in the Crimean War of 1904-1905. In 1918-1919, he was active at Stalin's side at Czaritzin. Budenny then answered Trotsky's call, "Workers, get on your horses!" and led the organization of the Red Cavalry. He fought on the Ukrainian front in the war with Poland in 1920. Episodes from the life of the formation of the Red Cavalry are immortalized in Isaac Babel's book *The Cavalry*. During the Soviet Union's war against the Nazi invasion, Budenny was made commander of the southwest front, but failed through lack of ability to cope with modern warfare, and was removed from command.

CHELOVEK (Russian): Man, person.

THE ELISHEVA EPSTEIN PRIMARY SCHOOL: Apparently one of the primary schools in Vilna where Hebrew was the language of instruction. The name "Elisheva" does not appear in the sources. Possibly the writer means Bat-Sheva Epstein, the wife of Dr. Josef Epstein, one of the founders of the Hebrew Gymnasium.

THE TARBUT HEBREW HIGH SCHOOL: In 1915, immediately after the Russian army left Vilna and as the Germans entered, Dr. Josef Epstein, a well-known doctor and public figure, founded a four-year Hebrew high school. After his death in 1916, his enterprise continued to grow, and in the 1930s, the Polish authorities granted it the right to award matriculation certificates to its students.

JEWISH POLICEMEN: The organized ghetto police force, set up on the initiative of the German authorities. Its task was to keep order in the ghetto, and to enforce upon the population the instructions of the *Judenrat* and the German authorities. In most of the ghettos of Eastern Europe, the Jewish police served as the executive arm of the German administration. Among the few ghettos where the Jewish police cooperated in acts of mutiny and rebellion were Minsk and Kovno. One

games. He remembered the field of battle in the wars with the *goyim: goyim* on the embankment on one side and Jews on the other and the sharpshooters with their catapults in the middle. They went to school in packed classrooms, wherever they could find a place, sitting on the windowsills, which were almost level with the ground outside, and on the floor, bare of carpets, and behind the stove. And you wouldn't find a boy in such places who would say "Sir, I couldn't do my homework, because I haven't any room at home." He ran his eyes over the entrance to the street of steps, which he used to enter and leave on his way to and from school, from his grandfather's house to the Elisheva Epstein Primary School[+] and later to the Tarbut High School,[+] there and back for eight years in a row, about an hour's walk, which he would shorten by jumping and skipping, whirling his satchel around his head like a chicken on the eve of Yom Kippur. He turned his gaze from the sight and from the visions that had been shattered, and stepped onto the wooden bridge, walking without looking to either side, until he came to the gate of the ghetto.

There was a line of people at the gate, waiting to go in, which extended along the whole street that went down to the ghetto and wound along the road perpendicular to the ghetto wall. About a thousand men and women had been crowded together here for some time, worn out from the day's work, and from cold and bodily weakness. It was a mystery why they were not allowed to enter, for the wicket was open and there were only policemen standing there. But the police owed no one any reason or explanation, for they were the law. Nearest the gate were the Germans, beside them Lithuanians and Ukrainians and members of other nations, as detailed by the daily roster. Inside the

of the steps taken in organizing the administrative institutions inside the ghetto, after setting up the *Judenrat,* was the formation of the Jewish police.

The deportation to the ghetto in Vilna took place on September 6, 1941. The following day, on September 7, 1941, bills were posted in the ghetto calling on young men to register for the Jewish police. The order was given by Franz Murer, a barber by profession, cruel by nature, in charge of Jewish affairs in the civic administration of Vilna. Appointed as chief of the Jewish police was Jacob Gens, who had been a captain in the Lithuanian army and was later head of the *Judenrat.* The Jewish police in Vilna was one of the forces that faithfully carried out every order and instruction issued by the Germans.

GROCZOW: A central training farm of the movement Dror He-Ḥalutz on the outskirts of the city of Warsaw, in the suburb of Praga. The farm at Groczow prepared many hundreds of pioneers for the Land of Israel and served as an educational center for the activists in the pioneer movements and as a permanent facility for seminars of Dror He-Ḥalutz. The Germans destroyed the farm in November 1940, and transferred all of the occupants to the Warsaw ghetto.

wall, Jewish policemen stood on guard. Fresh, bright snow covered their shoulders and the tops of their caps, blurring the identity of their uniforms and insignia. They were all tall and visibly burly, there too was a demand for bruisers and men handy with their fists. But the Jewish policemen[+] wore new boots, which squeaked as they trod the thin ice under their feet, with a ludicrous semblance of authority.

At that moment the street light at the top of the pole in front of the gate came on and the darkness suddenly thickened. From where he stood Sha'ul could no longer see clearly the faces of the people, who were wrapped in all kinds of rags and scarves and woolens; people wound whatever they could find round their throats and covered their ears to keep out the cold wind. The breath from their lips curled up from the shrouds like smoke climbing from chimneys. And the halo of light from the single lamp split into a fan of beams that spread slantwise and starlike snowflakes danced among them like large moths destined to be caught.

Exactly one year before he had stood like this at the gates of the Warsaw ghetto. They had stood there, crowded and frightened, he remembered. A promise had been made that permission would be given for the training farm to continue, and they had believed it. He had only gone to stay overnight, and on the Sabbath morning the building had been surrounded by Polish police. With a reaction conditioned by the experience of imprisonment, Sha'ul leaped over the rear balcony in his underclothes without delay. A shot was fired in his direction, which missed, and he turned back and crawled inside. The order was given to all the people at Groczow,⁺ except the Christian owner, to leave within fifteen minutes and move en bloc to the Warsaw ghetto. They were all pioneer youths, boys and girls, and they hastened to get dressed, to do as ordered, and leave. As they left, and throughout the journey, rumors jostled them. One rumor said there was great hunger in the ghetto. And the Germans intended to starve them to death. Another rumor was worse than the first and said that they weren't being taken to Warsaw, that the intention was to deport them to some far place. There was even someone who was convinced the destination was the Vistula,⁺ where they would be drowned alive. Maybe it would be possible, before they were handed over to the Gestapo on arrival in Warsaw, to bribe the "Blues" and flee. But where would they flee to, and how could the girls run? And it was actually one of the girls, Ruschka from Lodz, who had experience of the ghetto and of escape, who had found the courage to go back to the farm and pick up her kibbutz card, which she had left behind, and conceal it in her bosom, as her forefathers had done with pieces of Torah scrolls rescued from fire, in the days of Chmielmnitski.⁺ The Polish police suspected the Jewess of concealing gold and silver valuables on her person, and beat her unmercifully.

The look of Ruschka's face, smudged with dirt and blood from her battered nose, affected Sha'ul more than his grim experiences at the front or on his wanderings. When he was put into the ghetto that evening, he slipped away and vanished from between the walls. He had put some distance between himself and the ghetto and was already leaving the city, and still its sounds pursued him. He had hardly entered the ghetto when he was greeted by a chorus of voices: "Bread! Bread! I'm dying of hunger!"— the shouts of adults and children. Their faces were yellow and haggard. A yeshiva student in a fine capote was carrying a traveling bag. He was pale and stumbling. "One slice," he said. "Just a slice." Sha'ul cut a slice and held it out to the man. At once he was pounced on from all sides

by children, youths, and old people. And the screams . . . Sha'ul dropped the rest of the loaf in the spread of hands and immediately shut his eyes in pain and regret. For the fist fight that had broken out over his piece of bread was violent and unbelievably ferocious. For three months he wandered. For two weeks he found shelter with a Christian family he had not known before. As he warmed his frozen fingers over the flame of a stove, he caught sight of the picture of a young soldier above the mantelpiece. It was framed, behind glass, with a cold gaze. He asked if this was a picture of their son. They said yes. He heard the mother sobbing behind him. He assumed he was dead, but they told him no, he was missing. He asked if this was a picture of someone who had served with the Uhlan Regiment 241,⁺ most of whom had been taken prisoner, for he felt almost sure that he could identify the boy as someone he had seen in the prisoner of war camps, before the prisoners were transported to Germany. Naturally they suspected him of plying them with words of consolation, doing what seemed proper. He continued to tell them about the campaign, the period of captivity and his escape—he told them again that no one should be in too great a hurry to grieve as long as the war went on, and that not everyone who was missing and not heard from had actually perished, for the fortunes of war and the workings of Providence were devious, and private miracles sometimes happened.

One miracle happened to Sha'ul. He had some money in his pocket, but his hosts refused to accept anything from him; they gave him food and lodging, dressed him in a coat and warm socks, and suggested that he carry on living with them as a hired laborer—they would see to providing him with suitable documents. And on the fourteenth day, on a Sunday, when all the family were at the nearby church, the house was surrounded by Polish police and German SS men; Sha'ul saw them first through the window that looked out on the road coming from town, and forestalled them by going out the back door and hiding in the nearby wood, high up in one of the trees. From his perch he could see how the soldiers turned the house upside down, and ferreted about in the stables, in the whole area, and it was

VISTULA: The biggest river in Poland.

CHMIELMNITSKI: Bogdan Chmielnitski, Ukrainian anti-Semite who led the 1648-1649 pogroms against the Jews.

UHLAN REGIMENT: The Polish cavalry regiment.

WARTA: A river in central Poland, which flows westward through Poznan.

GESZA: A street in Warsaw, in a neighborhood once heavily populated by Jews. It is the site of the Jewish cemetery.

OHEL-PERETZ: A monument on the joint graves of three writers: Y. L. Peretz (1851-1915), Yaakov Dineson (1858-1910), and S. Ansky (Shlomo Zangvil Rapoport, 1863-1920). The monument, by the sculptor Ostrzega, was erected on May 20, 1925, the tenth anniversary of Peretz's death.

The words engraved on the tomb are taken from *The Golden Chain,* a play by Y. L. Peretz; they are uttered by Rabbi Shlomo in the first act:

And so!
That's how we go—
We great Jews,
In song and dance,
Our souls ablaze—
We Sabbath-and-holiday Jews.
Clouds split before us,
The gates of heaven open.
We sail into the cloud of glory
Straight to the throne of majesty.
We stand
Near the pure marble stone
Of the throne of glory.
We don't beg
And we don't ask for anything.
We proud Jews
Are the seed of Abraham, Isaac,
    and Jacob
We could wait no longer.
We sing the song of songs
And sing and dance as we go.

N.K.V.D.: Initials of Narodny Komisssariat Vnutrennikh Del (the National Ministry for Internal Affairs), the secret security police of the Soviet Union. Some years later the name was changed to K.G.B., the initials of Komitet Gosudarstenoi Bezopasnosti (the State Security Office).

clear from the thoroughness of their search that someone had been telling tales. They left behind an ambush to greet the family on its return from church. When they arrested the head of the family, the women attacked the Polish police and almost poked their eyes out before they were beaten back. The police took the fifty-year-old man away with them in shackles and Sha'ul never found out what became of him. Sha'ul carefully climbed down from the treetop and hid in the bushes; he wanted to visit the house in the evening and ask forgiveness of the wife and child before he left. He got up twice from his hiding place, but could not find it in his heart to do what he intended. So Sha'ul turned and made for the great lakes, and did not look back, and did not rest or delay, but wandered for two whole days and two whole nights without stopping.

And in the whole country there was no man so innocent of crime as Sha'ul, yet so plagued with guilt, which lay on his heart like molten stone. And events took their course and Sha'ul met three Poles, who had a young girl with them and were making their way through the mountains to sneak across the border. Armed with the documents his honest hosts had provided him, with his hair cut short and a mustache, Sha'ul fell in with them and came to Czechoslovakia; he saw a country from which it was still possible to reach the outside world, where young pioneers were calculating their chances of getting to the Land of Israel. Sha'ul made certain contacts in a small mountain town and told them what was happening to the Jews of Poland, describing in particular the suffering and the appalling conditions in the Lodz and the Warsaw ghettos, and everything he had seen between the Warta⁺ and the Vistula, hiding nothing, that they might transmit it beyond the borders for the world to know. The Poles urged him to go with them and he was almost tempted by them and their logic. But one night he rose and retraced his steps, not by exactly the same route, until he came to Warsaw and could pass on the information that there was a circuitous route, a way through the hills, and the bold could make their way to freedom. He did not enter the ghetto, for he was impatient to reach his home and his family, and perhaps this was the motive that prevented him from crossing the Polish frontier once and for all. But he had arranged to meet some young Jewish activists, to show them the route and explain its dangers. He waited for them at Gesza,⁺ by the Warsaw Jewish cemetery. They were late for the meeting, and he grew impatient. As he was pacing to and fro, he found himself stopping in front of a large monument with withered flowers lying on the stone. He realized he had found his way to Ohel-Peretz,⁺ and read with wonder and amazement the verses engraved there: "*un azoy geyen mir zingendik un tantsndik, mir shabes-yontefdike yidn.*"⁺ He showed the group of young pioneers who had slipped out of the ghetto the way to go in order to cross the border. He was happy to see that Ruschka was among the band ready to break out and find freedom, but his heart ached that there were so few who could do so. Sha'ul had seen Ruschka's suffering in Lodz and her resourcefulness at Groczow. He bade her farewell and embraced her. She said to him, "Come with us, Sha'ul." He told her, "I'm still looking for my mother and my sister."

The boundary between Poland under Nazi occupation and Poland taken by the Russians was the Bug River. And Sha'ul set off for the valley of the Bug, and had a good journey, for his mustache had grown and gave him a new identity to match the papers that had been forged for him; he no longer traveled by secret routes, but boarded crowded trains, harassed by emotion and the horrors that met his eyes.

But what satisfied the German soldiers, who admired anything stamped with the seal of an eagle carrying a swastika in its talons, was not good enough for the Russian N.K.V.D.⁺ Spy hunters by nature, they also suspected Jewish refugees of having no greater purpose than to sabotage and spy on the Soviet Union. They seized Sha'ul and, paying all due respect, moved him from one place of detention to another until finally they placed him on a high chair under an electric light that shone in his eyes day and night, so that he could unlock his innocent tongue and admit he had come to the land of the Soviets to spy and sabotage. In the prison of Lvov he got to know a young Jew whose sole crime was the holding of clandestine meetings where boys and girls of the Ha-Shomer movement could sing Hebrew songs and read "Zion, will you not ask."* He admitted this but the N.K.V.D. didn't believe him and asked what else he had done, and he admitted it again but they still didn't believe him and asked again, and then he confessed to what he had not done, and they didn't believe him. Then they told him to reveal who his comrades were, boys and girls, who were his followers and who were his commanders and who were his controls in enemy territory, and it were better for him to put all these names and addresses down on paper, in clear handwriting, and sign his name, and when he refused with a shake of the head, for his mouth was distorted by punches, they sentenced him to ten years, a middling punishment for such a serious saboteur. In their generosity the Russians eventually added another dozen years, so he was destined to spend twenty-two years in Siberia, the prime of his life, till the end of the war, till the last gasp of the dictator,* inclusive. The name of the lad, with whom Sha'ul shared the first cell in Lvov, was Mitek, and the Holocaust passed him by, but not the suffering.

And Sha'ul was liberated by German bombers; his jailers fled in the first hour of the attack, on the first day of Hitler's war against Russia,* before it became general knowledge. Again he was dragged by a tide of panic-stricken refugees, and he left them and traveled across unknown fields in a foreign land. And he came to Minsk,* the capital of Byelorussia.

While he was looking for some way to escape the maelstrom of hordes who had lost their way and their senses, Ukrainians, Poles, Russians, and Tatars, most of them shamefully accommodating to the invaders, a few of them fleeing from one disaster to another, the Jews were ordered into the ghetto.

Sha'ul looked at the Jews of Minsk, who were herded together and moved en masse like their predecessors, the Jewish families of Lodz and Warsaw, and the crowds flowed into the confines of the ghetto, and all was peace and quiet, with no fists raised or feet stampeding in flight. And he made up his mind: Come what may, I shall not go with them to the ghetto. And Sha'ul hid by day and moved through the fields and forests by night, and he had no friends or allies in these regions, only a rifle without a bayonet that a Russian soldier had abandoned, and five bullets. He removed the signs of rust that clung to the barrel, and wiped and cleaned every bullet, as if he had found five soiled diamonds in the mud. He had no idea that one of the five was a blank cartridge, the one he placed on top, in the breach, which was to save him from sin.

A new moon was playing hide-and-seek with the thatched roofs of a *khotor** between the marsh and the forest, when Sha'ul became aware of an unfamiliar figure. At once he cocked the rifle and aimed for the button shining from the breast of the German soldier's uniform. He heard the click of the bolt, but there was no shot. The blood throbbed in his temples; at that very moment he was aware of his mistake in the identification of the stranger. Only the jacket had belonged to a German soldier, but the rest, including the man's face, was something else entirely. "*Stoj, kto ti?*" (Stop, who are you?) he shouted with an unnecessary bark, as though to conceal his double confusion.

"ZION, WILL YOU NOT ASK": A poem of yearning for the Land of Israel, one of the best known of the poems of Yehuda Halevi, poet and philosopher (1075-1141). The poem is also to be found in the prayer book, and it was customary to read it on the Fast of the Ninth of Av:

> Zion, will you not ask how your captives are,
> Who seek your welfare, the remnant of your flock?
> From west and east, from north and south, accept
> Greetings from every side, from near and far,
> The blessings of this captive of desire
> Who sheds his tears like dews of Hermon, longs
> To have them fall upon your hills. When I weep
> For your torment I am a jackal, but when I dream
> Of your return from exile I am a lute for your songs.

THE DICTATOR: Josip Vissarionovitch Yugashvili, known as Stalin, 1870-1953.

ON THE FIRST DAY OF HITLER'S WAR AGAINST RUSSIA: June 21, 1941.

MINSK: The capital of Byelorussia. Before the 1917 Revolution, Minsk was a large Jewish center, vibrant with Jewish and Zionist activity. At the end of the nineteenth century, Jews constituted 52 percent of the population. Its Jewish character was blurred during the Soviet period, when it was cut off from the main body of the Diaspora. On July 20, 1941, the Jews of Minsk were sent to the ghetto. The Jewish underground in the ghetto had been organized even before the non-Jewish underground in town and had delivered 7,000 men, women, and children to the forests of the partisans. The last 8,000 Jews were murdered in Minsk in the fall of 1943.

KHOTOR (Russian): An isolated farm.

"*In the dead of night* the Lithuanians drove the Jews out of their houses. They did not yet know where the ghetto was. Thousands of guesses, theories, and questions ran through the minds of these people, whose slave drivers beat them like cattle. They were led through the streets and suburbs. Huge crowds of people, a chaotic medley of old folk and children, cripples who had to be dragged along, and infants in baby carriages. Men left the houses where they had been born, lived, suffered, and known joy, and made their way to an unknown destination. Of all their property, they were left now only with the meager bundle they could carry on their backs."

—RUSCHKA KORCHAK-MARLE

"*Along the street* known as 'The Street of Stephen the Little,' Lithuanian manhunters were leading a group of Jews, among them a very old man, the rabbi of the street (he lived at no. 21). His face and beard, white as snow, were stained with blood. He walked bareheaded and the red blood pouring down his handsome face made the very stones

"*Sovietski chelovek,*" (A Soviet Russian) came the reply, in an amused tone, and the man continued to draw near.

Sha'ul noticed that the holster of the Mauser hanging from the man's hip was open but he had not drawn the gun.

Now the man asked with authority, "*A vi, kto takoj?*" (And who are you?)

"A Russian," declared Sha'ul listlessly.

The softness of the mound they were standing on caused them to lurch toward each other and their heads almost collided, like two roosters in a cockpit. For a moment they stood thus, necks inclined, tense and grim-faced and altogether pitiful, to the point of laughter. The Russian's broad shoulders quivered, and with a burst of laughter he savored the simple reply–*chelovek*–tossing his head as if to inquire, "A Russian? Just a Russian, nothing more?"

The Russian, a man of forty, a little shorter than Sha'ul but stocky and thick necked, wiped the remains of the smile from his lips with his thumb and said reprovingly, with moral authority, "For a reply like that, Mr. Russian, you should get a bullet through the head."

The escaped prisoner of war, survivor of two ghettoes, who had sat through the humiliating tortures of N.K.V.D. interrogators, swung his head nervously from side to side, like a wild animal caught in an ambush.

"Go on then, try it," hissed Sha'ul with suppressed rage.

The future partisan general leaned his head back as though observing from a greater height, and silently regarded his junior by several years, who had grounded his rifle but still held it with his right hand ready for instant action.

"*Yevrei?*" (Jewish?)

Sha'ul nodded.

"Fyodor Gregoryevitch." He held out his hand with fingers spread. "I don't think one should waste a bullet on a comrade-in-arms!"

"The queue will never end," Sha'ul murmured to himself. New groups of workers were coming and joining the line by the ghetto wall. They filled the road to overflowing, as though swelling the thick human dough. They no longer had the appearance of live human beings waiting in line. Nothing human in their bearing. No clear gestures. As the snow piled up on their strange headgear, on their motionless shoulders, and settled on their eyelids, mustaches, and beards, a transformation took place. No longer were their shoulders draped in soft snow. The silent, stooping mass looked like a dense, well-pruned hedge, four square and sagging under the weight of the snow. Even the houses on either side of the road seemed beaten and collapsing in the darkness.

He did not know why his heart felt dead within him.

Orders were heard. With hurried steps, the mass began to move toward the gate. One and all they held their arms up. Their goods were searched. Their bodies were searched, the men and the women.[*] "What are you hiding in your shirt? In your underwear? Potatoes or margarine? Or maybe meat? Meat, eh? You'd better throw it down by yourselves, otherwise. . . ." A policeman with a voice like a broken whistle probed the people, scared and expressionless, who passed in front of him. "You, lady, open your coat wider. Ah! I told you you'd better . . . Don't blame me now." She begged him for the sake of her starving children. But his club felled her to the ground. Already she was being dragged out of the line. "Out!"

The German corporal and the SS lieutenant did not touch her. They stood to one side. The work was done by Ukrainians, Lithuanians.[*] And Jewish policemen, who were strict with their brothers, and quick to strike.

That day Reb Zalman Rogov was carrying two loaves of bread. Hitherto he had been careful. He had avoided any attempt to smuggle, so as not to put his son the policeman to the test.

to Jews, reserved for the exclusive use of pure Aryan feet. As they passed through the busy streets of the town, which they had not seen for many days, they looked around them in amazement, almost open-mouthed—they had forgotten there were things as shops and display windows and decorated horses harnessed to carts—and the passersby also looked at the Jewish children with surprise, as though they had never seen such creatures before.

A few old women made the sign of the cross, and hurried unsteadily down the street. And the column of children did not go through the main gate of the railway station, but were taken to a siding, far from the eyes of the curious, and the mothers were told to go no further.

Sonia saw the train and could not believe it was waiting for them. The carriages did not seem intended for human passengers; they were cattle trucks. And her heart fell. Two barbed wire fences crossed the area and the children were led between them, and in front of the carriages stood Germans in SS uniforms, each with a dog leash in his hand. And the dogs were Alsatians, each with its tongue hanging out. And the soldiers stood there in their boots, feet astride, five paces apart, for the whole length of the platform, from one end of the train to the other. And at the end of the train there was a carriage painted blue, full of soldiers, and in front of it an open vehicle with a mounted machine gun. Sonia heard her children shouting, "Mommy, save us, Mommy!" She ran to the dividing fence and fell at the feet of the officer standing at the crossing point between the barbed wire and the railway track, and she wept. And the officer, tall with the face of a youth, curled his lips with disgust; his boots flinched from contact with a moaning Jewess, and he said to her, "Get up, take your child, and stop screaming."

And Sonia rose to her feet and ran to the carriages, staring and confused, for from all the carriages came shouts, "Mommy, Mommy!" And Moreleh and Minaleh and Alyoshinke thrust their thin arms through the bars of their carriage and saw their mother running away from them, and they gave a great shout, "Mommy, we're here, we're here!"

She climbed up onto the ledge of the carriage, but as she was putting her foot on the top step, the officer touched her on the shoulder with the end of his whip and said, "But only one child, I said, you can choose." And thinking she had not understood, he warned her again, "Only one, Jewess!"

And Minaleh, Moreleh, and Alyoshinke stretched out their hands, and their fingers fluttered toward her and their voices merged into tears, "Mommy, save us, Mommy!"

The mother looked at the officer and she looked at her children, with upturned eyes. She could not speak. She chose none of the children. The soldiers removed her immediately from the carriage ledge and took her away, unconscious. And the train took the children to a place from which there is no return.

And there were no days harder for the Jews than those when the decree came for new *scheinen.*✦ For when new *scheinen* were decreed, the old ones were canceled. In the ghetto a man held a *schein* stamped with the seal of the kingdom of evil and it was as though he held a certificate of life for himself and his family. When the kingdom of evil suddenly declared that everything was null and void, tearing up all the documents like a crazy gambler in a fairground ripping up his marked cards, the whole world of the ghetto reverted to chaos.✦

Crowds of people would besiege the doors of the council, the *Judenrat.*✦ They would spend the night there, a night of prayer and fasting, and they would not budge, as if their lives were up for sale. And their hearts jumped with fear and panic, for they did not know what the new *schein* was like—though there were some who had seen it and it was actually yellow—nor who would be written in the Book of Life.✦ They did not know which occupations would be entitled to it, and which places of work could extend protection to their

SCHEINEN (German): "*Schein*" means "document." The *schein* indicated the identity of the holder, his rights, and restrictions. In the ghetto it served officially as a work permit. Without one it was impossible to live in the ghetto. A man without a *schein* was doomed. The *schein* was a devilish device, deliberately designed to sow envy between fellow Jews and hatred between those with a *schein* and those who were "*schein*-less"; it was a treacherous means of sorting out the inhabitants of the ghetto, confusing them, creating on the one hand false hopes and on the other despair. From time to time the *scheinen* were changed, in form and color. Each change was no more than a stage in the process of destruction.

"**The 'certificate'** is more important than bread, clothing, or housing.

The 'certificate' is one's hope for life, to live until after . . . to live until we reach . . . the certificate is life itself."

—MARK DVORZETZKY,
Jerusalem of Lithuania during the Revolt and the Holocaust

JUDENRAT (German): The Jewish council. A body of Jews appointed by the Germans, in all areas under occupation, to run the lives of the Jews in the ghetto.

WRITTEN IN THE BOOK OF LIFE: From the prayers for the New Year and the Day of Atonement, the period when, according to Jewish belief, a person's fate during the coming year is decided.

slave workers; whether there would be restrictions on sex or age or maybe even on place of residence, for the overcrowding in the ghetto was already endangering the health of the city. And though no one dared voice the thought, everyone understood that it was not for reasons of employment or greater efficiency that the authorities replaced one document with another, one piece of paper with another. Out of German bureaucracy came the *Aktion.*

And no man knew which was the fateful day. And if he knew, he would keep the secret, lest—God forbid—the rumor spread and the whole town be in an uproar. In time to come the men who knew would claim it was their consciences that obliged them to keep the dreadful secret; they had a sense of responsibility and pity for the people. What good would a general panic do for the Jews?

And the members of the *Judenrat* and their families, and the police, officers and men, and their families and dependents, and anybody in favor with the authorities received special *scheinen,* for they had to do their work with devotion, without a qualm; the law must be enforced, and they needed hearts of stone.

When the Jews were assembled in the square and there was an overflow into the neighboring streets, they were lined up in fives. Five heads in a row, and behind them five more, and the column of thousands grew and grew. And policemen passed among the rows to number the people. They would count and check their tallies, and do it again, for the German mentality cannot tolerate an error in arithmetic. And the assembly numbering thousands was as still as a burned forest, avenues of blighted trunks, trees struck by lightning, with hollow trunks and truncated roots—a slight breeze and they would fall.

After six hours on parade, the tallymen began sorting out who was for the left, who for the right. And Kreine Koussevitsky was standing arm in arm with her husband when by the wave of a finger she was ordered to the left. Kreine slowly withdrew her arm from her husband's warmth and, without looking back, moved as she was bidden. Meir Koussevitsky, one of the scholars of the city, a man who had seen life and the world, who never went on any journey or trip, so they said, without Kreine at his side, turned mechanically to the line on the right without even stopping for a farewell kiss. They parted and walked away as though hypnotized. And like them, hundreds and thousands crossed the hidden boundary between what they had been and what they would never be again, with senses numbed, with an appalling submissiveness.

There was a giant in the city, a real Jewish champion. It was he who had crushed gentile boxers in the ring, torn chains apart with his teeth, and bent iron bars; he was the pride of the Jews of the town and throughout the country. And when his wife Hinde was ordered to the left, she cried to him, "Noah! Save me, don't leave me!"

And Noah, of whom everyone was afraid, at the mere sight of whom anti-Semitic students in the bad old days would turn tail and flee for their lives, stood there motionless, and everyone could see that a paralyzing weakness had fallen on him. And when his wife's repeated screams struck his naked ears—Hinde, who had always had faith in his strength and resourcefulness—his colossal body suddenly shuddered and his head quivered like a pent-up lion, and he wrung his hands in grief and howled from the pit of his stomach, "And with these hands can I kill all the Germans?"

And he stood there with all his great height, with all his mass of muscles, his mouth gasping as though from lack of oxygen.

✦ CHAPTER EIGHT ✦

And Noah Was Caught Up
in the Stream

And Noah was caught up in the stream. But his column was for the right, and everyone on that side was marched out of the confines of the ghetto. And they stood around until after midnight. And when Noah, together with the other privileged workers, returned to his room in the ghetto, it was empty of Hinde. But the inside of his huge head was not empty of the sound of her voice. Mourning was forbidden. Investigating the unthinkable was impossible now. Noah rolled on the floor—a pair of his wife's shoes still stood there—and wailed with terrible force.

The next morning Noah arose and left for work, recognizable by his height, head and shoulders above all the other porters who carry the heavy loads at the airport. He joined the column going through the gate. He kept pace with them, step for step. And his thoughts remained behind. Hinde, Hindele, Hindeniu. Is he a widower? Like the rest of the Jews. Or just a miserable egoist beyond redemption?

And Sha'ul looked after his mother. And he built her a *maline** in a secret place under the garbage and contrived an entrance with great skill and ingenuity. And his mother went down there, together with three *agunot** and a young cripple, and they stayed there all the time. He took them down the few necessities of life. And they lived there and were saved. And Sha'ul said to himself: Now I know why I left the partisan dugout, my commander and my comrades, and came back to the ghetto. If I had come here just for this moment, it would have been sufficient. And Sha'ul did not put his trust in a hiding place within the area of the ghetto; anywhere in the ghetto was an invitation to catastrophe. He went out looking for a farm where he might hide them when it became necessary. And on the fourth day of the big *Aktion,* Sha'ul was caught and rounded up and stood in the assembly square with the rest, awaiting their fate. He had neither an old *schein* nor a current one.

And a member of the master race from Prussia, scarred but of a pleasant appearance, who had doubtless in his youth seen a democratic Prussia in its heyday, chanced to be in the ghetto that day and asked Sha'ul what he was doing there, "for you don't look a bit like a Jew."

And Sha'ul replied, "I'm a Jew, born and bred. But I don't look the way you imagine a Jew, any more than you look the way I imagine a German these days."

The German found the sharpness of the remark to his taste. Immediately he smiled sweetly and swallowed the reproach. He asked Sha'ul his trade.

He said, "I'm a welder, first grade."

He had a new *schein* issued on the spot for "his Jew"; men like that were needed for the repair of gun barrels.

When the *scheinen* action came to an end, it was followed by the shock of silence. The silence seemed redoubled: the number of deportees this time was twenty thousand, as many as remained behind. Every morning shutters were raised. Windows were opened to see if the guards on the ghetto had been relieved. People tried to hunt up some signs of consolation. The assistant to the manager of the public library saw a note that had arrived from the children's summer camp. Actually he didn't see it but he heard about it from someone who did. The old people had also been seen walking along the river bank. Had anyone seen a rainbow?

A student from the old scientific institute, who was now the assistant to the manager of the public library, was unable to linger and repeat again and again what he had heard from someone who had read it, since the time had come to open the library.

The library was what its name denoted: public and open. Although hard to believe, it wasn't long before our friend the deputy manager was able to post a large notice indicating that the one hundred thousandth reader had entered the library to borrow a book. The commander of the ghetto rounded up the surviving remnant of artists, writers, teachers, and intellectuals, and those bearers of culture known simply as *packentrager,** and urged them to organize and set up whatever they could in the way of art, entertainment, and moral education, to keep up the spirits of people who were at a low ebb. The assembly square, of grim repute, was converted into a sports ground. A well-regarded artist from the academy was not ashamed to stand on a sign painter's ladder and paint the outer wall with an eye-catching slogan, "a healthy mind in a healthy body," in Yiddish in Hebrew characters, with a young girl and a young boy runner on either side of the inscription. And hardly a week had gone by before—in the evening,

MALINE: A secret place for hiding from the evil eyes of the Germans during a search or deportation of Jews to the places of slaughter. Many people dug, many tried to hide. Their stories have survived.

AGUNOT (Hebrew): Wives whose husbands have left them, or are missing, without having granted them a divorce.

PACKENTRAGER (Yiddish): Porter, package carrier.

"On the thirteenth of November 1942, in the Vilna ghetto they celebrated 100,000 book borrowings from the library. The library organized a matinee in the ghetto theater. There were speeches, readings, and music. Gifts were awarded to the first reader and the youngest reader."

—HERMANN KRUK

YOUTH MOVEMENTS: Between the two world wars, youth movements flourished in the Jewish community in Poland. And just as the community was divided into streams, factions, and opinions, so too were the youth movements and their organizations. The biggest and first independent Zionist scout movement was Ha-Shomer Ha-Tza'ir (The Young Watchman), then came Freiheit (Liberty), and He-Ḥalutz Ha-Tza'ir (The Young Pioneer), which united with Dror (Freedom). Alongside them sprang up, each in its own style, other Zionist movements: Gordonia, Ha-No'ar Ha-Tzioni (Zionist Youth), Ha-Shomer Ha-Dati (The Religious Watchman), and Betar. In addition, the political parties organized or provided patronage for special youth movements: Communist Youth, Bund Youth (Tsukunft), Young Workers of Zion, and Zionist Workers of the Left (Borochov Youth). Within these movements grew the core of resistance and rebellion in the ghettos, and their leaders and fighters.

before curfew—the inhabitants could hear songs coming out of what were now public places, and they felt better. Hesitant study circles grew into classes and actual schools, some teaching in Hebrew and some still zealous for Yiddish, and there was no shortage of benches, for there were plenty of carpenters, but there was a great lack of teachers. Nevertheless, the educational leaders did sterling work and even competed with each other.✣ The Yiddishists claimed that they had the better teachers and the Hebraists, former members of Tarbut, were proud of building something out of nothing. And for future workers in the Land of Israel, enthusiastic teachers and youth leaders were found who in improvised accommodation taught Torah and right behavior, which the country—that is, the Land of Israel—would need. Though separated by thousands of miles of sea and darkness, the Land of Israel was present in the heart of the ghetto.

And the orphanage, which had been emptied of infants, filled up with older children; there was no shortage of abandoned orphans in the ghetto. For this they called upon the youth movements;✣ no matter how few active members had survived there were still youth movements, with a sense of responsibility greater than their numbers, who assigned voluntary youth leaders to the groups of street children to keep them from a life of crime. And the pioneering youth worked wonders, setting up a committee of young members to teach

A PEDAGOGIC POEM: Anton Semyonvitch Makarenko's book (1888-1939) in which he describes his educational experiment in a village for abandoned children. He stood for both discipline and warm-hearted sympathy, and restored a positive enjoyment of life to the souls of these children, who had already crossed the line into delinquency. The book was written in Kharkov (1925-1935).

"KINNERET, KINNERET": The reference is to the poem "And Perhaps It Never Was" by the poet Rachel (Blochstein-Sela, 1890-1931), which ends as follows:

And I never was purified
In the blue, undefiled
And serene
Of my Kinneret . . . Oh, my Kinneret,
Was it true, or merely a dream?

"OYFN PRIPETSHIK": Yiddish folk song.

In the stove a fire is burning
And it's hot in the stove
And the rebbe is chanting to the toddlers
The lore of the ABC.
Look, children, and please remember
What you're learning,
Say aloud and repeat:
E-A-T you say "eat."
And when you grow up, children,
You'll well understand
How much grief is in the letters
And how many tears!
When you bear the burden of Exile
And when you are weary to death—
You will draw strength from the letters—
Look at them and understand.

TCHAINA (Russian): Tea house.

the Jewish children of the ghetto a little democracy along the lines of *A Pedagogic Poem*.✣ They could be seen pushing wheelbarrows with creaky wheels to collect bottles, cans, and all sorts of rubbish fit for recycling. They also set up small stalls and sold sweets, their own make, not very tasty but with a different flavor from anything else in the ghetto. The street children began diligently to study arithmetic and languages. A historian of Jewish experience in the period of the ghetto would discover that the orphanage was one institution, perhaps unfortunately the only one, where both Jewish languages, Hebrew and Yiddish, had equal status as languages of instruction; children sang both "Kinneret, Kinneret"✣ and "Oyfn Pripetshik"✣ and emerged unscathed.

And the one soup kitchen, known as *tchaina*✣ and run by the community, proved inadequate and two more were opened, which belonged to recognized political parties. Every party strove to have its own soup kitchen, however small and cramped, for in the ghetto a soup kitchen was an institution of standing. Nor should it be thought that they were exclusive to members of the party. Anyone in need could come in and sit down and receive a plate of soup. And there were many in need, including some scroungers who moved from one soup kitchen to another, sometimes merely crossing to the other side of the same alley, pretending to be looking for a friend or a notice, grabbing and swallowing whatever was on offer in order to appease their great hunger. What had happened to shame?

In order to survive, a man must adjust to reality. With every active brain cell, with every fiber of his being, a man in the ghetto strove to hang on to reality. But reality in the ghetto seemed, on the face of it, the exact opposite of reality in life. So what should a man cling to? Cold, hunger, the stress of living isolated and cut off, death—they had all become part of the daily routine. And strangely, troubles that had worried ordinary people for years, like chronic diseases, were no longer a hardship in the ghetto. Physical weakness and spiritual depression, which normally invest an ailing body racked with fatigue and crumble it like a corpse, had vanished. When Sha'ul went down to visit his mother in her hideaway, after she had been living under the ground for two weeks, he could not believe his eyes, neither her surroundings nor what he saw in her face. Though Rosa was not yet sixty when she was confined to the ghetto, she had been sick a long while. Her weak heart and the swollen veins in her legs caused her distress, and filled the rooms of the house with the smell of medicine and groans of pain. When Sha'ul and his mother were reunited, he was shocked by her weakness and her poor sight; they had changed her appearance almost beyond recognition. Now the walls of the hideaway were decorated with hangings, which she had made from lengths of material, adding lace and embroidery, and making curtains or something like curtains for the imaginary windows. Her hair was combed, her clothes repaired, the network of wrinkles that furrowed her face had filled out, and her eyes, especially her eyes, glowed again with something of their original beauty. How had it happened? Sha'ul stared at her. Was it the first shock of the ghetto, or the taste of life, which had come back with the return of her son?

"Take it," was the first thing she said, "and try it on, the sweater I've knitted for you. Socks too. Nu, try it on. What are you standing there for, like a dummy?" with a sly smile. And not a word about what was going on above ground.

He remembered the old people's *Aktion,* what he heard and what he saw with his own eyes on that day, the day of the duped and the not-so-innocent. Grandmothers, like young mothers, wore dresses from the first years of their marriages. They had put colored ribbons in their hair. Sufferers from arthritis cast aside their walking sticks, held themselves erect as though by magic, and strode calmly to the parade. How simple it was for those who were not yet old to say that someone else was old and decrepit, and as good as dead. In a place where they were all as good as dead, they all, it turned out, discovered a tremendous will to live.

Later, he told Dvora, "The light came back to her eyes. They were the loveliest eyes I had ever seen." And when he told his mother that soon he would manage to find her a shelter in one of the villages, and then he would be able to return to the forests, she asked him if he had no feelings. After he calmed her down, he realized that it was not out of concern for herself that she was crying but from feelings of guilt. She had discovered that her strength had returned, she was once again living for herself, even if her husband, and Velvele, and Chaim-Ozer were no more. And she cried bitterly, and felt it was sinful that she did not wish to die at a time when her only son was going off to live among the wolves in the swamps of death.

Who knows the limits of suffering? Or how far human beings are capable of adjusting to the demands of a new reality, which is itself totally inhuman? Accepted truths become untenable within the walls of the ghetto, and the barbed wire. And revealed perhaps as the most untenable of all is the popular saying that when the cannons thunder, the muses are silent.

Not that there were any cannons thundering at the time, though the ghetto walls were likely to collapse and leave every living creature buried in the ruins. For death climbed through our windows every night.* But when all the lights were out, and all those who worked as slaves by day were sprawled on their beds, here and there in rooms full of snores and the smell of sweat, burned a candle, and another, and another. By the light of these candles Jewish poets sat up till the small hours of the night, for the poet of Israel shall neither slumber nor sleep. And they consulted with each other. Sometimes there would be enough

---

DEATH CLIMBED THROUGH OUR WINDOWS EVERY NIGHT: An allusion to the following biblical verses.

> Hear, O women, the word of the Lord,
> Let your ears receive the word of His mouth,
> And teach your daughters wailing,
> And one another lamentation.
> For death has climbed through our windows,
> Has entered our fortresses,
> To cut off babes from the streets,
> Young men from the squares.

—JEREMIAH 9:19-20

MINYAN (Hebrew): The quorum of ten adult men required for communal prayer.

to form a minyan.✝ And when the minyan was incomplete, those who remained still continued to write. And write. And write. They wrote on scraps of paper of every conceivable variety. And it is worth recalling that in this generation there were some poets who were keen on assonance and others who still stuck to regular, polished classical meters, and even for those who favored what is called free verse, poetry doesn't just flow, like running water; writing–any kind of writing–needs care and revision and polish. Lots of polish. In other words, diligence and hard work. And just as any self-respecting shoe repairer owes it to the shoe he is mending to see that it doesn't twist–God forbid–the wearer's foot, so every writer and poet, even if he doesn't admit it, feels an obligation to the raw material of his poem, and to his reputation, not to produce anything incomplete and below standard. And the poets did not rest from their labors in the ghetto, but appointed judges from their number to award literary prizes and thus keep alive the creative spark of the Jewish people. And the wick of Jewish life grew shorter and shorter and the flame barely flickered.

When Feivel Piasetski, the doyen of the theatrical profession, one of the survivors of the world famous Dramkreiz,✝ presented himself to the *Judenrat* and suggested setting up a theater in the ghetto, a real theater, with seats and tickets and premieres, a repertory theater of course, even the head of the *Judenrat* was somewhat surprised.✝

Feivel Piasetski was a timorous man, short in stature. The world is the world and the theater is the stage, but he had never been a negotiator, and had never in his life dealt with those in authority. Yet the moment he smelled greasepaint, he braced himself like a lion for the holy task. He took note of the grimace of the head of the *Judenrat,* and was alarmed by the twist of his lips. The commander of the ghetto stretched his muscular body uncomfortably in his upholstered armchair and gave the balding actor one of his rare looks of amazement. But within five seconds he had grasped intuitively the exciting principle behind Piasetski's idea. At the end of the year he would make a fighting speech in honor of the occasion. He would stand on a stage garlanded with flowers brought in by permission of the authorities, dressed as a civilian in dark evening dress, his officers in dress uniform sitting on chairs in the front row with their legs crossed, their broad-brimmed hats, decorated with silver braid, resting on their knees according to protocol, arms folded on their chests and gaze fixed on their commander in unbridled admiration.

And in the center, next to the wife of the commander, sat the eminent lawyer Sinolowski, recently appointed president of the autonomous court of the ghetto, though he was still unclear who or what or according to what code of law he was supposed to judge offenders; he wore a checked official hat, hastily put together, which too much resembled something from a Shakespearean production, and his remarkably tiny hands were poised for the expected rounds of applause. Behind them were the members of the *Judenrat,* officials, secretaries, leaders of the work force, and a large audience of invited worthies; and the commander would tell them that this cultural enterprise was a symbol of the vitality of the Jewish people, and the creative force latent in the ghetto. The theater was not just entertainment; in the present circumstance it played a role that went beyond art; it strengthened morale, it strengthen the spirit of the people, preventing it from giving in to these troubled times, "and I am happy to be the godfather to this wonder child." It was not clear whether he realized the ineptness of his metaphor. An actress who was sitting by his side at the presidential table, a woman whose daughter had been snatched from her arms during the children's *Aktion,* let her eyebrows fall over the bridge of her nose and bit her upper lip in a grimace of pain. A rustle passed through rows B, C, and D. But to the sound of appreciative applause, the commander gave the order for the curtain to be raised on the fifth premiere to take place. And the show went on.

The show went on, and there was nothing to disturb the warm, holiday atmosphere, which gave people back the dignity and sense of identity they had lost, which used to pervade the theater every evening, and especially at premieres. Only once did anything untoward occur. This was at a charity ball, when a mixed program included pieces of theater, songs, and recitations. Due to some hitch or other,

DRAMKREIZ (Yiddish): Abbreviation of "Dramatish kreiz," the drama group.

"Theater in the ghetto?"
"Yes," Wiskind confirmed, "we must do what we can. We must oppose the enemy with this weapon too. We must not give in even for a moment. Plays were presented on the stages of the medieval ghettos too. The annals of the Jewish theater draw inspiration from that period. Let's have theater– to encourage and cheer up the ghetto." —AVRAHAM SUTZKOVER, *Vilna Ghetto*

"January 1, 1942, Vilna, in the ghetto. Silence again in the room. A silence that no one breaks. Yet tears glint in dozens of young eyes. And a wave of feelings washes over their hearts. And fists clench. Suddenly a voice breaks out from the corner. Hushed and slow. The song grips everyone. Freedom is calling to their hearts and unites them all. No longer is one alone in feeling or thinking, for if one sings, sings with all his might, with all his heart, it is as though he filled the words with his own blood: 'To stretch out your neck to the sword—no, never!'

It seems our song will shake the ghetto walls."

—RUSCHKA KORCHAK-MARLE,
Flames in the Ashes

The unsaved are silently swallowed up,
Not a syllable is heard:
For it is a generation of evil-
 doers
And a time of wickedness.
Better heroic death
By the sword than to die as prey,
To offer your neck to the sword—
Why be alone in the corner—
A prisoner of suffering?
For as long as the spark
 ceaselessly glows
It will spread its light.
—NAHUM YOD

A cloister wall is high.
A wall of silence
 still higher.
A ladder leans at the side.
Tops of chestnut trees touch
 and recoil from the bell tower.
Three chestnut trees
 out of a land of lakes
And mud.
—ABBA KOVNER,
"My Little Sister"

TRASKEL: Some say *triskel,* a three-legged stool.

the solo singer had to give his performance in the first third of the program, almost at the beginning of the evening. His voice did not disappoint, and his choice of the first song from the stock repertoire of the folk singer was undoubtedly successful. And then the fellow began his second song, perhaps in innocence, perhaps out of stupidity—the underground historian of the ghetto was to note in his journal, "this was a performance which showed civic courage to the highest degree"—and in the presence of the head of the *Judenrat* and the police commander began the "Song of Rebellion." As he opened with the words remembered from other days, "*Oisstrecken dem haldez tsum messer—nein! A keinmal nein!*" (Stretch out the neck for the knife—No! Forever no!),* the commander leaped to his feet, his face flushing with anger, waved the forefinger of his right hand in a diagonal sweep from top to bottom—and the curtain came down at once. Few people caught what he screamed on that occasion, and you don't hold a man's anger against him. But everyone saw how he left the hall. His officers hurried after him before they could manage to put on their official hats. People stood there rebuked and embarrassed. Slowly, without a word, the large audience began to disperse and for quite a while the singer remained standing on the stage, stunned at the sight, like someone who had dropped the ball he had been playing with and, to his astonishment, heard it explode with a roar like thunder.

There was a man in the ghetto, Uri by name, young and wide eyed. It was in the days of the manhunts, when Jews were kidnapped in the streets of the city, and he escaped them twice. And a Christian woman brought him to a monastery, and the monks gave him shelter, and he lived among them. And every morning he would go to work in the fields, dressed as a Catholic monk. And from the monastery hill he beheld the Jewish city before him, and he came not unto it. And the monks were forbidden to enter the outside world, though their ears were attentive, and the father confessor came and went.* And he asked them, "My friends, what do your eyes behold?" and they answered, "A horse has eyes in his head." And the monks went with Uri to a horse owner on the other side of the river. And the name of this farmer was Zhezha, a man like Job, blameless and upright before his God. And he had two horses and one cart. He told them how the Germans requisitioned his horse for the "Jewish trips." On the last occasion they had requisitioned both the horses and the cart. And he told them also how they harnessed all the horses in the neighborhood, and there were huge convoys and they were not allowed to go as far as the forest, which was the destination, only to the green bridge, where they halted and from there the poor people, the Jews, were made to run.

And they also went to the train driver to ask, and he told them the name of the station, the destination of the train. And Uri questioned the train driver, whether this was the last station. And he told him, "The last one, sir."

"Of all the trains?"

"Of all the trains."

And Uri thanked him, and he turned and went. And he came to his cell within the monastery walls, and he took off his monk's robe and he sat on his *traskel** alone all night. And he pieced together one thing after another, and combined scraps of information in a cloudy jigsaw puzzle until suddenly the chambers of his mind were illumined as by a flash of lightning. And everything that had hitherto been wrapped in uncertainty became utterly certain, and what had hovered in the realm of unreality became now solidly real, what all the beginnings had hinted at, the explanation of the end. And he rose, and his eyes, always wide open, now stared and looked inward into his soul, and he put on his Jewish clothes and his yellow patch, and stuck one on his chest above his heart and the other on his back, and he returned to his brethren in the ghetto. Uri was twenty-three years old when he returned to the ghetto, and young men and women followed after him.

And Dvora found Sha'ul and said, "In two days time, when they are all at home, celebrating Christmas, we shall assemble in the hall of the large soup kitchen to hear another voice."

And Sha'ul came to the meeting place, and, as he was waiting for the men in charge of admission to close the doors, he could hear the sound of Christmas Eve carols rising in joy beyond the walls. Around him he saw many faces lit up, as though this were not the ghetto.✢ But Uri's face was pale from emotion. Standing alone behind a folding table, he began to speak. "If you refuse to ask yourselves the vital question, perhaps you will allow me to spell it out for you. This performance has a purpose and an end. I see clearly now both the purpose and the descending curtain. We are not the spectators and the players in this theater, we are the victims. And not only us. Do you ask how it is that so many good men see nothing, are all blind and stupid? They are neither blind nor stupid. But in order to see things as they are, you must first remove the glasses clouded with illusion and take risks. Take risks and go all the way, to the very end."

He read his manifesto from a crumpled piece of paper, covered with scribbled notes in neat, dense handwriting. Sha'ul listened enthralled, not only to the words of the man standing behind the folding table; his ears caught more than the clear, considered sentences that struck home like well-aimed blows from a carpenter's hammer.✢

There was something special about the tone of voice of the man, about the way he held the scrap of paper, about the eyelashes shading his prominent eyes whose gaze burned with an inner fire. From his whole appearance before this audience of young people, most of them his own age, emerged a profound consciousness that his fate and theirs were bound up in what was being said here and now. Leaning with their elbows on the bare tables of the soup kitchen, people continued to listen for a long time after he had finished speaking. It was clear that the man was no longer as alone as he had been when he entered. Something throbbed and flowed from wall to wall, girding with unseen bands the crowded listeners. From his place near the window, Sha'ul felt, like them, a common anticipation of some imminent, decisive event, not to be avoided, and beyond endurance. Though there was no smoking in this audience, the air in the hall seemed full of incense. And darkness everywhere. In spite of this, Sha'ul could see glowing in everyone's eyes, the same wonderful alertness, more than just the sign of a learned discipline found in a group of well-trained young men. It was the mark of a natural warm tension welling up from within, like the response of the vein to the hand that feels the pulse. Their eyes, filled with surprise and a sense of common identity, were fixed not only on the lips of their comrade—revealed to them at this very moment as their leader—not only on what he was saying here and now, but on what was bound to happen from now on. And as happens on such rare, authentic occasions, there was little talking. It was clear that they believed in him. He had won their unqualified trust, though he lacked power and authority. His words worked their magic upon these men because they spoke directly to the most painful, depressing things their souls had to bear—humiliation and impotence. No wonder the feeling of release was spontaneous

"**New Year's Eve.** The beginning of 1942. A yard in 2 Straszon Street. A large hall in semi-darkness. Dozens of young people have come together. Their cold, serious faces are tense and expectant. One hundred fifty pairs of eyes are fixed on one man's face, 150 are listening to one man. And that man's face is alight. His voice is powerful and full of pain as he utters the words he has memorized from the first manifesto."

—RUSCHKA KORCHAK–MARLE,
Flames in the Ashes

THE FIRST MANIFESTO

"Let us not go as sheep to the slaughter.

Jewish youth, do not place your trust in those who are leading you astray. Of the 80,000 Jews who lived in the "Jerusalem of Lithuania," only 20,000 remain alive. Before our very eyes our parents, our brothers, and our sisters have been torn from us.

Where are the hundreds of Jews who were taken to work by the Lithuanian press gangs?

Where are the naked women, the children, who were taken from us on the horrible night of provocation?

Where are the Jews of the Day of Atonement?

Where are our brothers from Ghetto Number Two?

Whoever is taken out through the ghetto gates never returns.

Every Gestapo route leads to Ponar. And Ponar is death.

Hesitators! Throw away your illusions: Your children, your wives, and your husbands are no longer alive.

Ponar is not the name of a concentration camp. Everyone there has been shot.

Hitler is scheming to destroy all the Jews of Europe. It has been Lithuanian Jewry's ill fate to be first in line.

Let us not go as sheep to the slaughter.

We may be weak and unprotected but the only answer to a murderer is self-defense!

Brothers! It is better to fall fighting as free men than to live at the mercy of murderers.

We will defend ourselves! To our last breath we will defend ourselves!"
—January 1, 1942, Vilna, in the ghetto

and collective. Sha'ul both loved Uri at first sight and felt animosity, as if for someone with whom he was destined to share a prison cell, their fates intertwined till the end of the road, and no redemption.

When he had finished, Uri hastened to make his way toward the exit from the hall, which was full to overflowing. Such an action could later have been interpreted as an error, or even blown up and judged as indicating a measure of superiority and scorn. But Sha'ul, who followed close behind, could see that the man was filled with the event, immersed in a kind of dreamlike impatience, and needed to be alone, in communion with himself and the grave task he had that moment undertaken.

The underground, which started out in the soup kitchen run by pioneering youth, began to spread, and was soon joined by everyone who was young at heart.* They set up cells of five or less. Three hundred loyal young men and women were chosen, without reference to former adherence or opinions, and thus was established the first Jewish organization that arose to fight the Nazis.

Though the underground was strict about secrecy for its actions and its members, and strove to preserve anonymity, anyone with eyes in his head could pick them out among the people in the ghetto, whether they spoke or remained silent. They wore no uniforms or semblance of uniforms, carried no weapons in public, did not even adorn themselves with badges sewn on their clothes, worn round their necks, or tattooed on their skin. But every young man and woman who was admitted to the underground immediately became imbued with a different spirit. Something different from the gray-green complexion common in the ghetto was visible now on their faces and in their bearing. Something strange entered their gaze, a hidden spark, even from their gait arose some covert message to the alleys. When a rumor began to spread—there were fresh ones every morning—and trouble people's minds, causing men and women to gather in the middle of the road and turning sensible individuals into an excited huddle, the mass of whom had lost their sense of judgment, their tongues interpreting facts that their eyes had not seen and their ears had not yet heard, fear and the power of imagination abetting each other with "oy" and "ah," at the same time next to the cluster of citizens stood a group of young people, merged with the crowd yet set apart as though they stood alone. And their reaction was different. Their faces were suffused with the calm and inner confidence only to be found among believers.

And they did believe. They believed they had found an answer. Not so decisive that it would straightway bring relief and salvation to the Jews. And certainly not an easy answer. But strong enough to turn a paralyzing hopelessness into a passionate devotion.

One evening Sha'ul saw them emerging slowly from a cellar full of junk, after weapon training. They peered around to make certain no evil eye had spotted where they were coming from, and then linked arms and walked down the middle of the street, drunk though not with wine. He heard them break into song. A sad song at first gave way to the rhythm of a march. Suddenly they halted and danced a *hora*. Only now, thought Sha'ul, have they come to terms with using a revolver or a grenade, in full awareness that many if not all of them have thereby accepted a death sentence, to die in a battle of few against many, and that's why they have let themselves go, like the high school students they used to be after the final examinations, as though intoxicated with a zest for life. Sha'ul let them go streaming joyfully past him and disperse. It was almost curfew time and Dvora had not yet come back. One day the story will be told of the Jewish girl who with a portable mine blew up a German army troop train; no one could believe the action came from prisoners in the ghetto. It was Dvora that the command had chosen to carry out the most daring of the acts of sabotage. She had been gone three days and nights, surveying the hills and the railroad

"**On January 21, 1942,** toward evening, a historic meeting was held in Josef Glassman's room at 6 Rodnitsky Street. Present were Itzik Wittenberg, Abba Kovner, Josef Glassman, Cheina Borovska, Nissan Resnik, and Major Frucht. At this meeting it was decided:

A. To set up an armed fighting organization to function as an underground in the Vilna ghetto. This organization would include all the federations represented at the meeting, with the aim of uniting all the organized forces in the ghetto.

B. The main purpose of the organization: to prepare for armed mass resistance to any attempt to wipe out the ghetto.

C. Self-defense is a national act: a people's struggle for its self-respect.

D. The aim of the organization: sabotage behind the enemy lines.

E. The fighting organization in the Vilna ghetto *de facto* joins the ranks of the partisans in order to assist the Red Army in their common war against the Nazi invader.

F. The fighting organization will spread the idea of self-defense to the other ghettos, and will establish links with other fighting forces outside the ghetto.

G. The activity of the organization will be coordinated by a command consisting of three members (Itzik Wittenberg, Josef Glassman, Abba Kovner). Itzik Wittenberg was chosen as the commander-in-chief.

H. The organization will be called F.P.O. (Fareinikter Partisaner Organizatsia)."

—RUSCHKA KORCHAK-MARLE,
Flames in the Ashes

tracks around the town, choosing the place for the action, close to a hiding place in the woods and far from any Jews at work. When she returned she feared she was too late to meet with Sha'ul, and when she left he feared for her. At war and in love, it was as though they had their own private clock, which measured a different time according to feelings and beliefs. The next day Sha'ul was sent on a mission. He went alone, his destination the other towns of the country, carrying with him news of the underground to spread among his brothers in distant ghettos. Sha'ul embraced Dvora, and said to her as they parted, "Look after my mother until I return, before the end of the first month of spring."

Dvora replied, "Don't worry about your mother. And bring me back a sprig of lilac." And she smiled, and in her heart made him swear he would return alive.

Circumstances at that time delayed his departure for three days, and it was during this unplanned period that a meeting took place, which was to trouble his mind for many days. There was a writer in the ghetto called Y. L. Markovitch. He was one of the survivors of the renaissance of Jewish wisdom in Eastern Europe in Yiddish and Hebrew. A shy man by nature, though renowned as a student of Jewish culture, a historian and a brilliant linguist, with a fresh, sharp mind, he hardly ever participated in the learned congresses that had recently become fashionable in Europe. He found no one there with any original ideas, though there was no lack of wheelers and dealers with a flair for publicity. And when his close associates pressed him and said, "Nu, aren't you interested in the opinion of the world?" he smiled his wry smile, replete with Jewish humor, and replied "Anyone who keeps his own company is the center of a whole world." The less he made his opinion known, the more his views were valued in the ghetto.

Y. L. Markovitch was not a member of any party. The Zionists of the city regretfully despaired of convincing him. Like his mentor Shimon Dubnow,✢ he believed completely in the power of cultural autonomy in the Diaspora to continue to exist. Until the rise of Hitler. From then on he was a confused man. Before the outbreak of war he managed to visit his only son on a kibbutz in the Jezreel Valley. What Markovitch was shown on Mount Scopus and in the National Library created conflict in him. And what he saw of the greenness of the Jezreel Valley and the blue in his son's eyes brought tears to his eyes. On his return from his visit to his son, he said to his wife, "*Rosa, mir haben a hemshekh*" (Rosa, we have a continuation).✢ Rosa, who was brought up in a house of eminent Yiddishists, from a long line of honest, anti-Zionist revolutionaries, for some unclear reason had not joined him on his journey to Palestine, either from weakness of health or some stiff-necked Jewish principle. Now she listened and understood. What she did not fully understand and did not ask to be explained was the sentence her husband then added, "If only we have the strength and time to endure."

Uri left the meeting with the writer happy and encouraged. "It's important, very important" he used to repeat to his friends on the kibbutz before he went to see him.

There were some who wondered how this accorded with the rumor that he had strengthened the hand of the head of the *Judenrat* after the last *Aktion* carried out by the Jewish police in the surrounding villages. "I hope he understood and will support us," Uri told them after the meeting. "Don't forget, he's a complex person, very complex," Uri stressed, wistfully. For the second, unforeseen meeting just two days later, he asked Sha'ul to accompany him.

And Y. L. Markovitch began by saying, "The ghetto now is passing through a period of calm. We're all like a sick man after a serious illness. Returning to life. Stability and

SHIMON DUBNOW (1860–1941): Jewish historian, thinker, and literary critic. Dubnow saw the development of the Jewish people through the generations as a migratory movement from one center to another. Dubnow saw autonomy as a satisfactory solution to the Jewish problem; the Jewish center would be in Eastern Europe, the Jewish culture would be largely secular, the language—Yiddish. In 1918, in order to realize this goal he set up the Volkspartei (The People's Party), which adopted his world view. He lived in Riga, Latvia, where the Nazis took him off to be executed, striding head erect, like one of his own forefathers who died as a martyr for the sanctity of the Holy Name.

"**Zelig Kalmanovitch** was a man of parts—an intellectual and a thinker, a scholar and a lover of Yiddish and Hebrew. I'll tell you something characteristic of his personality as eyewitness: I recall a certain unquiet morning in the ghetto. Prior to leaving, people were assembling in the yard near the gate. During the night there had been a hunt for old people— we didn't even know who was 'old'—there was an order to line up in threes before leaving, and suddenly the silence was broken by a loud argument from Kalmanovitch's 'three.' He was talking at the top of his voice, almost shouting at his friend Gordon, 'I'm not scared of them! I'm not scared of them! They can't do a thing to me!' And Gordon asks, 'What do you mean—you're not scared?' At this moment of silence, dozens of pairs of ears pricked up at this boisterous declaration in the street of Nazi Vilna, to know why he was not in awe of the Germans. And the answer that he gave in a more moderate tone, 'I have a son in the Land of Israel!'"

—RUSCHKA KORCHAK-MARLE, *Flames in the Ashes*

continuity are important. Continuity. If there is—God forbid—any danger of destruction, then it is acts of extremism that are liable to bring down disaster upon us." His eyes downcast, his fingers interlocked in front of him, the man in his slippers paced the narrow strip of floor from wall to wall with soft, measured steps.

They remained silent.

"I invited you"—and Uri seemed to hear "my friends"—"in order to remove any fear of misunderstanding. In matters of life and death, there must be no room for doubt. I thought about our previous meeting, and the suspicion entered my mind that you might have concluded that I was, as it were, in agreement with you. But all I did was listen. Just listen."

Sha'ul could feel how Uri had grown more tense. And they remained silent.

"No, no. I do not agree with you. By no means."

He came to a halt in front of Uri, who was a little taller, and, in what sounded like a note of apology, said as though changing the topic, "All the enemies of Israel have vanished in the twinkling of an eye."

"And is the ghetto also a matter of the twinkling of an eye?" Uri's astonishment seemed not to have got through to him. The man continued to weave the pattern of his own thought, "No, that is not what should matter for Jews today."

"What should matter for Jews today?"

"The affirmation of life."

Sha'ul looked at the writer almost with dread.

And as though answering a question that had not been asked, he stressed, "Acts charged with an affirmation of life."

✣ CHAPTER NINE ✣

A Man of Discernment

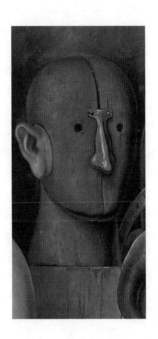

Seventy years old when he came to Terezin, with a white beard and high forehead, Baeck was an authoritative figure who inspired respect. Even someone who did not know that he was one of the most learned of his generation, versed in Jewish learning, philosophy, mysticism, and Christianity, felt his inner power; serenity radiated from him. At the end of three months Dr. Baeck began to serve as a rabbi, dividing his time between the dead (three of his sisters who had preceded him to Theresienstadt died before he arrived, the fourth died shortly after his arrival), the sick, and the thirst for knowledge. Among other activities, Dr. Baeck held a series of lectures on the history of philosophy, and about 700 to 800 people attended each lecture. Among them were most of the Zionist leadership, who came to hear about Plato, Kant, and Spinoza. At one of the smaller gatherings Dr. Baeck said to the people around him that the situation of the Jews was terrifying, but had to be borne in the faith that the Jewish people, who had managed to survive the tribulations of 2,000 years, would weather this trial too.

In August 1943, a Czech engineer by the name of Greenberg approached Rabbi Baeck and asked to speak privately with him. The man told Baeck that he had been awakened that night by a good friend whom he hadn't seen for years. Greenberg knew that his friend had not been sent to Terezin and therefore asked how he had got there, but the latter, very excited, cut him short, and asked him first to promise not to reveal to anyone what he was about to tell him: As a half-Jew he had been sent to Auschwitz, had passed through the 'selection' and had been sent to forced labor. Whoever did not pass the selection was taken to the gas chambers. This he knew for sure. Everyone at Auschwitz knew it. The man had succeeded in escaping from the work camp and had reached Prague, and, by bribing a Czech policeman had secretly entered Terezin in order to warn Greenberg and save his life. Baeck listened, horrified, to Greenberg:

And Sha'ul thought:

This man is discerning enough to know he is wrong. He is consciously avoiding the problem. But in order to change his opinion, a man must take tremendous risks. "If any of our intellectuals is capable of understanding us, it's Markovitch," Uri would say. The excessive respect that Uri paid to this aging writer annoyed Sha'ul, who had not read the articles Markovitch had once published on the response of the Jews to the rise of Nazism; he just happened to hear about them in the ghetto. Uri could quote from them by heart. Particularly impressive were the words explicitly addressed, without mentioning names, to Dr. Leo Baeck.✤ "Why this pride in passivity?" Markovitch bitterly asked the spiritual leader of German Jewry. The Jewish people had yielded millions of passive victims throughout its long history. But no nation can expect any recognition of its rights unless it is prepared to make active sacrifices for faith and freedom. A correct assessment. He gave his work the title, loaded with associations, *At the Crossroads.*✤

It was the year 1938. It was already too late. And still the words fell on deaf ears. If the two of them had been here—the thought suddenly struck Sha'ul—and met face to face, and Baeck had known what had not escaped the notice of Markovitch, that the yellow patch was the gateway to the ghetto and the ghetto was the passage to the valley of slaughter—what would they have said to each other, to their generation, to their people?

"Even if he doesn't actually join the ranks of the organization, undoubtedly he will lend us his moral support." For some reason, moral support was very important in Uri's eyes.✤

perhaps it was only a rumor, the fruit of a sick imagination? According to the rabbi's memoirs he was thrown into conflict: should he or should he not persuade Greenberg to tell his story again to the council of elders, of which Dr. Baeck was an honorary member—and finally decided against it; if the council of elders heard it, the whole ghetto would know about it within a few hours. In Rabbi Baeck's eyes to live in the expectation of being gassed was worse than the death by gassing itself. And anyway it wasn't that death awaited everyone: there was the selection for work, and maybe not everyone at Theresienstadt would be sent to Auschwitz. Thus Dr. Baeck arrived at the grave decision not to say anything to anyone and to keep the truth to himself."

—HANS ADLER,
Theresienstadt 1941-1945

"There is further testimony from an Auschwitz escapee, Siegfried (Vitezslav) Lederer. He tells how he escaped from Auschwitz at the beginning of April 1944, met Dr. Baeck on April 20, 1944 in Theresienstadt, and told him not only about Auschwitz but also about the murder of the transport of Jewish families from Terezin in the gas chambers on April 8, 1944. Dr. Baeck knew many of the people in this transport, which was composed of Czech and German Jews, and had arrived in Auschwitz in September 1943. No one was touched until they were all murdered together. The rabbi decided—again—not to warn the inhabitants of the ghetto. Leo Holzer, the head of Terezin firemen, who was present at the conversation between Lederer and Dr. Baeck, confirms its content."

—ERICH KULKA,
Briḥah Me-Auschwitz (Escape from Auschwitz)

AT THE CROSSROADS: A collection of the essays of Ahad Ha-Am, and also the name of a serious Yiddish journal (*Oyfn Sheydeveg*) that appeared in 1939 in Paris.

"To be a Jew means to live at all times on a high plane. The suffering and the blows that fall about Jewish heads are both transient and filled with meaning, they do not occur for no good reason, and they cannot humiliate a Jew. For a Jew is part of a threefold unity: Israel, the Torah, and the Holy One Blessed Be He—that is to say, the Jewish people, the Moral Law, and the Creator of the world. This threefold unity is firmly established and

"In order to see the danger straight—and not through us—you need intellectual integrity. He is one of the few, unfortunately, who have it." Uri had invested a lot of thought and feeling in preparing for this meeting. "I hope you're right," though in his heart Sha'ul was doubtful whether Uri was right about intellectual integrity. Firstly, Sha'ul didn't know exactly what it was. Secondly, in his time he had seen men not intellectually gifted, yet they were the ones who did the right thing in the right place at the right time. Sha'ul was ashamed at feeling a little malicious pleasure as he followed the course of this hopeless engagement between the two—strange, he thought, they look like father and son—as they moved inexorably toward the inevitable, decisive breach, which caused them both so much pain.

Uri crouched on his stool, which seemed once to have been a footrest, his knees raised, his elbows on his knees, his hands grasping his thin face. He was evidently confused.

"To die with honor—when we are all condemned to death—isn't that an affirmation of life?" Uri spoke the words quietly, as though wondering to himself, with no hint of challenge.

"Death and affirmation of life are incompatible. In death there is nothing of the holiness of life. Nothing! Nothing! Nothing!" Suddenly Markovitch realized his fists were battering an open Talmud. Alarmed, he stroked the book at once with moving tenderness, like a father passing his hands across the bruised forehead of his son, and bent over as though to offer a kiss. He placed his hands on the book with fingers spread, as in the priestly benediction. He was almost breathless. Until his vehemence returned. "I do not know what those evil men have decreed. What I know for certain is that the spirit is stronger than evil."

Uri returned his gaze. At once, as though the message had struck home, the writer also shifted his gaze toward him. Their eyes met.

A band of pallor spread across Uri's forehead and it was apparent to Sha'ul what an effort his friend Uri was making now before he spoke.

Then he said without taking his eyes off the writer, "And the children, the women, the old men, and all the thousands who have already lined up on the left, where was their spirit?"

"It does not suit you to be cynical."

Uri pursed his lips, and rose. "As far as faith is concerned, I am no cynic. But in God's name, the choice is not between life and death, but between passive sacrifice—now as throughout history—which we must make anyway, and resisting butchery."

A look of impatience flashed across the writer's face; he suddenly seemed much older than his sixty years. His gaze was veiled, as though he had remembered some pain that had not gone away. Had he suddenly felt a twinge of conscience for taking part in the meeting of sages called by the commander of the ghetto to get retrospective approval from intellectuals and Torah scholars for what the police had done during the last *Aktion?*

"And the commander is an honorable man," said Y. L. Markovitch, stretching his neck to look out of the window. The council building was visible through it. Suddenly he felt in the nape of his neck the frozen silence behind him. He approached them both, to within an arm's length, extended his right hand and, pointing an admonitory finger, seemed to look them straight in the eye. It was clear, however, that his gaze was somewhere far away as he said, like the teacher of a class of infants punctuating each word with his finger, "Just remain strong and survive, my young friends. Just remain strong and survive, I tell you."

The hour of curfew was approaching and the streets were empty of people as they went down the stairs and turned to cross the paved square.

"Did you notice," Sha'ul grinned, "that he was quoting Shakespeare when he said 'and the commander is an honorable man'?"* and he laughed aloud.

Uri was quiet.

"Why on earth did he think it right to say that? And to us?"

functions in history, it is a reality that has been tested time and again and has clearly proved itself. Our forefathers held to this threefold unity and drew from its power. And today too: the Jew who does not hold to this unity should be pitied; he is lost in an anarchic world, he suffers and can find no meaning in his suffering. In contrast, the Jew who holds firm to the threefold unity is not to be pitied. He is imbued with consciousness of the eternal Covenant. It is true our history is failing now, a war is being waged against the Jews; but the war is not with just one part of the threefold unity, but against the whole of it: against the Torah and also God, against the Moral Law and against the Creator of the world. Can there be any doubt which is the stronger side?"

—ZELIG KALMANOVITCH,
in the Vilna ghetto,
April 30, 1944

QUOTING SHAKESPEARE . . . The reference is to Mark Anthony's words in his famous monologue in *Julius Caesar* after Caesar is assassinated, Act 3, Scene 2: "And Brutus is an honorable man!" The tone is one of bitter irony.

Uri was quiet.

Sha'ul did not notice at first that his friend had fallen back. And had not heard his question.

"Are you all right?"

He ran to him. Uri was leaning his feverish brow against a telegraph pole.

"Don't take it to heart, Uri," he clapped him on the shoulder. "Intellectual integrity, or whatever you call it, is apparently not enough to distinguish between good and evil in Hell. A man needs all his spiritual forces in order to spurn false confidence in the wisdom of the commander, and take the risk of personal commitment like us."

"And if he's right?"

Sha'ul was destined to accompany Uri for many days to come. He would be by his side in good times and bad, but he would never see such an outburst of sudden anger. Without warning Uri grabbed him by the lapels of his jacket, digging his nails into them and shaking Sha'ul in the middle of the road as though he meant to throttle him. With the passion of despair he threw his words like stones in Sha'ul's face.

"I asked you. And what if he's right? I asked you. Why don't you answer me? What if he's right?"

"That will be for the survivors to say, Uri."

And on Friday Sha'ul reached his chosen destination. Through the window of the speeding carriage he could smell faintly the muddy earth that lay beyond the darkness. Dawn was breaking. Pine trees appeared. A small stream stitched the black plain fitfully with silver thread. His nostrils twitched as he sniffed the light through the mist and smoke; it bore the scent and glimmer of imminent winter.

The train jolted across a rackety little bridge and began to slow down. The monotonous clatter of the chains and the hoot of the engine pierced his heart as the train pierced its way through the landscape of his childhood. He closed his eyes and strained not to open them for as long as possible.

"Are you all right, young sir?"

Sitting next to his grandfather on the bench of the cart, as Francesca[*] charged

FRANCESCA: Here the name of a mare.

PRYPET: A river in the district of Polesje.

SHORTEST FRIDAY: The shortest Friday in the year usually occurs in the month of Tevet. Thus wrote Chaim Nachman Bialik in his story "Short Friday": "On short Friday there's no slacking. If anyone eases off, it ends (God forbid) in breaking the Sabbath. It's at the danger point that Satan strikes."

from the railway station toward the village center with the ease and rapidity of a professional runner, he used to love closing his eyes from time to time and opening them abruptly to surprise the landscape as it came speeding toward them.

He noted the inquisitive glance of the peasant woman, her good-natured eyes with no malice in them. He nodded in reply. The woman gathered up the ends of her gray head scarf and returned to her baskets.

What seemed at first to flow in the distance like a silver thread became a broad winding ribbon. The ribbon, passing between pine trees and bushes, gave way to a harness strap, a double harness strap that flowed, divided and encircled, a dry tongue that rose like a hump out of the thickets.

So this, he established with certainty, was the Sluc. From the edge of the dusty fields it extended up to the Prypet.[*] The small summer house his grandfather had built before the outbreak of war had exactly overlooked the tranquil confluence of the streams. The railway station—a peeling, two-storied building—crept past beyond the window. Carved wooden posts supported a small domed roof. The water tower stood on splayed legs, painted green. And there were the two giant chestnut trees at the entrance to this remote country station. Everything was just as it had been, drowsy, serene as in days gone by, as though no time had passed. And here was Pan Janowski, the man himself, with his black mustache and his red hat. Peace entered Sha'ul's soul, and he rested his hand on the lock. Surely, in God's name, nothing had changed for the worse in this lovely corner of the woods, in whose groves and cool waters, on the edge of the great marshes, he spent those summer months of happy memories when he was young.

It had been the shortest Friday of the year,[*] he remembered. A day like this in his Bar-Mitzvah year, and he was sitting on the bench of the cart. But Grandfather was being harsh with Francesca, urging her on and whipping her without mercy.

"Grandfather, why are you beating our Francesca?" he asked. And Grandfather replied that he was only a simple Hasid, not a man of exemplary righteousness.

At once he began to sing his favorite song about the rabbi coming home, who hurries along because any minute now Shabbat will come in. What does the rabbi do, he lifts his right forefinger—divides the holy from the profane and breaks through the middle:

fun eyn zayt—shabes, fun der anderer—vokh
un der rebi—fort in mitn.
ai-tshiri-biri-biri bim-bom
bim-bom
bim-bom
ai-tshiri-biri-biri bim-bom tshiri-bim-bom-bim-bom-bom.✣

"How can you help, I'd like to know?"

Startled, he stepped back. There was no one with him, only a sudden echo of Fyodor Gregoryevitch. He continued to look around. He had left here a youth and returned a man, with a mustache and a scarred face ravaged by wind and sun, *panicz*✣ boots on his feet, and eyes devoid of fear. Even Pan Janowski, who had been scrutinizing everyone coming and going for the past fifty years, would not recognize in this stranger the effete grandchild of Hershel the miller. Still, Sha'ul had learned to be careful. He crossed the main street, partly paved but mostly sand, with the beginnings of tarred pavements to the side. Not one extra meter had been improved. The same huts with straw roofs, the same houses built of wooden logs, with red-painted iron roofs. There were also some houses with walls of red brick, and tiles. One of them would be his grandfather's.

Nothing about the village had changed, from the cross at the road junction to the market square. Yet something seemed to have shrunk, to have lost height. The streets: were the houses drooping?

Could it be that today was the shortest Friday, and not a single Jew was in the whole neighborhood?

Hershel and Rachel-Leah had eleven sons and one daughter, Sha'ul's mother. In 1882,✣ Grandfather had been a *kheyder-yingele*✣ with Gershon the widower, a lean old man with yellow jaws and a straggly beard. Already they were speaking respectfully of Hershel as a definite infant prodigy. But he never learned anything beyond the Five Books of Moses. For that was the year in which he emerged from the empty rain barrel, in which he had hidden from the rioters, to see his father's legs sprawled under the counter in their felt boots. Sandor, who lay under the counter of his inn, did not move his legs. Fortunately, his face had been badly injured by the broken glass bottles and was drenched in blood, so that the rioters were fooled and took him for dead. The face of his mother, who was twenty years younger than his father, had turned to flawless wax, only from her slit throat oozed a thin trickle of froth. To the eyes of the child it looked so much like raspberry jam that had boiled over on to the ground that he almost licked his finger, which he had unconsciously dipped in the trail of his mother's spilled blood.

Before he extracted his whole body from the barrel, which luckily for him had been pushed into the shade between the gutter and the edge of the house, he caught a glimpse from eye level of the Cossack, with prominent yellow cheekbones, removing the trousers from their dying neighbor. Zalman Schneor the Bundist was lying next to the counter without his boots; the Cossack tossed the trousers on to the load of clothes already piled on his saddle and rode out of the square on his chestnut horse, cracking his whip and flourishing it in the air. At that moment the sun appeared from behind the clouds and bathed with bright patches the glowing flanks of the solid rump shone behind the quiet, assured movements of its short tail. The horseman

s'iz shoyn shabes, *vey iz mir,*
men vet shoyn bald nit torn,
un der rebi hot nokh
tsu zayn shtetl vayt tsu forn,
vos tut der rebe? nemt er
un shpant ayn dem ferd in shlitn
fun eyn zayt shabes,
fun der anderer— vokh
un der rebi fort in mitn.
tshiri-bim, tshiri-bom,
tshiribimbom, bimbom, bimbom,
ay tshiri biri biri bim bom
bim bom
bim bom.

—SONG IN A HASIDIC STYLE

Oy vey, Shabbat is here already,
No time for a stroll,
And the *rebbe* can't travel to his
   home town.
What will the *rebbe* do?
Oy vey, oy vey! Harness the mare to
   the cart.
On the right—Shabbat,
On his left—a weekday
And she gallops down the
   middle
Chiribim, chiribam
Chiribimbam, bimbam, bimbam
O chiri beeri beeri bim bam
Bim bam
Bim bam.

PANICZ (Polish): Yeshiva student. Here it means shiny, elegant boots, suitable for a young dandy.

IN 1882: The disturbances of 1882 were a series of pogroms that broke out in the southern and western regions of Russia in 1881-1882, known in history as "The Storms in the South." These disturbances began following a rumor that it was the Jews who had murdered Czar Alexander II, and the Russian government tolerated the bloodletting. The disturbances spread to all the Jewish communities—right up to Warsaw. Following the disturbances there was an increased wave of Jewish migration to the west, mainly to the United States.

KHEYDER-YINGELE (Yiddish): A child who learns from a rabbi in a *heder*.

STOLIN: A small town in Polesje, southeast of Pinsk.

RABBI ASHRUL (1765-1827): Rabbi Asher of Stolin, son of Rabbi Aharon of Karlin, and leader of the Jewish community of Karlin.

LAKHVA: A small town in the region of the Polesje marshes, north of Stolin, and south of Pinsk. There were 2,300 Jews in Lakhva at the outbreak of war. The influence of Zionist youth movements was considerable in the community. The ghetto was set up in 1942. Those who had been in the youth movements—and others—organized a fighting underground. The head of the *Judenrat,* Berl Lopatin, assisted in the uprising.

"DER STOLINER" (Yiddish): The man from Stolin.

ARENTER (Yiddish): A lease holder.

THE CUSTOM OF THE THIRD MEAL: The last formal meal on Shabbat, which usually takes place at dusk (between the afternoon and evening prayers). Kabbalists and Hasidim added ceremonies that had special religious significance, which they practiced with enthusiasm. In the evening, at the end of Shabbat, they would have a meal called *Melaveh Malka* (to "accompany the Sabbath Bride" on her way out).

IVREH (Yiddish): Knowledge of Hebrew and the source texts of Judaism—Bible, Mishnah, Talmud, and Midrash, with their commentators and interpreters.

SHABBAT ḤAZON: The Shabbat before the Ninth of Av, when Isaiah's prophecy is read (Isaiah 1).

CHERNOBYL: A small town in the Ukraine north of Kiev and south of Lahomel, which contained a Jewish community that was founded in the seventeenth century. In the eighteenth century Menahem Nahum, one of the disciples of the Baal Shem Tov, established the Hasidic dynasty of Chernobyl. During the German invasion the entire Jewish community of Chernobyl was destroyed. The town has become notorious as the site of the nuclear power station disaster of 1986.

dismounted by the dirt path that led to the river and the boy went in to his stabbed parents.

At the end of the seven-day period of mourning, his father said to him, "A Jew must learn how to die."

He was seven at the time, and in his heart he said, "Before I learn how to die I want to learn how to live." But he withheld the words from his mouth, and kept them locked in his heart. Hershel was thirteen years and two days old when he left his country, his birthplace, the house of his forefathers, in the Ukraine. And he passed through the great country that lies between the Dnieper and the Dvina, with much suffering and many wanderings, going back on his tracks, and much of this by night, and he dreamed more and more. He dreamed much, for only in dream does a person reach full awareness and see things as they really are, even though still a lad. He awoke in a cart, under whose tarpaulin he had climbed during a torrential downpour, after sleeping all night and half a day, in the marketplace of Stolin.✣ He was one of the first to visit the court of Rabbi Ashrul.✣ He did not leave without the rabbi's blessing, and the name of the place followed him around.

At Lakhva✣ they called him "*der Stoliner,*"✣ or simply "Stoliner" and only the Christian authorities recalled that in his documents the family name was Morgenstern. He was a fish merchant, and in those days his hands were coarse and sticky with scales. It's a wonder his young wife wasn't put off by the smell. But since the eye of the fish was not corrupted by man's first sin, it brings blessing, as everyone knows, to those who love it. When Hershel began to deal in grain, his fortunes prospered greatly and he became supplier to the duke. Duke Siniavski would openly admit that he had been an anti-Semite until he met the Jew, Hershel Morgenstern. Grandfather was ready to trust people, and always acted with composure. These two qualities are not usually found together in one person, especially in the body of a Jew. Even when he became an *arenter*✣ and almost the owner of an estate of his own, he continued to keep open house for the custom of the third meal,✣ bringing to the table what remained from the Sabbath evening meal, serving fish from his private pond, fish heads for the heads of the households and fish tails for the simple folk. And in a mighty voice he would sing Hasidic songs that contained only four or five, or sometimes only three words; the singing would go on for hours, with choruses of "ay" and "ay-ay" and thumps of "bim-bom" and lots of feeling. No man questioned the amount of *ivreh*✣ such a rich man possessed. His vitality was unbounded, and for the rest he was covered by the acts of charity of his lovely wife, Rachel-Leah, twenty years his junior. When they went to live in Lakhva, his circle of friends covered both sides of the river. Christians and Jews respected him and loved Rachel-Leah. Since God in his mercy had supplied all his material needs, and he had succeeded in everything he had done, he turned his mind to what a pious man had once preached on Shabbat Ḥazon, that the Messiah would come from Russia. Some say he was even more precise and said: "From Chernobyl."✣

In the year 5673, 1913 of the Common Era, feeling complacent, with the table laid for the Passover Seder, as he was wiping the rim of Elijah's glass to remove any specks before filling it with red wine, Hershel Stoliner raised an eyebrow and said, "And why not from Lakhva?" Rachel-Leah understood that all her husband had in mind was the unity of his far-flung family and quickly showed her whole-hearted approval by responding, "Oy, God willing. God willing."

Of his eleven sons, only four were abroad. As sons will, they had traveled far. Kalman, who had no love for the army of the Czar, had left in the dead of night for the Galicia of His Imperial Majesty,⁺ and soon found his way to Berlin, that most enlightened of cities. Sandor was sweating it out in the Sodom of New York. Each one was in exile where fate had sent him. The best of the sons, Zelig by name, was tilling the soil in the colony of Rishon Lezion, and Shrulik of the runny nose had become a teacher among the freethinkers. More than all the others, Rachel-Leah pined for her only daughter, dragged off by that Lithuanian to his stronghold of *Misnagdim,*⁺ a fate worse than America.

Rachel-Leah said, "If our daughter had been captured by the Lithuanians and there had been no war—*dayenu*⁺ (it would have been sufficient). If there had been a war and the wicked kingdom of Poland had fallen, and there had been no Soviet regime—*dayenu*. If there had been a Soviet regime, and the lovely big house had not burned down—*dayenu*. Now that the house is burned down, and the Bolsheviks have not deprived them of their land but left them to live in the small area that is all that remains, for it's better, according to the Soviet Russians, to be burned down than a landowner, how grateful we should be to the Almighty, Blessed be He, for His mercy endures forever."⁺ And the peasants in the district did not forget their straight dealing, and stood by them⁺ in time of trouble.

Sha'ul had made up his mind to bring his mother to Lakhva, after smuggling her out of the ghetto in a cart he would hire from peasants. Here he would surely find shelter for her. But he was too late.

Rachel-Leah's sister had a son named Yaakov. And the Soviets took him to work for the army, and he went to war. And when the Russians retreated in panic, he did not manage to bid farewell to his parents, and his mother almost went mad with worry for him. But the Russians did not get very far in their flight and Yaakov's whole brigade fell prisoner to the Germans. Three men from Lakhva escaped from captivity, and their luck held and they found their way home and changed their clothes. Yaakov had had a classmate named Berl, who had hoped to study law, but his dream was cut short. The Germans came and appointed him head of the *Judenrat.* It was not an easy thing to be a leader of the Jews at such a time. Every morning he had to get up and represent the Jews before the Nazis, and the Nazis before his fellow Jews. And everyone knew that the Germans had only set up the *Judenrat* so that the Jews themselves could help in carrying out the decrees. But how far would the decrees go?

When Berele Lopatin⁺ saw that his friend Yaakov had escaped from captivity by the skin of his teeth, he immediately hid him and prepared false papers for him and his companions, who had escaped with him. At the time he was well aware of the immense danger he was incurring. On August 16, 1941, Jewish men were rousted out of their houses to dig trenches. Trenches for what? To receive Jews who had been shot. Three days the trench duty lasted, and for three days and nights rumor drove people crazy. While this was going on, Lopatin was going round from house to house collecting gold from people with means. When he had gathered what he could,

HIS IMPERIAL MAJESTY: The Austrian Emperor Franz Josef I (1830–1916).

MISNAGDIM (Hebrew): The name given to those who opposed the Hasidic trend in Judaism and the Hasidic movement. This opposition came from the ranks of Orthodox Judaism, from those who zealously observed the commandments of the Torah. The father of the movement of *Misnagdim* was the Ga'on Eliyahu of Vilna, who regarded the existence of the Hasidic movement as dangerous for Judaism. At his initiative the Hasidim were excommunicated and all contact with them was forbidden. In the eyes of the *Misnagdim,* the Hasidim were a sect of deviant schismatics, mainly because of the changes that they introduced into the form of the liturgy, the joyful ecstatic singing and dancing with which they prayed, and perhaps also because of the scorn with which they regarded learned scholars and halakhic authorities who quibbled about halakhah. The tense relations between the Hasidim and the *Misnagdim* frequently gave rise to crises of personal relations, due to personal hatred, boycotts, and gossip. In the course of time the differences diminished and a measure of compromise was achieved.

DAYENU: "It would have been enough." From "Dayenu," a well-known song from the haggadah, the Passover liturgy. The song begins with praise for the good things that God has done for us. If He had merely taken us out of Egypt and not brought justice upon them (the Egyptians), it would have been enough for us (*dayenu*)—and so on, fourteen times.

"FOR HIS MERCY ENDURES FOREVER": Again according to the haggadah, the Passover liturgy. Quoted from Psalm 136.

AND STOOD BY THEM: Reference to a quote from the haggadah, the Passover liturgy. "And it [that same promise] stood by our forefathers and ourselves. For not just one man has risen up against us, but in every generation there are those who rise against us to destroy us. But the Holy One, blessed be He, has delivered us out of their hands!"

BERELE LOPATIN: Head of the *Judenrat* in Lakhva who assisted the underground. On the night of September 3, 1942, the Germans surrounded the ghetto, intending to wipe it out. With his own hands Berl Lopatin set fire to the first house and attacked the Germans. One hundred twenty people succeeded in breaking their way through to the forest.

MUSARNIKIM: Supporters of the Musar movement whose leader and spiritual founder was Rabbi Israel Lipkin, known as Rabbi Israel Salanter (1810-1883). The movement arose in the nineteenth century in Lithuania, as a reaction to the Enlightenment. Supporters of Musar emphasized the moral principles in Judaism, and insisted on unremitting effort in self-improvement and personal ethics. The ideas of the Musar movement penetrated the Lithuanian yeshivas and greatly influenced them. The ideal man was he who acted only after due consideration of the outcome of his deeds.

NOVOGRUDOK: A medium-sized town (about 200,00 inhabitants in the 1930s) in Lithuania, south of Vilna and east of Grodno.

KROPOTKIN (1842-1921): Pyotr Kropotkin was a Russian revolutionary, from an aristocratic Russian family, and one of the founders of the Anarchist movement.

HA'ARI, THE HOLY ARI FROM SAFED: The term for Yitzhak ben Shlomo Luria (1534-1572), one of the great sages and kabbalists, who became famous in his youth as a halakhic authority. While in Egypt, he made a profound study of the Kabbalah and its main text, the Zohar. In his last years he settled in Safed and was welcomed into the kabbalist community there.

THE GA'ON FROM VILNA (1720-1797): Eliyahu ben Shlomo Zalman, one of the greatest sages of Israel of all time. At the young age of six the Ga'on gave an address on religious law in the Vilna synagogue. He studied Gemara and Kabbalah, grammar, astronomy, mathematics, and geography. He was not officially nominated as Rabbi of Vilna, nor did he officiate as such. However, the comments, interpretations, and explanations that he noted down at the side of the pages of the Gemara are to this day a source

he ran at once to the appropriate place and paid a ransom. The next day the digging stopped, the men came home, and confidence was restored in God and in their Berele's ability to revoke a sentence of the Germans. On the first of April, on All Fools' Day, the ghetto was established. The Germans only included about 45 houses, most of them old and ramshackle, and the house of Hershel Stoliner was not one of them.

Hershel and all his family and the families of his brothers-in-law and his uncles went to the ghetto, and there were thirty-six of them in all. Not surprisingly, this single tribe of Jews contained everything to be found in the whole Jewish nation—factions and subfactions of Hasidim and *Misnagdim*, pioneers from Dror, and followers of Borochov, youngsters from Ha-Shomer Ha-Tza'ir and Betar, and a girl who was a secret Communist and a boy who favored the Bund and a heavily bearded yeshiva student who had spent time with the *Musarnikim*⁺ at Novogrudok,⁺ and two twins whose ways had diverged, the one who had been born on the right side of the bed had joined the left branch of Po'alei Tzion while the other remained a General Zionist. Nor was there missing a disciple of Kropotkin,⁺ and there was no lack of independents. And the independents were actually quite arrogant, for the phrase "independent"—both in Hebrew and in Yiddish—has a certain ambiguity, if you follow me. . . .

In earlier times, they could have been seen in the market square, between the old synagogue and the new and the study houses, clustered together in their shabby hats and caps, grabbing each other by the lapels and arguing heatedly. Local zealots praised the Rabbi of Karlin and by contrast, few but passionate, others told what they had seen with their own eyes at the court of Belz. Recent arrivals in short clothes would throw in comments to keep the fire burning, and the names of Ha'Ari, the Holy Ari from Safed,⁺ and Eliyahu, the Ga'on from Vilna,⁺ who had excommunicated the Hasidim, flew through the air like pancakes. Standing apart at the edge of the park, groups of young people gathered, wearing *rovashkas.*⁺ Some were leaning over a copy of *Haynt* and others over *Ha-Fraynd,*⁺ six or eight heads to one newspaper, and nothing to separate the young men from the young women.

The sun was playing hide and seek, and spring was late in arriving that year; rain poured down incessantly. Hershel found no consolation in the sight of all his family still with him, and walked the streets of the ghetto stooping and depressed. He could not get over the feeling of imprisonment, he could not get used to the ugliness of the two small ground floor rooms into which all his family were packed, the darkness, the dampness, the sight of the muddy rain coming through the broken windows and dripping from the rafters. He would pounce murderously on the bugs, and angrily chase the cockroaches, who were far too numerous to be bothered. And the hunger. The hunger. If only I could get free of this life. The end has come for the whole Jewish people. Only a madman can still

of inspiration for students. He vehemently opposed both Hasidism and the Enlightenment. He even imposed excommunication of the Hasidim. Because of the Ga'on, Vilna became the center of the *Misnagdim,* those who opposed Hasidism.

ROVASHKAS (Russian): Russian-style shirts or blouses. They are usually embroidered, with a high collar.

HAYNT AND HA-FRAYND: Two big daily Yiddish newspapers that appeared in Warsaw and were distributed throughout Poland. During the years 1935-1937, 27 daily papers and 100 weeklies were published in Yiddish. The daily *Haynt* was founded in 1908. Its general tendency was nationalist, slightly Zionist, and with an eye to the man in the street. It had a very wide distribution, possibly because of its serialization of novels. *Ha-Fraynd* was a Communist daily in disguise that came out in the late thirties (since the Communist Party was illegal in those days).

indulge in hope. Messiah now or suicide, said the sixty-seven-year-old, suddenly a broken old man.

"Messiah or suicide," he pounded with his fist on the eastern wall.

"Who ever heard of a Jew from our parts committing suicide?" This time it was the woman who protested. It was Rachel-Leah who had the courage in those times to wrap her head in a scarf like the farmers' wives from the banks of the Dnieper, and took her life in her hands to smuggle some flour and groats into the ghetto, sometimes even meat and potatoes, that her sons might live on after her.

Berele Lopatin sent two of his helpers to summon men he could trust, including Yaakov. They came and sat down and drew the curtains to shroud the light and locked the door behind them. Lopatin said, "There are no Jews left in Hanczowicz. And none in Dawid-Horodok. And Ignace Pitak, the cripple, followed his requisitioned horses as far as Kiev. He says he met no Jews anywhere in the Ukraine, and they talk there of a place whose name fills them with dread—a place called Babii Yar.*

The young men fell silent a while. Three of them were ex-soldiers. Lopatin turned to the three and asked, "What do you think we should do?" The ex-soldiers said they had to buy weapons and for that they needed gold. Lopatin summoned Schechtman, his assistant on the *Judenrat*. Schechtman said he would see to the gold. Dovidel said he knew two Russians who would be prepared to supply pistols in exchange for good Jewish suits, urban style. Schechtman said, "I'll bring the suits, you'll get the pistols." In the end the Russians took the suits but didn't supply any pistols. Dovidel didn't despair and went wherever he went and brought back word from another Russian called Poliakov, who was the commander of a unit of partisans, and was prepared to provide pistols in exchange for jackboots. A gun and ten bullets for each pair. As soon as he got five pairs, Poliakov disappeared. At that time Lopatin was summoned by the Gestapo, and reported to the officer, who demanded that he send away one hundred healthy Jews within two days.

Lopatin asked the officer, "Send them where?"

The German slapped the head of the *Judenrat* in the face, quite hard, and said, "None of your business, Jew!"

Lopatin replied, "If it's not my business, I send no Jews."

The officer slapped him twice more, and told him to go back immediately to the ghetto and not to leave its confines. As if he had any other alternative. Since the head of the *Judenrat* had come back to the ghetto at the cost of three slaps in the face and nothing happened, he was still alive and the hundred Jews were not sent anywhere, the Jews felt quite encouraged and Lopatin gained considerably in reputation.

Spring was over, it was halfway through summer and from the Lakhva ghetto no Jews had been expelled or killed. And Yaakov said to his friends, "In spite of anything our enemies may do, I shall raise a new family in Israel. On the twenty-seventh of July you, Berele, shall be by my side at my wedding." All his friends congratulated him—it was a good omen. A good omen.

On July 27, 1942, seven Jewish girls were taken while wandering around the neighboring villages looking for food for their families. Three German soldiers took the children and lined them up in two rows and shot them from close range. The first soldier killed three with one bullet and the sergeant killed four with one bullet. Among the dead was Mashka, Yaakov's sister. And Lopatin held up news of the slaughter till the evening, so as not to cancel the first wedding ceremony to take place in the ghetto, and that night the whole community was in shock.

From that day on the underground secretly stationed policemen by the gate of the ghetto to keep their eyes open day and night. And on the Eve of the New Year they saw the signs. When the Germans surrounded the ghetto,

BABII YAR: A beautiful valley on the outskirts of the town of Kiev, overlooking the Dnieper and its tributaries, and the site of the Babii Yar Massacre (See notes for Scroll 1).

No monument stands over Babii Yar.
A drop sheer as a crude gravestone.
I am afraid. Today I am as old in years
As all the Jewish people.

The wild grasses rustle over Babii Yar.
The trees look ominous, like judges.
Here all things scream silently, and baring my head,
Slowly I feel myself turning gray.
And I myself am one massive soundless scream.
Above the thousand thousand buried here.
I am each old man here shot dead.
I am each child here shot dead.
Nothing in me shall ever forget!
—YEVGENYI YEVTUSHENKO,
"Babii Yar"

the sun was just on the point of finally dipping in the river. The watchers counted one hundred and fifty Germans and two hundred auxiliary police. The Germans were armed with automatic weapons. Keen eyes spotted machine gun positions, which had been set up opposite the ghetto by the river crossings. Lopatin had known for three days about the pits that had been dug. Rukhchin, who trained the underground in the use of weapons, passing on what they had taught him in the army, divided the fighters into twenty-two groups and said, "Tonight we go into action. We have to break out before the Germans have finished their preparations."

MORDECHAI GERBERTIK (1877–1942): Popular Yiddish writer who lived with his family in Krakow. A carpenter by trade, Gerbertik lived in poverty. He wrote poems and set them to music. The song "Our Town Is Burning" was written before the war but was enthusiastically taken up by the young people in the ghetto, as an encouragement and a call to battle. On June 4, 1942, Gestapo agents surrounded the quarter where Gerbertik lived and arrested dozens of Jews and marched them to the railway station. On the way Gerbertik was killed by a burst of rifle fire.

Fire, brothers, fire!

Our whole town is burning
Black winds are storming
Flames of destruction are burning
No traces remain
It's going up in flame,
And you wring your hands without helping
Without putting out the flames
Of our town on fire!

Fire, brothers, fire!
The time is near, God forbid,
When the flames will spread
And will kill us all
Only the remains of walls will bear witness
To what was here.
And you wring your hands, etc.

Fire, brothers, fire!
Only you can help yourselves—
Quickly, stretch out a loving hand
And save yourselves from death.
Put out the flames with your blood,
Put them out with your blood, quickly—
Don't stand aside
Because the fire is mounting—
Don't wring your hands, there's a terrible fire!

—MORDECHAI GERBERTIK

Hershel Stoliner heard what was going on, took up his stout stick with which he used to walk the fields in the days of his *arenter,* put on his cloak which, thanks to Rachel-Leah, was still in good shape, and went to see Lopatin.

"Have you too cooperated with this evil company who wish—God forbid—to kill us all?"

"The Germans have come to destroy us."

"How do you know that?"

"The ghetto is surrounded, Reb Hershel, and there are burial pits."

"You have seen these pits with your own eyes?"

"The pits are there, Reb Hershel."[*]

"And what kind of death have you arranged for me and Rachel-Leah and the rest of the old people and babies who are unable to join you in a frantic dash to escape?"

"Are you of the opinion I should tell our youngsters to immolate themselves and make their way to the pits?"

"Berele!" The old man rapped on the floor three times with his stick. "I'm old enough to be your father, or your grandfather. Don't talk to me like that. I didn't say we have to walk to the pits. But pits were dug once before and by using your common sense you managed to close them."

"This time bribery won't help."

"Have you tried?"

"No, I haven't."

"Maybe they are just trying to scare us, to stop Jews from going off to join the partisans. They also pay with their lives for every escape from the ghetto to the partisans. You are the head of the Jewish community in the ghetto, not the leader of the savage beasts. For almost a whole year, thank God, we have survived in peace; maybe this time too the evil decree can be averted?"

"I fear I cannot stop them."

"If you don't stop the hotheads, I will. I'll stop them with my stick. I'll patrol the length of the wall and they'll cross it only over my dead body."

Lopatin summoned Rukhchin and they agreed to postpone the sortie till the morning. If the Germans allowed the Jews to go to work as usual, at five o'clock in the morning, it would be a sign that the surrounding of the ghetto was just a German troop maneuver, and the whole thing a false alarm.

It was not a maneuver. This was the day ordained for the destruction of the Lakhva ghetto. Had they been waiting for a weather forecast? The rain stopped at four and the river and the whole valley were covered with mist. There was no movement of Germans to be seen. At five the German bosses had not turned up to take their Jewish workers. At quarter past five the gate of the ghetto was still locked. And when a Byelorussian policeman on night duty said to Israel Dravsky, who had lit a cigarette for him and came to sniff by the wall, "Listen, man," the member of the *Judenrat* was surprised that a Jew had suddenly become a man in their speech, but didn't have time to marvel. "Give me your boots, after all, you won't need them any more after today." Dravsky ran panic-stricken through the streets of the ghetto shouting, "Jews, it's the end!" and what the discussions of the underground, the reports of the scouts, and logical argument failed to achieve—to anticipate the murderers by one hour—what Jewish brains couldn't do was brought about by the crude language of a Byelorussian policeman. All the men of Lakhva became a single company, they had flown into the air like hemp stalks in the wind and come down like a pile of twigs, dry of illusion, parched of hope: all that was missing was the match to start the fire.

Within an hour five military trucks had descended on the gate of the ghetto and the German commander ordered the head of the *Judenrat* to report to him. When Lopatin heard that the ghetto was due for destruction and only thirty highly skilled workers would remain—"And you too, and your family, and the members of the *Judenrat* can also stay"—he said to the German, "You are the masters, and you will wreak destruction. But you shall not kill us by installments." Thus spoke the head of the *Judenrat* to the German, and to the Jews who had banded together expectantly he said, "Brothers, this is the end."[*] And that was the signal for the uprising. It was Lopatin who was the first to set fire to his house and the others soon bravely followed his example. Israel Dravsky hastened to set his house alight and so did the doctor. Most of the houses caught fire in quick succession and the flames spread from street to street. Rukhchin crushed with an ax the head of the SS man who was barring his way to the fence and with two or three leaps had cleared the embankment and was racing to the river. A machine gun burst caught him half way across. Something blossomed on the water like a purple illustration in a calendar, and that was all that remained of Yitzhak Rukhchin, one of the leaders of the revolt in the smallest of the Jewish townships.

Hershel Morgenstern was running with the fugitives, stumbling in his galoshes, his cloak unbuttoned, his head bare, brandishing his stick. He had escaped from the blazing, smoking corridor and made his way to a side courtyard with a double entry.

On Sabbath Eve, as he was getting ready to go to bed, he had said to his wife in a faltering voice, "Rachel-Leah my darling, I'm a sick old man. My stay on earth is drawing to a close." And now suddenly the blood was flowing strongly in his veins. Where had all his family got to? Yaakov had passed him at a run, leading a tight band of young men and women armed with iron bars and axes. In Yaakov's hand he could see a revolver, which he was waving with arm extended over his head, like a man clutching a poisonous snake by the throat.

"Yankele! Yankele!"

But the lad ignored him, or perhaps the old man's voice didn't reach him amid the screaming and the shots. The men were charging out from the doorways of the houses, and attacking the Byelorussian policemen and the Germans who barred their way to the fence that led to the river.

The German soldiers withdrew hurriedly from the alleys of the ghetto to train their machine guns on the line of escape and the breaches in the fence. Dead and wounded were piling up near the fence. The crowd changed direction and tried to break through the fence from behind the cover of the houses.[*] Above the mad whirl of twisted faces and varieties of panic, Grandfather Hershel's white beard floated like a distress signal above a sinking ship. His heart filled with admiration for Yankele and his comrades who dared to wield axes against the heads of German soldiers. Again he caught sight of Yankele's silhouette at the end of the road and the butt of a rifle striking at it. Suddenly he felt abandoned and alone, swept along like a wooden log hurtling into the abyss.[*]

Within shouting distance Rachel-Leah was running and dragging along their granddaughter Manichka, who was crying bitterly. He could not hear her and the wave thrust her toward him and then hurled her away again. Her mouth was agape and her eyes distorted with fear and for the first time in her life she doubted whether her husband knew what was in store. Since the old man had turned in the opposite direction from the flow of the dense crowd and also seemed to be moving away from the sole hope—from the open gate—she summoned up the remains of her strength and with her free elbow strove not to be separated from him and to be by his side, even if he had lost his wits.

"We decided to sell our lives dear."
—PIONEERS IN KUNIN CAMP,
August 12, 1943,
Gustinin Notes (Poland)

You have not seen a city thrust on its back
   like a horse in its blood,
     jerking its hooves
   unable to rise

   Bells are ringing
   City.
   City.
   How mourns a city
   whose people are dead,
     whose dead are alive
   in the heart.

   Bells.   —ABBA KOVNER,
         "My Little Sister"

How will you be able to remember us
And our world, that the disaster
   made so inhuman?
Will a human world ever exist again,
That does not harbor the disaster in
   its breast?   —ANONYMOUS

✦ CHAPTER TEN ✦

As If by a Miracle

As if by a miracle, suddenly they found themselves beyond the ghetto, beyond the raging fire, beyond the range of the German bullets, as though in the eye of the storm: they were in a deserted courtyard that had once been the house of Jews, from which a hidden path led toward the river. Like a cunning fox, the old man turned round and saw his wife and the child. He waved to them to hurry up, for he had the idea of hiding here, perhaps under the pile of hay at the other end of the yard, until the danger was past and they could cross the river under cover of darkness.

The *goy* burst in, from God knows where. He stood on the pile of hay, legs swathed like a hunter, feet apart to keep his body steady, tall, with a tidy blonde quiff and a lock of hair falling over one eye. His face was in shade as the sun set behind his back. In his astonishment, Hershel didn't even crouch down, let alone manage to lie flat, when the bullet whistled past his right ear.

"Poleishuk! What are you playing at?" cried the Jew, gaining confidence as he recognized the marksman, a forester he had known from way back. "It's me, Hershko!"

Instinctively Rachel-Leah had recoiled, pressing her back against the door frame of the store room, pulling the child in after her and covering her mouth with her sweaty hand. She saw Hershel standing in the center of the courtyard, his hands lifted toward the pile of hay as though waiting for an answer, the wonder in his eyes, and the flash of his gold tooth. Suddenly he was stretched out on his back, his white beard resting on his chest, his feet extended, motionless, still. A rose of fire had split the center of his forehead.

Who can know where Rachel-Leah found the physical and spiritual strength to grab the child and straightway carry her far from the bullet-ridden houses and courtyards? She burst out of the yard and ran like a hunted animal, the child in her arms as though held in her teeth, and did not look back.

The gate of the ghetto had been broken open. Crowds of Jews had been torn away from their burning houses and were swarming into the market square as they broke their way out. This war of the Jews was no military engagement, and had no real command. When the signal was given each man acted on his own, as his senses told him, to the extent of his own resourcefulness.

The German wounded, who were screaming for help like any mother's child, were sorry perhaps that they hadn't descended upon the Jews in greater strength, and hadn't tricked them this time as well. Berele Lopatin had been wounded in both arms but was still fighting bravely. Rukhchin was right, he thought, we should have acted when it was still night. In the first minutes—it may have been only a few seconds—the Germans didn't fire a single shot, they were so startled and disconcerted. The Ukrainians and the Byelorussians as well. Only the dogs started barking furiously: and then the machine gun began to mow down the Jews.

Chaos was wild, complete. One of the lads—Lopatin could not identify his face—was wrestling with a German in front of the *Judenrat* building; the two rolled over on the ground, gripping each other by the throat. The soldiers withheld their fire.

The lad shouted, "Grab the gun! Grab their machine gun!" But they failed. Aharon fought with an Alsatian dog, crushing its head with an ax. Then they scattered in different directions. It was good they weren't running as a mob. Motorcycles roared by. It was already getting dark. The Germans were not equipped with torches. Berele skirted the last house before the slope and jumping over the pits raced toward the fading glow of the river. At that moment he recognized the figure that had been grappling with the German and had snatched his rifle. It was his friend, Moshe Leib Hefetz, whose brother had been shot in the first hour of the uprising. A thousand men and women had escaped from the ghetto in the storm of the outbreak. About half of them even succeeded in reaching the Reichin marshes, as far as the Prypet forests beyond the river bank.

For three days Rachel-Leah wandered with her granddaughter, quenching their thirsts on swamp water, chewing roots, and vomiting. Wherever they went they discovered the tracks of fugitives from the ghetto. Dead Jews and dying Jews as good as dead littered the forest paths and the marshes, the muddy furrows and the ditches. Babies turning blue crawled among the clods of soft earth. Rachel-Leah came across Cheina Moravchik under a pine tree. She kneeled and shook her to wake her up, and Cheina Moravchik looked at her but saw nothing. Her head lolled, she spoke but her words were soundless. Folded in her sweater, she held her dead child to her breast. No one from her family was with her. Those who survived the pursuit within the township plunged desperately through the swampy undergrowth toward the heart of the forest in the hope of finding shelter in its darkness, and partisans. All around them they saw those who had collapsed and heard the cry of those abandoned to their fate, and could offer no salvation.

On Wednesday evening, Eudokia Vasilevna Golovchik went out to feed the single piglet, all that remained after the German requisitions, carrying two buckets on a yoke. She put one bucket down near the entrance to the orphaned sty and carried the other with her to the well. She rounded the hut, drew the water from the well, and hurried back, for she could hear the piglet grunting greedily with impatience. And she saw a figure stooping over the bucket, avidly licking the pig swill and this figure with its filthy back and unkempt hair looked barely human, from some other world.

"Matushka," mumbled the figure. "I . . . I'm sorry I'm . . . it's me, the wife of Hershko the miller. . . ."

"Christ our Savior!" screeched the peasant woman, with no mind for the Jews, crossing herself in alarm as though banishing a ghost.

"Just a little milk perhaps?" Rachel-Leah was still kneeling by the pig bucket; one finger dripping with swill was pointing to the bushes beyond the ditch, "for the little girl?"

Eudokia Vasilevna Golovchik had been witness with her own parched eyes to atrocities in the wake of the wars of the White Russians against the Red, the Black, and the Blue, but she had never seen anything like this face.[*] She instructed the Jewish woman, frozen with fear, whom she barely recognized as the first lady of the town, to go back and hide in the bushes, and wait there till she could bring out a cup of milk, after dark of course, for her brother-in-law was in the house, "and he's not a good man." Her teeth still chattering, Eudokia picked up the bucket, which had fallen from her hand, half its water spilled. Pashka Kribonos had heard his sister-in-law's screech and was poking his head out of the doorway of the hut to see what had happened, perhaps the pig had gored the sow? He chuckled with amusement at the wit that sparkled in his

head, misty with villainy and vodka. At that moment a figure with a head scarf was crossing the ditch.

"Who's there?" he asked Eudokia.

Eudokia shook her gray head and shrugged her shoulders as if to say, "What did you see that I don't?"

Pashka Kribonos was a very sociable fellow. He was known in the villages for his skill as a pickpocket at fairs, and for his hobby of raising fallen horses. An ailing horse might fall in the middle of the road and not get up–but not with Pashka. Pashka would get it on its feet, even if it were already dead. Not for nothing did the Reds put him in charge of the reserve of horses for the cavalry squadron in Budenny's division. To the Germans he explained that it wasn't from any ideology that he joined the Reds, not even out of his well-known love of horses, but for the *lampasin.*[+] His soul craved for ribbons to be sewn to the sides of his trousers. How come the Germans hadn't draped one of those ribbons round his throat till his dying day? Some say Pashka redeemed his soul at the cost of the souls of Communist commissars. Nevertheless, he was a sociable fellow and there were thousands on the Prypet who loved him.

"My dear Eudokia Vasilevna, why are you lying to Pashka? That was a Jewess!"

Pashka took an ax and went out among the bushes. Rachel-Leah covered the child and stretched out her neck, without another move.

"Hold it, Pashka!" the old woman said firmly. "What's the point of you killing the poor things? Hand them over alive to the police and you'll get paid cash per head."

Pashka Kribonos snapped his fingers and said, "As you say, my dear Eudokia."

On the way they met Byelorussian policemen. Two policemen with two rifles were enough for a Jewess and a baby.

"Just a minute, fellows," Pashka stopped them, "I want a written receipt for my prize."

The Byelorussian policemen looked at Pashka, who had the build of an athlete and a small stubby head like a snake, and told him, "For the prize, brother, you'll have to take the trouble to report to the Germans." Even in Lakhva, which is a long, long way from Berlin, Germans remain totally German. And order must be preserved. According to the New Order, which Hitler wanted to introduce in Europe, perfect order would reign in the world forevermore. And the perfect example from among their actions so far was, of course, the death certificates.

The earth became corrupt before God; the earth was filled with lawlessness. When God saw how corrupt the earth was, for all flesh had corrupted its ways on earth . . .   —GENESIS 6:11-12

. . . Must the sword devour forever?   —2 SAMUEL 2:26

LAMPASIN: Colored piping down the side of the trouser legs. The piping indicated the unit and rank of the officer.

On the morning of April 29, 1945, a black GI from Louisiana entered a KZ[+] set up by the leading nation among the white race in Europe, and on the table of the chief clerk of the camp found an account of population movement, which the clerk had scrupulously maintained up to the twenty-fifth of April, inclusive, seven days before the total collapse of the Third Reich. Nowhere did the Germans forego recording their actions, or recording a blurred version of their actions, in precise detail: Entered–Left; Consignment Received; Dealt With; Written Off. The chief clerk, a *Feldwebel*,[+] said, "You arrived just in time. Today we have to complete the list of official returnees. By tonight we'll have no less than five hundred like that."

Pashka twisted his furrowed lips in evident disappointment; the expected prize money or its equivalent in goods had failed to materialize. There must have been plenty in those days who had earned prizes and all he got was half a kilo of salt. Why only half? Because Manichka was only seven years old and didn't count. Since he couldn't curse the Germans he went and abused his sister-in-law.

The street next to the market square was strewn with paper, pages from books, children's copybooks, trampled dolls, horse dung. Broken glass crunched under Sha'ul's feet: here was the ghetto gate. His heart beat strongly as he entered, almost at a run. The air was heavy with the smell of burning, decay, and Jewish fate. He marveled that he had not noticed the people before. They were scurrying from alley to alley, from house to house. Men and women were intent on raking through property. Women carried sacks full of jangling pots and pans, iron and copper, frying pans, saucepans, and buckets. One old man and woman were together dragging along a wardrobe with a large, shattered mirror. A pock-marked carter had shouldered a superb piano onto his cart, and was struggling to load the rest of his loot on its boards. Apparently the looters did not regard everything burned as destroyed. He wondered at the Germans, who had vanished. They didn't care for looting by private individuals. A man with the build of an athlete and a terribly small, stubby head like a snake went by carrying two shining, big-bellied samovars clutched to his chest, around his shoulders a chain from which dangled a chandelier. As he passed, his mouselike eyes glittered and like an old friend he said, "No doubt about it, they had a good life, those Yids."

Perhaps it was rash and stupid to make his way to the house of his grandmother and grandfather. The voice of reason warned him but his feet refused to listen. Almost running, Sha'ul left the warmth of the burned-out ghetto, as though harried by bats. The streets outside the ghetto were also almost entirely empty, for most of the inhabitants had been Jews. Occasional passersby would appear and glide away, elusive as though afraid of something. A shadow attached itself to him. "Where do you want to go, sir?" asked the shadow. Since it was the voice of a woman, not a policeman, Sha'ul did not reply. He walked on. Like one who knew his way, he went straight on. After the bridge he turned into a side alley and making a wide detour came back by another alley, back into the main street, in the middle: here was the house. His heart beat strongly and sweat trickled down his spine. He opened the gate, a string hung down from where a copper bolt had once been fixed.

He stood in the courtyard, enveloped by silence. The lock on the house was sealed with wax.

He walked round looking in the windows. The large kitchen table was standing in place, floury with dust. Even the chairs were arranged to take all the members of the family. Pigeons took flight in alarm, and silence returned and flowed through the windows. Straining his eyes, he examined every object, every detail he could discern in the inner gloom. The frozen stillness seemed about to swallow him up. A feeling of desolation and loss overcame him, and almost rooted him to the ground. Suddenly, a figure slipped behind the house and vanished.

He jumped after it and caught hold of an arm.

"Is it you who have been following me all the time?"

About sixteen years old, wrapped in an old woman's sweater, with startled eyes, the girl made no reply but asked, "Are you looking for one of the Hershkos, sir?"

"Yes."

"So let's go," she whispered, and pattered off on her bare feet.

They arrived almost at a run. Suddenly he stopped in amazement. The rusty iron gate of Uncle Reuben's leather workshop stood wide open, the silent courtyard totally deserted. Between the house and the rows of huts stood

---

KZ (German): Initials of the word *Konzentrationslager,* that is, concentration camp.

FELDWEBEL (German): Sergeant, a rank in the German army.

piles of foul-smelling garbage. The interior of the house had been emptied of most of its contents, only shreds of paper, broken boxes, and dismantled furniture remained, as though abandoned after a hurricane. This place had hummed with human voices, working, watching, running here and there, with children returning from school and running off to bathe in the river, Sabbath songs and summer quarrels with their neighbors the Hershkovitches. All this was now wrapped in the stillness of death, which Sha'ul's ears could barely find strength to endure. Suddenly he became aware of a clicking sound, as of one piece of wood being dragged against another, or perhaps a rat scampering between piles of rubbish. The girl led him along a concealed corridor to a cellar. Now he could clearly make out the sound and the words, "I want to go home. Wanna go home." Then he saw the thin arms and the disheveled hair.

"That's Manichka," said the girl.

The child was lying in a disjointed heap, her legs curled up on the straw and the boards. A lamp with a faulty wick was smoking in the corner. Moths were circling above it, blindly suicidal. The girl took off her heavy sweater and dirty blonde hair fell over her shoulders. Her name was Zoska Boivozha, the fisherman's daughter. She stood with her back to the wall.

"I was out with Marilka, whose father was a gatekeeper at Hershko's mill, gathering blackberries, when the convoys arrived. They were Jews who had come back after the escape; they didn't find the partisans and were dying of hunger. They came back to the ruins of the ghetto and the Germans rounded them up. They filled carts with them and the carts came back again a second, a third time, without end. When we heard the shots, Marilka panicked and ran away. I found my way to a hummock between pine trees, and I could see the trenches from there. It was strange. They toppled over like felled trees, with hardly a sound. They no longer had the strength to weep or shout. Suddenly I saw the old lady. She stood erect on the edge of the trench, and held the child. I knew Manichka and I was sure she fell into the pit without being shot. I saw how her grandmother had pushed her into the pit ahead of her just at the moment when she herself was hit. I hid until it grew dark and the Germans and the policemen had left the area drunk. Terrible fear gripped me as I felt the movement of the ground beneath my feet. Under the dirt that had been poured over the pits, life was stirring. I wanted to

run away, but my feet seemed paralyzed, they wouldn't move. I burst out crying and then in the intervals I heard other weeping answering me like an echo. It was Manichka. We crawled toward each other; she came out of the pit and I held her hand. She was covered in blood. Afterward it became clear that it wasn't her own blood; she wasn't wounded at all, as I had guessed. I hid her in the wood away from the place of slaughter and ran to Marilka. We carried her between us with arms linked, you know, like a birthday chair. Luckily for us no one stopped us."

"'Kh vil aheym. 'Kh vil aheym,'" the child was sniveling.

"What is she saying? She's been repeating those words nonstop for three days. Apart from that she doesn't say anything."

Till now it had not been clear whether Zoska had identified Sha'ul as a Jew or whether she was sure he was a Christian friend of the family. There was no point in denying that tears had formed in his eyes and his throat ached on hearing the two words, plaintive and exigent, which burst forth from the shapeless bundle. "She wants to go home, that's what she's saying, she's in shock."

Sha'ul tried to talk to her but she didn't respond. "Manichka, listen, you don't have a home, there isn't anybody. This will be your home. Zoska loves you."

When he stretched out his hand to stroke her, she let her head fall on her bent knees. "She's not mad?" asked Zoska in alarm.

"No. That will pass. A little patience and she'll regain her strength. Who knows about her apart from you?"

"Marilka. No one else. I haven't told anybody. We've been taking it in turns to look after her. But it's dangerous for her to stay here for long. I'm also a little bit fearful of Marilka. She's a chatterbox and likes to show off."

"Do you know the monastery on top of White Hill?"

"Sure. Once a week we supply them with fresh fish."

"Who takes the fish?"

"I do. In the cart."

"When is the next time?"

"Tomorrow."

"Tomorrow then, my dear, you must take the child to the monastery. Ask for the father superior. Don't give any details. Just that you found the poor thing near the pits. No name. They will take her in."* He undid a concealed pocket and gave her a bundle of notes and two gold rings that he extracted from the cotton purse. He told her to keep the money hidden and to use it only a little at a time, so as not

My sister's eyes search the wall
of the convent
for a scarlet thread. A candle
trembles
in the nun's hands.
Nine holy Sisters look at my
sister
seeing—ashes that speak.

—ABBA KOVNER,
"My Little Sister"

GRODNO: A port town on the banks of the Nemunas River and a railway junction, northeast of Bialystok. The Jewish community in Grodno was a large, thriving community and one of the oldest in the region of Lithuania. In 1912, there were 34,500 Jews (60 percent of the total population). In 1939, there were 60,000.

BARANOVICE: A town northeast of Slonim and the Scara River. Before the war Baranovice was in the Polish republic, but it is now part of southwest Byelorussia. In 1939, the town contained 12,000 Jews. During World War II most of the Jewish inhabitants were murdered.

BIALYSTOK: A town in the extreme northeast of Poland. A large administrative, cultural, and industrial center, and a railway junction, Bialystok became an important textile manufacturing center at the beginning of the nineteenth century. By the end of the century there were 230 factories in the town, which employed tens of thousands of workers, many of whom were Jews. In 1913, there were 61,500 Jews in Bialystok, making up 68 percent of the total urban population. At the outbreak of World War II, the Germans conquered Bialystok but returned it to Russia, according to the Ribbentrop-Molotov Agreement. In 1941, the Germans returned to Bialystok and set up the ghetto in which they concentrated 50,000 Jews. In February 1943, the Germans deported 12,000 of the Bialystok Jews to Treblinka. A rebellion movement arose in the ghetto, and on August 16, 1943, the movement called on the Jews to resist, but the community did not respond. A revolt broke out and continued for several days; it was put down with cruel fury.

to give the neighbors any cause for suspicion. "One day I'll come back here to take Manichka. Visit her from time to time, and be concerned for her. Remember I'll be back."

Her hands trembled as she held the bundle of money and her eyes gazed at him with fear and wonder. Sha'ul turned on his heels, held her head, and kissed her on the forehead. "God bless you, Zoska."

He made his way back to the railroad in the rain. As the train moved out, the roof of the tiny station disappeared in the mist. But thicker was the mist that enveloped the cells of his brain. "I wanna go home, go home, go home," his temples thumped to the mounting rhythm of the wheels. He made haste now to bring the manifesto of the underground to the besieged cities of Grodno,✝ Baranovice,✝ and Bialystok.✝

With a forged identity card and no money in his pocket,✝ Sha'ul stood on the road from Grodno to Lida,✝ his cough getting worse and his temperature rising from hour to hour. All morning he had striven to see his way clearly through the jumble of events he had lived through during his journey; at one time he would put himself in the place of the head of the *Judenrat* of Bialystok, who made decisions as if all the wisdom of his ancestors breathed through him, and then in the place of blue-eyed Batya, who made things difficult for her comrade, one of the leaders of the underground; why didn't they just go off to the forest, they and all the active members of the group, without delay; why did they have to feel any great obligation to a community that rejected them?

Shading his narrowed eyes with one hand and waving the other hesitantly at a truck climbing up the hill, all Sha'ul succeeded in saying to himself was, "The enemy spreads invisible nets over the whole country. The whole country."

"Climb aboard, man, if you want a lift," he was surprised to hear from the cabin. He blinked for a moment, pretending not to understand German, and then got on at once, repeating his thanks in Polish and school German.

It was an army truck, covered with a tarpaulin. From the easy way it rode along, it seemed it was not loaded.

A handsome *Feldwebel* with a severe expression was driving, and his companion was younger, higher in rank, and one armed.

"Heinz," the officer introduced himself and moved over to make room.

"I'm . . . Izzia Poliakov," answered Sha'ul.

"Poliakov, that means Polish?"

"No."

"Russian?"

"No."

"What then, for God's sake, are you human?"

"Karaite."

A penny less,
A penny more,
Hold your head high, man!
Be proud and alert,
And do not despair.

LIDA: A small town in western Byelorussia, northeast of Grodno. There had been a Jewish community in Lida from the seventeenth century, mostly of artisans and farmers. When the Germans entered the town, there were 15,000 Jews. Some fled east, but 8,000 were trapped in the ghetto, and of these most were shot in the killing pits outside the town. A desperate revolt by those being taken to be killed saved several hundred, who succeeded in reaching the areas under the partisans.

Among the shopkeepers and artisans of Lida were talmudic scholars. It was said of one that he used to sit engrossed in study all day long. When a customer entered and asked for something, the shopkeeper answered, "There aren't enough shops in the market, and needy Jews—you have to come here?"

KARAITES: A sect that originated among Jewish communities in Babylon at the beginning of the eighth century. Founded by Anan Ben David, the Karaites rejected the Oral Law (Mishnah and Talmud) and claimed that everything could be found in the written text of the Bible. Their watchword was "Look well in the Torah." Many Karaites settled in the Land of Israel, mainly in Jerusalem, but as generations passed they were dispersed among many countries (Egypt, Turkey, Russia—particularly in the Crimean peninsula—and Lithuania, with their center in Trakai). The Karaite reading of the Bible made a considerable contribution to commentary on the texts and the understanding of biblical grammar. At first there were many points of dispute between Karaites and Jews. These lessened as time went by. In the nineteenth and twentieth centuries the Karaites cut off completely from the Jews and declared themselves members of another religion. In 1932, there were 12,000 Karaites in the world. The Nazis recognized the Karaites as non-Jews and did not apply the "Final Solution" to them. When the State of Israel was established, the Karaites were persecuted in Arab countries, and many of them came to Israel. Today they number about 7,000, and are concentrated in Ramle and Ashdod.

ANTON (1900-1942): Austrian-born sergeant in the German army. Anton Schmidt was in command of a small military unit whose function was to administer a transit camp for German soldiers who had become detached from their units. In the cellars of the three houses that served the unit there were workshops for metalwork, repair of bed frames and mattresses, and sewing. Schmidt employed Jews to work in them, and during the ghetto actions he hid many of his Jewish workers in these cellars. He also moved Jews in German military trucks to White Russia. People of means paid him a lot of money, the penniless he moved for free. He also moved Jews to more distant places, such as Grodno and Bialystok. At the beginning he would smuggle out five to six people each time; later even twenty to thirty. In the second half of January 1942, Schmidt was arrested, accused of helping Jews, and sentenced by a German military court; he

"Karaite?* Hey, Anton,"* the officer beamed at his companion, "we haven't met one of those before."

"I have," said the *Feldwebel* bleakly, squinting quizzically at Sha'ul. "I hope he's not a relative of our friend Tamaroff."*

Cold sweat broke out on Sha'ul's neck and began to trickle down his spine. The lieutenant lit a cigarette and offered one to Sha'ul.

"And where are you from?" he asked.

"From Trakai,"* Sha'ul lied.

"And I'm from Dinslaken."

Sha'ul had no idea where Dinslaken was and the lieutenant explained. Suddenly his friendliness was cut short and his tone of voice changed. "Tell me . . . Poliakov, why do the people around here have such terrible relations with their neighbors, the Jews?"*

Sha'ul spluttered. Such a question from a German officer startled him so much; he didn't know whether it was the epitome of hypocrisy or a cunning trap.

"There are also decent people living around here," he replied, controlling his cough.

"There are also decent people among the Germans."

Sha'ul opened his eyes wide, "I haven't come across any." As he spoke, he felt as though fire had scorched the tip of his tongue. But the counterblast did not come. There was an embarrassed silence. On the knees of the lieutenant lay a burnished Schmeisser, and the palm of his false hand rested on the gun. He was about Sha'ul's age, with horn-rimmed glasses.

"What would you say if you came across a truck like this, in which a German was smuggling Jews out of the ghetto?" he said, blowing perfect smoke rings.

"Jews out of the ghetto—where to?"

was executed by firing squad on April 13. Yad Vashem awarded Anton Schmidt the title of Righteous Gentile.

TAMAROFF (1916-1943): Commander of the fighting Jewish organization in Bialystok. In 1937, Mordechai Tanenbaum-Tamaroff entered agricultural training at the Baranovice kibbutz, and later moved to Warsaw to teach. At the outbreak of war, he and some refugees escaped to Vilna, where he became the head of the He-Ḥalutz movement. Tamaroff was an activist, and made many dangerous journeys to areas under German domination, moving people from the "accursed" ghetto in Vilna to the "safe" ghetto in Bialystok. Gifted with daring and limitless devotion, he infused the movement's fighters with his spirit. Tamaroff fell in battle during the liquidation of the Bialystok ghetto.

"We parted from Mordechai, sure that we would meet again. But we never did. Mordechai surprised me in those last moments. Listened to the runners, who told of what was happening in the ghetto—listened without reacting. Didn't curse. I didn't once hear his favorite word: "Cholera"—is this Mordechai? Is this the nervous, dynamic Mordechai, quick to respond, easily enthused? Yes, his eyes are piercing but his movements are restrained and his answers clear and to the point. Decisive, conclusive, authoritative. Was this the Mordechai whose imagination dominated him, whose enthusiasm so often disturbed his peace of mind? This was a new Mordechai. He grew in stature and his position grew with him. This was the commander who knows why and for whom he is doing his job."

—CHAIKA GROSSMAN, *Anshei Maḥteret* (People of the Underground)

TRAKAI: A small town in Lithuania, in an area of lakes and forests to the southwest of Vilna. Trakai was the earliest and most important of the Karaite communities in Eastern Europe.

What have you done? Your brother's blood cries out to Me from the ground! —GENESIS 4:10

. . . the blood is the life. . . . —DEUTERONOMY 12:23

I will bring a sword against you to wreak vengeance for the covenant; and if you withdraw into your cities, I will send pestilence among you and you shall be delivered into enemy hands. —LEVITICUS 26:25

"That's a good question. Let's just say smuggling Jews from ghetto to ghetto."

"Why should Germans do a thing like that, what's the point, if you've decided anyway to destroy the whole race?"

"Is that what you all think?"

"I don't know what you mean by 'you all.' That's what I think. That's what I see with my own eyes."

The truck suddenly jolted, bumping over the ruts, clods like stones splitting against the metal fenders.

The driver swore with exaggerated fury, as though trying to stem his companion's flow of words. "Heinz," he said, indicating some point on the horizon.

From caution, Sha'ul asked to be put down before they reached the town. As he got down from the vehicle, he could see the roadblock in the distance and Gestapo officers coming toward the truck. Taking cover behind a building, he watched the armed soldiers surround the truck and drag the two Germans out of it.✤

Were they really Germans or just disguised as soldiers? he asked himself, with increasing bewilderment. That same evening Sha'ul was taken to the hospital in the ghetto. At first the diagnosis was pneumonia. His mother nursed him day and night. Even when he recovered, he still didn't know the source of the cream she brought him and fed to him with a teaspoon. Since she believed that cream was a sovereign remedy for conditions of the lungs, and feared her son had caught tuberculosis and was like a candle flickering before her eyes, she obtained the cream who knows how and gave him an oral infusion morning and evening. During the second month, Sha'ul was hurriedly transferred to the secret ward of the hospital; this time it was typhus, complicated by acute dysentery.

Yitzhak was fourteen years old when Sha'ul got to know him in the hospital. Wherever Yitzhak felt free, and hidden from the eyes of strangers, he would commune with his exercise book, writing in it and concealing it, writing in it and concealing it under his pillow. One morning he waited for Sha'ul to wake up, asked how he felt, and whether he had the strength to read something.

He stressed "something" as though sharing a secret. At once he took from its hiding place a double-sized pupil's

"May his soul be bound up in the bond of life. Anton Schmidt, a German *Feldwebel* from Vienna, who risked his life while saving hundreds of Jews from the Vilna ghetto and was a loyal friend to the movement and a companion to the writer. Killed by the Gendarmerie for his contacts with us."
—MORDECHAI TANENBAUM,
from a letter to friends in Palestine, Bialystok, April 1943

exercise book, leafed through it to the end of the manuscript, folded it and put it in Sha'ul's hands. Sha'ul read on from the point the boy had indicated, and did not stop reading, even when he came across signs he could not decipher.

A restless evening descends. The alleys are full of people. Holders of yellow documents report for registration. Anyone who can . . . goes into hiding. Hides in a cellar or an attic, to save his life . . . everyone in the house goes to the hiding place. We go with them. Little guest rooms . . . steps lead from floor to floor. The steps from the first floor to the second floor are moved aside and the entrance sealed with boards . . . you enter the hiding place through a hole in the wall . . . the hole is skillfully concealed by a kitchen cabinet . . . beside the hole a barricade of stones . . . quickly we too crawl through the hole into the hiding place. There are many people gathered together in these two floors of concealment. Like shadows they lurk by candlelight around the cold, exposed walls of the cellar. . . .

We are like wild animals surrounded by hunters. Hunters on all sides. Below us, above us, to the side. Shattered locks clang, doors creak, axes, knives. I sense the hatred underneath the boards I am standing on. Light from an electric bulb penetrates through the cracks. They are knocking, breaking, tearing. The sound of assault comes again from a different direction. Suddenly a child bursts into tears. Everyone groans with desperation. We're lost. In despair the child's mouth is stuffed with sugar, but to no avail. He is covered with cushions. The mother weeps. People cry out in frantic terror: suffocate the child! The Lithuanians bang more strongly on the walls, but eventually everything grows calm. We realize they have gone away. Then suddenly we hear a voice from the other side of the hiding place: you can come out. Your heart beats with such joy: I'm still alive!

"I see you're keeping a diary. You express yourself well, my friend," he warmly complimented the boy.

"I didn't mean to ask your opinion of the writing. I wanted to ask your advice, whether I should leave it?"

"Leave what?"

BARKAI: The Hebrew translation of the Polish name of the underground radio station (SWIT–Morning Star).

THE COMMANDER'S LAST LETTER

"Something has happened beyond our wildest dreams. Twice the Germans have fled the ghetto . . . we have suffered only one casualty . . . from this evening we go over to partisan actions. Three companies will move out tonight, their task–armed patrol and the acquisition of weapons. Know that revolvers are worthless, we have hardly used them. What we need are grenades, rifles, machine guns, and explosives.

I cannot describe the conditions in which Jews are living. Only the exceptional will hold out. Everyone else will perish, sooner or later, our fate is sealed. In all the bunkers where our comrades are hiding it is impossible to light a candle at night for lack of air. . . . Farewell, beloved comrades. Maybe we shall meet again. The main thing is that the dream of our lives has come to pass. I have lived to see Jewish resistance in the ghetto in all its glory and its greatness."

—MORDECHAI ANIELEWICZ

THE REVOLT OF THE DOVES

I have likened the community of Israel to a dove.

—BERACHOT 53:72

In incredible conditions ghetto Jews rebelled and took up arms in the communities of Vilna, Bialystok, Czestochowa, Sosnowiec, Krakow; in the towns of Tuczna, Lakhva, Mir; and many others, especially in Byelorussia, in the Minsk region.

And in the death camps of Sobibor, Treblinka, and Auschwitz members of the underground rebelled or fought back. The greatest battle was the uprising of the Warsaw ghetto, which has become the symbol of Jewish resistance during the years of destruction. It was the first mass revolt anywhere in occupied Europe, which broke out without any chance of relief by external liberation forces, with no possibility of retreat, with no hope whatsoever of military victory, solely out of a desire to achieve some retribution, no matter how little, and to save the honor of the Jewish people.

Just as the Holocaust was unique among all the disasters suffered by the peoples of Europe during World War II, so the Jewish underground was unique among the anti-Nazi forces. The Jewish underground had none of the characteristic advantages of the general resistance movement: no military training, no source of supply for weapons, no recognized status among the Jewish or the general public. The organization of Jewish

"You know, things like the suffocation of the child. It's awful."

"But it happened. You saw it yourself, didn't you?"

"Yes. But . . . I don't know into whose hands my diary will fall. One day they will read it and think the Jews were animals."

"The Jews were the victims. It is they who are the animals. Remember that, Yitzhakele, don't forget it. The victims have nothing to be ashamed of, no one to hide from in shame. Come what may, the Jews in the hiding places will have no share in the disgrace of the world."

"And do you think Jews outside will understand what happened to us in the ghetto?"

"I don't understand either how you suffocate a baby. And that's happened in other hiding places, not only yours. We have been thrown into hell, my son. Funny I should say 'my son.' But sometimes I feel already a hundred years old. When you grow up you'll understand there are things worse than hell. Living in a fool's paradise, for instance. We'll survive this hell and still be human. But for life in a fool's paradise, there's no hope whatever."

Sha'ul's words seemed a little obscure to the boy. Suddenly Sha'ul laughed, then looked around in embarrassment, seemingly not knowing himself what he was laughing at.

And on the night of the third day of Passover, at half past one in the morning, Uri knocked at the window of the hospital and was admitted. And he brought Sha'ul the news that the revolt had broken out in the Warsaw ghetto. Barkai* was the name of the Polish underground radio station on which Uri had just that moment heard the stirring news. The ghetto was fighting. The largest of the Jewish communities was going up in flames and Jews were smiting their German murderers with unbelievable heroism for the third day in succession.* So said the Polish radio, and Sha'ul, in his nightshirt, barefoot and forbidden contact with anybody, hugged Uri and the two young men held each other and cried like babies. And Uri hastened to the printing cellar and by dawn the underground leaflets were flying through the alleys of the ghetto, inspiring everyone with the awesome news.

From that day on the members of the local underground never had a moment free from the thought that their own time was drawing near. And they hoarded light and heavy weapons, whatever they could lay their hands on, and drilled and practiced with growing intensity. And their ranks filled with eager recruits, and their spirit was strengthened by the example of their brothers in Warsaw.* And Warsaw no longer answered. And the Germans spread their nets with cunning and ingenuity. And on the first day of the month of Elul, in August, the signal was given. That evening the members of the command headquarters were late in sitting down to their meeting in the office of the public baths when they clearly heard the agreed signal, three taps on the door. "Something is going on," said the messenger.

The late return of the head of the *Judenrat* from Gestapo headquarters in town, unwonted alertness on the part of the ghetto policemen at all stations, reinforcements of German soldiers and armed auxiliaries—it all left no doubt that something was indeed going on.

The messengers of the underground left their comrades on urgent missions. And the young men and women wasted no time. By first light each member was at his or her post, as planned in advance, and though they were used to meeting with the five members of their cell, they were surprised now to find out who their comrades were to be. For now the secrecy was broken and relatives, close and distant, who had not known till now that they were members of the same conspiracy, found themselves assigned together. While they were shaking hands, happy to greet each other in the holy brotherhood of arms, wishing each other "Be strong and of good courage," the streets were filling with the sound of shouting and a stampede of people fleeing from pursuit.

As though in a gale, windows and front doors burst open and people bleary with sleep poked their heads out to see what the news was. By that time rumors were already spreading, as rumors will in such crazy times, and the word "*Aktion*" reechoed from the walls. Even more terrible was the word "*liquidieren*,"* which raced through the courtyards like fire in a field of thistles. And the Jews saw that the danger was very great and bolted for their hiding places. And the sounds of running feet gathered in the streets and the echoes rose from the courtyards and the indoor entrances and were gradually swallowed up by the double walls and the cellars slammed shut in alarm.

"Happy is the man who prepared a good *maline* while there was still time, for the fateful day."

Was this really the fateful day? Since Dvora's orders were to slip into town and prepare their outside contacts, she was anxious to know and kept asking Uri for his evaluation of the situation. Would she be required to distance herself from the ghetto and from her comrades when their hour of destiny struck?

But the hour left no leisure for doubts and Dvora was not the girl to allow tears to blur the facts. She changed her coat and slid down the rope to the other side of the wall, removed the yellow patch from her clothing and hurried off to raise help.

And Sha'ul left the hospital without permission from the doctors, and kept close to the walls, for his legs were still unsteady. And he saw Choni sitting in his cellar. Outside it was daylight and in front of him a candle burned.

Choni was insane. Harmless and useless he wandered the ghetto. How he succeeded in evading the *Aktionen* and surviving together with those whose work was ostensibly useful to the Germans, God in His mercy alone knows. Here he was sitting in his *kaftan** in front of an old sewing machine, working and muttering.

Sha'ul stooped down by the broken window of the cellar and said to him, "Choni, man, everyone is in hiding, what are you doing, sitting there like that?"

"I'm also hiding," Choni replied without taking his eyes off his work.

Sha'ul saw what the man was doing, sewing together strips of paper, of the kind that served for galley proofs in old time newspaper offices, with no sign of any thread in the machine, the needle just making holes in the paper without stitching. These days it might be possible to imagine he was writing some computer language, but at that time in the ghetto these were merely holes punched by a madman.

fighters had no central command, neither sponsored by a government in exile nor an agreed-upon authority on the ground. In fact, there was no contact between the groups of rebels in the different places. Every act of rebellion and revolt needs time for organization and preparation. Time ran out for Jewish action before the first revolver was acquired.

By contrast with the leadership of the *Judenrats,* the underground offered no hope of rescue, and promised nothing except the hope of active resistance to the process of slaughter. Objectively speaking, there were not even minimal conditions for existence. The fact that it came into being at all, took shape, and reached the state of active resistance is a miracle: the revolt of the ghettos, and the 30,000 to 40,000 Jewish youths who escaped from the ghettos and joined the general partisan movement in the forests. Future generations can learn not only the story of deeds of heroism by brave young men and women, but also a message worth remembering: It was the rare feeling of a sense of accountability to Jewish history that guided the members of the Jewish youth movements in their fateful decision to set up a resistance movement and fight against superior forces.

On the evening of April 19, 1943, Passover Eve 5003, the German army entered the Warsaw ghetto in order to liquidate the largest Jewish community in the world. The attacking force was to be commanded, within two days, by SS General Jürgen Stroop, one of the veterans of the campaign in Poland and Russia, an officer with considerable battle experience. At his disposal were a reinforced armored regiment, a cavalry regiment, three regiments of German police, auxiliary units of Poles and Byelorussians, heavy artillery, and engineers. Against him stood Mordechai Anielewicz. Under Anielewicz's command were at most 750 young fighters with no battle experience, armed with three light machine guns, several hundred revolvers, fourteen rifles, several hundred grenades, and explosives. On May 4, two weeks after the outbreak of the revolt, Stroop was compelled to ask for reinforcements. On May 22 Goebbels, Hitler's minister of information, recorded in his diary, "The battle in the Warsaw ghetto continues. The Jews are still resisting." On May 24 the general reported capturing 56,065 Jews, destroying 13,929 of them, and demolishing 631 bunkers. Those still alive were transferred to forced labor camps in the Lublin area; some of them were wiped out at Treblinka. The ghetto was not quiet until the winter, in September, some say in October.

"LIQUIDIEREN": Elimination.

KAFTAN: A middle-length coat that could be buttoned up on either side.

"History will record your greatness, people of the ghetto. Your slightest expression will be scrutinized, your fight for man will inspire poets. The claims of your physical pollution and spiritual debasement will be reviewed and heard. Your murderers will be denounced and pilloried to all eternity. Humanity will gaze at them in hatred and fear and will strive to guard itself from sin."

—ZELIG KALMANOVITCH,
in the Vilna ghetto,
December 12, 1942

CAMPO DI FIORI (Italian): Flower Square. This is the square in Rome where the Talmud was burned in 1553. Italy at that time was the chief center of the Hebrew printing trade, and in the 1620s the famous Christian printer Daniel Bomberg published in Venice a complete edition of the Babylonian and Jerusalem Talmuds. This was brought to the attention of the Inquisition by apostate informers who went to Pope Julius III (1550-1553) and told him that the Talmud contained anti-Christian sayings. All the copies of the Talmud were confiscated, and the Inquisitorial Court of Justice ordered them to be burned in the Campo di Fiori. Fifty years later in this same square the Italian philosopher and cosmologist Giordano Bruno was burned at the stake (1548-1600).

MIKRA'OT GEDOLOT: The books of the Bible with explanations by the rabbinic commentators, early and late: Rabbi Saadia Gaon (822-942), Rashi (Rabbi Shlomo Yitzhaki, 1040-1105), Rabbi Abraham ibn Ezra (1089-1161), Radak (Rabbi David Kimchi, 1160-1235), Ramban (Rabbi Moshe ben Nachman, 1194-1270), Ralbag (Rabbi Levi ben Gershom, 1288-1344), and others, including the Aramaic translation by Onkelos. These books contain the medieval commentaries, a tradition that continued from generation to generation for approximately 400 years.

SHASIM: Shas is the Hebrew acronym for Shisha Sidrei (Mishnah), the "six orders." The reference is to the Talmud, comprising the six orders of the Mishnah: *Zera'im* (Seeds), *Mo'ed* (Set Feasts), *Nashim* (Women), *Nezikin* (Damages), *Kodashim* (Hallowed Things), and *Toharot* (lit: Purity).

HA-TEKUFA: A Hebrew quarterly, which first appeared in Moscow in 1918, then moved to Warsaw, Tel Aviv, and later New York.

ZALMAN SCHNEOR (1887-1959): Poet and novelist who wrote in Hebrew and Yiddish. He is best known for his long poems, some of which became famous among Hebrew readers: *Ba-Harim* (In the hills), *Im Tzlilei Ha-Mandolina* (To the sounds of the mandolin), *Vilna*. Schneor won the Israel Prize in 1955 for his life's work in Hebrew poetry, his monumental novel in Yiddish *Noah Pandre,* and his book *Anshei Shokolov* (The people of Shokolov).

"We have a great history,"* said Choni, fixing his gray, watery eyes, with upturned lids, on the head of the young man framed in the window. "And I'm hiding between the lines."

And Sha'ul felt pity for Choni and said to him, "Get up and run away, time is short."

"My dear young man," said Choni, "every man has his time. And mine presses on me to finish my report."

"And what is this report you are writing?"

"I'm recording the history of the ghetto. If you want to know the verdict of history upon us, wait for Choni to reveal all to the nation. Till then it's a secret. A total secret." And Choni pressed his naked, dirty foot on the treadle of the machine and the empty needle darted up and down. And his ascetic fingers held the edge of the paper and passed it carefully under the needle, as though sewing cloth to cloth.

About this time a company of Germans came through the main gate and the ghetto police ran ahead of them to summon the people to the assembly square.

From a position near the ghetto gate there was a burst of fire, to the great surprise of the soldiers. They gathered up their wounded and fled. Then they shelled the source of the firing, and the high building that housed the rebel firing post was destroyed. Higher up the street and in neighboring streets, members of the underground took cover behind improvised firing positions. The usual practice in the world is to prepare firing positions by piling up sandbags, for sandbags offer good protection. But there was no sand in the ghetto, just as there was no sign of a lawn.

Since the headquarters post was near the library, Uri decided on books.

It was strange. They had seen and heard of books being piled on bonfires, some of them with their own eyes and some in pictures from Berlin, and some remembered reading of Campo di Fiori.* But books piled up instead of sandbags were such an extraordinary sight that at first some were shocked by the very idea, which seemed an act of vandalism. In the first row they laid the encyclopedias, and the *Mikra'ot Gedolot** and the *shasim,** interwoven row upon row. Then came the volumes of *Ha-Tekufa,** and the large dictionaries and then the classics in leather bindings.

The famous Jewish public library was there, which lacked nothing of value, and every volume bore the fingerprints of generations of readers, young and old, lovers of books and language. Now they fetched them from the dim halls and carried them to the second floor balcony in the front of the building, which faced onto the main street of the ghetto, like building workers passing bricks from hand to hand. Sha'ul received them on bended knees, building the wall of books higher and higher and leaving firing slots. Last of all he laid Zalman Schneor's* *Im Tzlilei Ha-Mandolina** (Sounds of the Mandolin) and rested his rifle on it.

On the other side of the street a piece of a sheet was hanging, probably thrown from one of the windows and caught in the telephone wires. The linen was fluttering on the wire like a flag. Hey, why don't we have a flag, wondered Sha'ul.

"Uri, why didn't we think of a flag?"

Uri looked at him in amazement:

"The living need a flag, not us," he said dryly, and took the only pair of binoculars they had in the command post. There were no Germans to be seen in the street or by the gate. What were they up to now?

Suddenly she appeared, God knows where from. "Mother?" Sha'ul was moved to see her in her jumper. She had tried to enter the courtyard of the library and the guards had stopped her. Sha'ul hurried out to meet her. "What are you doing here?"

"Are they wiping out the ghetto?"

"Apparently."✦

"What should I do?"

"What happened to the *maline?*"

"It's full."

"But there's room for you there. I built it."

"Shaulik, will they burn down the ghetto?"

"I don't know, Mother. Maybe not."

A boy and girl were crowded in the entrance, loading a machine gun. Apparently they were transferring the priceless automatic weapon to another position on the other side of the street.

"God Almighty!" his mother shuddered at the sight of the weapon of destruction being carried like a pole between the two of them—she was pale and seemed scared to talk of the devil.

"Are you taking into account the size of the risk you are running?" She grabbed him by the arm, her lips trembling. "So what do you say, where am I to go?"

And Sha'ul could neither look her in the eye nor turn his face away.

"They are setting up cannons near the timber market. The ghetto is surrounded on all sides," Uri's voice was heard from the balcony.

And Sha'ul placed the palms of his hands on his mother's cold brow and commanded her, implored her, "Hurry, Mother, while there is . . ."

"While there is what, Sha'ul?"

"While there is still time."

And once again the Germans, who had used so many tricks in spreading their nets over the whole country, did the unexpected. They sent messages to the head of the *Judenrat* and all the scared Jews that the ghetto was destined for destruction but not its inhabitants. The whole population was to be transported to another country, by the seaside, not to meet a grim fate, but near the front, where there was a great need of labor, and anyone who traveled of his own free will, he and his family would be

---

IM TZLILEI HA-MANDOLINA: A long poem, written in 1912, that describes in its first part the collapse of the pagan world and the rule of the one tyrant God, his temples and his exploits. The second part describes the temple laid to waste by Titus: "Fire, the fire of Titus, opens all doors." What is the sound of the foreign mandolin in this context? It plays from the Book of Lamentations, and tells the story of the captives in Rome. Jewish men of valor had failed; men of the spirit had won: "Would you not rather listen to a holy book / Than the rustle of the Jordan or the tumult from Lebanon?" In exile the two cultures meet and clash. In the darkness of exile the melody of the mandolin reminds the poet of "the sound of the lyres which hung there, by the waters of Babylon"—actually, when he is lonely somewhere "Under the deep skies of Italy."

"To: **Those who build their new house.**
From: **Those who are about to die.**

When, after this deluge of blood, peace comes to the earth, the balance sheet for the Jews will be a sad one. This is not the first defeat suffered by a powerless people scattered over the face of the earth—but never before has the destruction been so comprehensive—no one extended a hand to the massacred Jews, or tried to help them in any way that would enable them to flee the danger of extermination—only a tiny few preserved a measure of humanity—we shall carry the heavy burden of this isolation to our dying day, and by its light we realize that the only true watchword is self-liberation—we have paid the highest price for being lulled by the affluence of Europe, or reliant on false hopes of liberation coming from outside—instead of preparing for independence we wasted incalculable energy in foreign fields. And who knows what the future of Jewry would be without the settlers in the Land of Israel—only this nucleus of a Jewish state guarantees the continued life of the people. There would be no point in our deaths, were it not for the feeling that when we are no more there will be living there those who will think of us with true emotion. And so, in spite of certain death, we join with them in the fight for the future. Every action of ours paves the way to freedom and brings closer the establishment of an independent motherland. Our insurrection is a protest against the evil that floods the world—our fight is a fight for justice and freedom that should be a light for the whole of humanity."
—From *He-Ḥalutz Ha-Loḥem* (The Fighting Pioneer), issue 29, the underground newspaper of pioneer youth, Akiba, in Krakow

What do I hear? Weeping? Song? The notes of a harp? The sound of war?

A waterfall? A quiet river?

A lowing herd? A lion's roar?

A psalm sung in tears and joy

By old and young, to this very day.

—YECHIEL LEHRER, who died in the Holocaust at the age of 46

SCHWESTER (Yiddish): Nurse, used here as a title.

"The first company went over the barricade. The words of the commander went with them: in one hour you will be on your way. For two weeks, while we have been standing here by the wall on our last barricade, we have been speaking less and less. Without words we have held the cold metal of our weapons close to our chests, and without God we have murmured our final prayer: Let the enemy draw near. Let him approach the wall.

Our strength is too weak now to reach the other side. Fighters! The barricade is sinking. We make for the bunker. Look! On the other side of the street the doors of the houses hang loose: all the windows look out from empty houses like gaping eyes. And see—on the pavements they move in groups, without weeping.

We loved those Jews. And disliked them. We fought with them, and roused them. Hardest of all to bear is the blindness that has struck them now.

And we, we go to a place where men fall daily in battle and perhaps it is they who will behold the day of liberation, those who are being transported and not one of us.

But we have not fought merely for life, but to give meaning to life, which had lost its meaning.

And those who remain alive, whether they know it or not, their lives will be hallowed by this death.

A cry that does not end calls to us from the earth: Go on!

Remember: Till the last breath—read our first manifesto. It was many, many days ago. Two years of bloody battle. We carry on till our last breath. And perhaps—till the light."

—RUSCHKA KORCHAK-MARLE

well treated, but anyone who refused or resisted would certainly be shot. And they withdrew the soldiers from the area of the ghetto, so that they should not be targets for attacks, and left the Jews to think it over till the following morning. And they went further and invited a delegation of worthies to come to the railway station and see for themselves that a train was waiting for them as planned, entirely made up of passenger wagons, not goods trucks.

The sun dying above the rooftops was slowly giving up the ghost, without suffering. Below in the ghetto, men ran about, their hearts cut off from reason, their souls wavering and divided. They put no trust in the Germans. The Jews naturally suspected that this was just another of the familiar Nazi ruses. They were too tired of lies to fall victim to false promises.✣

But time passed, hour after hour. And as the sands of time ran out, misgivings welled up from the depths of the soul. They wondered and said: perhaps. They said: who knows? They said: maybe this time they really mean what they say. "And what's the alternative?" interjected someone, with fearful glances toward the public library building.

This night will never end! thought Uri, lying sprawled on his back on a straw mattress by the entrance to the gun position on the balcony. With his arms folded under his head, he watched the winking of the stars in the sky, his ears and every pore of his skin absorbing the murmurs that arose from beneath the floors, behind the walls, from the attics. He heard the soft footfall of comrades violating the curfew. They were creeping into courtyards and leaving in the doorways the latest handbill of the underground, calling on all brothers and sisters not to go. Incisive, trenchant, it implored them to refuse to be caught in the fatal trap laid by the Gestapo, and to resist en masse. Even as he had written the lines he had been seized with doubt. Now as he thought what was bound to happen tomorrow he felt a sharp pain stab his breast. He squeezed a nipple to release the pain. Suddenly the figure of Masha loomed in the balcony window, a hypodermic in her hand.

Schwester-Masha✣ had been called to give him an injection. It was diphtheria or measles. He was six at the time, and thin "as a rake." As a young man, too, his thinness had embarrassed him. He loved the river but was shy about appearing in his swimming costume. He hated his body and suspected that everyone could see how ugly it was. To this day he avoided shirts that clung to his body . . . all skin and bones.

"No! Schwester-Masha, no!" he had screamed.

"In such soft flesh, love, it won't hurt at all!"

"I don't have any soft flesh for jabbing!"

Schwester-Masha bared her pearly teeth and laughed, "We have enough soft flesh for one little jab."

The bells of All Hallows Church were ringing. And it was evening and it was morning, the second day.

Three hours after daybreak, crowds of thousands were already thronging the assembly points. Their belongings over their shoulders, some of them arm in arm, they awaited the movement order without guns or whips, without shouts or screams. For on that day hope had vanquished wrath. The ghetto was rapidly dwindling away, like a reservoir that had developed long continuous cracks. Uri and his companions stood on guard at their posts and the crowds below flowed and flowed like water.

"Filth," said Feivke bitterly, thumping the rampart of books with his fist.

"They are Jews like us. Flesh of our flesh," Sha'ul reproached him.

"So what?" Feivke gnashed his teeth, "Life is filth!"

At the same time Uri had called a meeting of his headquarters staff in the bookbinding room of the library, and half an hour later he came out to the men and told them, "Today at fourteen hundred hours we abandon the ghetto. Our aim is to break through to the forest."*

And the order went out to all the fighters to leave their posts and come to the rendezvous. And they brought nothing with them but their weapons.

The mouth of the sewer gaped beneath Sha'ul. Half his body was within, his feet resting on projections in the steep wall. Only the upper part of his body rose above the entrance to the pit, leaning on his elbows. The muffled sound of footsteps trampling through the sewage water reechoed from the gloomy depths.

Sha'ul turned his head once more to see if any equipment had been left behind. A pinkish ray of sunlight flickered against the opposite corner of the unplastered wall, in a tangle of cobwebs. A German motorcycle screeched deafeningly past the wall, and silence trickled back into the deserted square. A button rolled past his eyes, within spitting distance, a small button, perforated, like the eye of a dying watcher.

An obscure desire impelled him to pick up the abandoned button. At that moment he saw a shadow swelling over a white door, which had silently opened. The cat discerned the searching eyes of the man in the entrance to the sewer and ran off in the opposite direction. He could make out the street—bathed in the faint, soft light of late afternoon—that was the main artery of the ghetto. The wide open gate to the house opposite was painted green, like the gate to his parents' old house by the riverside. And Sha'ul narrowed his eyes to a slit and focused his gaze to take in the splendor of the sight, the familiar scene, the last look of a man leaving his city never to return, a look that would haunt him for the rest of his life.

And then he saw what he had least expected to see—Y. L. Markovitch walking alone down the middle of the road. He was coming from a side alley, making for the main gate of the ghetto, with no sack over his shoulder, and no suitcase. He had two books, or one large volume, clutched in his arms, and his lined face was as pale as wax. As though held by the weight of the gaze, the man suddenly stopped moving in front of Sha'ul's gaping eyes. His form stood out against the passageway between two facades, and between the man standing on the sidewalk and the man descending into the sewer there stretched no more than fifty paces. The uninvited guest would have had to lower his eyes, look past the filth in the courtyard, the broken chair, the discarded galosh, and skirt the abandoned workshop and its silent machinery in order to make out the concrete manhole cover that had been moved from its place. But Y. L. Markovitch in his crumpled, ankle-length overcoat and his formal, broad-brimmed felt hat, the kind the Russian intelligentsia used to wear, lifted his head and raised his eyebrows at some stone relief work he had noticed on the cornice of the building; he stood there pensive, wondering, in the middle of the deportation, then bent his back again and walked on.

His face bore the dull despondency that the shock of baseless rumors, malicious tricks, and inauspicious signs of truth stamped on people whose minds had been deranged by living on the edge of doom to a state of total loss of feeling. And yet Markovitch's face had the look of a man who knows something for certain that is not a lie.*

Sha'ul remembered the failure of their meeting. How much he had disliked the man. "Ugh! These corrupt intellectuals!" He had spat as they left the doorway of the building and almost spat on Uri's shoes from anger and offense. Now it passed slowly across his face like the quiet flight of a bird moving across the screen, soaring slowly toward the hills.

"Fear stalks the streets. Promises that nothing evil will befall if the ghetto refrains from undesirable acts. But who knows what is desirable, if we are all–righteous and wicked alike–to suffer the same fate . . . something seems about to happen. Something is imminent. Something significant hangs over our heads. Hiding places are being prepared. Is it possible? I strive to show the neighbors I am not worried about the future. Really, trouble is enough now. . . . Without noticing you adjust to the mood of your surroundings, you breathe in shock from the air. People's faces look grim. Eyes look out upon vacancy. Each man inspires dread in his neighbor. I have had enough of enduring my fate. When I am alone there is no trace of fear in my heart. Complete confidence reigns. Is it complacency? No. I want to see clearly, and above all to tell the Jews beyond the ghetto what is happening. How does the Jewish soul respond on whom the heavy hand has not rested? What are the consequences for the life of the community? Will a heavy sledgehammer subdue steel?"

—ZELIG KALMANOVITCH,
July 13, 1943,
in the Vilna ghetto

For this stunted, skinny figure Sha'ul suddenly felt an attraction, as though an electric current ran through him as he moved away. Many good men will try to explain the events and fears of this period. Scholars will investigate and thinkers wise after the event will find it difficult to know how the people sat solitary between the walls, shouting in blood with no one to hear. If only we had built not *malines* when it was too late but one sure refuge in good time; if only the leaders had been real leaders at a time when everything could already be foreseen and they still held authority; and how would it have been if only there had been unity in the ghetto, not only of the perceptive but of the whole population, and in every congregation the leaders had helped to dispel complacency and had not outlawed courage—God Almighty!* We shall never know the solution to this painful riddle; would the result really have been any different? And Sha'ul, it was not this man who was your rival. You shared in the same disaster. "We'll crush you like dogs!" said the Germans, and in their eyes you surely looked like mad dogs. But you got nothing from them, neither Y. L. Markovitch nor you, and your comrades did not compromise. Too proud to feel humiliated, each in his own way tried to preserve his humanity. Thus you met your destiny. And thus you will render your account. The scroll of the destruction of this temple will be recorded in history according to the testimony of these two witnesses.

"Sha'ul?" Uri called again from the bottom of the sewer, "are you still there? We're moving!"

And they moved. Hands touching feet, they crawled on slowly, stomachs immersed in foul slime, revolvers between their teeth, one long, long line thrusting forward—a giant centipede winding its way underground, already under the ghetto wall, making for the outskirts of the city and deliverance. The sewage water dripped from open pipes that gleamed like the maws of insects, flowed into the stream in the central channel with a ring like tiny bells, the echoes reflecting off the vaulted tunnels built of stone and bricks, smooth faced and uniform like the skin of a leech. Someone stumbled and fell and a volley of excrement sprayed his face or splattered against his neck and slid under his collar. In the third hour after leaving the ghetto, the head of the line reached the exit from the sewer in the city suburbs, where Dvora and her companions were signaling from outside to guide them. And they spent that night in an old palace, and the city was surrounded by troops and immensely powerful searchlights swept the earth and the sky. And they were not permitted to fall asleep, only to rid themselves of excrement and slime. And they rose and set off on foot, making a detour through fields and ditches, and under army bridges, throughout the night, weapons in hand, with Uri at their head. And in the early hours of the morning Dvora, who was with the scouts, saw the dark blue mass on the horizon and her heart pounded like a sailor at the masthead and she cried out to those who followed her, "The forest!"

And the losses sustained in the escape from the ghetto were five. Four clashed with a patrol of soldiers and killed the officer; they were captured and hanged. And Dvora's childhood friend was the fifth, whom Uri had sent off before dark to reconnoiter the approaches to the forest, and she had been caught in an ambush and never returned. And Uri gave orders to stretch ropes across the river, which separated them from the forest. And the men went into the raging water in their clothes, holding their weapons in one hand and the taut rope in the other, and the clear water washed away both the filth and the despair. They moved ahead in a long winding column. The further they penetrated into the tall trees, the more the silence of the forest subdued them. And Sha'ul was left to himself. He watched his comrades pass him at the end of the beaten path, swallowed up in the dense forest that gave them cover, without noticing him. Kneeling, he leaned his forehead against a huge trunk, which must have been uprooted in a storm, and when the last of the survivors disappeared into the undergrowth, Sha'ul stretched out on the soft moss and burst into tears.

As though from close at hand he saw the market square, the neighing of the horses, the bellowing of the cows, the bleating of the sheep. The pigs tied to the farmers' carts, squirming as though in a fit. The hens crowing and the

---

"It should not be said that those put to death died ignoble deaths, even though they went like lambs to the slaughter. The living people of Israel will always remember them with respect. Their deaths will be the mark of shame for their plunderers. Their deaths redeemed the sins of their generation. People on this earth will know how God's innocent people were murdered. People all over the world will remember them, and their memory will be a sign for later generations, that if in time to come a tyrannical spirit arises to dominate people's souls, they will remember what a cruel tyrant perpetrated on the people of Israel and will be resolute to suppress that evil spirit before it spreads. Honor and value those with whose sacrifice came the birth pangs of salvation." —ZELIG KALMANOVITCH, July 12, 1943, in the Vilna ghetto

cocks singing solo and himself helping his mother carry tools to their cart.[*]

"How much for a scythe, brother?"

"How much for a cooking pot?"

How much for our lives?

I hear you, my son, even in your silence.

And his body writhed as he wept and the carpet of moss was soft as a cradle. His coat was drenched and heavy on him as an iron weight. His pistol was deep in his pocket, his fingers gripped the cold steel of their own accord. He may have cried himself out or ceased for some other reason. Suddenly with unprecedented lucidity he saw the oak trees with their mighty trunks towering above him, the treetops rising up to support the ends of the sky, the foliage golden in the soft light of dawn, the sheaf of rays whose light was scattered as from an upturned sword at the entrance to the secret garden, the quiet flutter of a mother bird returning to the nest, food in her beak for the fledglings, dewdrops hanging down and the glow of an autumn morning rising out of the mist. The hammers of pain ceased to throb in his temples and for the first time in his life he seemed to see the world that surrounded him as something becoming full, satisfied, and indescribably beautiful.

During their second year in the forest, General Fyodor Gregoryevitch set up camp opposite the camp of the Jewish partisans. And Sha'ul heard about this and went to see him and found him mounted on a horse. And he told him all that had befallen him, and Fyodor Gregoryevitch was lenient and did not treat his absence as desertion. Neither did he ask whether Sha'ul had succeeded in rescuing his mother or not. At one point in Sha'ul's story, the general wiped away a tear with a gray finger. They exchanged greetings and filled the cup like good companions, commanders sparing in speech, and they went their way. And one of the general's adjutants, a stocky, red-haired Jew, brought an exercise book wrapped in a cloth binding and said, "If you're Sha'ul, your nephew left this for you, for when you return. Velvele was here. The lad followed you and never came back."

> no one will carry my mother's bier with me
> no one will come close to my mother's bier with me
> come to the vast plains
> lead your eyes to the white river
> it scoops out its channel and shoves
> like the prow of a heavy
> ship in the ice
> and say with me
> imi
> imi
>
> —ABBA KOVNER,
> "My Little Sister"

✤ The Fourth Scroll ✤

Ash of the Heavens

Then I looked, but there was none to help;
I stared but there was none to aid—
So My own arm wrought the triumph,
And My own rage was My aid.

—ISAIAH 63:5

Does Birkenau Exist?

Is it a town?
No, it's not a town. There are no people.
What can you see through the crack, young man?
Black uniforms.
SS?
They're approaching the wagons. With whips. In their
    hands. Just a moment.
There's a sign.
What's written on the sign?
Bir-ke-nau.

Does Birkenau exist? We looked for it on the map and couldn't . . . The wagon suddenly opens. Dogs. Germans. Lined up. With whips. Get out. Get out. Everybody running. From all the wagons. Children crying. And women. I fell down. Run. A whip lashes out. Oh, my glasses. I must find them. Another whiplash. My eyes fill with blood. It's running down from my forehead. Thank God! Only one lens is broken. I can see the professor holding on to the sleeve of a man in a striped shirt, is he Jewish? The professor asks him, "Sir, does Birkenau exist?"

The man nods impatiently. At the same moment the SS push the old professor to the left. A mother picks up her child and gets a blow on the head from a truncheon. Left. Left. Professor Albert! I wave to him. He cannot hear.

Our line is pushed to the right.

✧ CHAPTER ELEVEN ✧

Passover in the Seventh Block

When the Nazis came to power, they needed concentration camps as an instrument of terror against opponents of the regime. When they occupied a country, they needed camps as a means of breaking the spirit of other nations. When prisoners of war were taken, they were needed as enclosures for slaves, for forced labor and starvation, and some of these prisoners also reached the concentration camps. When they began implementation of the Final Solution, the Germans invented death camps, the first in human history. And these shall be remembered to the end of time:

CHELMNO: A camp not far from the large Jewish working class center of Lodz. At first the method was to use gas trucks, and later crematoria. Here were slain 350,000 Jews from Lodz, Czechoslovakia, Germany, Belgium, France, Luxembourg, and Holland.

SOBIBOR: A camp on the banks of the Bug River. In nine gas installations surrounded by forest, 250,000 Jews from eastern Poland and other parts of Europe were slain. The remaining pris-

Nowhere in the world was

worse than Auschwitz,

except Birkenau.

And the seventh

block was worst

of all.✦

oners rebelled in 1943, and a few dozen succeeded in escaping to the forests and survived. After the revolt, the SS liquidated the camp and gave orders for trees to be planted over the ash.

BELZEC: A camp near the city of Lvov. Here were slain 600,000 Jews from Galicia and other Diaspora communities.

TREBLINKA: A camp in the Warsaw region. Here were slain 900,000 Jews from Poland, Germany, Austria, Czechoslovakia, Bulgaria, and Greece.

MAJDANEK: A camp near Lublin. Here were slain 350,000 people from 22 countries, 175,000 of them Jews.

AUSCHWITZ-BIRKENAU: A death combine. Near the Polish town of Oswieczim there were 40 satellite camps in the largest unit of the extermination system, which has become a symbol of Nazi atrocities. It was in Auschwitz that the gas Zyklon B was first used. Here 1,100,000 Jews were slain in the gas chambers, as well as 20,000 Gypsies and 230,000 other non-Jews.

The Story of Rabbi Raphael

This is the story of Rabbi Raphael Habib[*] from Salonika and Rabbi Nathan Cassuto, the rabbi of Florence, and the young man Gonda Redlich, of the Czech pioneer youth, and the boy, the one they called "the good-looking boy," who together with his father had been deported from France: they all celebrated Passover together in the seventh block of the largest death camp the Germans had set upon the soil of occupied Poland. "The seventh," *di zibele*[*] in the argot of the inmates of Auschwitz-Birkenau,[*] was the block for the sick, the last stop before the furnaces.

All night, in the faintest whisper, they had been telling the story of the Exodus from Egypt. With their legs hanging down from their bunks, they repeated by heart what they could remember, helping each other out; they had also begun by blessing the two wafers, a kind of matzah that they had prepared well ahead, fearfully and in great secrecy, "bread of affliction"[*] in every sense. They tasted nothing else, despite the gnawing hunger, and drank only the four measured sips of water they had set aside, no more; then they placed their elbows on their knees and began to sing the traditional songs.

Gonda held his chin in his bandaged hand. The others covered their sunken, unshaven cheeks. They could hardly be said to be singing, for only their lips moved soundlessly. Even so, it was clear from the movement of their bodies that each sang a different tune.

They could hear at intervals the thud of the guard's boots outside and the barking of his dog. And Gonda said, "The time is coming when released prisoners will return home. And the Jewish people will once again celebrate this festival of freedom properly with all due splendor. Will it be possible for Jews, in time to come, to sit around the Passover table and tell of the Exodus from Egypt without telling of the exodus from Auschwitz?"[*]

His companions were shocked by the acuteness of the young man, gaping at his question, visibly and inwardly, each of them silent. Eventually Rabbi Nathan answered, "A survivor will come and enlighten them."

The rabbi from Florence was still a young man. He looked less like a rabbi destined to be the leader of the slaughtered than a professor who had been involved in a serious accident. Not much was left of his tall, willowy stature, though the mark of nobility had not been effaced from his features, cleft and swollen by blows from trun-

---

RABBI RAPHAEL HABIB: Chief rabbi of Salonika. During the German occupation he swept the streets with the rest of the Jewish men, who were rounded up for this menial labor before they were deported to the death camps. Rabbi Habib refused to allow any attempt to be made to exempt him from this forced labor. He was sent to Auschwitz and perished there.

DI ZIBELE (Yiddish): The seventh. This is a name for a child born after seven months of pregnancy.

AUSCHWITZ-BIRKENAU: The largest Nazi concentration camp and death camp. It was set up in April 1940, in Galicia, west of Krakow and south of Sosnowiec and Katowice in Silesia. The first camp held Polish political prisoners. The second camp was called Birkenau (after the nearby Polish village). The commander of the camp, Rudolph Hoess, was assigned the main role in implementing the Final Solution, that is, the physical annihilation of the Jewish people. In September 1941, the first experiments with the gas Zyklon B were carried out. The first victims were 900 Soviet prisoners of war. In January 1943, the gas chambers, disguised as showers, and four ovens (the crematorium) for incinerating the bodies (instead of burying them) were built. Already in March 1942, the Nazis had begun the mass destruction of Jews at Auschwitz-Birkenau. Trains arrived from all parts of Europe, loaded with consignments of Jews for slaughter: from Poland, Slovakia, France, Italy, Holland, Belgium, Yugoslavia, Norway, Germany, Latvia, Austria, Greece, and North Africa. An underground sabotage movement was formed in the camp. With the retreat of the German army, Himmler gave orders for the gas installations to be dismantled and all traces of the slaughter to be erased (November 1944). More than a million Jews, Gypsies, and members of other nations met their deaths in Auschwitz. On January 27, 1945, the Red Army liberated the camp and the 6,750 Jews and others who were left there.

"BREAD OF AFFLICTION": "This is the bread of affliction which our fathers ate in the land of Egypt. Let all who are hungry enter and eat, and all who are needy come and celebrate the Passover. This year we are here, next year in the Land of Israel! This year we are slaves, next year free men!"

—FROM THE
PASSOVER HAGGADAH

CONSPIRACY OF SILENCE: The enlightened world fought against the Nazis, and only a few good men in this new Sodom, the Righteous Gentiles, did their best to save a few Jews. Was it just indifference to the fate of millions of innocent men, women, and children—or were the decision makers in the free world not untainted by a well-rooted anti-Semitic attitude? Even during the hardest days of World War II, long-range bombers took off from bases in England to bomb an isolated prison in France and help in the escape of British agents and members of the underground who were imprisoned there. The Jewish underground sent desperate appeals for the bombing of the railway lines to Auschwitz and not a single plane took off from the free world, not even in an attempt to bomb the crematorium, which in the last year of the war burned on average 1,000 Jews a day. It is not only in Germany that children have good reason to ask their parents difficult questions. After the war those responsible for this culpable omission had a wealth of excuses, military and technological. A few had the courage to admit that in their eyes Jews just did not seem sufficient reason for making such an unorthodox decision as bombing Auschwitz.

cheons. Gradually he straightened his back like a young palm tree freed from restraint and continued with passion.

"And I ask you, if he tells what happened to him personally, how will he enlighten them? What happened to one man cannot suffice to tell the story of our times, not even in summary. A few will survive, solitary embers. And if a survivor can tell no more than what he himself went through, how can he be a "witness for his generation"?*

His companions stared, Gonda too, wondering where his words were leading.

Nathan Cassuto continued, "In every generation a Jew has seen himself as the sum of all previous generations. Our forefathers did not hand down to us their personal experiences, or not that alone; what we received from them was the story of the people and the individual. It is the whole story that to this day has shaped our character. Perhaps each of us here and now is charged with the holy duty of hearing what happened to the others, not only to himself, so that when the time comes, whoever of us survives will be able to serve as a mouthpiece for the many, "for we bear witness before You"; and if we cannot be the sum of everything our people have undergone under Nazi rule, we can be the sum of this block in Birkenau."

The steps of the guards outside drew near. German called to German. Dog barked to dog. "So let us make this night a night of vigil; before we depart for the darkness of oblivion, let us share our knowledge, something we have never done till now. Let each of us place his story in the safe keeping of his companion's memory and, God willing, the last of us fated to survive will be the first to write the scroll of testimony for his generation. And let us say this to our brothers in the other blocks, and they shall do likewise."

His penetrating remarks were heard in total simplicity, entering their hearts like good news. The man from Florence gave the man from Salonika, who had said little, a glance of encouragement, raising his eyebrows and smiling in apology, lest what he had said sounded too pathetic.

"I am not sure you will understand, but on such an evening in Auschwitz you could see skeletons reciting poetry." —ANONYMOUS

TARBUSH: A felt or cloth hat with a tassel, similar to a fez.

If Only This Time: The Story of Rabbi Habib, Which Begins Far Off and Ends Behind the Wall

He moved his body in a strange way, like a palm leaf whose spine had cracked. It was some time before Raphael Habib began to speak, for his mind was elsewhere.

He was walking along the promenade like one of the grownups, holding his grandfather's hand so as not to go astray in the crowd. The whole town was there after the Sabbath luncheon, and everyone knew his grandfather and paid him respect: "*Shabbat shalom, El-Ḥakham, Shabbat shalom.*" On every side people greeted him with pleasure, drew near, and if they didn't actually shake his hand, they would make do with pinching Raphael's cheek. But Raphael was looking at the boats bobbing at anchor on the waves. All work in the harbor had ceased, including the Greek and Turkish firms, for Shabbat in Salonika was Sabbath for the whole town. As they were passing the White Tower, *El-Nono* came up to them; he was not old or perhaps old but not showing it, and everyone called him that, for he was the senior stevedore in the port. In the eyes of Raphael, *El-Nono* was like one of those bold Genoese sailors who had built the White Tower. The Genoese had lived hundreds of years ago but Grandfather told of their wonderful exploits as though they were still living. Grandfather still wore a tarbush,* a robe, and a fur cape in the old style, but *El-Nono* wore a tarbush with European clothes.

The foreman of the stevedores greeted Grandfather, kissed his hand, and said to the rabbi, "*El-Ḥakham*, let me tell you something that happened three days ago. There was a traveler, a Belgian. I was carrying his luggage from the harbor and I could tell from his bags that he was some kind of a professor, though he looked like a merchant. He was actually an amiable fellow, the Fleming, and he was trying to place the identity of this porter striding so easily, despite the load.

"'Are you Greek, monsieur?' the foreigner asked me in French.

"'No, monsieur, I'm a Jew,' I replied.

"'You mean a Greek Jew?'

"'No, monsieur, I was born in Salonika.'

"'In other words, a Turkish Jew?'

"He interrogated me the way professors do, and I replied, 'I'm a Jew, monsieur.'

"'Nothing more?'

SALONIKA: The main port of Macedonia, in the north of Greece. The Jewish community in Salonika was one of the most ancient diasporas in the world; Jews settled there in the second century B.C.E. and the community is mentioned in the New Testament (Acts of the Apostles 17). The major increase in Salonika's Jewish community took place after the expulsion from Spain in 1492. Thousands of families of Jewish refugees from the West came together there. Salonika opened to them the gates of commerce, trade, and other occupations. The Jews of Salonika were shipowners and sailors, fishermen, port workers and stevedores, carpenters, glaziers, blacksmiths, metalworkers, boiler makers, printers and bookbinders, woodcarvers, shoemakers, weavers, tailors, bakers, butchers, tanners, and specialists in the tobacco industry, among others. The Ottoman authorities were also well disposed toward the Jews, who worked wonders in all branches of the economy. There were of course difficult times brought about by blood libels, and during the Greek struggle for independence (in 1821, for instance). At the beginning of the twentieth century, Jews were the majority of the population of Salonika. After the revolution of the "Young Turks" in 1908, there was some emigration of Salonikan Jews to the West (to the United States, Argentina, and France). A huge fire in 1917 caused severe damage to the property of the Jewish community. Nevertheless, for many years the Jews of Salonika held the most important positions in the economic, social, and cultural life of the city—until the German occupation on April 9, 1941. From here on began the policy of extinction. The Jews of Salonika were concentrated in a ghetto, and in the summer of 1943 the slaughter of this ancient Jewish community was decreed. Nearly 60,000 Jews were deported to Auschwitz, where they were killed in the gas chambers.

LADINO: A Judeo-Spanish language also known as Judezmo, written in Hebrew script. The language originated in Spain and was widespread among the Spanish Jewish communities after the expulsion (1492), especially in Greece, Turkey, Bulgaria, Holland, and Israel. In Salonika there were Ladino daily newspapers.

PAPPAS: A Greek Orthodox priest.

"Imagine now a man who is deprived of everyone he loves, and at the same time of his house, his habits, his clothes, in short, of everything he possesses: He will be a hollow man, reduced to suffering and needs, forgetful of dignity and restraint, for he who loses all often easily loses himself. He will be a man whose life or death can be lightly decided with no sense of human affinity, in the most fortunate of cases, on the basis of a pure judgment of utility. It is in this way that one can understand the double sense of what we seek to express with the phrase: 'to lie on the bottom'."

—PRIMO LEVI,
Survival in Auschwitz

"At that point we reached the door of the hotel and I had already taken his sealskin leather case down from my shoulder.

"I wiped my hands on the back of my trousers and said, 'God be praised, nothing more!'

"The foreigner stared at the middle of my forehead, as though unable to believe there wasn't a third eye there."

El-Nono laughed aloud and Grandfather chuckled. And it had taken Raphael the whole of twenty years to understand why *El-Nono* and *El-Ḥakham* had been so amused in the middle of the promenade on the Sabbath before Passover.

Now the promenade is empty of Jews.

The White Tower, seen by seagoing Crusaders, Serbs, Turks, Bulgarians, and other seafaring nations as they rose and fell, looked out over a Jewish city, which had been thriving continuously for five hundred years. Could all that have been wiped out? Will they never again say "*Shabbat shalom*" in the streets of Salonika;[+] will hard-working, stiff-necked, barefoot dock workers never again leave the quayside talking Ladino;[+] will the great Hebrew day school be silent, and Jewish mothers no longer see their daughters leaving the Alsheykh and Alliance high schools talking happily as young people do; will the league of poets never get together again in the afternoon to sing both religious hymns and pioneer songs from the land of Israel; and on national holidays will Jewish guilds no more carry their banners proclaiming Torah and work as a way of life to the people of Salonika? Who will tell them?

Who will tell them about Kirya Ne'emana? This was no village, no ghetto. A Jewish republic almost, between the sea and the hinterland. Eighty thousand inhabitants, rich and poor. Woodcutters and workers from tobacco and textile factories. Doctors and nurses, lawyers and writers, and the fire brigade, renowned for their bravery. Above all respected merchants, not to be taken lightly, neither by themselves nor by anyone else, since, as they said in Salonika, Jews were capable of doing any work except being a *pappas!*[+]

And when they put them in the railroad wagons and slammed the doors and bolted them, the brave people of Salonika felt their spirits fall. The sudden transition from light to profound darkness was insupportable. Anybody who was taken one morning from his home nestling among the orchards, uprooted from a life of grace and security and thrown head first into a railroad truck designed to carry cattle to slaughter, felt crushed under a mountain.[+] Slowly the sound of voices died away and the clatter of the train wheels grew louder. Already they had traveled beyond the city limits, beyond the realm of the known. At that moment, when everyone was silent as though struck dumb, a woman's sobbing was heard from one end of the truck. It rose and cut through the air from one end of the truck to the other, unceasing.

"You may be right, Rabbi Nathan, that one day people will want to know what happened to us. They may also want to understand the nature of the experience we underwent. Tell me, will it just be Jewish curiosity that moves them or will they be genuinely anxious to know what lesson must be learned from all these horrors?

"So it may be important to remember something beyond the atrocities they are committing. Know, then, that that sobbing by an unknown Jewish woman at the end of a cattle truck full of crushed and downtrodden Jews was for me a blazing symbol of life. I suddenly realized that weeping—no matter how bitter—is the symbol of struggling humanity. At that moment it was as though I heard a voice calling in the words of Ezekiel, 'Live, in spite of your blood. Live, in spite of your blood.'*

With some effort I rose to my feet, for this was already the second day of our journey, and I, Raphael Habib, said to them, 'Weep, weep, my children. Weep aloud, weep bitterly, for there is nothing worse than despair that cannot weep.' And when they realized who it was that gave them this command, they all began to weep aloud. The sobbing and the wailing were earsplitting, you have never heard the like. The sounds of lamentation must have burst forth and been carried across the fields of Poland, whose borders the train crossed that night. And miraculously, when we reached the gates of Auschwitz, and the doors were thrown open, and there was no wagon without its dead—many did not have the strength to survive the journey—only in our truck were we all standing on our feet, terrified and exhausted, but all one hundred of us standing there, a stiff-necked people."

The father of the good-looking boy said, "That pile of bodies in the truck. The stench, after four days traveling, the perpetual gloom, the heavy breathing, the sudden pain in your loins. The shame. Replaced by lack of shame even more corrosive: you shut your eyes and let your water flow. Worst of all was the terrible pain in my ribs, broken by the rifle butt of the French Fascist at Drancy, when I refused to be separated from my son. I couldn't help kicking my neighbor in the stomach, an old Jewish merchant from Paris who was writhing on the floor of the truck with an attack of kidney trouble and almost crushed my wounded ribs. I held my son by the head, that he might have a little more room between my crossed thighs, and lifted his face toward the barred window and thought only of one thing, breathing. Ah, just let him breathe. My

friends, I am not by nature a strong man. But never in my life have I been so strong as on that four days' journey to Auschwitz."

"Five, Papa," said the son.

And he who had said before that he did not know who would remain to bear witness, and therefore it seemed to him important they should remember what happened to themselves and to each other, touched Raphael Habib on the shoulder and encouraged him to continue the tale from where he had left off. The rabbi of Salonika said:

"I remember Reb Arieh Geiger from Munkacz,* a simple Jew who was with us at the previous camp; he used to get up at two in the morning, touch me softly and press me to lend him my tefillin. At such an early hour he could say his prayers with devotion, dwelling on them as he used to in Munkacz. But by three there would be other Jews standing in line to use my tefillin, and so it would go on until ten past five, for at a quarter past five we had to be outside on parade for roll call. Sometimes I had to make do with a shortened prayer, when the tefillin came back to me, the last in line.

"Then came the day when an SS officer burst into the hut on a surprise inspection while it was still dark, and in the beam of his flashlight saw the figure of Reb Arieh standing against the eastern wall, something strange on his forehead and straps around his arm. The German tore the headpiece off and ordered the *Stube*⁺ to burn the tefillin publicly. Reb Arieh, a frail man by nature who now weighed less than forty kilo, was punished with twenty-five lashes, and almost breathed his last under the whip. Fortunately for us, this *Stube* was one of the criminal prisoners, and could be bribed. One of the young men who worked in the camp carpentry shop made a second set of tefillin, adding black painted straps to the boxes, and it was the fake tefillin that were burned at the stake.

"Yesterday there were two Jews here in the dispensary,

'LIVE, IN SPITE OF YOUR BLOOD. LIVE, IN SPITE OF YOUR BLOOD': When I passed by you and saw you wallowing in your blood, I said to you, "Live in spite of your blood." Yea, I said to you, "Live in spite of your blood."
—EZEKIEL 16:6

MUNKACZ: A town in the Carpatho-Russian region, in the eastern part of Czechoslovakia. The official name of the town is Mukacevo. Between the two world wars there was a large Jewish population in Munkacz, numbering more than 10,000. In the past Munkacz was a center of the Hasidic movement, founded by students of the "Seer of Lublin."

STUBE (German): Short for *Stubenälteste,* the term for the man in charge of the prisoners in one room of a hut.

MUSULMAN: Camp slang for a camp prisoner who is thin and physically wasted away from hunger, with no more strength, looking like a living skeleton.

KENDE: A term for the department where the workers in Auschwitz stored and sorted the clothes and property of the prisoners due to be destroyed.

BLOCK 27: The area of the punishment and torture cells at Auschwitz.

THE BLACK HUNDRED: Gangs of ruffians formed at the beginning of the twentieth century to serve as punishment units loyal to the Czar of Russia. These units were designed to "restore order" wherever revolutionary elements raised their heads and grew in number. Most of the activities of these squads were riots directed against the Jews, who were regarded as disloyal.

THE GREAT POGROMS IN RUSSIA: The pogroms of the 1880s that followed the attempt on the life of Czar Alexander II (March 1, 1881). The reign of Alexander III (1881-1894) was a period of grim and evil reaction, carried out by means of an organized, methodical system of crude and arbitrary administrative and police terrorism. In the months of April and May 1881, pogroms broke out in the southwest of Russia. In the spring of 1882 there was a large-scale pogrom in the town of Balata (northeast of Kishinev). The policy of the authorities was to stand aside and do nothing to stop the rioters until they had wreaked their will. And the rioters of course took the hint. A second wave of pogroms broke out 20 years later, following the attempt by revolutionaries on the life of the minister of the interior, the stern Pleve. Russian failures in battle (in the Russo-Japanese War, 1904-1905) caused a revolutionary ferment, which the authorities tried to divert against the Jews. They succeeded. Bloody pogroms took place in several cities—Zhitomir, Odessa, Kiev, Kishinev, Yekaterinoslav, Kamenetz-Podolsk, and several other places—right after the promulgation of the Czar's declaration concerning the granting of liberties and a constitution on October 30, 1905.

one of them was Geiger. I didn't recognize him. He leaned toward me and said, 'Rabbi, I'm the man who used to wake you up at night . . . now I have my own.' As he spoke, he touched a small swelling under his shirt, visible on the side of his heart. 'Apparently there was another set in the camp. You may not remember him, but the carpenter who made the fake tefillin? He was a *musulman*,* and before he died he gave me the set he had hidden. Honestly, Rabbi, I didn't steal them.'"

Gonda said, "I saw him as he left, fearfully fingering something under his shirt. He too is already a *musulman*."

"One and two.

"One and three.

"One and four.

"The boy lay stretched on his wooden bunk, his head hunched between his appallingly thin shoulders, his white arms limp beside his body. The rubber truncheon landed on his back like a blacksmith's hammer. I counted the blows, ritually, like the High Priest in the Temple on the Day of Atonement.

"Seven. Eight. Nine—

"And ten.

"The Gestapo officer from Camp B was notorious for his cruelty. Now he stood over the boy and it was clear he was in a fiendish temper. He could be heard counting, and frothing at the mouth.

"Twenty. Twenty-one. Two. Three—

"The bunk in Block 25 on which our boy lay prostrate had seen innumerable bloody whippings. But even this murderer of ours had never seen anything quite like this before. He stood, boots astride, huge, brawny, towering over the puny body of a boy of fourteen or fifteen, a worthless Jewboy, who took blow after blow, without crying out, without pleading for mercy—

"Twenty-seven. Eight—

"Was he still alive? Frozen to the spot, silent, other prisoners stood around. After the fortieth blow, the whipped body slipped to the floor. The German turned him over with the point of his boot. He was still alive.

"Now the truncheon landed on the boy's bare stomach, on his legs, and finally across his face. A strangled snort was heard, but no cry.

"Fifty!

"The German spat and left.

"His companions laid him on the straw mattress and sponged the blood with damp rags.

"'What did you do?' they asked. The boy was silent.

"They asked again, the boy remained silent.

"At last he opened his eyes and pronounced the words as though pushing them through his wounded lips, 'I found three prayer books in the *kende** and smuggled them in to the men in Block 27.*

"'*It was worth it.*'

"You told us about the power of weeping, Rabbi Habib. I have been thinking about the power of not crying," said Rabbi Nathan in summary.

"In books," began Gonda of Prague, "we read about the cry that was the last weapon of the victims."

His words were obscure. Perhaps few in Florence, Paris, or Salonika had heard of the Black Hundred.* The movement youth leader reminded them of the origins of the great pogroms in Russia.* How the Jews would shut themselves in their houses whenever the galloping hooves of the Cossack horses were heard approaching the settlement. How from a whole village, secure behind lock and bolt, an unending cry would arise, wailing that continued all night and the next day and another night, wave upon wave, so terrifying that the galloping horses would stumble in their tracks, rear up, and paw the ground, unwilling to advance, and in the end this awesome scream would put the murderers to flight before they could do their worst.

"But our persecutors are worse than the Black Hundred. They have a heart of stone, they know neither fear nor mercy."

Gonda left no time for wonder. Clearly he wanted to make his point. "There was a member of the block with me in Birkenau, younger than me, making out he was a man, who saw a large transport arrive from Hungary. Among those who were rushed straight from the trucks to the *Himmelstrasse** was an old rabbi, Shalom Eliezer Halberstam.* When the old man had stripped he saw this boy collecting up the clothes and seized him by the arm.

"Pointing to the gas chambers, he asked, 'My son, have you been inside there already? You're dressed.'

"My friend was startled by the look on the old man's face and replied with eyes lowered, 'I'm from the *Sonder,** Rabbi, I work here.'

"'Where are you from?'

"'Kruke.'"*

"'The birthplace of the holy Rabbi Moses Isserles!* Are there any Jews left in Krakow?'

"'No, Rabbi.'

"'*Oy veh!* My brother was there—Rabbi Yeshayele Matchikow—you've heard of him?'

"'Rabbi Shayah is your brother . . . then you must be the *tzaddik* from Retzfert?'

"'How do you know that, my son?'

"'I am from a family of Hasidim. Holy Rabbi, pray for us!' the boy cried with feeling. But the old man had suddenly started to shiver. His whole naked body trembled as he held my friend by the shoulders.

"'Is it true that evil men beat people in there?'

"'No, Rabbi, there are no beatings in there.'

"'Are you sure?'

"'I'm sure.'

"'God bless you, my son.'

"By that time the Hungarian deportees had finished undressing and the huge crowd was being pushed toward the gas chambers.

"As they were moving the rumor must have spread about the nature of the showers awaiting them behind the massive doors. The herd of naked men began a blood-curdling scream.

"'Holy Rabbi, say your confession,' the boy pressed him.

"'But I'm naked,' said the old man in his innocence.

"'Holy Rabbi, hurry up and pray,' the boy urged.

"Suddenly the old man realized what was in store. His eyes closed and he could be heard praying. His voice rose, he sang with joy, it was like rain falling on a fire—at once the screaming of the crowd died down. Now they moved quietly, only the rustle of their bare feet accompanied the rabbi's prayer.

"My friend, whose hand was held between the rabbi's fingers, almost failed to notice he was being dragged by force inside. At the very last moment the rabbi opened his eyes and pushed him away. 'You will survive, my son, and you have a duty to tell . . .' and said no more. They were on opposite sides of the threshold."*

HIMMELSTRASSE (German): Literally, the street of heaven. *Himmelstrasse* was camp slang for the corridor leading to the gas chambers.

SHALOM ELIEZER HALBERSTAM: A Hasidic rabbi and sage from Racapart, Halberstam was the son of Rabbi Chaim Halberstam (1793-1876) of Zanz, who was regarded as the foremost halakhic authority of his time and leader of the talmudic sages, and the brother of Rabbi Yeshayeleh of Chakhuyov. Halberstam perished at Auschwitz.

SONDER (German): Short for *Sonderkommando*, a special unit of Jews who worked in the crematoria. The members of this unit were the last to be designated for slaughter, but their turn too would come. On October 7, 1944, the members of the *Sonder* at Birkenau rebelled, blew up one of the ovens, killed a number of SS men and tried to escape. They all perished. In the wake of this event four Jewish girls, who had helped them obtain explosives, were arrested, tortured, and hanged (see the testimonies on p. 123).

KRUKE, POLAND: Krakow (Kruke) was the capital of Poland from 1320 until 1609. There was an ancient Jewish community there, which reached the height of its fame in the Jewish world during the sixteenth century, during the lifetime of Rabbi Moses Isserles, who played an important role in the development of Jewish autonomy in Poland. In the years before the Holocaust, Jewish and Zionist organizations and cultural institutions of all kinds were active in Krakow.

RABBI MOSES ISSERLES (1525-1572): Head of the Krakow Yeshiva and a recognized halakhic authority.

"I do not consider myself an author or writer of literature. This is a chronicle from Planet Auschwitz. I was there for about two years. Time there is not like time here on Planet Earth. Every fraction of a second is measured by cogwheels of a different time. The inhabitants of that planet had no names, no parents, and no children. They did not dress as we do here. They were not born and did not give birth. They breathed according to different laws of nature. They did not live and die according to the laws of this world. Their name was a number."

—KA-TZETNIK (Yehiel Dinur)

"One day 52 Jewish boys were taken to the gas chambers to be killed. Stripped of their clothes, they stood naked in a circle, holding hands in the presence of approaching oblivion, and burst into song: 'Purify Our Hearts.' And so they were gathered unto death, with pure Jewish hearts, praying to their Maker."

—RABBI MEISELS, chief rabbi of Belgium

SATMAR: A town in northwestern Transylvania, near the borders of Czechoslovakia and Hungary. The original name was Satu Mare. Between the two world wars, 11,530 Jews were living in Satmar, approximately 25 percent of the total population. There were many synagogues, Hasidic courts, and houses of study in Satmar, and all trends of the Zionist movement were active. At the command of the Germans, the whole region was annexed to Hungary, and many Jewish men were deported to forced labor camps in the Ukraine. With the occupation of Hungary by the Germans in the spring of 1944, 20,000 Jews–local inhabitants and refugees–were incarcerated in the ghetto. Several weeks later the transports to Auschwitz began. In the heat of the summer, thousands–men and women, children and old people–were marched in dense columns to the railway station. All along the road stood Hungarian citizens, who gazed at the endless column of deportees and the cruel harassment by their armed Hungarian escorts. And these close neighbors of the deportees stood by the side of the road with no expression of sorrow on their faces. At the railway station the Jews were loaded in consignments of 1,000, 80 to 100 in each cattle car, and sent on a three days' journey to the Polish border, to Auschwitz. Eighty-five percent of the Jews of Satmar perished there.

Sunday

Everyone beaten to death.

Even on their own holy day they do not leave us alone.

Monday

All day long–truncheons.

Tuesday

My feet are like blocks of wood. How will I get up tomorrow?

Wednesday

I try not to speak aloud, to make do with moving my lips.

Can't drive the flies away.

Don't think about food any more.

Can still walk

But the body wants to be earth.

Thursday

I've been transferred to the *Sonder*. A transport from Satmar.* Another transport from Hungary. God, we have no common language with our fellow Jews!

Friday

I accompanied the old rabbi to the gas chambers.

Saturday

We finished early. Some are playing cards, others treating the soles of their sore feet, or busy with some paltry business dealings. The father and son are walking between the huts, side by side, deep in thought, they seem to be pacing out the limits of our existence.

I can't stop seeing the figure of the old rabbi. And then he's replaced by the figures of my father and my grandfather. And back again.

When the doors of the crematorium opened, I heard God moving above the smokestack.

It gets dark quickly. Above the smog, stars are emerging, clean and pure. Will you understand how here stars and ashes are all one?

"That's all that remains of the boy from Krakow," said Gonda. "He caught typhus and died. He must have written more but all I got was this one page."

The SS dog barked near the door of the hut and inside they fell silent in sudden fear. Rabbi Nathan closed his eyelids, but his thoughts knew no peace: Almighty God! Have You abandoned the jewel of creation to a pack of dogs and madmen? Here we lie in this place, the last station before the crematorium, with no curses to utter, no execration. We merely speak in praise of Your children, immersed in the final desolation. But worse than death is the feeling we are abandoned and forgotten by man and God.

Rabbi Nathan started back from the black hole into which his thoughts were plunging him. He bit his lips and said, "I remember when they hanged the girl. Do you remember the parade in front of the gallows?"

Only Gonda Redlich was not present on that occasion. The others of course remembered, to the last detail.

Ten thousand men were assembled on the parade ground in front of the gallows. Forbidden to move, they did not move. Forbidden to look down, they did not look down. Even if they had turned their heads and closed their eyes, they could not have avoided witnessing what unfolded before them.

Reinforced by detachments from neighboring camps, the SS staged the parade with their familiar well-oiled efficiency. The commands came over the loudspeakers:

"Parade, atten . . . SHUN!"

"The noose was placed around her neck. The executioner seemed pleased with himself and at ease. He joked with his victim, leisurely drank a glass of beer, lit a cigar, smiled. He was relaxed. The moment must be recorded and spoken of, written down and described with extreme brevity, as brief as the days that remained to us to live, told with point and sharpness, as sharp as the knives aimed at our hearts. That some memory might remain in the annals of Jewish sorrow, that our brothers in freedom might learn some lesson. One prayer only was on our lips: 'May it be Your will, even if You do not hear the sound of our weeping, that our tears be stored in Your vessel, the vessel of existence, and so reach hands of faith and find redress.'"
–K. L., Auschwitz, January 3, 1945

"We found out that Rozha Robota had brought explosives to Birkenau and this material was handed over to the *Sonderkommando* – and the *Sonderkommando* informed us that they were about to rebel. They rose up in rebellion on October 7, 1944. They blew up the crematorium, killed several SS men and their *kapo*. As far as I know, none of them remain alive. As a result of the work of the inquiry committee, Rozha Robota was arrested and severely tortured – Noah Zabladozocz came to her at night and she gave him a piece of paper, which reached us, on which was written that we had nothing to fear, we should continue with the work, she knew that she was going to die but no one else was in danger–she and three other Jewish girls were hanged, and Rozha Robota's last word, heard by the girls who were standing at attention, was 'Vengeance.'" –ISRAEL GUTMAN, evidence at the Eichmann trial

And twenty thousand pairs of wooden clogs had to respond with a click of heels. The Germans loved military drill, so the loudspeaker repeated the command again and again until the thousands of clogs came together with a single . . . CLICK!

"Hats . . . OFF!"

And all the prisoners in a single movement took off their caps with their right hands and held them against their hips. When this had been performed for the third time in a manner that satisfied these perfectionists, the condemned prisoner was brought onto the square.

"Raizel." The word passed from mouth to mouth through sealed lips.

"Raizel."

"Rozha,"✤ came a correction.

She was a girl of twenty-three. Two guards supported her bound arms. She could hardly move her feet toward the gallows platform.

Sealed lips continued to pass information from row to row.

"Seven hours they interrogated her, a wolfhound standing over her, his front paws on her shoulders. Two days she lay unconscious."

Something happened to her as she passed the upright pillar of the gallows and saw the huge silent crowd. She straightened her head and her bruised lips parted. She wanted to say something to them, perhaps she said it, but at that moment the loudspeakers screamed, "Atten . . . SHUN!"

Dangling from the noose was the small body of the young girl, apparently caught smuggling explosives out of the nearby factory to blow up the crematorium. Who had sent her on this mission was still unknown. The Gestapo had tortured her but had failed to break her spirit.

"You remember," Rabbi Nathan said at last, "how we stood there, ten thousand men, in the light of the setting sun, in the presence of that brave girl, until her body stiffened and we were allowed to disperse. Do you understand what I am getting at?"✤

said something aloud. Not a curse. Nothing bitter. A cry. But more important than this cry was what she did not say before she mounted the scaffold."
–ABBA KOVNER, *Encounter Beyond the Darkness*

ROZHA ROBOTA (1921–1944): Robota served as a youth leader in the Czechanow branch of Ha-Shomer Ha-Tza'ir. She was brought to Auschwitz in November 1942 with the rest of the population of Czechanow. Robota was executed together with her companions Ellen, Toussia, and Regina after the Gestapo had failed to break their spirits.

". . . everybody heard the cry of the doomed man, it pierced through the old thick barriers of inertia and submissiveness, it struck the living core of man in each of us: '*Kamaraden, ich bin der Letz!*' (Comrades, I am the last one!)

I wish I could say that from the midst of us, an abject flock, a voice rose, a murmur, a sign of assent. But nothing happened. We remained standing, bent and grey, our heads dropped, and we did not uncover our heads until the German ordered us to do so. The trapdoor opened, the body wriggled horribly; the band began playing again and we were once more lined up and filed past the quivering body of the dying man.

At the foot of the gallows, the SS watch us pass with indifferent eyes: their work is finished, and well finished. The Russians can come now: there are no longer any strong men among us, the last one is now hanging above our heads, and as for the others, a few halters had been enough. The Russians can come now: they will only find us, the slaves, the worn-out, worthy of the unarmed death which awaits us."

–PRIMO LEVI, *Survival in Auschwitz*

"I was at Auschwitz in 1961. Not the Auschwitz of terror, but the Auschwitz of inanimate objects. I approached the scaffold. The sun was shining. I closed my eyes and suddenly I felt my body shiver. This is where they stood. On this square. And saw the girl mount the scaffold. And they stood. And stood. The lives of those men who stood here were worth no more than the tail of a German dog. So profound was their helplessness. So total their paralysis. Theirs. Everybody's. And she was the first to mount the scaffold. They say that as she went up she turned and

DR. MENGELE (1911-?): Josef Mengele was a Nazi doctor and war criminal who served as doctor of the Auschwitz death camp and conducted medical experiments on the prisoners as if they were laboratory animals. When a transport arrived, Mengele was among those who sorted out the prisoners—who was for life and forced labor and who was for immediate death. At the end of the war he escaped to South America. His life and fate (perhaps also his death) are shrouded in mystery and rumor. In 1986, a body alleged to be his was subjected to pathological examination. To this day there are no definite conclusions.

WARSAW: The capital of Poland. At the outbreak of war in 1939, Warsaw contained nearly 400,000 Jews, about a third of the population of the city. Jews emigrated to Warsaw at the beginning of the fifteenth century, and the Jewish population there began to grow significantly at the end of the nineteenth century, following the pogroms in Russia and the stream of refugees from there. From that time on, Warsaw became the largest Jewish community in Europe. The Jews of Warsaw were active in all branches of the economy, culture, science, and religion. In particular, there was a flowering in the use of the language of the people, Yiddish, which found expression in a wide-ranging press, a thriving literature of all varieties and genres, in theaters, libraries, and educational institutions. There were enthusiasts for every trend and political party and youth movement, from the Bund to the various kinds of Zionists, from the "autonomists" to the "territorialists," from yeshiva scholars to university students, from assimilationists who adopted Polish culture to those who remained faithful to Jewish tradition. A varied network of welfare institutions, hospitals, and charities completed the picture of a quasi-autonomous Jewish community. On October 12, 1941, the Jewish ghetto was established there, the largest within the area under German rule. The story of the Warsaw ghetto, with its suffering, struggle, fight for existence, and the great rebellion that broke out before it was destroyed, has been recorded in many documents and records.

Everyone was silent for a while. Gonda Redlich had heard the story for the first time and his voice trembled. "The Warsaw ghetto, the revolt there, what conclusion can we draw from that?"

"I was there," said Rabbi Raphael unexpectedly.

His companions stared at the Rabbi of Salonika in apparent disbelief. He explained, "It was the Eve of the New Year at Auschwitz-Birkenau and we were suddenly called on parade. These sudden alarms did not bode well and each of us prepared for the worst. One glance from Dr. Mengele* at a group of naked men could determine who was for death and who had gained a remission. Ten days earlier fifteen hundred veteran prisoners had been dispatched to the furnace. This time a thousand were chosen.

"When I arrived in Auschwitz I was met by a man from Salonika, who had been taken in a previous transport. He managed to warn me at the gate by saying, 'Rabbi, when they ask you what you do, tell them you're a port worker and speak only Greek.' I was astounded. I thought the poor man had taken leave of his senses. But I did what he told me and I was saved. Those who declared they were teachers or clerks or, above all, rabbis were sent to the left; their doom was already sealed. I was attached to a group who tarred roofs. My whole body was bruised and sore from the rigor of the work and the blows of the overseers. But gradually my muscles hardened and I became a seasoned laborer in every way. But by the end of 1943, we were all considered *musulmen*. Nevertheless, I was selected with that thousand and sent to the camp at Auschwitz. There about a thousand more were waiting for us. By the time we had been loaded onto the cattle wagons, the rumor had spread that we were being transferred to another camp. With the keen eye of convicts, we checked up and discovered that the one thing in common among the whole transport was that though we were from different countries, none of us were Polish Jews.

"After a whole day's journey, the train stopped somewhere in the middle of the night and through the barred windows of the sealed wagons we could make out faint lights shining through the darkness. Surrounded by SS, we were marched to a large square with mountains of bricks on all sides and ruined houses barely standing.

"'Warsaw,'* someone said.

"Many people throughout the world will remember the name Warsaw, but no one who was not there to see what we beheld that dawn is capable of describing the horror of that sight—a city beaten to death.* "Of all those streets, which had contained half a million Jews, keepers of the faith and men of action, the largest Jewish community in the world, nothing remained but a pile of stones. Stupefied, we looked in all directions—only heaps of rubble. A sea. Yet the corpse of the ghetto still seemed warm. Above the stones holy spirits were whispering. Each had once been the soul of a living Jew.*

"The German in charge of us was a man of forty, sturdy, with a skimpy beard, almost a dwarf, with the eyes of a cat. His cheeks were flushed despite the morning chill, and in his hand he spun a lead-tipped whip on a short strap. A smile never left the lips of that dwarf. I have never seen such a wicked smile.

"There were two brothers with us. One came from Greece, the other from Paris. The one from Greece had not known his brother was alive, for he had been missing since the beginning of the war. And I had seen them recognize each other on the parade ground at Birkenau; it came to them as a complete surprise.

"They fell into each other's arms and wept and were

so overcome with longing for each other, they could not feel the lash of the whip. The day after we arrived in Warsaw we were housed in Gesza, the great cemetery, which still remained, and from there we went off to work at cleaning up the ghetto. At midday the soldiers searched the belongings of the prisoners and in a sack of straw that the two brothers had prepared for sleeping on they found some American dollar bills. When we got back from work, there was a surprise inspection and the dwarf—with that wicked smile on his face—asked the two brothers which of them the dollars belonged to.

"The one called Elis said, 'Me, sir.'

"The second brother, called Henri, quickly said, 'Me, sir.'

"The dwarf whose smile never left his lips waved the green bills under the nose of the first brother, 'Do I understand correctly that half are yours and the other half are his?'

"'No, sir,' Elis insisted, 'all the money is mine, because I found it.'

"Henri told the same story. 'I found it, sir. All the money is mine.'

"Henri was younger than Elis but a head taller. And three heads taller than the SS man. And all the prisoners from Auschwitz and Birkenau stood by the wall of the Warsaw cemetery following with bated breath this case of 'two who lay claim'* and all knew who was the judge.

"The dwarf turned his head in order not to lift his eyes and look straight at the Jew who was taller, merely touching the tip of each brother's nose with the leaden tip of his whip and suddenly screaming in an access of rage, 'And you both want to be heroes here?'

"The two brothers burst into tears, but would not change their story. One said, 'Have mercy on my brother; he is not to blame,' and the other said, 'have mercy on my brother; he is innocent.'

"At once the German ordered them to stand against the wall, and shot them both. He ordered us, 'Clean up the mess. Work well and you'll stay alive.'

"So we gave a Jewish burial to the two brothers who in their lives were separated but in death they were not divided."

And Raphael Habib continued to tell his story.

"They called the clean-up squad the *Kartoffelkommando,** on account of the secret stock of potatoes they found in the area, among the ruins. These caches must have been laid up by the inhabitants of the ghetto in preparation for the revolt. The Germans ordered them to comb the whole ghetto, collect every potato that remained, and stack them in one central spot. What necessity the Germans saw for scrambling among the ruins for moldy potatoes is beyond human comprehension. But evil men think differently. Perhaps they thought there were still Jews in hiding, skulking somewhere among the cellars and the sewers, and sought to deprive them of any source of food that might still sustain life. It soon became clear that this was no mere suspicion.*

"One of the workers, whose foot had been crushed under a block of concrete, had gone back early to the camp of the *Kartoffelkommando* in Gesza. As he was leaning forward to bandage his injured toes with a rag, something like a lump of mud rolled over and fell on his hand. He saw that it was a potato. Since they were forbidden to bring potatoes into the camp, he wondered where it came from and what it was doing there.

"When he picked it up, he noticed a leaf stuck in it, but a leaf of a plane tree, not a potato leaf. He removed the leaf from the body of the potato and saw that it was perforated with pinholes in the shape of a Shield of David. Our comrade was startled and looked around, but couldn't see anybody or anything. He calmed down with the thought that it must have been one of the members of the squad who had done it to amuse himself, for a joke

Let us remember
Our brothers and sisters,
The thousands of Jewish communities,
Families of human beings,
The whole of Jewry
Doomed to slaughter
At the hands of the Nazi butcher
And his helpers.
Let us remember
Those who clenched their fists
And took up arms,
The weapon of vision, despair, and revolt,
Men of heart,
With open eyes,
Who laid down their lives
But were powerless to save.
Let us speak out,
Let us not be mute,
Until our lives are worthy
Of their memory.
—ABBA KOVNER, from "A Memorial Prayer for the 27th of Nissan"

"I bequeath to my son: Do not forget! Do not forgive!"
—LAZER ENGELSTERN

"TWO WHO LAY CLAIM": Tractate *Baba Metzia* of the Babylonian Talmud begins the story as follows: "Two lay claim to a prayer shawl, one says: I found it, and the other says: I found it. One says: It's all mine, and the other says: It's all mine . . . and they cannot agree."

KARTOFFELKOMMANDO (German): A *kartoffel* is a potato. The reference is to the unit of prisoners whose task it was to supply potatoes, and maybe other food.

Which hunger
    is hard,
    harder,
    hardest? . . .
they asked in the camp, and they used to answer:
After you've eaten your ration of bread, it's hard.
Before you eat the slice of bread, it's harder.
When you have a crumb left in your pocket, it's hardest.

that could well cost him his life. For there was no knowing what the SS dwarf was ready to kill a man for, between breakfast and lunch. Before very long our comrade felt quite sure that there were eyes following him out there in the dark. His gaze combed the bushes again and saw the glow of pupils behind a gravestone just above ground level. Imagine the depth of emotion he felt when he beheld a Jew emerging from a grave. His age was uncertain, though he seemed young, his hair like the roots of a bush, his face the color of earth from the bottom of a pit, and a stench worse than anything you can imagine. But alas, our comrade was from Salonika and they had no common language.

"There was a Jew in the squad name Goldmintz, born and brought up in Warsaw, who as a young man had found his way to Paris, the promised land for any man with the soul of an artist in his shabby clothes. He was arrested in Paris and handed over by the French to the Gestapo, along with the rest of the Jews of Polish nationality. The Gestapo took him to Auschwitz. As I said, to clean up the Warsaw ghetto the Germans chose Jews who did not speak Polish or any other Slav language, but they made a mistake with Goldmintz. He was the one who first called out 'Warsaw' on the night they arrived.

"Goldmintz was like a man in a dream the whole time he was there. From the moment he realized that his feet were standing in the town of his birth, he was like a man floundering in a whirlpool threatening to drag him down into the abyss, as he clapped his hands in sorrow, grasping at wooden beams and broken branches. His fingers turning blue with cold, he turned over every stone he could stoop over and pick up, in case it concealed some friend or acquaintance, some limb or object of value. Sometimes in the middle of work he would stand up in some deserted square that was once a thriving marketplace, his head bent, inclined to one side. His gaze would rest on blocks of concrete, sprayed with whitewash, his eyes—which in any case were dark—gloomy and secretive as the entrance to a well. 'Warsaw, my Warsaw' he could be heard muttering, and mumbling other words, disjointed or meaningless for those who knew neither Yiddish nor Polish. Suddenly he would fall onto a pile of bricks, crawl on his belly like a snail, and disappear into the darkness of death, into the ruined houses.

"We could only guess what was going on in the soul of Goldmintz. But we shared his joy on the day he returned from one of his dangerous forays concealing in his hand an object of priceless value: a silver candlestick he had found under the rubble in the courtyard of his home, crushed by the displaced lintel of his childhood room, which he recognized by the special mezuzzah his father had once brought back from Berlin. When he showed us the candlestick, he burst into tears like a lost child who has been found by his mother. No one was more scared or more delighted than he when he managed to bring the candlestick concealed on his body through the gates of Auschwitz. One morning he woke up with a cry of despair; the candlestick had been stolen from under his pillow during the night. The thief, probably one of his fellow prisoners on the block, did not respond to his entreaties, did not repent or confess, had no pity. Goldmintz banged his head against the wall, overturned his bunk and his meager straw mattresses, screamed and shouted until the *kapo* came and took him off to the punishment cell, from which he never returned.

"There was no need of the camps to teach us that men are capable both of doing great good and extreme evil. But only in the camps did the difference between humanity and inhumanity become so terribly, transparently clear. There were some who would steal his only slice of bread from a fellow prisoner on the block, from the next bunk, who shared his fate. At a time when a man's life depended on a thin slice of black bread, stealing it was tantamount to sending a comrade to his death.

"And yet thefts were a daily occurrence. The victims would wake in the morning, extend trembling hands toward the hiding places near their heads and turn pale as the whitewash in the lime pits when the hands returned empty. Hatred and suspicion would spread through the hut of condemned men, even harder to bear than hunger."

Gonda Redlich, the pioneer youth from Terezin, said, "But we have also seen in the camp how a man can become indomitable, able to share his last cigarette butt, his last breath."

"Oh, yes," added Rabbi Raphael. "With God's help, not everybody dies in a state of ignorance. We have seen man at his worst and at his best."

"Outside a light summer rain was falling and inside—in the mortuary in the cemetery of Gesza—Jews from Greece, Belgium, and France sat in silence listening to the survivor from the sewers. Goldmintz translated the young man's words from Polish for the man from Salonika who understood French. And he passed on the story to his fellow townsmen in their language.

"From time to time there would be a hiss from the watcher at the door and total silence would reign indoors until the guard, the flashlight, and the dog had passed.

"With a trembling hand Yashiu—that was the boy's name—raised the spoon to his lips, sipping the soup we had brought him. He drank the weak brew with extreme care and answered our questions. At times a faint grimace would twist his lips and he would stop the flow of words, his thoughts plunging inward."

There is neither time nor space to include the whole story within a story that the rabbi from Salonika heard translated by Goldmintz, that this "last of the Zealots"✢ revealed that night, and the two following nights, in the shadow of the grave of Y. L. Peretz, known to this day to the local Jews as Ohel-Peretz, in the Warsaw Jewish cemetery.

Yashiu was Yehoshua ben Zvi. He was one of the zealots who took part in the revolt of Jewish youth in Warsaw on the Eve of Passover 5703 (1943), determined to carry on their fight to the end, without the slightest doubt what that end would be. And the cry of the flame-wracked ghetto struck the windows of the Polish inhabitants of the town beyond the walls and was thrown back by the smog and the clean consciences, the cries of the besieged returning to them like ricochets off the rock.

Yashiu was not from Warsaw; he was born in Kalisz in the west of the country. He and his comrades and followers had fled Kalisz and made their way to Vilna during the first year of the war. And he had recrossed the border at a time when the Germans had spread across the whole continent and there was no longer anywhere to flee. Yashiu came back to Warsaw, bearing the manifesto of the fighters of Vilna. From Warsaw he moved on to Czestochowa, the holy city of the Christians, which led the way in persecuting its Jewish fellow citizens. In Czestochowa Yashiu roused the Jewish youth to self defense and managed to reach Warsaw at the outbreak of the revolt.

This is the story of Yashiu and what befell him.

He was twenty-one when he left home. He left Kalisz, and he left Vilna, and he left Czestochowa and came to the gates of Warsaw on the Eve of Passover 5703. The revolt broke out on the morning of the first day of Passover. Yashiu had a beautiful girlfriend named Dvora, like his sister, from whom he had been separated by the war, just as he had been separated from his mother and father and the rest of the family, and wherever he went he found no trace of them. On the fourth day of Passover his girlfriend Dvora was still standing by his side at the window of a tall building that served as a lookout for the fighters, from which they could block the entry of the Germans into the heart of the ghetto. A German soldier saw her there and shouted out, "Look, Hans! A Jewess firing!"

On the last day of Passover Dvora was killed, gun in hand. When the strength of the fighters above ground gave out, they went down into the depths of the earth, in order to attack the enemy from the ruins and the sewers. They carried on the desperate fight, the few against the many, the doomed against the victorious. From one of the sewers of the Polish capital Yashiu emerged, at the behest of his commander, seeking asylum for the remaining fighters. When he returned from his mission, pursued by the smell of burning from above and the stench of urine and feces up to his knees, his comrades from the revolt were nowhere to be found. All exits from the central bunker had been sealed off by falls of earth caused by German grenades and the place still reeked of the poison gas sent in to suffocate the leader of the revolt and his staff, one hundred and twenty young men and women, the flower of the slaughtered Jewish people.

The name of the place was Mila 18.✢

"LAST OF THE ZEALOTS": The Zealots was the name given to those Jews in the Land of Israel who rebelled against Roman rule during the first century C.E. The movement began among the Jews of Galilee, who called for opposition to the census held for the purpose of imposing taxes (in the year 6 C.E.).

"The fighters began to concentrate at the new and the last rallying point—Mila 18. The bunker at Mila 18 was not only a shelter for Jewish suffering and a base for squads of fighters, it was also the headquarters of the fighting organization. It was the center of the rebel movement: threads stretched from here to all the fighting positions in the ghetto; runners and fighters came here to deliver reports, orders from headquarters issued from here. Every night, as darkness fell, new life began to throb bravely in the bunker. Mordechai Anielewicz made a significant contribution to shaping our daily lives in the bunker. He was the nerve center, all the threads from the actions of all the squads were concentrated in his hands, in the bunker. He listened to the opinion of every man, was attentive to his views on events and tactics. Everyone knew him, his very existence gave us all strength." —TUVIA BUZHIKOVSKI

"The Germans did not grant them a quick death. They introduced a small amount of gas and then stopped, in order to depress our spirits by a slow, protracted suffocation. Arie Wilner was the first to call upon all the fighters to commit suicide and not be taken alive by the Germans. That's when the suicides began. Shots were heard within the bunkers—Jewish fighters were taking their own lives. Thus perished the flower of the Jewish fighters of Warsaw. A hundred met their deaths here, including Mordechai Anielewicz, the courageous, handsome leader, upon whose lips played a smile even in the hours of dread." —TZIVIA LUBETKIN

MOKOTOW: A suburb of Warsaw.

"When I think that all the concentrations of our people will disappear from the face of the earth and nothing will remain of everything we hold dear, not even a trace—as God is my witness, I yearn only for death. I do not wish to be a survivor among graves. I cannot live among the ruins of my people, I do not want that."
—GUSTA DAVIDSON

GUSTA (JUSTINA) DAVIDSON (1917-1943): One of the leaders of the Jewish Fighting Organization in Krakow. She left a diary (*Justina's Diary*). She perished with her husband, Shimon, a leader of the fighters, in the winter of 1943, at the age of 26.

THE GREAT RIVER: The Vistula.

UMSCHLAGPLATZ: The name given by the Germans to the square in Warsaw, near the railway, where the Jews assembled before deportation to the death camps.

A SONG OF ASCENTS

Out of the depths I call You, O Lord.
O Lord, listen to my cry; let Your ears be
    attentive to my plea for mercy.
If You keep account of sins, O Lord,
Lord, who will survive?
Yours is the power to forgive
    so that You may be held in awe.

I look to the Lord;
I look to Him;
I await His word.
I am more eager for the Lord than watch-
    men for the morning, watchmen for
    the morning.

O Israel, wait for the Lord;
    for with the Lord there is steadfast
    love and great power to redeem.
It is He who will redeem Israel from all
    their iniquities.   —PSALM 130

Hear O Israel, the Lord our God, the
    Lord is one. (*once*)
Blessed be the name of his glorious king-
    dom for ever and ever. (*three times*)
The Lord is God. (*seven times*)

        —From the closing service
        for the Day of Atonement

And Yashiu continued to flee. In a daze he stumbled around beneath the surface of the city, seeking a way out of the sewers, without the strength anymore to lift the concrete manhole over his head. A Polish driver happened to be passing, saw his fingers fumbling, pulled him out, hid him in his lorry, and moved him to a small wood near Warsaw, where he joined a group of partisans formed of survivors from the revolt. Yashiu did not know the name of his rescuer, only that he was from Moko-tow.✣ It did not take many days for the Germans to pick up their tracks in the wood and decimate the group of Jewish ghetto survivors;✣ there were only two left alive, Yashiu and the pharmacist's son, who had hidden in a water conduit. The pharma-cist's son, who had been a nursing orderly in the ghetto, still had a few bandages and medicines left, but nothing to cure his own blindness, for he had lost his spectacles in the flight. Yashiu led him like a blind man from one temporary hiding place to another. They took to the dark woods and the villages on the other side of the Great River,✣ but found no rest or shelter, either because of the Germans or the Polish informers who made their living by hunting Jews. When they had been driven from their place in the woods and the dog kennels by the farm gates, the pharmacist's son placed his right hand on his companion's shoulder and, stout stick in hand, the two of them made their way back to Warsaw, the lame leading the blind.

In the middle of the night they found their way into the cemetery, all that remained intact of the whole Jewish town, and took up residence in a grave pit, which the underground had once converted into an arms cache. From the end of the revolt there were German patrols combing the ruined ghetto quarters day and night, and firing at anything that moved. Yashiu took his life in his hands every time he emerged from the pit to rummage for scraps of food for the two of them and secrete them in the hiding place they had dug between two graves.

"They had already spent three whole months there before we suddenly appeared like ghosts," said Rabbi Raphael, "and doubtless they are there to this day, for there is no lack of rats to eat."

"Rats?" the father and son said in one voice, appalled.

Raphael Habib nodded and said, "I must tell you that if the Germans on patrol had suddenly burst upon the scene, we would hardly have noticed them. Sitting round this living corpse, we were totally absorbed in what he was telling us. We had com-pletely forgotten that we too were the living dead. And as Yehoshua, called Yashiu, explained to us how they took it in turns to snatch a little sleep, for fear the rats would eat them alive—they had already gnawed at his foot—and how they had vom-ited everything the first time they had been compelled to eat the flesh of a trapped rat, for all their stock of food had been used up and he did not know what would hap-pen next and his companion was sleeping all the time from total exhaustion, tears formed in the eyes of all his listeners; grown men were not ashamed to weep aloud. And I asked them to save their tears for tomorrow, for the Day of Atonement prayers."

The men from Auschwitz said Kol Nidrei secretly in the tool shed of the *Kartoffelkommando,* and fasting was the eas-iest thing to bear, for they were accustomed to starvation. In a place called Umschlagplatz,✣ from which three hundred thousand Warsaw Jews had been carried off to extermination, they spent the whole of the following day in forced labor, and in another square, behind the former community center, they stood in fear and worshiped.

It was the Day of Atonement. On that awesome day, Raphael Habib and the remnant of the Salonika congregation stood among the ruins of Jewish Warsaw.✣ They made haste and cut out some of the hymns. Among the congregants was Rabbi Shemuel, the cantor from Salonika, and deeply moved by all they had undergone, he asked to end the Closing Service with a special prayer, according to the custom of the Salonika Jews who had come from Aragon, but his strength failed him—just as his mouth opened to chant the prayer—and he collapsed unconscious. They moistened his lips with a little water, and the man who for years had been a practicing cantor opened his eyes immediately, and continued to pray from the point where he had broken off and everyone heard the special prayer: "O God of Abraham, Isaac, and Jacob, from the depths I cry unto You, from the fires of Auschwitz, from the ruins of the Warsaw ghetto, we raise our prayer to You. Guardian of Israel, preserve the remnant of Israel, let not the last of Your children perish, who give up their souls for . . ." Fortunately his voice gave out in mid sentence and he lost consciousness a second time, from weakness and emotion. For the keen ear of the commandant of the *Kartoffelkommando,* the cruel dwarf, had picked up from afar the melodious voice of the *ḥazan,* who had begun to chant the first of the seven repetitions of the affirmation "The Lord He is God," and the congregants had time to wind up the day of judgment and disperse before the murderer could make them wind up in the punishment cell.[*]

One of the camp searchlights suddenly went out and the face of the rabbi telling his story was swallowed up in darkness.

"And now that I have given you, my friends, a full account of everything we saw and heard in the ruins of Warsaw, the essence of what the memory can bear, I must fulfill my obligation to tell you the last request of those two young heroes, the request they made before they returned to their sepulcher and we went back to this Vale of Tears, Auschwitz. Soaked in the pouring rain, Yashiu led me to one of the corners of Ohel-Peretz, near the northern face, where he had buried a tin in the ground containing two documents, his own ghetto journal and some early poems composed by his comrade in Hebrew. We shook hands as I gave him my word I would tell my fellow prisoners. And whichever of us lives to see the day of redemption, let him not forget to visit the grave of Peretz and open that container and publish this relic of a life."

Gonda Heard

Gonda Redlich heard about the journal hidden in the Warsaw cemetery and his heart ached. He too had written a journal in the ghetto of Theresienstadt, and left it with his friend Willi. What had happened to it? He could see the final lines now, though his seared eyelids were closed.

> It seems to me they want to wipe out the ghetto, just leaving old people and people of mixed ancestry. In our time the enemy is not only cruel, but cunning and malicious. They make promises but do not keep them. They send away little children but their baby carriages remain here. Families are separated. The father is put on one transport, the child on a second, and the mother on a third. It will be our turn tomorrow. God grant our salvation is at hand.[*]

Gonda Redlich was twenty-six when he arrived in Theresienstadt from Prague. And he was on the last transport to leave Theresienstadt for Auschwitz. He took with him the baby carriage he had bought for his newborn child.

"What's that?"

"A baby carriage for my son."

"For your son? And where do you think you're going with it?"

"In the camp at Theresienstadt, you could . . ."

"Birkenau is not just another camp, boy."

It was a Jew who was standing in front of him. Why was his tone of voice so malevolent? He had pointed his finger at

---

"**Throughout its long history,** this people has found again and again that after every holocaust its faith remains invincible."

—MANES SPERBER

It was the last, the last of the last,
And so replete, bitter and
   multicolored—
Which perhaps, somewhere in the
   glow of fragments
Of white stone, seems yellow—
And as it raised its wings to soar aloft,
Flew to kiss the last remnant of my
   world.

I have been here seven weeks—
"Ghettoized"—
My loved ones found me here.
Here too the dandelion calls to me.
The chestnut in the yard with its white
   blossom
Holds out its arms to me
But I have seen no butterflies here,
That was the last, the last of the last.
For butterflies cannot live
   in the ghetto.

—PAVEL FRIEDMAN,
one of the children in
the Theresienstadt ghetto

ACHTUNG! (German): Attention!

SCHNELL! (German): Quickly!

A new king arose over Egypt, who did not know Joseph. And he said to his people, "Look, the Israelite people are much too numerous for us. Let us deal shrewdly with them, so that they may not increase. . . ."

—EXODUS 1:8-10

YAAKOV EDELSTEIN (1903-1944): One of the leaders of Socialist Zionism in Czechoslovakia. After the Nazi occupation he used all his influence to prevent the deportation of Czechoslovak Jewry to the East. He realized correctly that deportation meant death. He thought that a ghetto within the "Protectorate" (Czechoslovakia under German occupation) would prevent deportation and so regarded the Theresienstadt ghetto as the lesser evil: even if Jews had to live in conditions of slavery, they could hold out until the storm had passed. Edelstein was one of the leaders of the community of prisoners in Theresienstadt. At the end of 1943 he was removed from the leadership. The Germans had decided that with his strong personality, his influence over the young people, and his bravery in the face of the Germans, he was likely to prove too dangerous. He was arrested on November 10, 1943, on a charge of "helping escapees" and in December was sent to Auschwitz. In June 1944, he was executed by a firing squad, together with the rest of his family.

OCTOBER 7-8, 1942: "We are in a huge trap. If we escape some time, we shall remember with fear and trembling everything we have seen here, all these terrible things. They break up the family, kill, torture, and give to everything the mask of rectitude. I would like to fall asleep and wake up only at the end of the war."

—EGON (GONDA) REDLICH,
A Kind of Life (a diary)

the tall chimneys. Smoke wreathed with flames was curling up from their mouths. "That's a chariot of fire, not a baby carriage."

In time he came to learn of the existence of the Jewish *Sonderkommando*. The condemned. They too fought their battle of survival. Had he expected some other welcome at the gates of Birkenau? Something soothing, encouraging, deluding?

Old Professor Albert, what was he hoping for when he asked one of the *Sonder* who had just been taken off to work at the crematorium, "Does Birkenau exist?"

And the man who had been working at the crematorium for who knows how long, what was he supposed to reply? No, Herr Professor, Birkenau is a fiction! That's what Professor Albert was hoping for. Like the old lady, a relative of Gerhart Hauptmann, taken from Berlin to Theresienstadt, who sat on her sealskin traveling bags, crying and lost on the camp parade ground, begging to be told that everything that had happened to her was just a mistake!

And how was he any different, leaving on a transport for the east carrying a baby carriage? These were questions after the event. Standing in the throng of bodies winding their way through the gates of Birkenau, he asked no questions and did not think about what he was doing. "*Achtung!*"* came the command over the loudspeaker. "Leave all baggage at the side." He no longer had the baby carriage. But his wife and child were still by his side.

"Watches, bracelets, jewelry, gold, and money—to be left here, at once! I repeat: all gold and money, filthy Jews!"

"Czech money too?"

"Czech money too, you idiot!"

They obeyed. Without uttering another word, they parted from all their belongings. They pulled off their bracelets and medallions without a final look at the portraits of their loved ones inside. They grew anxious if the clasp got stuck. They threw them on the pile. They wanted to breathe deeply. A scream, "Don't throw them, bend down and place them neatly, you swine!"

"Women and children to the left! Men to the right! *Schnell. Schnell!*"*

The men cringed. They kept close together, like a herd under the whip. Suddenly Gonda felt totally alone in the midst of the huge crowd. Never in his life had he felt so terribly alone.

The whole time he had been at Theresienstadt he had been involved with people and they had loved him. He had a stubborn determination not to give in. Theresienstadt had been the final destination for many old people. Thirty thousand of them had been buried there.

Day after day they died like flies in the heat but the young people in the ghetto remained buoyed up by hope. He inspired them not to be resigned. They organized theater productions, opera, even cabaret with political asides too subtle for their square German overlords to catch the intent. And they laughed, artists and audience of intellectuals, that they too, like Pharaoh, had been able to say, "Come, let us be too clever for them. . . ."*

Gonda and his companion Yaakov Edelstein,* his former youth leader, now appointed head of the ghetto by the Germans, a man of integrity who remained deluded to the end, were sure that at this time being a pioneer meant going along with all the Jews, strengthening their spirits in evil times and serving as leader of the deportees when the fateful day arrived.*

They tried to understand the logic of German actions. To divine their intentions. After a while it seemed it was easier to get along with a tall German and harder with a fat one. From time to time they would give a cry of surprise and disappointment, "Oh, that's impossible. Impossible, Herr Professor." And you could never know what might be hidden, for good or ill, in the next decree. Everyone tried to do whatever was right to protect himself from being sorted, from selection. But how could one protect oneself against evil? Once there was a theory that the sick were not sent east, since what was needed in Poland was a healthy labor force. People were in a hurry to fall sick or in other words, to feign sickness. One morning all the sick, the genuine and the malingerers, were taken from the clinics and loaded brutally onto trucks covered with tarpaulins. About the old people in Theresienstadt the Germans used to say, "They have the right to live and die in peace in the ghetto." And some days it was they who were the first to be deported. And the police and the heads of the ghetto thought themselves immune from wanton misfortune—until they too were taken by special decree. Every personal detail seemed fateful—age, sex, occupation, refugee or citizen of the Reich—but no one knew which detail would seal his fate when the day arrived.

"You be responsible for educating the children," Yaakov suggested to Gonda. "That's a job with importance for the future." Gonda took on the task with enthusiasm. He sat down at once to learn Hebrew, for teaching Hebrew to the Children of Israel in the ghetto seemed to him not merely teaching another language but providing hope. And the convoys of transports to the camps in Poland were unending. And since Birkenau was not to be found on any standard map of Europe, Birkenau did not exist. No one uttered the words "death camps." Only east. To this mysterious east went the Jews who had been deported from the big cities, a source of special status in Theresienstadt, and that was a good sign. Many of them were assimilated Jews who had long blended in with Germans, Austrians, and Czechs. They failed to understand why they were incarcerated in Theresienstadt, and had no idea that being sent east meant being doomed to extermination.

Had no idea? What about the rumors—constantly circulating—the farewells on postcards, the hints, the information that filtered through from there?

And the name that thrust its way into their minds with the awesome force of an electric drill:

Birkenau: Birkenau: Birkenau: Birkenau: Birkenau.

"Julia Fradkin was taken to a transport during the last week of rehearsals. The drama group was working on a play by Cocteau. Julia, a promising dancer, seventeen years old, was very beautiful. As she was standing on the platform of the railway wagon leaving for Auschwitz, she asked with tears in her eyes, "Will you be able to manage without me, guys?"

They managed without her. Julia went to Auschwitz, and Gonda and the members of the troupe hurried back to the improvised theater to find a replacement for her.

The first performance took place in Theresienstadt on schedule and the young people were proud. They didn't see themselves as convicts who had committed a crime. Since they were innocent, they rejected the idea of punishment. So if the ghetto was not punishment, it should be ignored, life should be lived to the fullest, it was one's duty to rejoice and give the downtrodden cause for joy. Gonda knew no greater joy than the day the Zionist commune was founded, which he and his fellow pioneers-to-be saw as a means to preserve the spirit of man, who was created in the image of God, within the ghetto walls.

His joy redoubled when he got to know Greta in the commune.

Why hadn't he passed her the baby carriage when he saw her being pushed to the left? What happened to him that he didn't even lift a hand to wave goodbye?

"And your diary, you said you wrote it in Hebrew?" Nathan Cassuto asked with respect.

"In Hebrew. Except on Shabbat, when I wrote in Czech, so as not to violate the Sabbath."

Gonda sensed the amazement in their looks—at his naivete or the strength of his belief?

"We must learn to enter the ghetto as Zionists and leave as Jews," he had written in the journal that remained in Theresienstadt.

But here, in Birkenau, nobody left.[*]

For a while the shock of the death camp had paralyzed his will, which he had fortified with such obstinacy at Theresienstadt.

He remembered the time and the place when despair had almost got the better of him. They had been standing in line in the commando ready to go to work. The sun had just risen and the chief *kapo*,[*] one of the longtime criminals among

"For human nature is such that grief and pain—even simultaneously suffered—do not add up as a whole in our consciousness, but hide, the lesser behind the greater, according to a definite law of perspective. It is providential and is our means of surviving in the camp." —PRIMO LEVI, *Survival in Auschwitz*

KAPO (Italian): Head. This was the term for a prisoner placed in charge of a group of prisoners in the Nazi camps. In time it became a synonym for one who collaborated with his murderous overlords.

PONTE VECCHIO: "The old bridge" on the Arno River in Florence.

DEL CARMINI: A Carmelite monastery in Florence.

In 1938, Fascist Italy adopted the German race laws. The Jews of Italy, whose lives had remained unaffected by the turmoil of the times and who had not been harmed by the course of events in World War I, nor by the many years that Mussolini had been in power, were shocked by the decree that fell upon them.

A Jew whose family had been for 20 generations in Italy would climb into bed at night, equal among equals, and wake up in the morning deprived of his rights, with no livelihood, no chance of providing his children with an education, inferior in the eyes of the law, socially humiliated, helpless. In the absence of any warning signals, the shock was complete. Jews who believed in the sincerity of the declarations of the regime that the rights of the Italian Jews would be unconditionally preserved, and collaborated with the Fascist government with a loyalty acquired over generations, suddenly found the ground cut from under their feet. Of the 47,000 Jews in the country—Italian citizens, recent immigrants, and refugees—5,500 succeeded in leaving the country after the publication of the race laws. Five thousand converted to Christianity, in the hope that leaving the Jewish people would stand them in good stead in these perilous times. Many committed suicide. Nearly 8,000 were sent to Auschwitz. And the deportation did not spare the 1,800 Jews of Rhodes, even though Rhodes was administered by Italy.

the German convicts, had sorted out three rows of five men each. He told the Jews to follow him. Gonda was in the second row of five. As they marched off, he thought to himself he would not come back alive. This *kapo* was a cold-blooded murderer. There was frost outside. They were moving toward the center of a snow-covered field where wooden beams marked out the area as a building site. Two hundred meters away there was a road. Trucks were arriving loaded with sacks of cement. He saw the first five men take the sacks on their shoulders and the *kapo* order them to cover the distance to the building site at the double. The first two prisoners stumbled but they had the strength to start running and cope with the load. The third almost dropped his sack and when his neighbor tried to help him he caught a vicious blow to the head from a whip. The first of the second group of five was a yeshiva student from Karpato-Ros, not yet eighteen, who immediately collapsed under the weight. The seam of the sack split open and the cement spilled on the snow. He tried to rise. A shot rang out and the young man crumpled. As Gonda passed he caught a glimpse, from under his sack of cement, of the pool of blood and cement seeping into the snow.

Already during the previous night, Gonda's head had begun to ache and his temperature to rise. When they left the square, he doubted whether he would have the strength even to reach their destination. As he ran with the first fifty-kilo sack of cement, he didn't believe he would last out the first two hundred meters. Rings of fire and darkness danced in turn before his eyes, and he felt like lying down and putting an end to the vile story. At that moment the figure of Greta appeared before him, with their firstborn in her arms. Perhaps they still lived? The image of his wife or the sight of the crushed head of the boy from Karpato-Ros achieved the unbelievable. Gonda completed the fateful two hundred meters seven, ten, twenty, innumer-

able times in the course of the day. And as he ran with the sacks of cement on his neck, across his shoulders, he knew he was fleeing from death.

"Apparently," Gonda seemed to be muttering to himself, "one can overcome death. Peter Ordner overcame death."

"Who is this Peter?" they asked.

The groans of the dying filled the air in the other, the harsh wing of the seventh block.

"Peter was a blind artist in the Theresienstadt ghetto. When he became blind, he began to fashion things from wire. We would collect scraps of wire for him and with this material he would make the most marvelous objects. As he waited his turn to be sent on a transport, Peter filled his wretched space between the walls with works of art that blazed like stars. I was privileged to see them. And the fact that I think about them and remember them here—somehow, it seems, Peter continues to live, in me."

This is the end of Gonda Redlich's account. Rabbi Raphael Habib has already told his story. Now it is the turn of the man from Florence.

On the Banks of the Arno

I.

In the evenings light mists were still rising like steam, hovering above the River Arno. But the beginning of September saw the end of the blazing summer of 1943. And with it faded the hopes of the Jews of Florence for a speedy redemption.

Allied forces had landed in Sicily and obscure goldsmiths on both sides of the Ponte Vecchio[+] prophesied with typical Florentine enthusiasm that the war would end in September. Monks from Del Carmini,[+] who spoke little of everyday affairs, were heard whispering, "Italy, at any rate, will be out of it [they did not say surrender] in a few days. The Lord have mercy on our sinful souls. Amen."[+]

And the Di Gioacchino[+] family added very, very quietly, "Please God, by the Eve of the New Year. Perhaps our prayers will be answered already during the Days of Penitence."[+]

Like a man in torment, Nathan was counting the days that remained of a life of suffering. The respected Cassuto[+] family had been hurt by the adoption of the laws of racial purity in Italy. His father was a professor at the University of Rome; his sister Milcha taught Latin and Classical Greek at a government high school; Hulda, his second sister, was due to begin teaching mathematics, having been placed at the top of the list of candidates. Leah, his third sister, had also trained as a teacher. And he himself had just started on a career as a promising ophthalmologist when they were hit by the Nazi race laws. The Cassuto family table, the hopes of its members blighted, presented a picture typical of many Jews in Florence, not merely blessed with talented, hard-working sons and daughters but well integrated in the life and culture of the people of the country. Greater than the immediate adverse effect of the decrees on their physical existence was the way they were left spiritually dazed. Worthy citizens of Florence of Jewish origin saw themselves as mortally insulted without cause and felt totally at a loss.

There was one ray of light in the Cassuto household. Nathan's family and that of his wife, Chana, the Di Gioacchinos, of the tribe of Zebulun, had been for many generations steeped in Jewish tradition, love of the Land of Israel, and loyalty to the Zionist ideal. The coming of the laws did not weaken their own sense of dignity and self-respect; though they were humiliated, their stature was not diminished in their own or their children's eyes.

2.

How did the evil tidings spread throughout the land? Constantly, persistently, grim rumors filtered down from the north, tapping on the doors of the forty thousand Italian Jews, bringing secrets of ghettos, camps, and killings. Here and there Jewish refugees could be seen in town seeking refuge. They came from there. They brought evidence and they passed it on, but what they told was better unheard.

Nathan was dismissed from the government clinic. He straightway found alternative employment when a post of rabbi became vacant in Milan. From Milan he was asked to take over as rabbi of Florence. Nathan Cassuto revived an ancient tradition of rabbi-physician in the Jewish communities along the Mediterranean coast. He was thirty years old. His sisters had been expelled from the government schools. They got together and worked enthusiastically to set up a Jewish high school, which soon became the pride of the community in its reaction against the race laws. It earned a fine reputation and the members of the community adored their young rabbi. They saw him comb the city, from the outskirts to the inner suburbs, trying to track down refugees in need of aid. The Jews of Florence had always been hospitable and welcoming to guests, and whatever was needed to help their brothers in distress they did efficiently, without ostentation. But when their young rabbi brought up the evidence he had heard from the clenched lips of the survivors, and his words were meant as a warning, the members of his flock politely but firmly rejected his dire forecasts and answered with one voice that "here, in Italy, it won't happen here!"

3.

Nathan Cassuto removed his glasses, wiped the cracked lenses, and carefully put them back on. The fresh scar that furrowed his brow, the tufts of hair on his cheeks, the wild beard, and the dark rings under his large eyes gave him the look of a man of indeterminate age.

Strange. The young man from Theresienstadt had told about the old professor and his glasses at the gates of Birkenau, and something very similar had happened to him. Old Professor Zevi had carried bundles of books in his bag and would not be parted from them, even in the sealed cattle truck. Dazed and unable to keep their balance after five days' travel, they had stumbled when they jumped from the wagons on arrival at Auschwitz; the professor had fallen flat on his face in the mud and all his books had scattered. Nathan had bent down to help him and a blow from the leaden tip of a whip landed on his forehead. Worse than the blood that streamed into his eyes was the fact that his glasses had been sent flying. The crowd, harried by rifle butts and screams from the SS, almost trampled him to death.

Crawling around like a mad dog, he scrambled feverishly with his fingers and did not stop, not even when he heard

DI GIOACCHINO: Name of a Jewish family in Italy.

DAYS OF PENITENCE: The custom of the Jews of Italy, like that of the Sephardic Jews, was to begin the reciting of penitential prayers at the beginning of the month of Elul, not on the first day of the last week before the New Year.

CASSUTO: Name of a Jewish family in Italy.

LA DIVINA COMMEDIA (Italian): *The Divine Comedy*, the name of Dante Alighieri's famous trilogy composed of 100 poems arranged in three sections: "Inferno," "Purgatory," and "Paradise." Dante was born in 1265 to a noble family in Florence.

"Dawn came on us like a betrayer; it seemed as though the new sun rose as an ally of our enemies to assist in our destruction. The different emotions that overcame us, of resignation, of futile rebellion, of fear, or despair, now joined together after a sleepless night in a collective, uncontrolled panic. The time for meditation, the time for decision was over, and all reason dissolved into a tumult, across which flashed the happy memories of our homes, still so near in time and space, as painful as the thrusts of a sword."

—PRIMO LEVI,
Survival in Auschwitz

PIAZZA STATIONE (Italian): Station Square.

DUOMO (Italian): A cathedral, a large church.

a voice in German ordering him to get up immediately or be shot. And a miracle occurred. His glasses were cracked, but he had found them.

A fellow citizen tapped him on the shoulder:

"*Divina Commedia!*"✣ said the naive Florentine. Like Gonda from Theresienstadt, Nathan Cassuto had had his breaking point in the camp. During his very first week in Auschwitz he had caught dysentery, which left him dispirited before they broke his back with hard labor. On the brink of exhaustion, unable to mask his pain, he asked to be transferred to the sick ward. Those were days when men were falling ill and dying like flies. Anyone who reported sick was sent at once to the seventh block. At first sight it looked just like any other block in Birkenau. Bunks lined every hut, three high, so packed with invalids that you could hardly breathe. They had stopped bringing food, just let them die. When the number of prisoners exceeded capacity, they came early in the morning with trucks and took the superfluous invalids straight to the gas chambers. Those condemned to be gassed were thrown out into the yard while it was still night, exposed to the cold and rain and stripped of all their clothing. When Nathan heard the whimpering coming from the yard of the seventh block, he gathered his strength and returned to the workers' hut.

The next morning his dysentery went away.

"It's a miracle," commented Enzo, a man from Assisi.

"I don't believe in miracles," replied Doctor P., "but at times like these things do happen contrary to clinical experience, quite beyond comprehension."

Perhaps this time too a miracle would happen and he would get out of here in good health and live to see Chana and his children?✣

4.

The railway station of Florence was as busy as ever, and when he came back from Milan he noticed nothing special until he emerged into the city streets. Trucks with their tarpaulins rolled back, loaded with armed soldiers, were concentrated between Piazza Statione✣ and Piazza Bettini. Helmeted military dispatch riders tore off with terrifying screeches in the direction of Avenue Cavour. Germans! He left the *duomo*✣ on his left and made his way to Piazza della Signoria.

Chana was about to give birth and he hurried to make arrangements for her to be accepted by the hospital under a fictitious name. Then he went to the nunnery of Della Calza to meet his children and his sister. After wearisome efforts the Mother Superior had agreed to take in the children and his sister on the express condition, apart from payment, that the children learn like adults to respond only to their new names and not be choosy about whatever food they were served. Without hesitation he gave the nuns his consent and felt great relief. He had found secure shelter for his children and sister.

But within a week he was summoned to the nunnery. The Cassuto children had suffered stomach upsets at the sight of the nonkosher meat served at the nuns' table and had not touched their food. Worst of all, they refused to tell any lies!

David was the most obstinate. "Don't want to be Amato Fanfani. I'm David Cassuto!" screamed the little six-year-old.

"You're my son David Cassuto, and you always will be. But it's necessary to deceive wicked men."

"And I won't eat their pig meat!"

"But didn't you get used to eating nonkosher meat at home?"

The boy shuffled his feet. "But this isn't home, this is a nunnery!"

He would never forget the scared faces of the children as they crowded together in the dark bedroom set aside for the snatched meeting with their father. When he saw they could not be convinced, he laid down the law and said, "As your father and as a Jewish rabbi I give you permission to eat nonkosher meat and to tell lies in order to save your lives and not endanger your parents and the kind-hearted nuns. In Hebrew this is called *pikuaḥ nefesh,* the saving of lives, do you understand?"⁺

They accepted his ruling at once and promised to do as they were told.

He in turn promised them that soon he would come and take them away and the whole family would be together again.

The little boy David wiped away his tears and asked, "Don't you ever lie, Papa?"

Was the child prescient? He felt a stab of pain in his chest. He smiled and said, "You have a baby sister now, called Eva."

The dark bedroom in the nunnery of Della Calza all at once filled with cries of joy and sparkling eyes.

His wife had given birth. The children's rebelliousness died away. The rest of the family had found refuge with friends in villages, in concealed apartments in town, or within the walls of the monasteries.

That same day he set out for the San Marco monastery to meet Father Ricotti.

5.

Florence was full of refugees from the northern districts. And as they slipped through Bolzano and Como,⁺ a further stream came through Grenoble,⁺ fleeing from France. With no documents and no knowledge of the language they pressed south, toward freedom, impossible to attain without the mercy of heaven and a helping hand extended across the frontier.

Sometimes things of value have their origin in distress: three Florentines were taking counsel together about how to come to the aid of their brothers in need. In the attic apartment were Raphael Cantoni, Signor Carpi, and Nathan Cassuto. Once they had got things started, others came and joined them. Very quickly the Welfare Committee set up in secret became a meeting place for the town worthies. There was no lack of Christians and men of the Church. Since priests and monks were taking part, the Church too was generous in financing support for the host of refugees.

By the time of the Ten Days of Penitence two hundred Jews—men, women, and children—had found temporary shelter.

The rabbi and his assistants rented them apartments under assumed names, a few were hidden in houses that at the time seemed immune from search, like the private residence of the cardinal of Florence; one family of Jewish refugees found shelter in his library, between two walls, behind a picture of the Holy Family. But most of them were hidden behind monastery walls, which fortunately were not scarce on either side of the Arno.

"My dear Padre, don't you feel well?" His friend's appearance frightened the young rabbi. For a long while the monk had not raised his eyes to look at him. He sat hunched on the inner steps of the Church of San Marco, and it was clear he had undergone a painful experience.

Father Ricotti had been on his way to an apartment where a Jewish family had found refuge and were waiting urgently for medicine for their child, who had had an attack of asthma. Two Fascists accosted him at the entrance to Via San Fradiano. The older of the two, with plucked eyebrows, laid his hand on the monk's shoulder and said, "We know you're helping the Jews. If you don't stop, we'll burn down your church. This is your last warning!"

"**I received an answer** to the question 'Who is a Jew' from one of the children in the ghetto—and it was confirmed again and again by other children. A teacher of religion from the ghetto school told me from her own experience. The children listened with interest to holy stories from ancient Jewish history, from the Pentateuch. And one child, who had studied previously in a Polish school and spoke Polish at home, began now to study the Bible stories with great enthusiasm. When they reached the weekly portion Toledot, which includes the story of Jacob and Esau, the boy suddenly opened his mouth and said: 'Teacher, we come from Jacob, but they—the people who are bad to us—come from Esau, isn't that right? It's good; I want to belong to Jacob, not to Esau.' Man has the imagination of a free man. No walls can stifle it. An inhabitant of the ghetto can imagine being presented with an alternative: to strip himself of his abject, persecuted Jewish self and assume the self of the ghetto masters. This Jewish child instinctively chose to remain a Jew."

—ZELIG KALMANOVITCH,
April 30, 1943,
in the Vilna ghetto

BOLZANO: A town in southern Tyrol, on the border between Italy and Austria.

COMO: An Italian town, north of Milan near the border between Italy and Switzerland.

GRENOBLE: A town in the center of the French Alps, on the Isère River. Between November 1942 and September 1943, it came under the rule of the Italian army, which favored the Jewish refugees. A Jewish underground movement was organized in the town, composed of the Zionist youth movement M.J.S., the organization for the rescue of Jewish children, and the Jewish Scouts, assisted by sympathetic elements in the local Catholic church.

Cipriano Ricotti was a hefty man, made without fear, but there was still a tremor in his voice. It was not his own fate that caused him anxiety, but the weight of his responsibility for the monastery and the church.

The cardinal had instructed him to get away from the city for two weeks, till the storm had passed.

"All right," said Rabbi Cassuto, "hand over all your arrangements to Don Leto Cassini; in the meantime we have to find accommodation for a group of children who are coming across the border tomorrow."

That same day the young rabbi went to see Don Leto Cassini. He made arrangements with the priest to call a meeting of the committee for the twenty-sixth of the month. Don Cassini had bad news to tell about Professor Levy's two daughters in the Piazza Senioria. The two girls were wearing nun's habits but the Fascists lying in wait recognized who they were. Eyewitnesses reported that they had both been handed over to the Gestapo. The young rabbi knew them both, one was from his year at school.

"The true evil," he murmured in pain, "is the nature of those who commit evil."

6.

But true good must also be seen to be done. Anna Maria Agnelotti had already converted to Christianity and removed herself from the Jewish people before the bad times. From the day she volunteered her services for the secret committee, there was no one more zealous or devoted. But she too was caught in an ambush and handed over to be tortured. They did not break her spirit and in the end they shot her.

Nathan Cassuto had no premonitions on the twenty-sixth of November when he set off for the committee meeting. There had been a drizzle since early morning and he was thinking he ought to get the worn-down soles of his shoes repaired without delay. The meeting with the cardinal had been set for noon; he would raise the problem of getting a group of refugees across the Swiss border.

A gust of wind turned his umbrella inside out and as he looked up to restore it to shape, he saw out of the corner of his spectacles the barrier at the entrance to the street.

CARABINIERI (Italian): A term for the police in Italy. Literally, "rifle carriers."

ATTENZIONE (Italian): Watch out, be careful!

The committee met at 2 Via Puzzi. At first he was sure it was only Italian *carabinieri*.* By the time he noticed the black Mercedes it was too late to retreat. As he was being dragged forcefully through a gateway left a little open to allow one man to pass, and hustled along a gloomy passageway, his head throbbed like a compressor. But even before he heard the voice behind him, he understood that he was held by the arms of a friend.

Don Leto Cassini explained the meaning of the activity outside in the street, and the need for him to follow along a secret path to a small apartment he had prepared in advance for a time of danger.

"Do you understand exactly what's going on out there? Surely there must have been an informer?"

The priest blanched but controlled himself. Slowly and with reluctance he took out from under his cloak the printed manifesto. "Declaration No. 5 of the Ministry of the Interior of the Italian Fascist Government hereby proclaims that all Jews living in Italy, whatever their country of origin, must report to the following concentration points in order to . . . on 30 November. . . ." In other words, the persecution had begun today.

When he went back into the street, saw the helmets of the soldiers running through the gates of the houses, and heard the squawking of the loudspeakers, "*Attenzione, attenzione,*"* he instinctively walked around the truck, empty of soldiers, which blocked the entire width of the narrow road and began to turn in the direction of Piazza San Giovanni. But at once he pulled himself together and went toward the three men, who did not notice him at first: the Italian officer, Mario Gazzini, who had shot Anna Maria, a German SS man, and a Fascist youth guiding them. Nathan knew the boy and his family.

"That's him, the man with the beard," the boy pointed at him and quickly hid behind the officers.

7.

"Didn't you regret giving yourself up?" asked Gonda, the man from Theresienstadt, and Nathan Cassuto said nothing.

Suddenly he felt sad about Don Cassini. The priest had also been arrested that day and only through the efforts of the cardinal was he released from prison. Anyone in those days who fell into the hands of the Italian police had to consider himself lucky. Everybody knew that "our Fascists" were nothing like those revolting members of

Himmler's⁺ Gestapo. After all, Italians could be bribed. He wouldn't be surprised if this subtle distinction was also clear to Don Leto Cassini. An Italian interrogation was more amateurish. There were differences in method, in technique, but there was no difference in the nature of their malice. If he lived to come back to Florence, then every Shabbat Ḥazon⁺ he would preach a sermon on the theme: "The ultimate evil is those who commit evil." He repeated this to himself again and again, as though trying to inscribe the words on the tissues of his brain. On that day the Germans had rounded up more than a thousand Jews and sent them to the death camps, carrying out their orders with a precision not to be found among Florentines and Romans. The priest was two or three years younger than he: "Signor Cassuto, don't go. Those are Germans there. Gestapo."

They were standing in the shadow of oleanders and poplars in this unfamiliar courtyard, and only the water bubbling from the fountain broke the silence within its four walls crowned with bougainvillea. "We need you. Your family needs you."

Where were they? What was happening now to his wife Chana? Eva!—was there a hint in the name that one day they too would be expelled from Florence, but for what sin?

He felt himself suffocating with profound emotion. Perhaps he should go first to his wife and family to protect them, at least to consult them. "The poor of your own city come first";⁺ how much more so one's own family. There are critical moments when a man's whole world disintegrates, and when he is most in need the gates of counsel and prayer are closed in his face.

As these thoughts revolved in his fevered mind, his glance fell on the carefully cultivated oleanders growing opposite the blue marble basin. He remembered his father telling him how in the Land of Israel oleanders grew wild in wadis and along the banks of streams. Maybe his father was sitting now on a terrace wall above Mount Scopus,⁺ his gaze turned toward the hidden horizon, trying to send him a message from afar. Or perhaps at this hour his father was to be found in the National Library, among the hush of books? The sound of firing and voices shouting broke the calm of the patio.

"The first members of the committee to arrive are being taken now."

"*Dottore,* go up to the room I prepared for you and have a cup of coffee. Then you can decide whatever you will."

He noticed that Don Cassini had called him "*dottore.*"

"But I'm also the rabbi of Florence. And it is my fellow Jews who are being taken away."

He asked his friend to take note from afar where they took him and to try to tell his wife and family at once to change their hiding places.

"Quickly, my dear friend!" he urged him and turned toward the gate.

But Don Leto Cassini had not done as he was bid. No sooner had the rabbi left than he stole out after him and passed him on the other side. Again it was the priest who tried to pull him by his coat toward the vaulted residence of the cardinal. Cassuto regretted the impatience and rudeness with which he had rejected the proffered arm.

Those nights in custody he did not shut his eyes. Men, women, and children lay strewn there like broken tools. He was overcome by a feeling of unreality: Was this just a nightmare? Could it really be happening? he asked himself, his eyes glowing in the light of dawn.

They took them away in the early hours of the morning, before the city had woken from sleep. In a long column, accompanied by armed *carabinieri,* the people trudged, bedraggled almost beyond recognition. Very few inhabitants encountered them en route. But by the time they reached the railway station there were more and more, especially in the Piazza Statione: workers, clerks, shopkeepers, waiters. People did not react. Like strangers they

HEINRICH HIMMLER (1900-1945): One of the leaders of the Nazi Party, who carried out Hitler's orders. Himmler was commander of the SS and thus in charge of the Gestapo. If there is anyone who can be held personally responsible for the destruction of the Jews of Europe, Himmler is the man. With the collapse of the Nazi regime and the conquest of Germany by the Allied forces, Himmler was arrested. He committed suicide once his identity was discovered; he did not stand trial.

SHABBAT ḤAZON: The Sabbath before the Ninth of Av is also known as Shabbat Eikha, since the word "*eikha*" (how) is read three times:

How can I bear unaided the trouble of you, and the burden, and the bickering?
    —DEUTERONOMY 1:12

How she has become a harlot, the faithful city that was filled with justice, where righteousness dwelt—but now murderers. —ISAIAH 1:21

How doth the city sit solitary, that was full of people. She that was great among nations is become like a widow, the princess among states is become a thrall.
    —LAMENTATIONS 1:1

In Yemen it was called Shabbat Yagon (affliction).

Your own poor and the poor of your city—your own poor come first. The poor of your city and the poor of another city—the poor of your own city come first. —BABA METZIA 81 (a tractate of the Mishnah)

MOUNT SCOPUS: A mountain in Jerusalem.

VIA DOLOROSA (Latin): Literally, way of sorrow. A street in the Old City of Jerusalem that leads from the Lion Gate, through the Moslem Quarter, to the Church of the Holy Sepulcher in the Christian Quarter. According to Christian tradition, this is the path that Christ took from his place of trial to his place of crucifixion.

"On the back of my feet I already have those numb sores that will not heal. I push wagons, I work with a shovel, I turn rotten in the rain, I shiver in the wind; already my own body is no longer mine: my belly is swollen, my limbs emaciated, my face is thick in the morning, hollow in the evening; some of us have yellow skin, others grey. When we do not meet for a few days we hardly recognize each other."

—PRIMO LEVI, *Survival in Auschwitz*

". . . THROW MYSELF ON THE WIRES": Commit suicide by contact with the electrified fence that surrounded the camp.

LA GRANDE ARMÉE: The great army of Napoleon Bonaparte, organized for his march on Russia in 1812. It consisted of 600,000 troops and was the largest force ever mobilized in those days. Not all the soldiers were French; there were also a large number of Italians, Poles, Swiss, and Germans.

were quick to pass them by. They saw them clearly but had nothing to say, for good or ill: better to ignore them.

"And I thought it was different with you," came a voice from the end of the hut.

Father and Son

The father and son had refrained from speaking, as though wishing to preserve their remaining energy. Everyone in the block knew what had happened to them. But you do not.

The father and his son, who was known as "the good-looking one," were Auschwitz veterans. Their eyes had seen practically everything that long-standing prisoners of the death camps could see, winter and summer, summer and winter. But you, my distant relatives, which winter were you at Auschwitz?*

The winter of 1942 was colder than usual, and the days of frost began earlier. The frost hit the prisoners like the blade of an ax cleaving through hollow trees. Every morning, when the working parties moved off, they left behind those whose strength had failed them. They lay degraded in the snow, strewn along half the length of the Via Dolorosa,* the main avenue between the huts, or folded in grotesque postures by the entrance to the block itself. The living had to step over their comrades, whose bodies still twitched. Some tried under their own power or with the furtive help of a neighbor to crawl back into the hut. But the *Stube* would be on the watch and with a few kicks roll them back into the frost. And they lay stretched out in the cold of minus 20 degrees till ten in the morning. That was when trucks with trailers drove through the gate to make the daily round of the huts.

The helpless were thrown in to the trailers like bales of hay. Men in that condition did not cry out, though many of them still had a breath of life.*

One night the father woke up in pain. In order not to disturb the troubled sleep of his son, Eli, he carefully crawled outside the hut, past the threshold. The sun had not yet risen, only the pale white of the frozen snow shone from the roofs like dead days.

The son found his father lying in the snow, his plan only half accomplished. His father implored him, "Leave me, son. You still have strength. I am finished."

The son said, "If you do this to me again, I'll throw myself on the wires."*

Since then they had been inseparable, neither by night nor by day are they apart. Every night, the father's right arm lies under his son's head to form a soft pillow till the boy falls asleep. In his heart he prays, in German, "Merciful One, grant that I may live to lie down with my son alive again tomorrow night."

Until Eli turned up in Paris, Dr. Sternheim had been running like a frightened animal, trying to save his own life. His morale had been high all the time, as he had written to his sister who had been compelled to stay in Germany while he had succeeded in getting safely to Paris. After three years of exile, when he went to volunteer for the French army, his morale was still very high. He still believed in France, even when he joined the grim stream of defeated, humiliated soldiers trudging along in disorderly retreat. He, the Jewish doctor, the refugee, was supposed to encourage these descendants of La Grande Armée,* to teach these sons of Brittany and Lorraine that while they may have lost a battle, no nation can be defeated on its own soil as long as its sons are ready to give up their lives for the motherland.

He saw their devotion and admired the spirit of France and its culture, even though the officers of his regiment were already disposed to justify the law soon to distinguish between true sons of France, taken prisoner by the enemy, with all their rights and dignities protected, and stepsons, abandoned to their persecutors.

His morale remained high whenever he thought of his wife with little Robert in a safe place in Nice[+] and Eli his elder son working on a farm at Moissac in the unoccupied zone of southern France, where he and his youth pioneer companions were preparing themselves for their forthcoming *aliyah* to Palestine. Perhaps, he thought, God willing—to his surprise the phrase from his childhood came to mind—he too would follow in his son's footsteps.

Dr. Sternheim answered to the name Philo alone, though his great grandfather, whose name he bore, had the original double name: Philo-Yedidiah,[+] appropriate to the son of an eminent rabbinic family, descended from the great Rabbi of Rutenberg.[+] But there are limits, he thought, to the use of history as a symbol!

Were there limits to fear? One by one, imperceptibly, his fellow exiles had disappeared. Benjamin,[+] Weiss,[+] Hasenclever.[+] What had grieved him more than anything had been the death of his companion from his youth, Carl Einstein.[+]

The homes of his friends in Berlin were fresh in his memory. But his parents' home in his birthplace, a small town in Lithuania, existed only in the dim misty levels of his memory: from home too he had been exiled while still young.

To his fellow students in Lvov he was "Philé," the eccentric yeshiva student from Novogrudok;[+] in Berlin he was affectionately known as the *Galicianer,* and in Paris they took pity on the refugee from Germany. An eternal wanderer, how he envied his Berlin friends living in rooms with furniture that never changed, where the walls breathed tranquility, where stability enfolded the people who dwelt there. Whenever he crossed their threshold, he felt something reassuring, an aura of security, as though he leaned against the trunk of a stout tree.

And those walls! When he saw the portrait of the head of the family looking down at him from the heights of the plush-covered wall, side by side with earlier forefathers in their heavily gilded frames, he knew that the man was ensconced in the place he had wished to remain in forever, he and his children and his grandchildren after him.

And they deserved to remain there, for there was no one more loyal, more industrious, or more productive. They believed they had finally achieved the ideal balance between being minimally Jewish and thoroughly German. Two days before the time of the trains, he had seen an essay by Hermann Cohen[+] in the library of Karl's father. It's doubtful whether any German had ever written such words of admiration in the German language for German culture and the German spirit.

The trains sped across France. It was difficult to avoid seeing them. And it was impossible to mistake the identity of the load they carried in sealed wagons.

Imagine a winter's evening around the fireplace in the home of Dr. Charles. At noon that day his golden-haired daughter Louise had become engaged and now for the last time, before it was prohibited, she was being petted while she sat on Papa's knees. Papa Charles held a glass of champagne between his fingers, which he brought alternately to his own lips and to his daughter's. The glow of flames from the fire flickered

---

NICE, FRANCE: Nice came under Italian rule from November 1942 until September 1943 and was full of Jewish refugees protected by the Italian army. In September 1943, after the surrender of Italy, it was occupied by the Germans, who began a hunt for all the Jews. About 1,000 men, women, and children were seized and transferred via Drancy, a camp near Paris, to Auschwitz. The rest escaped, thanks to the French Jewish underground and French sympathizers.

PHILO-YEDIDIAH (20 B.C.E.–50 C.E.): Philo of Alexandria, a Jewish philosopher, born to a wealthy Jewish family that was connected with King Herod. Philo wrote in Greek and was well versed in classical literature and philosophy. Many Jews at all times have called their sons "Philo" or "Yedidiah" (literally "beloved of God").

THE GREAT RABBI OF RUTENBERG (1215– 1293): Rabbi Meir bar Baruch of Rutenberg, one of the spiritual leaders of German Jewry in the thirteenth century and an important author of Tosafot (comments on the Talmud). He was also known as a fighter for social justice, and gave expression to the sufferings of his contemporaries in the elegies that he composed.

WALTER BENJAMIN (1892-1940): German philosopher and literary critic (See notes for Scroll 1).

ERNEST WEISS (1884-1940): A writer, friend of Kafka, who cut his veins in a hotel in Paris on the day the Germans entered the city.

WALTER HASENCLEVER (1890-1940): Poet and playwright, who committed suicide in the detention camp at La Mille.

CARL EINSTEIN (1885-1940): A critic of German art, who drowned when fleeing from the Gestapo.

NOVOGRUDOK, POLAND: A town east of Grodno.

HERMANN COHEN (1842-1918): A German Jewish philosopher, Yehezkiel Hermann Cohen defended Judaism against anti-Semitic attacks.

against the young girl's full breasts. The father saw the cleft of her breasts and suddenly became aware of a desire to sprinkle there a drop or two of his champagne. Inexplicably he burst out laughing. Mademoiselle approached, carrying a tray loaded with sandwiches of goose liver, which his nephew had brought from La Mille. As he was leaving the town, or more precisely as he was passing the fenced camp there, crossing the field and the railway line, a train went by.

At the front was a carriage with French gendarmes and Germans in black uniforms. The windows were full of soldiers, bareheaded in the wind. They sipped from the bottles of beer they held and sang "Lily Marlene."[*] After the passenger compartment came sealed cattle trucks. Where heads of cows should have been seen there were thin arms of children, their fingers clutching the bars. He saw a hand waving like a sprig of lilac in the wind. When the nephew said "like a sprig of lilac in the wind," Louise looked at him in astonishment. At a curve in the embankment, where there was a small bridge, the train slowed down. Then he distinctly heard voices crying "Maman, maman." From the front carriages came the sound of "Lily Marlene" and near at hand, before his eyes, the cry of the children was answered only by the squeaking of the brakes.

The nephew from La Mille described what he had seen with genuine emotion. To his hosts' credit it must be said that the surprising revelations of their guest from the provinces left them heavily silent. Young Louise hugged her papa with her bare arms and the muscles of Dr.

"LILY MARLENE": A well-known German song, which German soldiers were already singing during World War I, and continued to sing during World War II. It was translated into English and sung by British soldiers as well.

ALEXANDER HERZEN (1812–1870): A Russian writer and thinker of socialist and radical views.

NIKOLAI CHERNISHEVSKY (1828–1889): A Russian writer, critic, and thinker who was active in revolutionary circles.

THE SANCTITY OF LIFE FOR THOSE WHO ARE ABOUT TO DIE: Because of the topographical conditions, the French resistance movement's main sphere of activity was within the towns. During the day its members would go to work and only at night were they active in the resistance. Jews played a great part in this movement.

On September 29, 1943, the underground made an attempt on the life of one of the senior German officers in Paris, Julius von Reuter. He was shot at the corner of Rue Petrarche and Rue Reservoir by the commander of the unit, Marcel Raimand. An informer betrayed 23 fighters and they were all sentenced to death after a show trial. In the statement made by the Resistance in memory of the 23, it says: "They were one Spaniard, three Frenchmen, one Romanian, two Armenians, three Hungarians, five Italians, eight Poles." This is not accurate. Among the eight "Poles" there

Charles's face quivered. They were unable to forget that their guest was a Jewish refugee, for Dr. Charles had served with Sternheim in the same unit of light cavalry and after the German invasion had helped him find the man who forged his papers. And made him a fully-fledged Aryan. And if there was any meaning to what he now did, it was only an attempt to dissipate the man's suffering, for he said, "Let's see what else our dear nephew has brought from La Mille, maybe some goose liver, as in the good old days?"

Dr. Charles was only trying to do something positive; as they say, one must take a positive attitude.

And on his bed that night, Philo-Yedidiah Sternheim, who according to his forged papers was Alphonse de Vernet, preferred to remember the comradeship of battle, when he had forged links with several high-ranking members of the aristocracy, and the great culture of France, and the thinkers who in the Russia of Herzen[+] and Chernishevsky[+] were called the "intelligentsia" and in France were "les intellectuels." No more than twenty-four hours would elapse before Dr. Sternheim would be forced to realize that the France of Descartes and Racine also held Vichy and the gendarmes.

It was an albino gendarme, with plucked eyebrows, who had once happened to visit the field hospital of Captain Sternheim. It was he now who lit a warning light under the Porte Saint-Denis, by the pedestrian crossing, in broad daylight in the heart of Paris, when he said, "*Bonjour, cher Docteur.*" The officer bared his teeth in a grin from ear to ear. Sternheim continued on his way without turning left or right. He could feel the breath of the gendarme on his neck as far as the Rue du Temple.

Automatically he felt for his breast pocket, for the papers that bore the pure Aryan name Alphonse de Vernet. Suddenly he felt the tips of his fingers singed by fire.

Fortunately there are whores in Paris in peace as in war, and in this district there was no lack. One of them was hanging on the neck of the gendarme, who seemed to prefer the sweetness of honey to the strength of the lion, and allowed his Jewish prey to escape.

On Sternheim's return from work the following day he was told by the concierge that some characters in civilian dress had been looking for him and asking questions. With the impulse of a frightened animal, he packed two or three shirts, a spare suit, and the best of his books and went down the iron stairway to the back entrance, with no intention of coming back.[+]

Sternheim did not need his address book in order to examine his options. Naturally he would turn to those of his French friends, worthy citizens, whose favor was sought even by the conquerors, because of their reputation and public standing.

It is not easy for a man to accept that his illusions have been shattered. The couple named P. received him in their garden with their usual warmth, speaking quietly and calmly on their home ground. There are houses in Paris that from outside are in the bustling heart of the metropolis but once inside, they are like the country landscape of the Loire. The couple named P. were considered intellectuals and until the German invasion used to host in their salon exiled writers and artists from Germany, in the flattering words of Madame P. "from the true Germany," until the Germans dragged off to the concentration camps those of them who had not managed to commit suicide.

It was evident that Monsieur P. was moved, even somewhat embarrassed, by the visit but Madame P. did not conceal her thoughts, merely expressed her desire in a whimsical rhetorical question that it was impossible to refuse. "My dear Phil," she told the Jewish refugee, "surely you would not wish to endanger your good friends at a time when those madmen are suspicious of everybody and everything and our Emile, as you well know, has heart trouble?" He didn't know. And he didn't stop to ask. The impulse of a frightened animal took him straight back outside, straight into the snake pit.✣

It had been a stormy night when he had been called out to attend to the only son of the ambassador, who had escaped from captivity, wounded and feverish. He had found him on the brink of cardiac arrest. The writer-diplomat had said to him, "You saved my son's life and I am at your service, at any time." He had been moved to tears to hear this representative of the nobility and French honor repeat with emphasis, "At any time."

Well, the time had come.

When he set off for the home of the high-ranking dignitary, he was not thinking only of saving his own skin. The training camp had broken up and the young pioneers in the south of France had hurried to try and cross the Pyrenees; some of them had succeeded in stealing across the Spanish frontier. But the rear guard had run into an ambush of gendarmes and been captured. By a miracle Eli had escaped his pursuers. When he heard his son's voice on the telephone, speaking from some gas station in the suburbs of Toulouse, telling him he couldn't wait to be reunited with his father, he realized that a disaster had occurred. But he was still saved from full knowledge of his fate. Fortunately the high-ranking dignitary was in Paris. That same morning Sternheim had seen his name mentioned in the society gossip column of *Le Figaro*.✣ The writer-diplomat lived near the Quai d'Orsay.✣ There was a feel of ancient grandeur about the rooms, hung with tapestries and lined with books. Behind the marble columns, which surrounded the entrance hall, gleamed masterpieces from the sixteenth century. A butler he recognized from before opened the carved door.

To his surprise the butler asked him, "Whom do you wish to see, Sir?"

"His Excellency, Pierre, *mon vieux.*"

"Do you have an appointment?"

"Certainly," still confident.

With visible embarrassment the butler turned toward the inner marble staircase. Still clutching his umbrella, Sternheim waited in the entrance hall. Despite his inner tension, he could not help feeling some relief at the sight of Holbein's "Portrait of a Woman," which he never tired of seeing. The butler returned and asked the doctor the purpose of his visit. Now the visitor's embarrassment was greater than the butler's.

He looked at the blank expression on the butler's face and could find no words to define the reason for his visit. "Tell your master, Pierre, that Dr. Alphonse de Vernet needs to see him urgently."

With professional skill the butler banished a sly smile

---

was only one Pole; seven of them were Jews, including the leader, Marcel Raimand, age 20, a man of many exploits, a native of Warsaw. From his letter of farewell to his mother: "My darling mother, I can tell you only one thing: I have loved you more than anyone in the world and I would wish to continue to live for you. I love you and embrace you, I cannot find words to express my feelings. Your Marcel, who admires you and thinks of you in his last moments—*vive la vie.*"

A German Jewish refugee in France, who had been called to the front to fight against Hitler's army, asked his commanding officer after the defeat, "Why are you taking me, in French army uniform, to a concentration camp? Why are French soldiers taking me?"

The French officer replied, "*C'est parce que vous avez trop aimé la France*" (Because you loved France too much).

LE FIGARO: A widely circulated Parisian daily newspaper.

QUAI D'ORSAY: A street in Paris, bordering the Seine, on which the French Foreign Office is located. Hence the use of the expression *Quai d'Orsay* as a synonym for the Foreign Ministry.

and walked softly away. Sternheim was angry with himself for allowing a note of entreaty to enter his voice. Half a floor above the glass door of the ambassador's room opened and over the balcony loomed the figure of his sister. She may never have cared very much for the company of Sternheim but her manners had always been impeccable. She was about forty, unmarried. Tall in stature, wearing a heavy brocade dressing gown and a strange headdress, with the clear complexion of an angel, she seemed to have stepped straight out of the gilt frame of Holbein's portrait of Princess Christina.

She stood over the white marble, leaning on both arms, and hissed down at him, "At a time like this. Making a nuisance of yourself. Such vulgarity. Typical egotism. Typical! How could you!"

When the heavy carved masterpiece of a door closed behind him, there were plenty of addresses left in Dr. Sternheim's address book, but very few chances. Nevertheless, he still felt hopeful. The exit doors from France had narrowed to a crack: the sole remaining hope was Murphy, the American consul in Paris.

After so many separations, father and son were once again reunited: they slept on the same mattress, in the same hut, in the same concentration camp at Le Vernet.✛ By an irony of fate the "Aryan" ancestry registered in his forged papers came from the same place where there was now a concentration camp. But things could have been worse. Blows were a daily occurrence here, but at Dachau men were beaten to death. Winter had begun and they had no blanket to cover them. Eventually the son obtained a torn blanket for the two of them, thereby joining the happy 40 percent who had a blanket for the winter chill. In Dachau, they said, prisoners were chained and abandoned to the frost at night. His uncle Emmanuel was sent to Gurs.✛ He was expelled with all the Jews of Baden and the Palatinate✛ and together with twenty thousand men and women imprisoned in the worst of the French concentration camps. The camp at Gurs was established with malicious intent on marshland.

LE VERNET: A concentration camp in the southwestern region of France, near the camp at Gurs, not far from the Spanish frontier.

GURS: A concentration camp within the area controlled by the Vichy government, near the Franco-Spanish border, south of the Bay of Biscay.

THE PALATINATE: A region in western Germany, also known as Pfalz. It is located on the west bank of the Rhine, with the French border to the south.

"LIEBE HERR DOKTOR..." (German): My dear Doctor.

The rain turned the whole area into a sea of mud. Even before the French had managed to hand over the mass of prisoners to the Gestapo, thousands died on their hands of typhus, malnutrition, and dysentery.

"How are you, Herr Professor?"

"How did you pass the night, Herr Advokat?"

Unwashed, smeared with slime, smelling of mold and decay, in old torn clothes, the prisoners always addressed each other by their former German titles, as though trying with their last grasp to hold on to this flimsy bridge to civilization.

"*Liebe Herr Doktor,*✛ would you be so kind as to tell me the time?"

But the worst was yet to come. Their train would speed across the French countryside, stopping at out-of-the-way places, in God-forsaken railway stations, where new wagons would be attached. Into these cattle trucks women and children, old people and invalids would be loaded by the gendarmes with blows from their rifle butts. Even cripples with their wheelchairs. First the deportees would be searched and anything of value taken from them, then a head count would be taken, not less than fifty to a truck. Since there was a war on and the Germans had been ordered to economize on transport, no train was to cross the German frontier unless loaded with at least a thousand heads; once the twentieth truck was attached it could continue to speed east. The trains raced on and the wagons clattered and once again the convoy was inexplicably held up at night. The number of dead in the cattle trucks mounted and the cargo of corpses and horde of half-suffocating living left behind them a trail of lamentation, and if the sky were parchment and all the waters of the Rhine were ink, the cry of the innocent might have been inscribed on the body of Germany and never expunged till the end of days. Yet German railway workers and German farmers, overseeing their Ukrainian forced labor, maintained in days to come that when the trains went by they saw no screaming faces, heard nothing, were aware only of a cloud of nauseating odor, totally without explanation. Perhaps they really saw nothing, heard nothing. For in every sealed truck there was a Sternheim, and one was enough, to tell his fellow sufferers to stop screaming at soundproof walls, since every scrap of breath would be needed in what remained of life.

Even in the wagon that carried them to the menace of the unknown, Dr. Sternheim's morale was still what you might call high. As long as he could still say to his brothers "keep your spirits up" and his son was in his embrace, the worst was still to come.

On the fourth day of their journey, Eli saw a feathery sky through the bars. The doors were opened and they were allowed to leave the trucks. Some jumped. Some climbed down holding on to bolts and brackets and some fell on their faces. There was a strong smell of birch trees. A forest of mixed coniferous and deciduous trees stretched before them, and above it a range of sharply defined mountains glowed white. In the distance they could see a settlement, with a long road and roofs thatched with straw. Cows gazed at them without moving, probably people too. According to a wooden sign left lying by the side of the embankment, they were standing on the soil of Poland.

"We have arrived," thought Sternheim.

"Doesn't the greenery gladden your heart?" cried Eli. "Look at the splendid range of mountains, Papa, that has been provided for us!"

Nearby a shot rang out and the strangled cry of a victim. It was Julien, a young sportsman, who had not dropped his training even in Drancy.* The door of his carriage had stopped exactly opposite a bend in the stream and it didn't take much, just the fierce passion for life of a man of indomitable will like Julien to jump across a few railway sleepers and slide down from the embankment almost unseen to the bank of the stream. It's not clear whether or how much fresh water from the stream the lad managed to drink before he was shot in the head. They saw the upper part of his body floating on the stream and from his skull oozed a trail of blood in the clear blue water.

The soldiers of the escort handed out spades and shovels. The bodies of those who had died on the journey were dragged out from the darkness of the trucks and piled up between every three trucks. Why three? Don't ask.

"The members of the first party to finish burying will each receive an extra quarter of a loaf!" Since eyebrows were raised in disbelief, the Ukrainian chuckled, "This is genuine Socialist competition. A promise is a promise."

The men from Drancy, Berlin, and La Mille couldn't see the joke. It was only now that they noticed that their guards had changed. The Germans had been joined by squads of Ukrainians instead of French gendarmes. Unlike their predecessors, who liked to sit inside their compartments, the Ukrainians clustered on the roof. They sat there with their machine guns pointing down, like hunters in the saddle waiting for rabbits.

"Julien's alive!" Dr. Sternheim almost gave a cry when he drew near to the body lying in the mud and saw that the skull was intact and the wound superficial. Julien opened his eyes a slit and with a look implored him to be quiet.

"What shall I do now?" thought Sternheim.

"Bury me last," whispered the wounded man when he leaned over him to pick him up, "and leave a little opening for air. I intended to run away in any case."

And that's what they did. They had known worse things to happen since, and many times as they lay awake in their huts in Auschwitz-Birkenau the father and son had asked themselves over and over again whether they had buried a man alive or saved a condemned man from death.

"We have arrived."

Five whole days the journey had lasted and toward the end the wail of people begging for water grew louder. The Ukrainians heard the cries of entreaty rising in waves from inside the trucks and tried to hush them with bursts of machine gun fire from above. There would be silence and then the cries would return: "Water! Water!"

Almost inaudibly Sternheim would repeat from his corner, "In a while they will give us water, just as yesterday they gave us bread. It means they need us, for work."

Had he consoled his son in his blanket or did he have a dim feeling that this was not the worst?

Finally the train stopped at a large station and there was no longer any doubt they had reached their destination. Sternheim was incapable of saying any more.

The large sign in front of his eyes said Auschwitz.

You cannot say Sternheim had never heard of Auschwitz. Nor can you say he knew what Auschwitz was.

Those nearest the bars passed on the message. As they looked out they described what they saw; this was no rumor.

"A large camp."

"Very large."

"Lots of fences all around."

"No civilians. Apart from Germans, only prisoners in pajamas."

"Pajamas?"

The doors were not opened till the following morning. Spades, shovels, and bundles in their hands,

*DRANCY: A detention camp southeast of Paris, through which passed most of the 100,000 who were deported to the death camps.

they were told to run. The first thing they saw was the long whips in the hands of the officers.

"Get down!"

"Quickly!"

"On the double!"

"Quickly!"

Anyone who took his time was whipped—on the head, in the face. People streamed out of the other trucks. Women and children too. Everyone had to move on the double. They came to a wall. There were clerks sitting there. Germans. And armed soldiers standing along the wall. Above the gate was a giant slogan: "ARBEIT MACHT FREI."[*]

"Men to the right! Women and children to the left!" Some of the scurrying procession fell to the ground and were trampled on. The lines divided in different directions. It was impossible to understand the reason for it. And there was no time to pay heed to what was happening. In that winding stream they seemed not even to feel the pain of separation.

Out of the corner of his eye Sternheim saw mothers shudder as they hugged their children and men call out to them with a wave of the hand, "Goodbye. See you at the station."

Even as the frightening chorus of commands fell like shadows across their ears, they continued to examine the unfolding sights of the camp. Reinforced blocks of huts in reasonable condition. A pattern of roads. Everything perfectly clean and well ordered. The impression was of a busy, well-organized beehive. Dr. Sternheim, who was driven to distraction by anything illogical, found some

"ARBEIT MACHT FREI" (German): "Work makes you free." The cynical slogan of deceit that flew above the gate of the Auschwitz death camp.

"If there is hope, great and clear, it is not for us."
—ANONYMOUS GRAFFITI

"I have loved thee, my people, even dressed in rags."
—GERTRUD KOLMAR

Someone will say it lasts but a year,
Three times four months;
I say those are days and nights
That are endless.
Every day—twelve hours,
Every night—seven hundred minutes,
Every minute—sixty seconds,
Each second with its load of pain and suffering.
—Written in Polish by an unknown Jewish girl
and found lying around at Auschwitz

consolation in the appearance of the place: Auschwitz was a camp designed for mass labor. The line of men went through the gate, ran past the wall, and arrived at an empty square. Sternheim dropped, exhausted. The moment's respite ended and Eli did as ordered and added their personal belongings to the general pile, lending his father support as they moved forward. They were standing now in groups of five and straightened the ranks. Armed guards moved among the ranks and marked off five groups of five. These were marched off to one of the blocks. Eli prayed their turn would come quickly. His father's body hung slack, reaching for the ground. Eli held him without the guards noticing. But they stood waiting more than an hour and his strength was running out. Eventually their turn came and they were marched off between the huts. As they crossed a wide avenue they happened to meet some veteran prisoners. At the risk of a whipping from the guards, Eli turned toward the men passing by and pressed them with questions. The camp dwellers made no answer, no one stopped for him. He could see they were busy with some task. Some were carrying food containers and some blocks of wood. Tottering and running. They called out monosyllables to each other, as if they spoke some secret language. They all wore peakless caps. He now saw the camp as unending. A camp within a camp within a camp within a camp, crisscrossed and surrounded by electric fences. They marched forever.[*]

Sternheim's face had turned green and Eli could not understand how his father could still march with his eyes shut. Eli's eye were open but he could hardly breathe and a cold sweat bathed the back of his neck.

They passed through gates and moved between rows of SS carrying Schmeissers. The salt from his sweat seared his neck, his whole brain seemed to have turned into a block of salt. Strange, it was just at this moment that sights from the farm came unbidden to his mind, trivial incidents during his training. There was a large iron bar hanging from a post in the middle of the farm camp, which served as a bell. They would ring it for meals and meetings. He asked them to get rid of the spine-chilling thing. But the youth leader said this was the way things were done on a kibbutz in Palestine and nothing from Palestine could be alarming, only heartwarming. Three shots were heard and a single cry.

They passed through one gate, and then another, and then they saw two huts, identical in size and design, each of them as big as a cargo ship. Above them chimneys rose to a great height.

There were concrete pillars every two or three meters. Wire fences encircled the camp and divided it into quarters. White insulators made it clear that the fences were electrified. In an instant the voices died down, the orderly ranks reeled suddenly as from a blow, were swept roughly aside as though hit by a hurricane.

Someone shouted "Gas!" and the ranks took up the cry. "They're going to burn us! Gas!"

"We won't go in." Eli tightened his grip on his father's arm, digging his nails in confirmation. "Come what may, we won't go in," he whispered between his teeth.

A burst of fire from the side and another from the rear put an end to the incipient revolt.

Where could they go? How could they flee?

Pushed from behind, the son led his father toward the entrance of the long, narrow building. Those who had gone in ahead of them were already milling about in the nude. At once he helped his father undress as ordered, and was himself late in standing against the wall naked as the day he was born. He expected to be whipped. But this time the *kapo* made do with a hearty curse. Eli picked up his clothes and his father's, folded and sorted them, and placed them on the appropriate piles, a pile of singlets, a pile of briefs, a pile of shoes, and a pile of hats. For some reason shirts and sweaters were put in separate piles. They were packed together in one huge dense mass, standing in the space between the piles of clothes, along the walls on both sides. Then they saw the raised dais at the end of the hall and the officer towering there, booted feet astride. He had a large Mauser strapped to his hip and a whip in his hand. He snapped the whip once and there was a hush. Though the guards told them to close up they kept a certain distance apart, as though each man recoiled from touching his neighbor's nakedness. The German had already bared his lips and was about to begin speaking when an unexpected noise made him look round. An expression of surprise and disgust spread across his moon-shaped face. His paunch seemed about to burst out of his uniform.

Below him, almost in the center of the front ranks, an old man was standing and urinating. He stood there gaping like a man in shock, his fingers shielding his private parts. The stream was impeded by the callused fingers on his penis and dripped like rain around his ankles. His bare feet were plunged in the middle of a puddle from which hot vapor was rising. Unluckily for him, the floor was lower at that point and the bounds of the puddle were broken. A trickle of urine was creeping down the slope right toward the dais. If the men had been able to spare any thoughts for compassion and an intelligent response, then those around the old man, who must have been suffering from prostatitis or involuntary panic, should have drawn closer and concealed his shame from the murderer. But the men flinched and instinctively withdrew from contact with this accursed individual. He was a man of seventy, with a full beard, and skin of a shade between parchment and a shroud. Large hot tears were now falling across his cheeks, but he did not ask for mercy, he made no sound.

To make matters worse, compounding the offense, one doesn't actually have to be malicious. The first of those standing near who couldn't help laughing was certainly not evil by nature, and it's doubtful whether he did what he did with any intention of hurting another victim. When he realized his mistake, he suppressed his giggles and wiped his trembling lips with the back of his hand. But it was already too late. From all sides came a response. Even the distant ranks who didn't understand exactly what had happened joined in the laughter. The wave of sharp hysteria swept through the naked throng. It seemed as if the fear that had caused one sick old man to urinate in the least amusing place in the whole world now prompted hundreds of men with bare buttocks and shaven heads to give vent to wild laughter, freeing deep-seated restraints of shame, totally oblivious both of themselves and of the SS man looking down from the dais.✣

The German had not moved an inch. He stared at the Jews whose limbs shook like willow branches waving in synagogue on Sukkot, and only his chin quivered.

"Jewish swine," he said at last, almost in a whisper, and pointed his middle finger.

Two burly guards pounced on the wretch with clubs. They dragged the old man by an arm out of the hall, though not before rubbing his face two or three times in the pool of urine, just as you do with an untrained cat. At once the ranks reformed and straightened up. Silence returned and was cut like a knife. The German said, "You have

How can you remember us,
and the world,
which disaster has
rendered inhuman?
Will a human world ever exist
which does not conceal
disaster in its breast?
—ANONYMOUS

come here to work. God help anyone who doesn't carry out orders to the letter. No privacy. If anyone conceals anything of value on or inside his body, he'll pay for it. Order, cleanliness, and efficiency—that's all we require of you here. And now, forward march, you shits!"✢

Eli stretched his neck to see over the shoulders of those marching in front of him, to see where they were going. He could see his companions being swallowed up in the dim maw of the next building. In between, just at the space between the huts, shots were heard from behind the wall. Two or three shots in all, enough to save an unidentified Jew from the expected passage through the forty-eight gates of hell.✢

As they passed into the second wing they were seized by the powerful arms of the barbers. There were about twenty of them in all, and it's doubtful whether any of them had been a barber by trade. Certainly their tools were not fit to be used on human beings. They were dressed in striped pajamas, like those they had seen earlier in the camp, and were in charge of shaving. It was their duty with their blunt instruments to complete a massive quota of shaven heads, armpits, and groins, to remove every trace of hair from the bodies of the new prisoners. Since their time was limited and slowness could cost them their lives, they paid no heed to the pleas of their "customers."

Can pain be measured? The screams heard in the first wing as blunt clippers plucked hair out by the roots, and scraped away a little skin here and there were no less frightful than the cries of those condemned to die in the last wing. Both there and here there was no one to hear. When it was Eli's turn to stand in front of his squat, toothless barber, he crammed his fist in his mouth and bit it, so as not to cry aloud. As he silently cursed his torturer, he forgot that the man was only another prisoner who had once been inspired to lie and thus be registered as a bar-

ber, with no desire to hurt or torture anyone, only to save his life, since members of the intelligentsia like him, with no productive occupation, were doomed to go to the left. Now he was on duty from morning to evening and, like the instrument he wielded, had no will of his own.✢

There was a corridor, as in a railway train, with cells along its length. The second wing was for bathing. By the time he had realized the nature of the muddy liquid, Eli had already been pushed into the bath up to his knees. The trough that had been dug out of the center of the cell was full of Lysol or some such disinfectant, which gave off a nauseating smell. Eli feared for his father, who might collapse and sink down in this cesspit, but was not allowed to hold him or even stand next to him. He was ordered immediately to turn around while another prisoner, whose job was decontamination, wiped him with a rag soaked in the same material. The rag was tied to the end of a stick and the prisoner who held it wiped all the suspect areas with brusque efficiency: armpits, groin, skull, back, and buttocks.

After the decontamination cell the door opened onto the third wing. It was larger than the previous rooms, with bare walls and in the ceiling you could see round holes like the ends of pipes. White wisps of steam curled around the edges of the holes. When the last of their group had been thrust inside, the iron door slammed behind them with a loud clang. The agonies of the shaving and the smarting and feeling of nausea brought on by the decontamination bath were replaced by cries of terror, "Gas!"

"Right. Gas!"

As their cries redoubled and they moaned with despair they became aware of steam bursting through the holes in the ceiling. Within seconds, streams of hot water were pouring through those dread apertures. The men were quick to cover their shaven heads, or their genitals, with their hands lest they be scalded by the hot water. There were still some "*oy*"s, but it was only water and actually the heat and the fog were reminiscent of a steam room in a Turkish bath on the Sabbath eve.

At the wave of a magic wand the atmosphere had changed from one extreme to the other. The men slapped each other on their bare backs, plunging in the startling torrents of water, and there were bursts of laughter from the decontaminated, now feeling a little embarrassed. As though frozen to the spot, Dr. Sternheim stood in their midst, his arms hanging by his sides, his head lolling for-

"**Perhaps my ancestral lineage** rolls around in the sand and is effaced." —MIRIAM ULINOVER, killed at Auschwitz

FORTY-EIGHT GATES OF HELL: Kabbalistic literature speaks of the "forty-eight gates of impurity." Mendele Mocher Sefarim says, "Their soul sunk in the forty-eight gates of crude passion" (In the *Vale of Weeping*, Book 7, Chapter 1), but here the forty-eight gates are substituted for the seven circles of Hell.

For My plans are not your plans, nor are your ways My ways, declares the Lord. (Isaiah 55:8) —A dedication written on the frontispiece of a Bible by a Catholic priest, a native of Florence, and given to the daughter of Professor Cassuto, in lieu of a reply to a "silent question," February 13, 1944

ward. The son heard the strangled sobs of his father above the splashing water and it was heartrending.

"Papa, you're washed, you're clean now. Papa, it's only a shower."

His father's shoulders quivered with his weeping. Eli stroked his father's bare back, a warmth from some other world flooded his fingertips as they caressed, and he choked. With difficulty he whispered, "Soon, I'm sure, they'll give us new clothes. I think they need us."

A door opened and they were pushed through. Dr. Sternheim did not react. He seemed resigned to his fate. Just let the time in this hell be brief. To their surprise they found other prisoners there. Just like them. These were dressed in striped pajamas. Father and son walked unthinkingly toward piles of clothes. Behind each pile stood a prisoner. They were told to stretch out their arms. They did so. The prisoner placed shirts, striped trousers, cloth sandals, a peakless cap, a metal bowl, and a battered mug in their arms. They spread out along the wall and put the clothes over their scalded skins.

"Sir," a lanky Jew was urging Dr. Sternheim, "perhaps we can exchange. These do not fit me." Sternheim stared with eyes empty of expression and did not understand what he was being asked. On all sides arose voices of entreaty, passionate pleas to do a deal. For a moment they seemed to be standing in the heart of the Flea Market in Paris. Some were offering tomorrow's portion of soup in exchange for a cap that fitted. Rising above the persistent voices, someone burst out wailing hysterically, "These trousers keep falling down!" Suddenly men at the entrance to hell felt miserable on account of their trousers!

They were pushed out into the open square. Other prisoners were sitting cross-legged on the ground, indistinguishable one from the other. Uncomprehending, they found themselves in front of a long wooden table loaded with huge steaming cauldrons. Behind them stood hefty prisoners, presumably specially chosen, who poured soup into their bowls. Sternheim held his metal bowl with trembling hands and took a long breath, smelling the muddy liquid. A *kapo* brandished his whip and the soup spilled on the ground. They were allotted one minute to drink the soup and anyone who didn't manage was punished. Dr. Sternheim stood there with his arms hanging down, the remains of his soup dripping from his trembling lips. Eli quickly picked up the precious bowl and moved out of range of the vicious blows of the guard.

Again they were being pushed toward a gate in the fence. Eli had given up counting the gates. Only one thought was blazing in his mind: to lie down. Just to lie down a little. His feet could no longer support him. And what about his father? If they had decided to kill them, why all this ill treatment? Was it some sadistic game, or did they want to reduce them to a state of total surrender?

They were ordered to stop in front of a line of huts surrounded by barbed wire. "Sit down." They had to sit in ranks, in marching order. Quickly they arranged themselves as bidden. No one moved right or left. Eli saw his father flop to the ground. With some effort he sat up as required. His head drooped toward his knees. That's all right, thought Eli, and put one arm around his father. In the other hand he held both their eating utensils. He didn't yet have a lace or a piece of string to tie them together. Later Eli would talk to his father about what they saw at that time. And his father would state forcefully that it had never happened, it was all a product of his fevered imagination. But Eli knew what he had seen. They had probably been sitting like that for several hours, for it was getting toward evening and his head had fallen onto his raised knees. With the remains of his strength he kept drifting in and out of a dulled state of mind, trying to shake off drowsiness in order to follow closely what the Germans and their dogs were doing, clearing the ten large huts on the other side of the road of their Gypsy inhabitants.

The Gypsies[+] were still bunched together in families: men, women, old people, and lots of children. Their dress was colorful, the sole patches of color against a sea of black and stripes. Moving out clearly took them by surprise. Some tried to fight their guards. Their heads were smashed with lead batons and the screaming of the women and children shocked the whole area. Eli saw one or two of the Gypsy men striking the baton-wielders in the face, wresting the weapons from the hands of the Germans. Trained dogs sprang at them and sank their teeth in the throats of the brave

GYPSIES: A tribe of nomads, originating in northwest India. The Gypsies reached Europe in the fifteenth century and spread throughout almost all the countries of Europe, even reaching North America. Most of them were concentrated in the Balkan countries, Hungary, Italy, and Spain. Their language belongs to the Indo-European family. There were about 5 million Gypsies in the world. The Nazi authorities decided to destroy everyone they defined as being of mixed German and Gypsy blood, beginning in 1941, and during the war they murdered hundreds of thousands of Gypsies—men, women, and children.

Gypsies. Shots were heard. There was instant silence and the long lines rolled on like the incoming tide toward the fences. A bitter, muffled wailing still hung in the air long after the Gypsies had disappeared from sight.

The evacuation of the Gypsy camp—they were taken off to the gas chambers—went on to a late hour. All this time Eli held his father's shivering head; his father had not woken from the moment he had sat on the ground among the thousands of men cowering like him, ravaged by nightmares and lack of sleep. When eventually they were packed into the huts, four hundred to each hut, there was still a smell of the previous inhabitants.✢

Their eyes roamed, searching every corner of the gloom. Someone found a knife and spoon, left behind in the flurry of evacuation, and quickly hid it inside his shirt.

The *kapo* came in. He strode to the middle of the hut, looking to either side, and climbed on to the ceramic furnace. He spread his feet, leaning on the end of his stick, his fists on his hips. He was a tall Pole with a stubby neck, broad shoulders, and small, glowering eyes whose pupils gleamed like glowworms. He began speaking abruptly.

"Don't think you have come here to work. You'll stay here a few days and then leave by the only route that leads out of here," he waved his stick in the direction the Gypsies had taken, "up the chimneys." Now he came to the point of his address.

"Anyone hiding anything of value on or in his person is hereby warned, he'd better hand over any gold to me here and now. He'll save himself a lot of trouble, and in any case you don't need anything anymore." He hinted at our impending encounter with Moses in heaven, "And this Moses of yours, by what I hear, was not all that keen on the golden calf." This pleasantry had hardly left his moist lips when he let loose a thunderous roar quite terrifying and

totally incomprehensible. But the Pole was already yelling again.

"Lie down, I said, you scumbags lie down!"

Eli shook his father out of his stupor and pulled him down to the muddy floor. The men were looking at each other in astonishment. Armed guards jumped into the middle of the hut. The Jews crumpled and buried themselves in the floor, body alongside body. They stifled their groans. The *kapo* made a sign to those guards who were trigger-happy, indicating that they wait. He alone stepped down, and trod on the heads of the prostrate. He pushed head against head, body against body, sometimes with his stick, sometimes with the toe of his boot. Finally he gave a grin of satisfaction: the whole floor of the hut was covered with human bodies lying in grotesque postures, motionless. Since they had not given up any gold when he asked for it, he moved among the heads of the men lying there, fuming and striking indiscriminately. Anyone who moaned or cried "*oy*" received a double portion.

The next day they were tattooed. As he bared his arm, Eli saw that the man behind the table holding the tattooing needle was young and baby faced, with particularly thick lenses. This was the reason, Eli assumed, why he was here instead of at the front. This German from Alsace was proud of his French. Dr. Sternheim, after his first terrible night in the hut of the Gypsies, seemed to have recovered from the shock of entry to the camp and shaken off his paralysis. He dared to ask, "We were told, sir, that we are not intended for work, sir, so what is the point of the tattoo? Sir."

The baby face rose to stare in amazement at the garrulous Jewish intellectual, whose autonomy had been so completely eliminated, and for a moment the young German's face took on an expression of innocent decency. "First of all, I'm not an officer, only a corporal. Secondly, who told you this nonsense about not being here to work? What do you think this place is? Baden-Baden?"✢

Eli screwed up his eyes in pain from the stabbing tattooing needle. And perhaps it was convenient for him to shut his eyes for another reason. One question did not cease to trouble his mind: which of the two was lying, the Pole or the German? When he opened his eyes a red stain covered his swollen arm and on the punctured skin a black number glowed, which would henceforth erase his name and family: A254809.✢

The next day nothing happened. And the day after that

"As for the destruction of antisocial elements, Dr. Goebbels is of the opinion that we should totally eliminate Jews and Gypsies, as well as Poles sentenced to three or four years hard labor, Czechs and Germans sentenced to death or life imprisonment or preventive detention. The idea of destruction by work is the best."　　—From official German archives

BADEN-BADEN: A famous spa in southwest Germany on the banks of the Rhine frequented by tourists and holiday-makers from all over Europe and beyond.

"My daughter, listen to your mother's plea, flee for your life. Run away, my daughter, maybe you will succeed and at least one person will remain alive to preserve our memory." 　—DVORA HANDLEMAN née FINKELSTEIN, to her 14-year-old daughter, in the Belzacz death camp

again nothing happened. For five days the same routine recurred: once a day they drank muddy water that looked like soup. Most of the hours of the day they did no real work. They merely obeyed pointless orders. In the evening, having finished whatever they were doing, they were returned to the hut where they lay on bare boards, side by side, till morning. Anyone who caught dysentery was put outside the hut. Every morning prisoners harnessed to carts would pass by the doorways to collect those who had died during the night.⁺ They carried out their task skillfully and in perfect silence and disappeared. From time to time the *kapo* would feel like hitting somebody and lash out in all directions. The *Stube* screamed. The dogs barked. And it was evening and it was morning, the fifth day.⁺

And on the fifth day the word was uttered that transformed the camp into an anthill against whose entrance a red-hot stone had been placed. At morning roll call the rumor was already going around that this was the day they would register for work. It was not yet clear what kind of work. Who and where? Was it good for the Jews or bad? All the men were obsessed by the fear: would it be first come first served? And could anything be worse than hanging about the camp doing nothing?

Sternheim and his son went to register. One at a time they entered the office hut and pretended not to know each other, lest they be separated out of malice. There was a long table and behind it three Germans and a *kapo,* apart from the armed guards. Luckily for them, the Pole who knew they were father and son was not there. Eli looked too young and Dr. Sternheim too fragile to be part of any special work force. Those who were too old and those who looked too worn out were removed from the line and taken off somewhere by the guards. The number was recorded of all those who were taken off.

"Barber," replied Dr. Sternheim without blinking an eyelid, on being asked by the German for his profession.

"Metalworker," said Eli.

The officer looked with suspicion at his hands. "You don't look like a metalworker."

"Since I was a boy, sir, I've been working in a metal workshop. My father and grandfather were metalworkers."

"And where are they?"

"My grandfather's dead. And my father—"

The German wrote down "Metalworker's apprentice."

"Oh, God. I hope I'm not inviting disaster," muttered

Eli and bit his lip as his father was taken off and marched away with about two hundred men past the fence to some unknown destination.

He was not left to suffer alone. About a thousand men were taken to the parade ground, where they waited long hours and the weak fainted and collapsed. Toward evening their escort appeared. The Germans took charge of the occasion, their dogs strained at their leashes, and the men were ordered to form up in fives. As the column began to move off, someone jabbed his elbow in Eli's ribs and as though impelled by an invisible hand, he was moved out of the inner ranks and pushed to the side. An older man immediately took his place. Some secret code seemed to be at work without a word being said. Little by little the younger prisoners were being moved to the outer ranks and the old and infirm were taking their places in the middle. It wasn't long before the matter was explained to Eli in all its grim necessity.

The column of prisoners marched between two lines of SS men brandishing whips and batons, with *kapos* standing beside them, block seniors, armed with truncheons. Anyone who wasn't marching in step with the command—left-right—was beaten. Not that anyone who was in step escaped unscathed. The Germans lashed out with pleasure and the more the blows from their weapons were answered by moans and heartrending cries, the greater grew the delight of the perpetrators in their mischief. From now on this was a regular routine that took place almost every day, from now on the younger men took their places in the side ranks in order to protect their older comrades. Were the Germans and their helpers aware of this silent expression of solidarity by condemned men? Dr. Sternheim was not among the marchers in the middle when his sixteen-year-old son interposed his head to shield an unknown Jew from an SS truncheon. When they had run the gauntlet of the blows, the old man touched him on the shoulder, "Are you badly hurt?"

"The sound of singing was heard. A male voice. We really went crazy. What's going on here? Here, in the cemetery, above the island of the dead, a song of life bursts forth? Can it be that here, in the death camp, any human being could possibly of his own free will give voice to song, and even win some curious listeners? After all, here we are in the midst of a kingdom of ghosts, where everything operates in complete opposition to human reason." —From the writings of ZALMAN GRADOWSKI, a prisoner at Auschwitz

And there was evening and there was morning, a fifth day.
—GENESIS 1:23

Eli felt his neck and said, "It could be worse."

The old man said, "Thank you, my son."

Eli said, "I thank you."

The old man said, "What do you thank me for?"

Eli said, "For giving me the feeling that I was protecting my own father."

"Where is your father?"

"We've been separated."

"God grant you see him again alive and well!"

He wanted to respond: Amen. He pursed his lips and was just nodding his head when the sound of music of Mendelssohn[+] burst forth from somewhere, like an aural illusion from some other world. There was an orchestra standing in the square. About a score of men, wind instruments, strings, timpani, and cymbals. Some of them were artists who had recently been acclaimed in the concert halls of Berlin and Vienna. They stood in a circle, all alike in their striped uniforms, caps askew on bald scalps, eyes glazed as they followed the beat of the conductor's baton—one of the greatest conductors of his generation—who stood on an upturned box in the center of the circle. He must have had special rights, since he was the only one bareheaded; he and his orchestra played the "Wedding March" to greet those who came to their "liberating work" in Buna-Auschwitz.

The *kapo* at their head stopped yelling left-right and allowed the orchestra to set the pace. They were passing a huge structure that looked like an industrial complex. The installation was surrounded by an electrified wire fence with an observation tower.

The end man in the row behind him pulled his shirt. "Hey, man. The old man's dead."

THE MUSIC OF MENDELSSOHN: The work of the German composer Felix Mendelssohn-Bartholdy (1809-1847), the grandson of the Jewish philosopher Moses Mendelssohn (1729-1786).

DOLEK (1912-1942): Aharon (Dolek) Liebeskind was born in a small town near Krakow. He grew up in Krakow and studied law at the university. An observant Jew, he was placed in charge of the *hakhsharah* and *aliyah* departments of the Akiva Zionist Movement in Krakow. During the German occupation he influenced the movement to revolt against the Nazis: active resistance, including the ambushing of German soldiers in Krakow, which involved killing them and taking their weapons. Liebeskind forged an organized fighting force and became a central figure in the fighting pioneer underground in this part of Poland under German occupation. Among other actions, he was responsible for the attack on the Tzignaria, a café frequented by SS officers. The fighter who, on December 22, 1942, under the general command of Liebeskind, attacked the Tzignaria was Idek Lieber. Dolek fell in battle on December 27, 1942.

"What?" He shivered. His old man, his father, was not with them. "Who's dead?"

"Your neighbor."

"What do you mean dead—I was talking to him a minute ago?"

He turned his head and saw him lying on his back. A muddy froth covered his lips and his eyes were open.

"You have to keep trying." He stooped over the corpse.

"Keep trying what? I should only have such a death!"

The next morning he was taken to a large metal workshop, after they had all been allotted to "trade squads," and set in front of lathes and other machines he couldn't recognize. The SS officer in charge of the workshop looked at him with suspicion.

"What are you?"

"A metalworker, sir."

"Do you intend to continue standing idle undermining the war effort?"

"I haven't been told what to do, sir."

"Haven't been told? Make me a holder like this, for flowerpots. It's my wife's birthday today, and I want something like this." He took out a piece of an illustrated newspaper with a photograph of a metal container with rings and decorative wrought-iron leaves. "It'll look nice in the drawing room. Get it?"

"Yes, sir."

It could have been his last day in Buna-Auschwitz, or anywhere. To his left, at a large lathe, stood Sashka Patrashina. Sashka was a Russian prisoner of war, one of the veterans of Buna-Auschwitz; his torso was clothed in a striped shirt and for trousers he wore the remains of his Soviet army uniform. On the other side of the table Dolek,[+] known as the *Zigeuner,* was working. Eli assumed he was one of the last remaining Gypsies. Actually Dolek was one of the survivors of the Krakow ghetto, one of the leaders of the fighters. At one time Sashka the Russian had come to the aid of Dolek, who by posing as a metalworker had gotten into the squad, and had taken him into his team and gradually taught him how to work at a lathe. Dolek covered for Eli and told him to sweep up the filings from the lathe. He and the Russian made a glorious pot holder, with wrought-iron leaves and everything.

Eli was engaged in painting the container black to make it shine when the SS officer came back into the workshop. With evil intent, he strode between the machines, tapping his boots with his baton. And then he stopped,

stopped, open mouthed, incredulous. The murder in his eyes died away. At once he stretched out his arm and reversing his baton, patted the boy on the shoulder. With his other hand he took out a packet of good quality cigarettes and gave them to "our young master craftsman" as a sign of his appreciation.

Eli saw the officer's good mood and dared to ask, "Please, sir, my father is in Buna-3. I have a great favor to ask, sir, would it be possible to transfer him here so that . . ."

"Shut up!" the SS man's voice returned to normal. "Jewish swine. Give them a finger and they'll want the whole hand."

Eli shared the cigarettes among the workers in the shop and left none for himself. Any cigarette of this quality was equivalent in value to a quarter of a loaf of bread. To Sashka and Dolek he gave two each, not much but all he could do to show his gratitude.

But Dolek took the two cigarettes to exchange for something else. They were now living in the same hut and their friendship had been welded tight from that first moment. The workers with trades had special permission to be outside their huts and Eli saw his friend hurry off and come back and then do the same again. From the beginning of the curfew Dolek would sit on the edge of his bunk and take out a few crumbs of something from his shirt. It looked to Eli as though this was some delicacy that Dolek had bought in exchange for his cigarettes.

There were many concentration camps in the area, all of them satellites of Auschwitz. In one of the women's camps, across a field of waste ground, some young Jewish girls were imprisoned, companions of Dolek's youth, who like him had been captured in Krakow, in the wake of the underground action. These young women would get together in a corner of their hut—which was full of Poles, Russians, and girls acknowledged or unacknowledged as Jewish—and celebrate the Sabbath Eve.

"With light and hushed singing."

"A Sabbath Eve celebration in Auschwitz? You must be joking."

"Why should I be joking?" Dolek replied with pleasure, and showed him the wax he had obtained in exchange for the cigarettes.[*] From this wax he would mold candles, which he would get to the girls' camp by means of a *kapo,* in exchange for the second cigarette, "and this is like a sign of life between us, the biggest present we could give them, candles for Friday night." Eli did not yet know that Dolek had been one of the young leaders of the movement, and that when he said "give them these candles" he was expressing not only joy in his own resourcefulness but the strength of the obligation he felt toward his comrades, boys and girls, even if his hands were tied and there was little he could do to save them, separated as they were by seven electrified fences. That winter Dolek was taken away. Not from the lathe but at dead of night. By a special command. In the absence of any clear reason, there was no way of knowing whether the Gestapo had discovered his true identity or whether his die was cast. For several weeks Eli made a habit of putting aside some of his bread in order to get wax from here and there and used the same route to send Sabbath candles. And the girls did not know whether the candles came from Dolek alive or Dolek dead, living in the heart of his young friend, the good-looking boy from Paris, as Dolek used to call him.[*]

Millions of people at that time were longing for the end of winter. Every year when spring comes, hope revives in the human heart, and the song of the dove seems to herald the coming of salvation. But in Auschwitz the skies clouded over in March. Disaster after disaster beset the various camps, near and far.

In Auschwitz-Central and all its daughter members, the foremen, managers, and overseers of the extermination complex changed overnight. The old evildoers gave place to

"There is no way back. We tread a path to death. Remember that. Anyone who seeks life will not find it with us. We have reached the end of the day. But not the twilight of the setting sun. The end means death, toward which a strong man strides alone."

—DOLEK LIEBESKIND,
quoted in *Justina's Diary*

It was a Hasid from Warsaw who composed the melody to Maimonides's "Ani Ma'amin" (I believe) on a train of deportees to Auschwitz. And since the cattle truck was full of scared and anguished people, he taught them the melody and they sang it at Auschwitz. There were two young men among them who tried to jump from the speeding train and the Hasid encouraged them, saying, "Whoever gets away should try to reach America and give the tune to my rabbi and he will earn a share of the world to come." One of the two men who jumped was shot but the other escaped and did reach America. He handed on the melody as bidden, and thus it spread throughout the world:

Ani ma'amin,
  be-'emunah sheleimah
  be-viyat ha-mashiaḥ.
Ve-'af 'al pi sheyitmahmei'ah,
  'im kol zeh, 'achakeh-lo
  b'khol yom sheyavo.

I believe
With perfect faith
In the coming of the Messiah.
And even though he tarries—
Despite everything
I will wait for him
  each day, believing
  that He will come.

new ones. And with untiring energy the latter applied themselves to carrying out the mass selections that came along in waves.

It was at this period that Sternheim arrived in Buna-1 and father and son were once again united for a while. There was no way of knowing whether it was the miraculous hand of chance or whether finally the German officer had met the "impertinent" request of the "young master craftsman." On that early morning before dawn, when there was a tap on the window of the block and there came in, frozen but alive, he who was thought to be dead, father and son fell into each other's arms and it seemed there were no people in the whole universe happier than that couple. Once they had overcome their joy, their will to survive redoubled and they gave each other support in every possible way. Until once again they were separated.

That was the day when the Jewish quarters were separated from those of the rest of the detainees in the camp, and the officer in charge called Eli and told him, as though sharing a secret, "In three days time there will be a football match between Buna and Auschwitz-Central in the presence of officers and guests. You will be the goalkeeper for Buna, and you must strive to do a good job in goal. It will be crucial, if you understand me."

"Yes, sir. I understand, sir." Eli shivered all over; he understood very well what the German's words meant. Yet one could never guess the enormity of their guile. Tremendous emotion gripped the camp as the game drew near. Eli and his comrades were awake all night on the eve of the match, which would decide the fate of the group, who would live and who would die. Because of his age or inexperience or the inefficiency of his defenders, Eli let in five goals and the opposing team, Auschwitz veterans, won by a wide margin. But the next day it was the winners and their supporters who were led off to the gas chambers; the fate of the cremated had been decided, it appeared, before the game began, at the morning briefing in the office of the management, over a cup of coffee and cream.

Eli survived, but five days later his own private catastrophe occurred. Even the Germans could not believe that planned sabotage was the cause of the great explosion that destroyed half the building and killed five people, including the *kapo*. Nevertheless, members of the team of boilermakers were sentenced to death, as guilty of criminal negligence: three of the four were executed at the scaffold,

their faces and bodies scarred by burns. Eli was pulled out of the ruins, his leg injured. Sashka the Russian, like a nursing orderly on the battlefield, cleaned the wounds and applied dressings, but did not realize that in addition to the burns the hip was broken. His fellow prisoners from the hut supported him at morning roll call and his coworkers covered for him during work hours and at night he suffered as his temperature rose and a bout of shivering tossed him like a falling leaf.

Dr. Sternheim was lying in Buna-3, the third branch of the Buna camp, one of the satellite camps in the death complex of Auschwitz. Over the prisoners' grapevine Dr. Sternheim had heard the news of the explosion at Buna-1, the deaths, the hangings, and the wounded, and it seemed ominous. He had no doubt that his son was among the wounded; he was convinced that his son needed him.

Dr. Sternheim had three gold crowns on his teeth. Fortunately for him, they did not glisten in the front of his mouth but were concealed. With his own hands he succeeded despite terrible pain in extracting two of them and gave one of them to a *kapo* to arrange his transfer to his son's camp and the other to a *kapo* to transfer both of them to the seventh block at Birkenau, for there was a well-known surgeon working in the sick ward at Birkenau. It was not only Philo-Yedidiah Sternheim who knew that a full professor of surgery requires a bribe before he will give an anesthetic to a patient awaiting an operation. The truth is that chloroform was extremely precious in Birkenau. Still, a measure of chloroform was within the power of the chief of surgery to obtain. Sternheim extracted the third crown and gave it to the professor. But this time he did himself serious injury, either in damaging the nerve or from the traumatic reaction of the vocal cords, which left Dr. Sternheim practically speechless, unable to utter anything but frantic scraps of wordlike groans.

Professor L. kept half his promise. He gave Eli an anesthetic, but not the required amount. The operation took place to the accompaniment of screams from the boy, immediately stifled by a cloth between his teeth. Sternheim clenched his fists and pressed with all his force on the temples of the boy in anguish, whose arms and legs were tied, and hardly knew what first to ask of the Dweller on High: whether to take his own life in absolution for his son or to strike the cursed doctor dead five minutes after the operation. One way or another, there was no one to hear his prayers.

Five days after the operation, Eli and his father were in the block of prisoners classified as fit for work, one with half a voice and the other with half a hope. On the seventh day, between Purim and Passover, they stumbled back into the "seventh"; the gangrene on the boy's leg was spreading menacingly. There were no more crowns in the father's mouth. Now he prayed for death, wishing only that his son have no awareness of his approaching end.

Sternheim raised his body above the bunk so that Eli could lay his head on his chest. With the tips of his fingers he stroked the blonde hair on the boy's head, which was beginning to grow again, and listened tensely to his flow of words. He recalled hut number 8. When they were together there in the winter, the prisoners in the neighboring bunks had mocked the father who every night cushioned his son's head with his arm. In their eyes, Eli was a man in all respects. But Sternheim would look to see if his child had fallen asleep. It was only yesterday that they had snatched him from the arms of his mother in Warsaw at the beginning of their travels. He had but one prayer in his heart, that they be able to lie down together on these boards the next night as well. "We'll stick it out, Son," he would say at the end of every day, though his own powers were ebbing. Standing beside the heavy press, he could hardly find the strength to last out the day at work. One Tuesday from the end of the hall Eli saw his father leaning his head against the iron doorway. He ran toward him to prevent him from collapsing, but the new SS man got there first. He was quickly followed by the *kapo*. They saw that Eli had left his own place of work in order to help his father, and both of them struck him repeatedly on the head—one with a thick stick and the other with his braided whip. They had difficulty that night lifting him into his bed. Some of the blood had congealed but most of it was dripping from his forehead down his cheeks. He wasn't even capable of swallowing his slice of bread. His father applied cold compresses to the wound and said to him through tears, "Why, why did you do it? You're still young, you must live, but I . . ." and Eli placed his hand on his father's lips and would not let him finish his sentence. Sternheim was only forty-three, and the next day it was Eli whose strength failed him at roll call. He ran to the corner of the next hut and collapsed. His father ran up and bent over to revive him. He covered his prostrate son with his body and said to him, "If it's the gas chambers, we go together." They waited for the end and nothing happened.

Actually a miracle happened. The overseer hesitated and the boy rose to his feet. That night on their bed the boy withdrew from his father's embrace and expressed the pain in his heart, "Why, Papa? What are we really struggling for?"

And his father replied, "To remain men created in the image of God, though in the house of bondage."

Words from another world. Strange, like phrases from early childhood recovered from oblivion: house of bondage. Created in the image of God.[*]

"We shall vanquish death," his father said with emphasis and kissed him.

It was in that harsh winter. And Eli was dying on his bed. His only son whom he loved.[*] In the final analysis, does our ability to suffer have any meaning? When at any moment some degenerate can come in and send one off to the gas chambers, or put a bullet in the head of either of those two righteous men who spent the night awake together?

In the meantime it was as if Eli had been given a new lease on life, with renewed vitality he continued to talk, telling what had happened to him and his companions in the camp. His father peered at his glowing eyes and knew that this was the final outburst, all that remained of life.

Many of the things that Eli now revealed were new even for his father, especially what had happened since they had been separated. In a whisper, but in words that came out remarkably clear and lucid, Sternheim asked, "These girls you sent candles to, do you know their names?"

Eli didn't. Suddenly he turned his head to where Gonda was sitting. The young Czech, who had become dear to him, was about ten years older than Eli and younger than all the others. Eli turned to him and said, "When one day you meet survivors of the Krakow ghetto, ask about the girls who celebrated Sabbath Eve in Auschwitz. Tell them it was I who continued to send candles after Dolek had gone."

His father hastened to speak and this time it was broken words that emerged, "When the time comes, *mon cher,* you

---

And God created man in His image, in the image of God He created him; male and female He created them. —GENESIS 1:27

. . . take heed that you do not forget the Lord, who freed you from the land of Egypt, the house of bondage. —DEUTERONOMY 6:12

And He said: Take your son, your favored one, Isaac, whom you love, and go to the land of Moriah, and offer him there as a burnt offering on one of the heights which I will point out to you.   —GENESIS 22:2

DR. KORETZ (d. 1945): Rabbi Dr. Zvi Koretz was the chief rabbi of Salonika, appointed head of the community in December 1942.

As on my bed I recall the malice of my heart and all my guilt

I rise and come to the house of my God, to his footstool.

And as I lift up my eyes in entreaty to his heavens, I say:

Be judged by the hand of God, for great is His mercy.

To You, my God, rock of my strength, my refuge in adversity,

In You, my hope and my expectation, my Lord in my exile,

All the wishes of my heart are for You, my desire is for You.

Redeem the slave who cries out to You from the hand of his oppressors.

Be judged by the hand of God, for great is His mercy.

Answer me O Lord, answer me as I call from my distress,

Let it be known among the nations that You are all powerful.

Do not despise the suffering of the poor man who cries aloud at his enemy's rage,

Who freely admits the sins of callow youth.

Be judged by the hand of God, for great is his mercy.

—A propitiatory prayer, according to the Sephardi rite. First printed in a prayer book for the New Year, according to the usage of the Jews of Aragon, in Salonika, 1869.

will find them and tell them yourself." The eyes glowed beneath the feverish brow of the young man on his deathbed. Eli smiled but said no more.

The moon shone through the window. It shone on the brows of those present as it shines on tombstones.

All was silent.

There was a sudden outburst of terrible screams, like the screech of an electric saw grinding against a nail. Gonda and Nathan jumped up and went to the head of Habib's bed. They tugged at the rabbi's shoulders and neck, raising his head to make him more comfortable. Habib was suffering from fever. He mumbled in the half-light, "Go to Dr. Koretz.* Tell him not to spare me from sweeping. The roads. Roads. Of Salonika. I do not agree that Dr. Koretz should exempt the son of Chaim Habib." The listeners did not understand the meaning of his words until a *musulman* from one of the upper bunks, a member of Habib's community, leaned over and explained to them.

Gonda wiped Habib's forehead with a damp cloth: "He's burning like fire." After several compresses, Habib seemed to sink into a deep sleep. His companions returned each to his own boards, his own thoughts. And after a while they turned their heads in the direction of the rabbi. Gradually all the inhabitants of the "seventh" came awake.

Habib was sitting up straight in his bunk, his face radiant, singing in a voice that made their hearts tremble. From all corners heads emerged and joined in with him quietly, "As on my couch I recall my heart's malice and its sins."*

And Philo-Yedidiah Sternheim heard the chant for the first time and for some reason burst into bitter tears.

And when Raphael Habib reached the words "Be judged by the hand of God," he fell silent.

When the door of the hut burst open and with much commotion a *kapo,* a dog, and two further escorts armed with rifles charged in, all the inhabitants of the hut, apart from Raphael Habib, knew that the man standing before them, feet astride and baton held in both hands, though his face was in shade, was none other than Dr. Mengele, the Satan of Auschwitz.

✤ The Fifth Scroll ✤

To Be at Home

Say to the silence: My people.
Say to the silence: Here is the fire.

The finish but not the end
of the Scrolls of Testimony.

"And more than I have told you is written here."

—MISHNAYOT YOMA 7:1

✤ CHAPTER TWELVE ✤

Here We Are

✦ Chapter Twelve: Here We Are ✦

1. Around the Campfire

On Friday evenings the sad weight of memories oppressed the partisans more than on other days of the week, which were packed with activity and self-oblivion. Those who remained in camp, or returned from their missions while it was still day, both the healthy and the sick in their filthy bandages, preferred to lie around the edge of the warm embers before crawling into the trenches, camouflaged by trunks of dead trees, and curling up to sleep, steeped in the smell of sweat and musty clothing, on beds of earth and straw, covered by sheep skins swarming with hungry lice.

The rain had stopped and the damp branches, smoking in the center of the dying fire, were crackling fiercely. From under the embers, blue and yellow flames flicked out as though sniffing the air. There was a pungent odor of boiled resin. The forest had subsided.

Pelek and Zavka were quietly roasting potatoes and the sticks in their hands, moving slowly and precisely backward and forward across the embers, served to focus the attention of the partisans who lay around in a variety of postures. With dull eyes half-closed, wearily they watched each blackened potato as it was removed from the fire. No one pushed forward, no one tried to get ahead of his neighbor. Aware of the need to take turns, the one nearest the edge of the fire rolled the charred tuber toward the man lying next to him, and turned his head slightly to hear if the jacket of the potato crackled to show that roasting was complete.

"HEY DOLYA, MOYA DOLYA" (Russian): O fate, my fate.

URSA MAJOR: The Great Bear, a group of stars prominent in the summer sky. Also known as the Plow.

"Is there no singing in the forests? Oho! And how. . . . But not songs of war and heroism. They sing, but only songs of longing for one's home, one's beloved, one's mother. No songs of battle . . . it's strange and wonderful to see heroes, toughened as oak in the forest, who do not flinch from slaughter and destruction and loss . . . and here, matching the mood of an evening around the campfire, they become gentle as women given to sentimentality, softening and joining in the song, expressing the desires and yearnings of their hearts. Often they are songs that they themselves have composed, or changed and adapted from melodies well known before the war."   —SHMERKE KACHERGINSKI,
'*Kh Bin a Partizan*

"RAISE YOUR EYES AND LOOK ABOUT": They have all gathered and come to you. Your sons shall be brought from afar, Your daughters like babes on shoulders. —ISAIAH 60:4

"MAYN KIND, DU BIST SHOYN ALAYN" (Yiddish): My child, you are already alone.

Hassia stopped singing. But everyone seemed to be listening for the words of the chorus to rise up with the sparks:
"*Hey, dolya, moya dolya.*"⁺

She had a full, rich voice, Hassia, which did not fade away at the end of the song. The partisans accompanied her with a murmur of harmony, some from ignorance of the words, some from a desire to hear the words that she articulated so clearly, thinking her voice would continue to ring out, but she suddenly fell silent, as though suddenly short of breath or overcome by a surge of nostalgia.

"*Hey, dolya, moya dolya*"—and no more.

The two end stars of Ursa Major⁺ glowed like candles. Mother covered her face and her lips moved.

Hassia had been too young to ask, and had never even wondered what Mother saw when she closed her eyes in front of the Sabbath candles.⁺

In the damp darkness of the forest, time slipped by without protest. Yet something did cry out from the black vacancy, between the seven torches of Ursa Major: was there no other way?

Again and again the same questions. Again and again the same inadequate answers to cover the wounds:

"Raise your eyes and look about."⁺

They too had left their mothers behind. And not only their mothers!

But she was so young. Mother could have been taken for a partisan. She could easily have been one of us.

So little did we know what awaited us in the forest. Summer, autumn, and a winter of sickness have passed and again it is spring. And we are alive. Most of us. We went to war and did not die—who could have thought it?

"Mother! I cannot take you with me to the forest. But I don't want to be alone!"

"*Mayn kind,*" said Mother, "*du bist shoyn alayn!*"⁺

The frozen wall of forest swallowed up in dark silence the dancing sparks of fire, like moths straying near the gaping maw of a predatory toad. Leaning back against the trunk of a pine tree, Motke continued to whittle the pipe that he would never finish. Sha'ul suddenly broke the silence and said, "It's Friday evening, Shabbat. Anyone who didn't tell his story last time should tell it now."

He looked around and when he noticed the unit's chronicler, a former Hebrew teacher, sitting somewhat apart from the circle, his arms clasping his knees and his

RABBI ISRAEL SALANTER (1810-1883): Also known as Israel Lipkin, Salanter was born in Lithuania to a family of rabbis and Torah scholars. He was the spiritual leader of the yeshiva at Vilna, and later founded a yeshiva of his own. The Musar movement, which arose and followed his teachings, stressed the study of Torah and halakhah, along with ethical behavior and personal moral improvement. Students of Salanter founded yeshivas in the spirit of his teachings in Lithuania and Russia. When cholera hit Vilna in 1848, Salanter was at the head of those who provided aid. He stipulated that Jews were obliged to concern themselves with *pikuah nefesh*—saving life—even on the Sabbath, and even if it meant eating on the Day of Atonement.

The thirteen principles of Israel Salanter:

Truth—To say nothing that the heart does not approve.

Dispatch—Not to waste a moment in idleness.

Diligence—To carry out one's decisions with devotion.

Respect—To respect one's fellow man, even if you do not agree with him.

Calm—To do nothing out of panic. This is spiritual calm.

Ease—The words of the wise are heard at ease.

Cleanliness—To keep one's clothes and body clean and pure.

Patience—To remain serene in the face of every trouble and obstacle.

Humility—Not to overstress your fellow's faults and to acknowledge your own.

Order—To do everything in a disciplined, orderly fashion.

Justice—In essence: give way.

Frugality—To make do with little.

Silence—Think carefully about every utterance before you speak.

chin resting on them, like a tired but alert hunting dog, he added, "And comrade Shmuel will place his notebook on the tree trunk and write it down."

Perhaps at that moment Sha'ul recalled the story of Rabbi Israel Salanter,⁺ who permitted public eating on the Day of Atonement on account of the plague of cholera, and cleaning his trousers by slapping his hands against them, he pronounced half in jest and half in earnest, "By the authority of the Almighty and the times,⁺ the words of brands plucked from the fire may be written down on the Holy Sabbath."

And some say he chanted the words like a cantor.

2. Eliahu Began

Eliahu, known as Alyosha, began by saying, "There were three *Judenrats* in our town. The first was set up by order of the *Gebietskommissar*.⁺ Its members were the local bank manager, one of the town's respected lawyers, three tradesmen, four merchants, one industrialist, and Dr. Kantor. Mr. Lichtman, the headmaster, also joined them. And Lichtman was appointed head of the *Judenrat.*

"In his time the Germans destroyed the large imposing synagogue, the pride of the town, and the Jews—old and young, even the children—were ordered to take it to pieces with their own hands, brick by brick.

"Every day the Christians came to buy the bricks removed from the holy building and the German overseers slipped the ransom into their pockets. The process of destruction lasted several weeks until in the end there was no sign of the place where once had stood the house of God. Mr. Lichtman, who had taught history, said the Temple in Jerusalem must have looked like that when the Romans plowed it under after the rebellion. But we did not rebel, we only wept.

"During the time of the first *Judenrat,* young Jewish men were taken by the German officers to serve as hunting dogs. They would go out hunting rabbits in the neighboring countryside, with the press-ganged Jews chasing the rabbits. But those were the days when we were allowed to fetch tableware, beds, and chairs from our former houses—things were a little better for the Jews. Whenever a new decree was imposed on the community, Lichtman and his associates did what they could to soften the blow. They were servants of the public; in their time shelter was given to many refugees who arrived secretly in Lida⁺ from the Vilna ghetto. The leaders of the *Judenrat* were brought to account for this, and, in accordance with ancient Jewish tradition, the leader of the community was the first to be killed.

"Two days after the murder of the members of the first *Judenrat,* the second *Judenrat* was set up in Lida. It included men of resource and initiative.

"In their time, almost out of nothing, dozens of workshops were set up in the ghetto, small businesses and light industry, by metalworkers, tinsmiths, carpenters, tailors, etc.

"BY THE AUTHORITY OF THE ALMIGHTY . . . ": The utterance is based on a quotation from the opening of the Kol Nidrei service on the Eve of the Day of Atonement, when the rabbi declares: ". . . by the authority of the Almighty . . . we declare it permitted to pray with the transgressors."

GEBIETSKOMMISSAR (German): District commander.

LIDA: A town in the Novogrudok district, northeast of Grodno and now part of Byelorussia. There had been a Jewish community in Lida since the seventeenth century. In 1940, there were 15,000 Jews in the town. Most of them earned their living in small factories and agriculture. The Germans bombed Lida on the first day of the war. In 1941, the entire leadership of the Jewish community was executed, followed by the great majority of the Jewish population. Many of the young people managed to flee to the forests and join the partisan units. The most famous of these was the band led by the Bieletski brothers.

"My sons, my spiritual heirs, remember to do the right thing, at the right time, and to make decisions courageously. I did not know, I was too late."
—An ordinary Jew, after the Day of Atonement, 1942

ZITL, KOZLOVSZCZINA: Villages in the hinterland of Novogrudok, a region that now forms part of western Byelorussia.

DR. ATLAS (1913-1942): Doctor and partisan leader. Yehezkiel Atlas's family was murdered in the village of Kozlovszczina. He himself fled to the forest and organized a band of Jews who had fled the Drachinets ghetto on the day it was liquidated. He obtained weapons, trained his men, and formed a fighting unit of 20 men. He and his unit joined the Soviet brigade in the forest of Lipczani. Dr. Atlas organized attacks on Drachinets (August 1942) and Kozlovszczina (September 1942), sent a band of saboteurs to blow up the railway lines from Lida to Grodno, and burned down a bridge over the Nemunas River. He led his men into action against the Germans, who attempted a reprisal action, and brought down a German reconnaissance plane, which had to make a forced landing. Dr. Atlas was killed when the Germans hunted him down in the forest.

"We moved on through the village of Vola, along a track parallel with the river. As usual our leader, Dr. Atlas, marched at the head of the band. Mines exploded nearby with a tremendous noise, bullets flew over our heads. From time to time we had to fall to the ground and creep forward on our stomachs in order to exploit the short pause when the enemy diverted his fire to a different sector, and then jump up and advance another few meters. Atlas walked with a crouch and only very rarely did he fall to the ground. This scorn for danger of his was amazing, it seemed like scorn for life itself. Suddenly he stumbled and fell. We thought, it's a trick, a strategy, and did likewise. But suddenly we heard someone say, "Atlas has been wounded!" Barak and Avraham Lefkovitz cared for the wounded man until he died. According to them he passed away half an hour after he was wounded. His mind was clear until the very last moment. Before he closed his eyes for all eternity, he turned to the two of them and said, "Tell the boys to fight bravely!"
—From *Pelugat Ha-Doktor Atlas* (The Squad of Dr. Atlas), from the Hebrew Holocaust bibliography at Yad Vashem

A start was made on the manufacture of electrical accessories, vehicle spare parts, textiles, and furs. Men of talent established jewelry cooperatives and created clever toys to gladden the hearts of the *Gebietskommissar* and his men, some of whom were fathers of children. The Germans marveled at the products of our artists and *Herr Gebietskommissar,* an amiable potbellied Westphalian, even deigned to praise his tribe of hardworking slaves and remind them how two thousand souls were dependent upon them. And the members of the *Judenrat* believed them and repeated after them, 'Jews, your security is solely dependent on your hard work!'

"But they were slaves of illusion. On the first Friday in May, 1942, at four in the morning, the first 'selection' took place. Out of a total of 6,700 Jews in the ghetto, 5,200 were taken. They were led to pits that had been dug on the edge of the forest and shot in batches of forty.⁎

"When the turn of the third batch came, a crazed voice arose from among the condemned '*Yidn ratevet zikh*'—Jews, save yourselves! Immediately there was a wave of screams. Women shrieked. Men shouted. Above them all rose the sobbing of children. Suddenly a hail of stones and clods of earth was hurled at the heads of the Germans and Byelorussians. They began to fire, at first with their rifles and then with bursts of the machine guns. Thousands of Jews started running, in ragged files fleeing for the forest. Hundreds were cut down; many were seized alive and beaten to death. At night dozens who had made it to the forest started coming together, my father and my sister Zelda among them. For four days and nights they hid there, with nothing whatever to eat. About two hundred of those who had gotten away returned in secret, exhausted and despairing, to the closed ghetto of Lida. They included Zelda, who was in urgent need of an operation. She perished in Majdanek with the rest of the Jews of Lida. My father never came back.

"The third *Judenrat,* which was set up after that black Friday, was headed by Windisch, an SS officer. I don't remember the names of the members of the third *Judenrat,* the slaves who saw the end.

"One night I dreamed that my father was urging me to get out of bed. I got up, dressed hastily, and fled by myself from Lida, before there was a further *Aktion*. I reached the ghetto of Zitl⁎ on foot, ready to drop, and entered the house of the rabbi. He was a member of the family. That evening Dr. Atlas⁎ was in the house; he had come to say *Kaddish* for his father and mother and all the members of his family who had been shot at Kozlovszczina. When I found out that this Dr. Atlas had organized a unit of partisans, I fled from Zitl with another Jew in order to join them. But by then Dr. Atlas was no longer alive."⁎

At this point Eliahu, known as Alyosha, disentangled his legs and, gently moving the head of the girl who was leaning against his thigh, said, "I met Dvora for the first time at Lida, when she was looking for some way to cross the frontier and get to Vilna, and I nearly went with her. But her rate of progress seemed to me quite insane. I never thought we should meet again in this world—if you can call this morass of a forest part of God's creation."

Dvora listened to Alyosha, the back of her head resting on the grubby edge of his mantle, and said nothing.

3. *Speak, Lenz*

One damp branch was still smoldering in the middle of the campfire. The wall of pine trees surrounding the tiny clearing grew blacker. The heavy branches of the trees were silent, darkness enfolded in darkness. Swaths of silence seemed to enwrap the partisans in the circle, deepening the intimacy among them. With the heel of his boot Pelek thrust a few stray twigs that had not been consumed back into the embers. Once again yellow tongues of flame began crackling cheerfully. Dvora moved aside to whisper to Lenz, her right-hand neighbor, urging him to tell how a young man from Vienna had found his way to their forests in Byelorussia.

Lenz was grateful to her for calling him a young man, not a boy or a kid, the way some of them would taunt and insult him, for he looked even younger than he was. He told her he was not from Vienna. He had fled to Vienna when the SD came to Dinslaken. He was then deported from Vienna to Zbaszyn, since he was the son of a Polish citizen. In the camp at Zbaszyn, also known as Niemandsland, he got to know Dr. Ringelblum, a volunteer from Warsaw, who did what he could for him and brought him to Warsaw. There he learned Yiddish and could already chatter a little in Polish. And when the Germans occupied Warsaw, he fled ahead of them to Vilna. In Vilna he had an uncle, whose daughter Cherna was then still alive.

In June 1941 he fled from the Germans once more and got caught up in the retreating columns of Russian troops, and almost lost his life because of it. The Germans were dive-bombing the columns and decimating them. He almost reached the gates of Smolensk,[*] but his strength gave out. For a year and eight months he preserved the hope that he would return and see her again—he did not know that Cherna, that lovely girl, was lying in a pit at Ponar.

He had never managed to bare his heart to her. But there was no point in talking about all that, and everything else, to those who were sitting around the campfire. Every one of the partisans bore his own scars from his own encounters with the fire. He caught a glimpse of the unit chronicler, whose spectacles flashed as he opened his notebook to a new page, and remembered the notebook he had left behind in Vienna, in the storeroom of Klein und Krever. If both the notebook and he himself were to be lost, it was just as well that some account should survive in the records of Dr. Shmuel Brandt, who saw this as his war service.

"What I'm going to tell you now will sound like a figment of my imagination, totally unbelievable. But you and I know that there's nothing left in the world that is unbelievable. The Russian forces were in retreat and I was with them when we almost reached the gates of Smolensk, where we were surrounded and taken prisoner. I was unconscious when I was picked up by armored forces of the Wehrmacht. For three days I did not open my eyes. But someone else had his eye on me. There was a second lieutenant among the wounded in the military hospital who was surprised to see a boy in civilian clothing among the piles of soldiers, lying in the gloom and mumbling in German. Perhaps my face reminded him of somebody, and when after two days I had still not regained consciousness and no one could tell him who I was or where I came from, he searched the pockets of my jacket—I had a very short leather jacket, from my days in Vienna—and found an envelope containing a letter from the director of our institution in Dinslaken, asking about me. The young officer almost went out of his mind when he saw his own father's signature on the letter. Heinz, that was the second lieutenant's name, had been studying in France before the war and had received letters from his father about what was going on in our institution at the time of the Nazis' rise to power, and in one of the letters his father had mentioned Leo der Junge, that is, me."

Heinz had been put in charge of a rear echelon transport base, and Leo went with him to Minsk and Kovno. To his comrades and superior officers the young officer introduced Leo as the son of a *Volksdeutsch* farmer who had been kidnapped by the Russians. Since his parents, so the cover story went, had been killed during the air raids, everybody felt sorry for the poor boy "taken prisoner by those barbarians," and showered indulgent affection upon him. Foremost among them was the wife of the commander of the Einsatzgruppen in Kovno, who wanted to adopt him. But her husband, the *Obersturmführer*,[*] hated the idea of adoption, and loathed abandoned children, what-

SMOLENSK: A town of 250,000 inhabitants northeast of Minsk and southeast of Vitebsk. Smolensk was captured by the Germans during World War II, and they ruled there from 1941 to 1943. The Jewish population was isolated in a temporary ghetto and murdered at the end of 1941.

OBERSTURMFÜHRER: (German): An SS officer equivalent in rank to a captain.

ever their race, sex, or religion. Heavy-bosomed Mathilde, still childless, had to be content with emotional embraces and stroking the blonde hair of "our little Lenz." For Leo was no longer Leo der Junge, or Arieh Morgenstern, but Lenz, the name of a fellow from Upper Silesia—Herbst Lenz, according to the crumpled scrap of a document that Heinz had obtained for him. But let's not get ahead of ourselves. Events did move rapidly, but Lenz's legs were still dragging slowly, still painful from the shrapnel that had lodged in his ankles when the bomb had overturned the Soviet truck and its fleeing occupants.

"From now on I'm Lenz. Ten kilometers from Minsk there's a place called Malitrostinyetz, where the SD had set up a camp. Deportees from Vienna were concentrated in this camp, among them my Uncle Arthur. Six hundred of them had been transported from the railway station of Vienna, half the distance in proper passenger compartments and from Poland eastward in cattle wagons. When they were thrown out of the wagons, Arthur was among the eighty-one chosen as fit for special work. Why precisely eighty-one?—that's what the SD wanted. The Minsk ghetto held seven thousand Jews from Vienna, Bremen,⁺ and Brno.⁺ There were a thousand more at Malitrostinyetz, and they were all gassed in trucks at the side of the road on the way to Mohilev.⁺ The drivers of Heinz's unit told him about Kharkov⁺ and Kislovodsk⁺ and the valley of Drovitski, which was full of pits stuffed with Jews, and a field called Babii Yar. And Gunther used to tell of a place called something like Mineralwasser,⁺ which the Russians had

BREMEN: The oldest port in Germany.

BRNO: A town in western Moravia, Czechoslovakia, also known as Bren.

MOHILEV: A town in Byelorussia, east of Minsk. It had a Jewish community numbering 40,000 and was the scene of mass destruction during the Nazi occupation.

KHARKOV: A city in the Ukraine of a million and a half inhabitants, with a large Jewish population. It served as a center for Yiddish culture and research. During the German occupation (1941-1943) tens of thousands of Jews were murdered by the Germans in Kharkov.

KISLOVODSK: A town in the Caucasus. The Germans slaughtered 7,000 Jews there.

MINERALWASSER: The reference is to the spa, Mineral'nyje Vodi (Russian for "mineral water"), where 2,000 of the Jews of Kislovodsk were executed.

"I TOO WAS THERE AND DRANK SOME BEER . . .": A conventional ending, recurrent in Russian legends and folktales.

SLOBODKA: A poor quarter in Kovno. It was the site of yeshivas and Talmud Torahs and, after the German occupation, of the ghetto.

left full of antitank trenches, and the days when the Jews from Kislovodsk had been collected there and saved the trouble of digging their own graves. Once while Gunther was filling up with gasoline he had seen three Jews who had been arrested—a doctor of about fifty, his wife, and their daughter. They had tried to escape the rounding up in the market square by killing themselves. Since they did not have enough morphine for everybody, they had cut their veins. The *Sturmbannführer* had ordered their bleeding wrists to be bandaged and explained very courteously to the doctor that Jews were forbidden to commit suicide, since a Jew committing suicide was taking the law into his own hands. When their wounds had been dressed, the three of them were given hot coffee and then taken off to the aforementioned trenches and shot. Gunther, a reserve soldier with stubby ears, a fat little man who was usually fairly cheerful, pulled a dark bottle out of his haversack and said, 'Nu, this is what the Russians call *kvass* and it tastes like horse piss. Anyone who likes horses and Russians can join me in a drink.'"

"My hand was already on the bottle," said Lenz, "when I suddenly saw that Heinz was looking at me and I didn't have the courage to continue. So you see, I too was there and drank some beer⁺ with the Germans."

It was the end of October 1941. In the home of the mayor of Kovno they were drinking tea. The maid opened the window and was brewing a second samovar of tea when a young German officer outside blew her a kiss. Blushing to the tips of her ears, the Lithuanian girl leaned out of the window frame, carefully keeping her eyes on the hand that was waving to her from the other side of the street.

There were three of them and they turned toward the narrow streets that led to Slobodka.⁺ "I think it's all over, son" said Heinz.

When they reached the ghetto and were allowed in along with the German bosses who had been called to extract their essential workers from the mass of Jews destined for "selection," the crowds were still standing in the square, filling it to capacity. There were tens of thousands of all ages—women, old people, and children.

They had been expelled from their houses in the morning and had already been standing in the square for seven hours without food or drink.

They were lined up in solid ranks. In the first rank stood the members of the *Judenrat* and their families. In the next the ghetto police and their families. Then the members of the various forced labor squads, with the squad commanders at their head. And the infants sobbed and squalled in their mothers' arms. The square was encircled by regular soldiers and SS men. And a double circle of Germans and Lithuanian Ypatingas from the special unit surrounded the ghetto from the perimeter down to the river bank.

Many thoughts hammered at Lenz's brain, threatening to drive him out of his mind. Marching between the lieutenant and the *Feldwebel,* he strove to appear indifferent, as much a German as he possibly could. In the square, packed with bodies and revolting smells, the Jews were being counted. Despite the overcrowding they had been warned not to step on the sidewalk but to leave it free for the soldiers and the police. Arrogantly, with measured stride, SS officers patrolled the square. Occasionally the crack of a whip was heard, accompanied by a scream, as the *Meisters*✦ urged their employees to form up in groups on the right of the square. Behind the squad of workers from the airfield Heinz found his own crew. There were ten of them. But twice the number were clustered around them. Jews whose bosses were not present, or whose indispensability was in question, clamored to be assigned to his *Stelle,*✦ thinking the lieutenant was not like the others. Some swore they were automobile mechanics, others claimed to be metalworkers, or drivers, anything concerned with vehicle maintenance. And others never opened their mouths but just filled their chests and flexed their muscles.

Lenz found himself in a winding alley, which led off from the square, and in an opening between a courtyard and the street saw two people struggling. A small woman was badgering a man more than a head taller, though still a youth. After she had managed to get him into a coat that was too long for him, she fastened a belt around his hips, hoisting the slack. The boy squirmed in her grasp, trying to get away, and kept mumbling:

"Auntie, it won't work. Auntie!" Sweat oozed beneath her thick layer of face cream. Her hair was gathered behind her neck, and tied in a bow with a pink ribbon. With amazing deftness her bony fingers smoothed out the creases in the overcoat, straightened his tie, and pulled down over his eyes a gray cap of the kind worn by respectable householders. Without another word she pushed him from behind, urging him across the square.

"To the left!" one of the ghetto police directed him, waving his baton under the boy's nose.

"He's my husband!" The woman jumped between them, trying to push the skinny lad forward.

"He's your husband like I'm your boyfriend!" The policeman laughed in her face, without moving his baton, which lay across the boy's larynx. The boy stammered but his aunt-wife would not give up.

"I swear by all that's holy, he's my husband!"

"There's nothing holy today. Don't lie, woman. Move!" The policeman prodded the trembling boy with his baton. "To the left!"

"He's not going to the left!" The woman grabbed the policeman by the sleeve. "Please, sir, be kind."

She wept.

They had been speaking a soft, rich Yiddish, and Lenz listened and held his peace.

The policeman roughly shook off the unfortunate woman and brandished his truncheon above his head, for the boy was taller than him. "You scum!" screamed the aunt-wife, "may you burn in hellfire and never be consumed!"

"Leave him," said Heinz, "he's one of my men."

The selected workers were already hurrying through the gate, some on foot and some in vehicles, en route to their places of work; this time their speed seemed less from compulsion than for salvation. For the thousands who remained, columns of trucks covered with tarpaulins waited.

Did the people know what awaited them?✦

The counting and sorting went on. The women, the old people, the men without patronage, the children, and the youngsters would stand in the ghetto square ten hours until the end of the *Aktion.*

It didn't end that day. The next day thousands more were taken off. When the men came back from work, they ran from house to house, now emptied of their inhabitants, looking in vain for their wives, their mothers, their children. At

MEISTERS (German): Master craftsmen, tradesmen, leaders of their particular profession.

STELLE (German): Job, place of work.

My horses slowly
Climb the hill,
The dark of night
Envelops all.

My wagon creaks
As though loaded
With thousands of dead.

I send a silent song
Abroad in the night,
May it travel far.

My horses listen
And slowly climb.

—DAVID FOGEL,
"Before the Gate of Darkness"

four in the afternoon, when the column of deportees was marched out through the gate and loaded on the trucks, the rumor began to spread beneath the tarpaulins that the destination of the convoy was the "Ninth Fort." Young men jumped over the tailboards of the trucks and began running madly toward the river or back to the ghetto. They were all shot. The machine guns barked a while and the bodies of the daring littered the streets of the neighborhood.

Heinz stayed where he was in order to ensure the departure of his workers and of the extras he had managed to add to his squad, and later spoke of what he had seen. Far worse, apparently, was what had taken place at the Ninth Fort. In groups of three hundred the condemned had been stripped naked and forced to run up to the firing emplacements. Many children had been thrown into the pits alive.

"If there were a God, he could not have let such things happen," said Heinz.

Lenz followed him, his gaze frozen. The son of Dr. Marten from Dinslaken moved back and forth in the uniform of the Wehrmacht, in the suburbs of Kovno, his right hand holding a mug of beer and his left fist clenched and striking his forehead. "That day," said Lenz, "I became convinced there is no God."

But he said to himself, "And yet miracles do occur." He felt a strong desire to get up from the edge of his camp bed and embrace the German. But at that moment, without knowing why, tears burst forth and flowed uncontrollably down his face.

"You mentioned another German," mused Sha'ul, as though bothered by a memory. "Who was the third man?"

"A Viennese, Anton Schmidt, that was the name of the *Feldwebel*. He was the one who brought me the news of the murder of my cousin, Cherna, in Ponar."

"That evening," added Lenz, continuing his story, "it was suggested that I go to Berlin."

"To Berlin?" Eliahu from Lida was dumbfounded. And Pelek, who was in charge of the campfire—one roasted potato extracted from the ashes was worth a little of his friendship, two potatoes were worth a homemade cigarette, five cigarettes were worth a nip of vodka, a bottle of vodka was worth its weight in gold, and his word was worth more than anything—Pelek lowered his gaze to the

HAMANN: A reference to Haman, the villain in the Book of Esther. A Franz Hamann was in charge of one of the Einsatzgruppen in Lithuania.

tongues of flame rising and falling, pursed his lips in a whistle, and then said, "If you got to Berlin, my lad, I advise you to hold your tongue. The forest has ears. But no one will believe that in all innocence you traveled to Berlin and came back to join us."

Lying on his stomach, Lenz held his chin in his two hands and said calmly, "I didn't get to Berlin."

His voice sounded weary, as though pushing through a heavy curtain of memory.

The startling idea of sending him to the school for Hitlerjugend came from the shrewd brain of the commander of the Einsatzgruppen in Kovno. Unbelievably, the name of this *Sturmbannführer* was Hamann,⁺ and when he had had some beer and was feeling relieved after the successful completion of an operation involving the mass destruction of Jews in many of the Lithuanian ghettos—"and you can't imagine what a feat of organization and complicated logistics that was, how much thought, planning, and efficiency I had to invest in the job"—his eyes suddenly alighted upon the glowing head, in front of the blazing fireplace, of "our little Lenz." Already the plan was hatched in his "logistic brain" in all its detail, and there was need to hurry because "this young lad," said Hamann with prophetic emotion, "is destined for greatness."

When the *Sturmbannführer* uttered these words, it sounded like an offer that could not be refused. He exchanged the mug of beer at once for a glass of fine French cognac and as he raised his glass in his stubby fingers, this German Haman said he had the sensation that today was destined to be one of the great days of his life. It was not only that he was still basking in the wonderful feeling left by the past day, when his loyalty and ability had reached their peak, but also that from today on his name would surely be linked with such great achievements of the Reich as the elimination of the Jewish enemy from Ostland. It was also because this moving experience of destruction was augmented by a mysterious intuition that something was about to come into existence, that he, childless Franz Hamann, with his own hands was planting, in the shape of Lenz, the future spiritual leader of the Hitler Youth!

Within three days Lenz found himself on a military train en route to Berlin, in his lap a basket full of cookies baked by Frau Hamann. He managed to stuff his pockets with honey cakes and biscuits before he got off the train the second night, when it slowed down at some unidentified country station.

"That was the beginning of the coldest winter nights I have ever known. It was in frost and snow on the banks of the Volga and the Neva[+] that the fate of the war was decided. But before the frost could deal with Hitler's forces, my own limbs were gradually freezing between the Bug and the Vistula. By the light of day I skirted villages, by night I lurked in fields and crossed streams, making my way steadily toward the southern frontier of Poland in order to reach Czechoslovakia. I walked with no guide or map, alone, and losing my way on the confusing roads of a treacherous 'foreign' country. At a place where I hoped to find a settlement of Jews, fellow-sufferers, I fell into a trap of anti-Semites called 'Shmaltzovniks,' who lay in wait for any who had survived the deportations, and with the sharp eyes of informers, showing even greater skill than the Germans themselves, exposed Jews who were trying to hide. My progress became more and more erratic. My fevered brain lost count of the days, and then I reached a place called Januszew.

"Believe me, I had no intention of telling you the story of my life. I just wanted to tear out a page here and there and get them into the notebook that Dr. Brandt is filling with records for those out there, who rightly will want to know what happened to their fellow Jews here. Anyway, the small town of Januszew was already empty of Jews, as I had realized while hiding all day among the damp bushes. When night fell I reached a work camp not far from here. According to the story of a shepherd boy, the men had been taken from Januszew and were working in the mines and at other forms of hard labor. The women and children had been taken by the Germans to Krasnik,[+] to die. A large lamp bathed the entrance to the camp in its rays, but there was no guard to be seen in the watchtower and no one called upon me to halt. There was nothing but silence and trees without end. It was hard to realize that I was standing in front of a concentration camp. What amazed me was not meeting a single human being, no police and no prisoners, even when I went inside and moved between the huts, skirting—still cautiously—the main avenue of the camp. Only a scrawny dog suddenly gave voice from some obscure corner, and its barking sounded to me not so much threatening as a yelp of lament."

Strange, but precisely as Lenz was uttering these words, from beyond the swamp a bark shattered the night. At once all the dogs in the area, near and far, joined in and there was a chorus of barks, high-pitched and whining, surrounding the partisan camp in a chain reaction and echoing round for a radius of three to five kilometers, and those seated around the campfire smiled at the coincidence.

Lenz raised his eyebrows and continued to describe how he entered a hut whose light filtered out through the window coverings. Seized with fear of the strange silence in the camp, as though it were populated by ghosts, he opened the door of the hut with his left hand and with his right cocked the Beretta pistol he had received from Heinz as a farewell gift.

A man holding a single candle was shielding its flame with his beret. The interior of the hut was filled with dozens of silent people. They stood with their heads inclined and their eyes gleamed in the light of the flickering candle. At first Lenz did not notice that each of those standing in front of him was holding a bundle of belongings under his arm. There was nothing threatening about their glances, but Lenz recoiled a step toward the door—instinctively he felt sudden terror at the sight of dozens of silent figures waiting, tense.

"Thank God!" the man holding the candle broke the silence. "You've come back!"

"I knew as soon as I heard the dog bark," another voice exulted.

"You came to take us, right?" An old Jew gripped him by the shoulders. "Bless you, my son, I knew a Jewish soul was not made of stone."

"Take you? Where?" said Lenz, astonished.

"What do you mean where? To the forest!"

"I didn't come from the forest."

"But you're one of Reuvke's men, one of the partisans. We saw you—"

"I don't know who Reuvke is and I have no idea what partisans you are waiting for."

If the roof of the hut had collapsed and fallen in, the shock, the sorrow, and the despair could hardly have been greater. Their heads drooped, they stood there with arms and shoulders sagging. Many listlessly dropped their bundles on the floor with a dull thud. They still could not believe it.

"Who are you?" they asked him, their eyes full of fear.

"I'm a Jew."

"Where from?"

NEVA: A river in northern Russia near St. Petersburg.

KRASNIK: A village near the south of Lublin, Poland.

"From far away."

He soon found out what had happened, the solution to the riddle. A short while before there had been a band of partisans there. They had ambushed a wagon of camp guards en route to the camp, got the better of them, driven into the camp in the wagon, and eliminated the Ukrainian in the watchtower. They killed one policeman but didn't destroy his dog. They were Jewish partisans from the neighboring villages, led by Reuvke from the village of Rakhov. He had marched straight into the quarters of the camp commandant, who had not had time to draw his Mauser.

The camp commandant was a German called Peter Iganov, who had been living for years as a mole among the Jews of Januszew, a teacher in the rural school, regarded as a Pole in all respects, moderate in his views, a friendly fellow. And when the Germans came he removed his mask and showed his teeth.

Iganov had been alone in his large room, occupied with the radio set on the cupboard, apparently trying to make sense of the squawking voices coming from nearby Lublin and longed-for Berlin, and when he turned toward the door, which had opened without a click, he was too late in drawing his revolver, which lay on the table in its bright pigskin holster.

Reuvke, the son of a blacksmith, was wearing a *papachas,* a Cossack hat, with a five-pointed red star above his forehead like a third eye. He seemed to open his mouth to say something to the *Oberscharführer,*⁺ perhaps he intended to do it in the German's own language, as he had seen in films when a condemned man is executed. But he remembered helping his father shoe Pan Iganov's horse, which was called Aniolek.⁺ And it was Aniolek's hooves that had pursued him when he dragged his father through the village at the time of the first *Aktion.* So Reuvke stuck the barrel of his sawn-off rifle—he called it *Otrezka*⁺—between the teeth of the Nazi and said to him in between-the-wars Polish, "For our mothers and our fathers, you son of a bitch!" and pressed the trigger just once, so as not to waste more than one bullet on him. But his three companions also fired at the lifeless target.

When the camp inmates, who had been confined to their huts, found out what had happened, their joy and amazement burst forth, clashing like sparks in the smoke above the chimney of an iron foundry. The people of Januszew were very proud of Reuvke; from the neighboring village of Rakhov, the leader of their avengers and they touched him and fingered the Russian hat on his head. The sharp-eyed also noticed that the rifles the men carried were more like scrap iron than military weapons, though they too proved capable of killing the enemies of the Jews.

Many were clustering around the pile of loot that the partisans had dragged out of the camp storerooms and Iganov's house. It had been plundered from the Jews of Goscieradow, Januszew, and the district, and Shaulik Popover recognized his grandfather's silver candlesticks, the work of a Caucasian silversmith. Since he had heard that in the forest anything of value was to be used for the acquisition of rifles and ammunition, the boy bit his fingernails and made no claim. And when he had chewed down his thumbnail, he said, "I'm coming with you."

Reuvke, the group commander, told him, "You're too small, Shaulik, I know you."

Shaulik, a well-built lad of sixteen, said, "I'm not too small for hard labor. Why am I too small to be a partisan?"

The blacksmith's son shrugged his shoulders. But many of the bigger men spoke up and there was a confused outburst of speech.

"Take us all, Reuvke, take us all."

And one of the partisans who, terrified, had seen the first "selection" in the ghetto, remembered the sound of his elder brother's voice, and those of his father and his uncle, as they pressed around the German leader of the work party and begged him, "Take us, Boss, take us." And how he encouraged them with a nod of the head, as if to say yes, yes. The partisan's name was Leibel Musikant, and his belt was stuffed with a grenade with a long wooden handle.

Reuvke looked reproachfully at Leibel Musikant and said, "Damn it, stop preaching at me. I'm in charge here, not you. You must understand, comrades. With all my heart, I would love to take you. We are all one blood. But there is a Russian commander in the forest and there are Russians and Ukrainians in the squad fighting with us. The captain gave us Iganov's head, but expressly forbade us to take any unarmed men into the forest. 'If you do, it will cost you your head,' he told me categorically. You have to realize that the forest is not a shelter, it's not a bunker,

OBERSCHARFÜHRER: A low rank in the SS, equivalent to sergeant.

ANIOLEK (Polish): Literally, little angel. Here it is a horse's name.

OTREZKA (Russian): Literally, cut off. Here it refers to a rifle with a shortened barrel.

without a rifle a man's as good as dead, without a rifle a partisan cannot exist."

"Can we continue to exist here?" asked Pesach, whose hands were bruised from working in the mines.

And one man, a former worker for a charity organization, Rabbi Hershel, went further than asking questions. He came up close to the partisan blacksmith's son and beseeched him, poking him in the chest with a black forefinger, "But you killed Iganov. You killed him."

"Did you expect me to have pity on the murderer of my father and mother?"

"You should have pity on us, we're alive. If you didn't come to take us with you to the forest, why are you leaving us burdened with this corpse? He'll cause us more trouble now that he's dead than he ever did when he was alive."

There was a menacing murmur of agreement from the crowd of desperate men, and Reuvke took another step back and stood with his back to the wall.

At once he turned his gaze from the doomed men to the free men and ordered the partisans to take the plunder and break off contact forthwith. Only when he had crossed the threshold and was outside did he turn and say, "We'll lock and bolt all the huts, leaving only this one open. Early in the morning, run to Goscieradow and tell the Germans what happened. How you were locked in and saw nothing. And tell Lazarczik, the commander there, that it will be his turn soon, you heard the partisan leader say so."

They took the butcher with them and two other men from Rakhov, Reuvke's village, and the doctor, Dr. Gross.

"And they left and you came," they told Lenz. "You looked like one of the partisans, and we hoped they would change their minds, because we could hear their voices in the distance, arguing among themselves. We were all ready to leave, with gold coins in our hands that we could contribute for the purchase of weapons, for we had heard that rifles could be obtained for Napoleons; we should have spoken to Reuvke before about the gold. Now we're lost. In another hour or two, the SS and the Gestapo will be here." The Jew who said all this to Lenz was a burly fellow with long ears and a shaven skull.

Outside the window, night was a black pillar. The man sat crosslegged on the floor, his hands between his knees, his body swaying as though reading Lamentations on the Ninth of Av.* The words poured forth from the lips of a mourner. He was in great distress. Both for the time when he had gone and for the time when he had not gone. The

first occasion was in the market square. The German bosses in charge of the work squads were still standing around, sorting out those who were fit for work. Everyone understood that this was a "selection" and that those who remained were doomed. That's why so many were crowding round the German officers, begging them, "Boss, please, take me." He had felt strangely listless, his senses dulled. He asked for nothing, and did not join the unfortunate. His brain seemed split in two, half here in the market place with six hundred to a thousand Jews being counted and half at home with his sick wife Rachele, his only daughter, and the rest of the family. How could he leave them without his help? If their fate was unclear, did he have the right to save his own life? Part of his mind dimly took in the activity around him and froze, the other part was feverish. He had just reached a decision when his brother Avrahamke, who had been chosen by the boss, dragged him with him by force. The German gave him a glance and gestured with his finger for him to join the group. The quota had been filled. A hundred men in all had been chosen; the operation was quickly over. His name, Gershom, was taken down and he was given permission with the rest of the chosen to run home and return to the assembly point with a bundle of clothes, a blanket, and some soap. Rachele did not cry, but pressed him to go. If he had insisted on staying, she certainly would not have prevented him, neither she nor his mother. But he did not insist, just gave them both a hurried kiss, handed his wife the little money he had in his pockets, and did not kiss his only daughter. Early next morning, through the window of the hut in the camp, they could see the strip of road beyond the valley leading to Krasnik, and their families, wives, and children, bundles of belongings on their shoulders, walking into the unknown. Strangely, there was no armed escort. No soldiers, no police. They plodded on, a disorderly rabble. They could have broken ranks and fled. Where to?

"Perhaps," the husbands and brothers in the hut sought comfort, "it means that what awaits them in Krasnik is a camp, not death?"

The man sat crosslegged, his hands between his knees, sobbing soundlessly. If the partisans would take him, he would go with them. Why shouldn't he follow them? Why shouldn't they all go?

THE NINTH OF AV: The Jewish fast day commemorating the destruction of the First and Second Temples, when the Book of Lamentations is read in the synagogue.

"Who is for life and who is for death*—who can know?" he redoubled his Jewish dirge. Lenz's expression had changed, he no longer looked at all surprised, only a boundless pain was reflected in his shrouded eyes, which he fixed again on the barred windows, where night hung like a curtain of fear.

"But here," Lenz told him, "certain death awaits you. They'll come back and take revenge."

"Do you intend to leave us?" Gershom asked.

"Yes."

The man looked at him again and it was as if only now did he really see him. He was twice as old as Lenz, if not more.

"You have no wife, daughter, mother, and sister in Krasnik. When I didn't join them before, maybe I caused them disappointment, but if I flee with you now, I'll bring disaster upon them. Don't you think so?"

Lenz shrugged his shoulders and did not reply.

"WHO IS FOR LIFE AND WHO IS FOR DEATH . . .":
On the First Day of the Year it is inscribed
And on the Day of Atonement it is sealed and determined,
How many shall pass away and how many shall be born,
Who shall live and who shall die,
Who at his appointed time and who not at his appointed time,
Who by water and who by fire,
Who by the sword and who by wild beasts,
Who by hunger and who by thirst,
Who by earthquake and who by plague,
Who shall rest and who shall wander,
Who shall be tranquil and who shall be harassed,
Who shall be at peace and who shall be tormented,
Who shall rise up and who shall be cast down,
Who shall become rich and who shall become poor.
—From the *Musaf* (Additional) Service on Rosh Hashanah (The New Year)

"Pour out Your wrath upon the heathen that have not known You, and upon the kingdoms that have not called upon Your name. For they have devoured Jacob and laid waste his dwelling place. Pour Your anger upon them and let Your wrath take hold of them. Pursue them and destroy them in anger under the heavens of the Lord."
—FROM THE PASSOVER HAGGADAH

Some who had caught the end of the conversation asked him if he knew the way. He told them he did not, that this was a foreign country for him. But since he had already crossed half of Europe on his own, he had every hope of crossing the other half and "either I'll come to an end or Europe will," he laughed.

And Lenz left, and took Yitzhak and Shaulik Popover with him, both of them sixteen years old. After they had gone others broke out and at the very last moment, just before Lazarczik and his Gestapo cronies arrived, another twenty took to their heels.

Under the long domed roof, between plywood walls lined with black, greasy tar paper, the majority of the prisoners stayed on. Few had made their beds and only one or two managed to fall asleep. With his bundle in his hand, each man sat on his cot, alone with his sorrow. At first they had spoken, reciting the names of those who had run off, not knowing whether to add "God preserve them" or "May they rest in peace."

All the inhabitants of Januszew were transferred to the same camp, tortured, and shot in the valley known as Novi Rakhow. And Lazarczik, also one of the *Volksdeutsch,* after he had buried his friend Peter Iganov, took personal command of the death pits.

Januszew is a small place and it doesn't appear on the standard maps, but the trials of the Jews of Januszew were not yet over. The fugitives hid in the forest. From the forest they fled to the marshes. From the marshes they fled to the scrubland. And from the scrubland hunger drove them to seek shelter with farmers. The farmers took their gold coins and in exchange handed them over to the Germans; singly and in groups they were caught and taken to Goscieradow, where they were murdered. Their brethren in the camp at Goscieradow saw them cut down like standing corn. And Lenz skirted the villages and strayed deep into the forest. One morning in the pouring rain he came across Leibel Musikant. The lad who had been with the partisans who had broken into the camp at Januszew was unrecognizable. Filthy, shabby, and stinking, he was living in a cave like a hunted animal. Leibel Musikant told him what had happened to the Jewish partisans.* Seeking to raise the stock of his unit in the eyes of the local Jew-haters, the Russian captain had expelled the Jews from his bands and cunningly stripped them of their weapons. He had thrown out Reuvke, their brave commander, leaving him his rifle but taking his pistol. This had happened a short while after the operation at Januszew. There were many Jews in the Zalesje area, fighters and remnants of families in hiding. Those who had been expelled from the partisan forces and the families in hiding were ambushed by the Polish partisans and slaughtered. The leader of the Polish partisans who hunted down Jews in the triangle of the Gocieradow-Kremenets-Zalesje forest was called Gregosz Kurczinski, who later became a general in the Polish army.

"Leibel Musikant advised me to go east, as far as possible from the centers of Polish activity. He himself, the sole survivor of his band, would stay in his cave, with no more strength. I was alone again, hardly able to stay on my feet. The soles of my feet were covered with suppurating sores, and every step was like walking on fire. With the help of my stout stick, I made my way toward the Bug. One night I knocked at the house of a farmer, and when he opened the door and a wave of hot air struck my frozen face, I fainted on the threshold. The father dragged me to the cowshed and hurried back to his hovel, where he had guests, including a policeman.

"When I came to, I was covered with a pile of straw and behind me in the corner of the cowshed a dog was whimpering. Later I found out that the same morning the dog had been shot by a German patrol, and the farmer had sworn and cursed the damned Krauts, using every oath in the book, and it may have been his hatred for the Germans on that day that saved my life. But all this only became clear to me after midnight, when the farmer's guests had left. Meanwhile I was stroking the wounded dog, whose whimpering was heartrending. The sorrier I felt for the dog, the sorrier I felt for myself. For the first time in my life I felt worse off than a dog. After all, for the dog you could call a vet, but I had to dress my own wounds and hide my tears.

"The rest of the way, as far as the vicinity of Lida, I traveled—you won't believe this—in an army truck belonging to the supply corps of the Wehrmacht, for once again I was Herbst Lenz, the lad from Schleswig who had been taken prisoner by the Bolsheviks. When we were held up by a bridge that had been blown up, I knew I was in partisan country and when night fell I got away. Unfortunately, I headed straight into the marshlands."

And Sha'ul said, "You faint too much, my lad. It's a good thing there's still some romance left in the partisan forests and someone chose to seek solitude in exactly the spot where you were lying sprawled."

As though the lumps in their throats had dissolved, the partisans chuckled and giggled. When their laughter died down, Lenz turned to Dvora and said, "I regained consciousness long before I opened my eyes. I heard footsteps and I was afraid there was a German, a farmer, or a wolfhound standing over me. I never imagined it would be a girl, a Jewish partisan. And then I heard you say, 'He has the face of a *sheygetz* but he moans like a real Jew.'"

His story had come to an end, and he fell silent. And Lenz remembered that to his father and mother his name was Arieh Morgenstern, and there was no longer anyone who knew his name. The graduates of the orphanage would remember Leo der Junge and Mathilde Hamann would mourn for Lenzi, who vanished without trace, and the milkman's daughter on the banks of the Dvina would think of the boy she had insisted on calling Lobuchka. He turned his gaze to the whispering embers and wondered whether he was the hero or the victim of his story.

At that moment Uri approached the campfire with a lamp in his hand. Its beam of light fell on the glowing embers and the commander said, "Masters, the time has come for morning prayers.✶ Go and rest, you have a long march ahead of you. Tomorrow you're going to blow up the bridges."

"MASTERS, THE TIME HAS COME FOR MORNING PRAYERS . . .": A quotation from the story at the beginning of the Passover haggadah, where it is said by the disciples of the rabbis in Bnei Brak, who stayed awake all night speaking about the Exodus from Egypt.

✣ CHAPTER THIRTEEN ✣

The Death March

Suddenly, at the height of the death march,

the war came to an end.

✤ CHAPTER FOURTEEN ✤

Crossing the Sea

Somewhere in southern Italy.

No, Ruth, I don't want to tell you about the sea breeze gusting against the cracked house. Or the worn shutters creaking on their hinges. Or the salt smell of seaweed mingling with the fumes of kerosene heating and stale sweat. The door behind my back (it's one o'clock in the morning) is ajar, opening on a long, gloomy dormitory, like the baggage hall in a deserted railway station. Across the solid darkness I sense the breathing of men, women, and children, a fitful stifled murmur from two hundred seventy homeless Jews, prevented from reaching the Promised Land, almost two years after the end of the World War.

No, Ruth, I don't want to tell you about the anger swelling in my throat at the sight of the storm lantern that started rattling as though in response to the thunder of the sea crashing against the rocky shore, at the sight of the roof that has suddenly started leaking, the bundles on the moldy straw mattresses and the hands of the people fearfully pulling the blankets over their heads in a desperate attempt to find space between the cold rain pouring from above and the nightmares convulsing their sleep from within. On the bunks, in stacks of three installed by soldiers of the Jewish Brigade,[+] lie sprawled side by side people who have come from Gross-Rosen,[+] Auschwitz, Bergen-Belsen, and the rest of the death camps whose names we have never even heard of, whose survivors streamed to us across the Alps, through the Brenner Pass,[+] as well as ghetto fighters and partisans who emerged from the forests of Russia and Yugoslavia. Near the door are Minna, Flora, and Fania, three who survived the death march that began at Stutthof[+] on the shores of the Baltic Sea (gradually they are recovering their hair and their looks) and opposite them men whose hair and bodies to this day still smell of graves and sewers. The most wretched of them all seems to be Krisia. While still a baby she was handed over to gentiles, in some remote village in the marshes of Polesje.[+] A note that her parents threw out from the death train was found by a priest who was crossing the lines early one Sunday morning on his way to mass at a country church near Rakhov. The priest handed the note in Hebrew characters to a monk who had escaped from the slaughter at Mir. From him it passed to a member of the Briḥah, the Jewish escape organization, in Lublin. And the note found its way across Czechoslovakia and Romania to Budapest, where two soldiers from the Jewish

Brigade were on their way back to Italy, after a wonderful meeting with Jewish partisans who had come to see them from the other side of the Carpathian mountains. One of these Palestinian soldiers came originally from Krisia's birthplace; her father and his father had lived in adjacent houses in the market square! Some of our men traced the note back to the marshes of Polesje and found the girl—she was five years old by now—and she no longer answered to the name Mirele, which her father and mother had given her, only Krisia, the name given her by the gentiles. It was a goodhearted farmer and his wife who had raised her as their daughter and even baptized her in a Russian Orthodox church (at the beginning she had been hidden with their relatives on the other side of the Bug). When our boys went to take the orphan from her father and mother, she refused to part from her foster parents. The childless couple and the frightened child both cried bitterly. From that day Krisia has not removed the crucifix from her neck and has not spoken. She is quiet by day and sobs by night and her voice echoes from one end of the building to the other, "I want Papa. I want Mama!" Krisia writhes like a small fish stranded on dry land and refuses to accept what we keep telling her, that the parents who are alive are not her real parents and her real parents are no longer alive. And Krisia-Mirele has an uncle on a kibbutz in the Emek[+] who is waiting for her and the meeting that might save her is being delayed. It's unbelievable! You just can't believe what the famous British navy has been doing since the victory over Hitler. Anyone who reads one day the history of these times will just find it hard to believe that captains, who with immense courage escorted rescue convoys across the frozen sea to Murmansk,[+] are now working

THE JEWISH BRIGADE: The brigade of Jewish soldiers from Palestine that was attached to the British army and served with the infantry in the invasion of Italy and the battles against the retreating German forces. Soldiers of the brigade came in contact with Jews in the DP (displaced persons) camps and organized them into units for immigration to Palestine.

GROSS-ROSEN: A concentration camp in Germany, south of Berlin, and near the Czech border.

BRENNER PASS: A mountain pass in the Alps, connecting Innsbruck in Austria with Bolzano in Italy.

STUTTHOF: A concentration camp on the border between Poland and East Prussia, on the Baltic Sea.

POLESJE: A region in Poland.

EMEK: A valley in Palestine.

MURMANSK: A port in the center of the northwest of the former Soviet Union, on the Barents Sea.

overtime on the bridge of warships and destroyers hunting down Jewish war refugees!

They investigate us at all the ports of embarkation. And the representatives of His Majesty's Government are not choosy about their methods—terrorizing, intercepting, and sinking. They sank a boat we were waiting for before Pesach (fortunately there were no passengers and the crew, most of them American volunteers, were rescued). The sea did not divide for us. There was no miracle. And rain covers the land. The sky is stripped of stars: between the sheets of rain I hear the sobbing of Krisia.

I was told a story by our friend, Eliahu Klatzkin, who as you remember was among the first to liberate Florence. The town was still divided, the Germans on one side of the Arno and our forces on the other. That morning Eliahu had met the rabbi's son. The boy's father was the rabbi of Genoa, known for his activities on behalf of the prisoners of Ferramonti Tarsia (a concentration camp for Jewish refugees in the south of Italy even before the time of the Nazis!). In 1943 the rabbi was deported to a death camp in Poland. A few months later the widow, the rabbi's wife, was also caught and transported. The boy (oy! I've forgotten his name!) was seven years old and he and his younger brother, aged five, found shelter in a convent. When the besieged city was cut in two, the inhabitants were left without water. Army tankers, among them tankers from the Jewish Brigade, would bring water to the liberated area. The rabbi's son was sent by the nuns to fetch a bucket of water. He was nine years old and couldn't tell who the soldiers were who were distributing water, Italians, Germans, or Americans. Machine guns were whistling overhead as he huddled in the line behind the tanker. And that's when Eliahu saw him. Eliahu didn't know the boy was Jewish and the boy didn't know who this soldier was. Suddenly he noticed the Star of David on his badge. "As if hypnotized," Eliahu tells the story, "the boy left the line, his empty bucket in his hand, his eyes fixed on my badge. He was

about two paces away when he stopped and whispered, *Shema Yisra'el.*'" Eliahu, who is from Beit-Alfa, a Ha-Shomer Ha-Tza'ir kibbutz, was so moved, he could hardly control his feelings. That same day he had already taken two orphans from the

BENGHAZI, LIBYA: The Jews of Benghazi were a thriving, well-organized community, but in February 1942, 2,600 of them were deported to forced labor camps in the Jado Desert in western Libya, in Tripolitania. Five hundred of them died of hunger and disease. After the war, most of the Libyan Jews immigrated to Israel.

convent in Florence and transferred them in his jeep to Rome, where he handed them over to relatives of the rabbi who had remained alive. Eliahu collected children who had survived and formed a *hakhsharah* group for those who wanted to go to Palestine; he was both father and youth leader to them. I worked with him for a time.

There was a boy in the *hakhsharah* group called Josepho. Once I asked him, "Josepho, why do you keep quiet when the others are talking?" He used to sit on the edge of his upper bunk, dangling his feet, his head tucked into his thin shoulders. Josepho was swarthy; without looking at me he murmured in Hebrew, "My name is Yosef."

"I'm sorry," I said. "Where are you from, Yosef?"

"Benghazi,"* came the reply. I asked him where he had learned Hebrew and he cut me short, "in Benghazi." I didn't know they had taught Hebrew in Cyrenaica. "They taught us Bialik too, you know!" he answered rudely.

Suddenly he softened and continued of his own volition, as if to placate me. "Do you know," he asked me rhetorically, "what was the last celebration I took part in before we went to the camps? (My God! I never knew there were concentration camps in Libya.) The anniversary of Tel Hai."

On the tenth of Adar, in Benghazi, Josepho-Yosef had read *Yizkor*, the memorial prayer, for Trumpeldor and his comrades. Josepho had joined the *hakhsharah* after being hospitalized in Naples. I asked him whether he had caught typhus when he was in the camp, and wondered where the camp had been.

"Do you know where Jado is?" (I didn't.)

Josepho was born in Benghazi. He and his father had been transported from there, packed in trucks like cattle, three thousand kilometers deep into the desert. On the day the edict had been published, his father had been in Tripoli. His Italian employer had not known he was Jewish, and his father had told him he had received a telephone call that the Jews were leaving Benghazi. His Italian employer said to him, "Do you know where the Jews are going? To a bad place." Josepho's father replied, "Wherever my family and the rest of the Jews go, I go too." And his father reached Benghazi exactly at the time his family were being ejected from their house. They traveled right across the desert, and many of them collapsed and there was no truck without its dead. They spilled them out of the truck into the courtyard of an ancient fort on a high stone cliff.

Josepho's sister had fallen sick on the way, and the doctor in the camp gave her an injection but she died the same night. The camp commander saw how the father and son dug a grave for the girl and ordered them assigned to the grave squad.

"Dozens died of hard labor and typhus, and we had our hands full with work."

When there was an announcement on the radio that Rommel[*] had reached El Alamein, the Italian commander burst into the camp with a platoon of soldiers and asked for a rabbi. There was a room in one of the huts in the camp, which the inmates had fitted up as a synagogue. They hauled the rabbi out of there and dragged him by his beard to the parade square like an ill-used goat. At once all the Jews were assembled in the square and the commander proclaimed, "We didn't bring you from Cyrenaica just to stay here. Now that we have conquered El Alamein, your time has come. In three days' time, on Sunday, you're going to Germany. And from there to destruction."

The Italian said just that: to destruction.

"Three days and nights we sat, weeping and praying. On Sunday morning we rose early for our last morning service, and there was no camp commander and no sign of the guards."

At midday there was a huge cloud of dust and an English patrol appeared. They saw the people imprisoned there, but they also saw the notice warning against typhus, and the patrol went straight on without even stopping. One soldier made a sign to them with his fingers that the army was on the way. Josepho was impatient and he went out to meet the liberating army.

"I walked a long way before I met them. I must have looked terrible. To judge by the expression on the face of the soldiers in their jeeps, they weren't sure whether it was a human being or a phantom in the dust cloud."

Josepho suddenly noticed the word "Palestine" on the insignia of one of the soldiers. The boy asked him in Hebrew if he was a Jew.

The startled soldier replied, "Yes, a Jew from the Land of Israel. And you?"

Josepho nodded in assent.

The soldier wondered at there being any Jews in Libya.

"Yes, and they speak Hebrew. I said this to the soldier from the Holy Land, and he collapsed."

Josepho stopped talking.

An education in the Palmaḥ[*] has its obligations. I controlled my overpowering emotion and said with a smile, "You're a lucky fellow, my son. You'll cross the Mediterranean twice!"

The boy from Benghazi looked at me distractedly (I was amazed by the turquoise shade of his eyes) and said, "Life has taught me not to rejoice too soon. When I got back to the camp two days later in an army jeep full of canned goods, my father had died."

That's what he said, and I wanted to apologize, but I didn't. Something within me was struck dumb. At that moment it was not clear to me which of us was the adult and which the boy. Do you understand me, Ruth?

Is anything else needed to make one understand the fate of the Jews other than the fate of this one Jewish boy? Could any writer use his imagination to create a greater story? Many clever sayings and wise maxims have lost their force. Who was it that said that one drop of water contains the whole ocean? Here you have three. Three crystalline drops: Krisia the foundling, the boy from Florence, and Josepho from Benghazi.

Every single drop seems like a new sea. Or Leo! I told you in previous letters about his flight from an orphanage in Germany on Kristallnacht, how he managed under his own steam to get to Copenhagen, and he wasn't yet ten years old. (Just imagine one of our own kibbutz children of the same age!!) At the age of fifteen he was smuggling Jews into Sweden within

ERWIN ROMMEL (1891–1944): A German general who reached the rank of *Feldmarschall*. Rommel served with distinction during World War I, and he began World War II as commander of an armored division in France. In 1941, he was appointed by Hitler to be commander of the Afrika Corps, on the front that the Germans had opened in North Africa. There Rommel scored many successes on the battlefield and was nicknamed the Desert Fox. He advanced as far as El Alamein, near the Egyptian border and the port of Alexandria. After a successful counterattack by the British army under Field Marshal Montgomery, Rommel was compelled to retreat from the Egyptian border deeper into Libya. In 1944, Hitler made him responsible for the defense of France, in anticipation of the invasion by the Allied forces. In the summer of 1944, he was apparently one of the supporters of the generals who conspired to assassinate Hitler. The would-be assassins had ceased to believe in a German victory and regarded Hitler as the main obstacle to the future development of Germany. The conspiracy was discovered and Rommel was forced to commit suicide.

PALMAḤ: The elite force of the Israeli army during the War of Independence.

the framework of the Danish underground's great rescue operation (we'll find an opportunity to talk at greater length about this wonderful work of the Danes), when he was caught by the Gestapo.

Tortured and forlorn, Leo arrived in Auschwitz. Since childhood Leo had been physically well developed (he said there were three boys named Leo in the orphanage, and they called him "*der Grosse*," the big one) and his tall stature saved him from the first "selections." I wrote "forlorn," but that was not accurate. Leo found friends in the death camp. One of them, who had been a youth leader in the Theresienstadt ghetto, several years older than Leo, extended him his patronage. This youth leader from Theresienstadt taught his young friend to read Hebrew in Auschwitz. The second of his new friends was the rabbi, Cassuto. (Does the name Cassuto mean anything to you? Yes, he's the son of Professor Cassuto from Jerusalem,✢ whom you met in the house of Gattegno. And then you studied Torah with him at the university. The sound of that name did something for me too!)

You know, when out of the dark, anonymous sea of people a familiar name suddenly shows up, it does something to you, like a close-up appearing on the screen. Very few at Auschwitz knew that Cassuto was a rabbi. The Germans knew him as an Italian eye doctor, which was how he escaped the fate of the crematorium (according to Leo, his friend was in the hospital block in a serious condition from dysentery and exhaustion, and the hospital block was called by the inmates the "corridor to the gas chambers") and it was the Devil himself who saved him at the last moment.

Dr. Mengele (apparently that was the name of the head butcher at Auschwitz) took Cassuto out of the clinic and had him fed and strengthened, since Mengele's deputy urgently needed a doctor to help him, even a Jew. Rabbi-Doctor Cassuto was "privileged" to join the death march. In other words, to hold out till the last winter of the war, when the Germans had already dismantled the camps, blurring any traces of the slaughter, and were marching hundreds and thousands of prisoners from camp to camp across

PROFESSOR CASSUTO FROM JERU-SALEM (1883–1951): Moshe David Cassuto, linguist and biblical scholar, who was a native of Florence. Cassuto was ordained as a rabbi and became professor of Bible studies and Hebrew language. He immigrated to Palestine in 1939, and was for many years a lecturer in Bible studies and did research in Ugaritic literature at the Hebrew University of Jerusalem.

Germany. One morning, before the start of the evacuation, the youth leader from Theresienstadt had fallen victim to the malice of the *kapo*. His glasses flew from his nose and the *kapo* in his anger trod on them. Without his glasses the lad was as good as dead, certainly incapable of marching even the first kilometer of the proposed march. Somehow Cassuto managed to extract from the store of belongings of those who had already been cremated two pairs of glasses, one of which fitted the boy's eyes.

"God is in Heaven." The young Czech, whose face had not lost, even in Auschwitz, the delicate features of a young Jewish intellectual, covered the borrowed glasses with his hands and said with emotion, "I feel as if someone is looking at me through these glasses." And he tortured himself worrying whether it was permissible for him to take them. Cassuto in his capacity of rabbi fortified him, saying, "It is permissible. That is the meaning, for our time, of the words of Ezekiel, 'live in spite of your blood.'"

When they set off, and many stumbled in the mud and snow, and shots cut down the faltering and did not cease all day, Cassuto took Leo's hand under his arm and bade him to make a holy promise. The boy asked, "What do you want me to promise, Rabbi? Is there anything that in my present state I'm capable of promising?"

"The only thing you can promise, my son, is that you won't give in."

He also demanded that the young man from Theresienstadt keep going. But the young man's feet had swollen, through the new glasses on his eyes he could see blue and yellow rings and he muttered, "Keep going—what for? So that I can tell them all about these horrors?"

"No," Cassuto was holding him by both arms, "so as to survive. To survive."

But the young man from Theresienstadt did not survive. Death struck him down on the far side of the Polish frontier. Ice covered the roads and his feet could no longer support him. He attended the first inspection on German soil "sandwiched."

"When he died, his corpse was leaning on me in a standing position."

When Leo saw how amazed I was by what he was saying, he added, "You've never heard of dead men standing for inspection in the morning, have you?"

I hadn't. How could we? So I heard.

In December 1943, the temperature in Birkenau reached 25 degrees below zero. The inmates had no clothes except their striped uniforms, shabby tattered rags, and they went off to work in them at first light and came back at sunset. Before and after there were marches. Ruth, I do the men a tremendous injustice when I try to reconstruct in a letter what I heard from their lips, which is itself only a pale reflection of what they went through. That morning Leo was leaving the camp at five o'clock when it started raining. At that time of the year the rain turns the clothes immediately into a covering of ice. The rain didn't stop all day, it just changed the direction of assault from time to time, sometimes it scalded like fire from the left, sometimes from the right. Strange, he spoke of a feeling of burning, of fire—in the frost. Six of the occupants of Leo's block breathed their last en route to the work site and they carried the bodies back with them on their return from work. It was getting dark and after the march they were ordered to get into the huts immediately. Usually the meals—a slice of bread and some muddy coffee—were given out while they were standing outside. What was going on? They wondered: maybe the SS felt a spark of humanity and had decided after such a terrible day to let them eat inside the hut, which was somewhat protected against the wind and cold. Even when they heard the shrieks of the *Älteste*,[*] ordering them to undress at once, there were some who thought it was so that their clothes could dry. But immediately they were told to go outside in the nude. The SS and the *kapo*, dressed in raincoats, hoods, and high boots, beat the naked men with their clubs. Cries of pain and suffering arose from all the blocks in the area. Crowds of naked men were being run up and down the parade ground.

"Dance!" came the order. "You wanted to get warm—so dance!"

And the poor wretches danced. Leo moved and twisted among the bodies that clustered and pressed to hide in the middle and thus avoid exposure to blows from their oppressors. Every time the runners revolved in the dance, more men collapsed. Few of them managed to get up again. It was a Sabbath eve. When he awoke on the Sabbath morning, eight of Leo's fellow prisoners in the hut were dead. Within moments they were supposed to be outside on morning parade, and the senior prisoner in the hut would as usual have to report the deaths.

"Let us be too clever for them,"[*] Leo voiced his crazy idea, and everyone realized what he was getting at. He stirred them into putting berets on the heads of the deceased and wooden clogs on their feet. They went on parade, and the dead men "marched" in the inner ranks. And when they heard the *kapo's* whistle, they straightened the lines. They stood there solid as a wall on the parade square, and the dead stood in their usual places, furtively supported by their comrades, erect. Mercifully the snow descended and covered their faces, which were turning blue. With their dull eyes, the living were indistinguishable from the dead as they all stood there, silent and motionless. And the Germans completed their head count, and distributed the rations of soup, bread, and margarine for the following day in accordance with the number on parade.[*]

Four more died on Monday and during the course of the week the number of corpses in the hut rose to twelve. No report was made of any of them, they all went on parade, the living and the dead, and the snow and the cold were a help. And the rumor spread among the blocks, and other huts were emboldened to do likewise, and Leo proposed they set up a common pool into which the bread of the deceased would be placed and then shared out equally. And they agreed.

One Hasid, a survivor of the slaughter at Trzemeszno,[*] who always said the blessings over his food, could hardly believe it when he received an extra slice from the rations of the dead. He turned to Cassuto (who put his bread aside on the Eve of the Day of Atonement and everyone saw that he didn't touch it until the end of the Fast). "Rabbi," said the Hasid

THE ÄLTESTE: The term for the senior prisoner on the block at Auschwitz and the other concentration camps.

"LET US BE TOO CLEVER FOR THEM": Pharaoh's comment on the way to deal with the Israelites. See Exodus 1:8-10.

Numerical distribution of the ashes of extermination:

Albania	200
Austria	52,000
Belgium	28,900
Bohemia and Moravia	78,150
Bukovina and Bessarabia	250,000
Crete	260
Danzig Free Port	1,000
Denmark	77
Estonia	2,000
Finland	11
France	83,000
Germany	140,000
Greece and Rhodes	67,000
Holland	100,000
Hungary, within the 1941 borders, including Northern Transylvania	560,000
Italy	8,000
Latvia	70,000
Libya	562
Lithuania	143,000
Luxembourg	1,950
Norway	700
Poland	c. 3,000,000
Romania	40,000
Russia (Soviet Union)	1,100,000
Slovakia	68,000
Yugoslavia (including Macedonia)	60,000

TRZEMESZNO: A small town in Poland, northeast of Poznan.

from Trzemeszno, "isn't this, God forbid, like a heathen sacrifice to the dead?"[*] I don't know what reply he reveived from the incognito saint of Florence. Suddenly there were heard in the hut strains of *El Male Raḥamim*.[*] The Hasid from Trzemeszno had the fingers of one hand spread across the bread on the edge of his bunk like a spider's legs frozen over its prey, and with the other he covered his eyes. He began quietly, and as he continued his chant grew louder. When he reached the words "the soul of . . . ," it was like a wave striking a rock. Everyone fell silent, as he cried through his tears, ". . . the souls of our comrades who have gone to their repose, and with their bread have given us strength to vanquish the kingdom of evil, even if for but one hour . . . and may the Merciful One . . ."

Stifled sobs broke up the chant and obscured the words of the prayer. From that day on the bread of the dead at Auschwitz was known as the Bread of Eternal Life.[*]

My dear Ruth, I don't know whether you are reading this over lunch, a demanding time (isn't that the time when the mail is distributed?), or whether you put the unusually thick envelope to one side to read at your leisure. I imagine you sitting in our new armchair, your tired feet in yellow house slippers or tucked underneath you as you squat in the oriental style you love (is it comfortable in the seventh month?), the water sprinkler outside tapping quietly, rhythmically, refreshingly against the shutters. A clear, peaceful evening. Have I made you cry, my dear? My hand does not tremble, as they say, as I write these words, but my eyes stream with tears, hot and incessant. Strange, I didn't cry when I heard them tell these stories (did you ever see me cry?), only now, when I put it into writing, does it happen. Can writing do such a thing to a man?

I suspect I shall not come away from these encounters the same man. I fear that when I return to the kibbutz I shall feel a stranger—in my own home. You raise your eyebrows? What are you saying, it's not nice to talk like that? What's happened to you, Hezi? Actually, something had already happened, on my last visit home.

Do you remember the evening when we were all together in our apartment? You had gone to the trouble of roasting peanuts and there was plenty of tea. Everything was very jolly. The Tokers were there, Yankele and Miri, Ahuvaleh and Gilead, Shushu, the whole gang. I was asked to tell how I was doing, what the people were like, and the operations and above all whether it was true that there was friction between our boys from Palyam[*] and the workers and envoys from the institutions, and what on earth was Doveleh doing in Paris. As I said, it was all very jolly, lots of laughter, and I didn't say anything about the people. Apart from mentioning the pogrom at Kielce.[*] Just before I sailed there had been a large wave of refugees from Poland, eyewitnesses to what had happened. With photographs. For me it was quite a shock. I just couldn't take it in that something like that could happen there—in Poland—after everything that had gone before. You all listened with half an ear. The discussion of the call-up of the youth group, finding out the truth about the impending break-up of Tzivia and Gabi, the latest kibbutz gossip, all these things quickly overshadowed my report of the pogrom. Later, when we were alone, you said, "Hezi, you should tell Yakush tomorrow." Yakush?—I didn't get it—tell him what? "*Nu*, you said something about Kielce. Yakush is from there."

That's just it. He's from there, and we—aren't we from there any more? That's why there's such insensitivity. I felt it plainly myself. Tell our friend G., Ruth, whose voice is not confined to the editorial board of the party newspaper, to stop talking about the refugees as men of dust and dry bones that we have to restore to life, so to speak. That is harmful, humiliating nonsense. Such terrible destruction may happen only once in a thousand years. But only once in a thousand years will a people renew itself after such a catastrophe the way this stiff-necked people is likely to. What vitality they show, these Jews, who fought so hard to survive. If only they can be enabled to reach a safe harbor! Sometimes I think they are not the survivors—they are the ocean.

". . . SACRIFICE TO THE DEAD": Honoring the dead by providing food, offered to him or eaten in his honor. The custom was widespread in the ancient world, especially Egypt. In the Bible the expression is found in a pejorative sense, in the context of idol worship: "They attached themselves to Baal Peor, ate sacrifices offered to the dead" (Psalms 106: 28).

EL MALE RAḤAMIM (Hebrew): Literally, O Lord full of compassion. It is the name of a prayer of remembrance for the soul of the dead, recited after burial, on Remembrance Day, and whenever a grave is visited.

BREAD OF ETERNAL LIFE: A reference to the end of the prayer *El Male Raḥamim*: ". . . and let his [her] soul be bound up in the bond of eternal life."

PALYAM: An acronym from the Hebrew for "naval force," a unit of the Palmaḥ whose main task was the bringing of illegal immigrants by sea, carrying out sabotage operations at sea, and serving as the nucleus of the future Israeli navy.

KIELCE: A small town in Poland, east of Czestochowa. On July 4, 1946, after the establishment of a People's Communist Democracy in Poland, riots broke out against the Jews in Kielce, most of whom were refugees. A pogrom took place and 42 Jews lost their lives.

ELKIND (1897-1937): Menachem Elkind immigrated to Palestine from Russia in 1920, and was one of the leaders of the "Work Brigade" named after Josef Trumpeldor. In 1927, he returned to Russia with the intention of establishing a commune there. During the purges of the 1930s, he was arrested and all trace of him was lost.

SPANISH CIVIL WAR: Civil war broke out in Spain in July 1936 between government republican forces and loyalist rebels who sought to overthrow the government by force. The Spanish aristocracy and the clergy supported the rebels, who opposed the reforms that the Popular Front government—which contained Republicans, Socialists, Syndicalists, and Communists—wished to introduce. The rebels were led by General Franco and his followers from the Fascist Phalangist Party. The Soviet Union supported the government and Fascist Italy and Nazi Germany supported the rebels. Forty thousand volunteers, including Jews from Palestine, came to the aid of the Spanish government from the countries of Europe and the United States: they formed the "International Brigade." In April 1937, German planes bombed the small town of Guernica in the Basque region, an event that has been immortalized in the great painting by Pablo Picasso. In January 1939, Franco occupied Barcelona, the Catalonian capital, and by the end of March of the same year, Madrid, the capital of Spain. The regime established by Franco lasted until his death in 1975.

THE RESISTANCE: The underground movement that opposed the Nazi occupation in France. It was led by General De Gaulle, who established a Free French Government beyond the borders of France. The Jews, who constituted only one percent of the population, were represented in

Ruth, as I was thinking of the relation between the drop and the ocean, I was reminded of Eliahu Klatzkin. He told me another story, this time about his emotional meeting with a childhood friend who had left Israel for Russia with Elkind[+] and his group. He took part in the Spanish Civil War,[+] continued in exile in France, and was among the first to join the Resistance.[+] In 1943 he was arrested, along with a key unit of the Maquis,[+] all of them Jews. Some say it was their comrades in arms who betrayed them. This friend's name was Bolek Chaimovitz, and he had been through hell at the hands of the Nazis. Now he has a full beard and answers to the name of Bar-Chaim. Eliahu from Beit Alfa asked his old friend from Ramat Yohanan, "Explain it to me, how could it happen. In an enlightened Europe, in the middle of the twentieth century—how could it happen?"

The man replied, "It happened because we didn't believe it could happen! I was on the Ebro,"[+] he told him, "and I saw what was going on behind the backs of the fighters who still believed with perfect faith in the brotherhood of nations, the solidarity of the workers and their comrades in arms. Three years after the rise of Hitler to power and three years before the outbreak of World War II you could already read the writing on the wall; there were signs in the sky that foretold the coming storm (from the shadow of Göring's dive-bombing Stukes[+] up above to the black and brown legions from Europe assembled in Franco's[+] camp down below) and we just couldn't imagine what was going to happen within a mere three years. You ask how we could be so blind. We truly believed that with our own hands we were building a new world, fashioning a new, improved man, establishing a better, more just society. We were unaware of the simple, painful fact that we represented nothing but our own dreams!"

And this man from Ramat Yohanan had a friend whom he had met in Paris in the days of the underground, a young philosopher, a Jewish genius by the name of Yankelowitz, who said to the man back from the banks of the Ebro, "*Mon ami,* be careful. France is like a calm sea. The polished mirror of its surface conceals waves and depths. Even in the Resistance there are shoals of anti-Semitism." It would take five years of mental and physical anguish before Bolek would fully understand Yankelowitz's trenchant comment about the stepsons and Cassandras who passed as intellectuals but were nowhere to be seen wherever and whenever there was need of real courage.

Courage is no success story. I would like to remember young men like Rudi. Who was

much higher proportion in the underground movement and its fighting units.

THE MAQUIS: The name given to the evergreen shrubs widespread in the hilly regions of France near the Mediterranean coast and on the island of Corsica. "Maquis" also referred to the bands of law breakers who found refuge from their pursuers in the scrubland. During the period of the Nazi occupation, the term "maquis" was also used for the underground fighters who engaged in active resistance to the Germans.

EBRO: A river in the eastern part of Spain. Here the reference is to the International Brigade, which fought against the Fascist forces during the Spanish Civil War.

STUKE: A German fighter plane.

FRANCISCO FRANCO (1892-1975): A Spanish general who gained control of Spain during the Spanish Civil War (1936-1939), after leading the army, which rebelled against the Republican Government. After victory he was proclaimed sole leader and ruler (*Caudillo*). He set up a Fascist regime in Spain on the Italian model. During the World War, Franco did not join the Axis Powers, even though he had received massive support from them during the Civil War. However, Spanish volunteers were sent to the Russian Front. His anti-Communist stand was explicit. On the other hand, his regime behaved with a fair measure of tolerance toward the Jewish refugees from France. In 1969, Franco named the exiled king of Spain, Juan Carlos, as his successor after his death. The king used his authority after the death of the dictator to restore Spain to the family of democratic countries.

Rudi? I had just got back from Ferramonti-Tarsia with a load of blankets. Leo was by my side. Yes, the one who fled the orphanage at Dinslaken and passed through twelve(!) concentration camps and is still a young lad, with his carefully groomed ginger beard, the appeal of his wild quiff, freckles, and open expression, which suddenly make him look like a *Palmaḥnik.*

I said to him, "Leo! You haven't got to Israel yet and already you look like one of the *jima'ah.*"*

He asked me, "What's the *jima'ah?*"

I told him.

He said, "No, Hezi, between me and the *jima'ah* there will always fall the shadow of Rudi."

I asked him who Rudi was. It was an October evening. Leo opened the window of the cabin and let the fierce wind blow in his face. I glanced in surprise at the lad, who was not yet twenty, and saw that his gaze was wandering far off in the frozen darkness. For the next two hours, as my Studebaker swallowed up the rows of lights reflected off the tarmac, he told me things, which to my sorrow I'm incapable of recalling except in part, in essence.

At the beginning of February 1945, Leo and the remnant of the prisoners from Auschwitz reached Germany without knowing where they were finally being taken. Of the three friends who had set out together on that murderous journey and sworn together that they would not give up, only Leo remained alive. The youth leader from Theresienstadt, a brother as much as a friend, had died, as you remember, supported on the shoulders of his companions.

Out of some feeling of thanksgiving that once again he was on the soil of the *Faterland,*+ the soldier escorting them allowed them to bury the corpse of their comrade. And all they had was their nails and the ground was February-hard, frozen solid. They hid him near an oak, covering his face with damp leaves and lots of snow, and Leo took his spectacles. Two nights later, Rabbi Cassuto disappeared. When they were woken in the morning by the shouts of "*Schnell! Schnell! 'Raus!*"*—and the rumor was that the next stop was the camp of Gross-Rosen—the rabbi was not in his place. There had been no shots fired during the night and no one had heard him cry out. Probably the rabbi had felt that his time was approaching, and wished strongly to

JIMA'AH (Arabic): Gang, band.

FATERLAND (German): Fatherland.

"SCHNELL! SCHNELL! 'RAUS!" (German): Quickly! Quickly! Outside!

meet his Maker in peace, without receiving the coup de grace at the hands of a German. Cassuto had crawled away, dragged himself apparently to a ditch or some undergrowth in the forest and, when the chill of death gripped his limbs, must have tried to fill his dull eyes with the cold radiance of the stars before passing over to the other side, appearing before the Supreme Judge and giving Him a report on this world of crematoria. Probably a man like Nathan Cassuto would ask the God of Abraham, Isaac, and Jacob why He had planted within us an unconquerable soul when the body lay dying.

The boy who had been orphaned at birth suddenly felt the full weight of loneliness. For in Cassuto Leo had acquired a father, and the young man from Theresienstadt had been like an elder brother. Leo was now going from Gross-Rosen to Buchenwald, alongside the other marchers, making no attempt to hide himself from the whips in the hands of the guards. The last days before they reached Buchenwald brought an unending harvest of blood. One after another the men toppled like dominoes. Isolated shots marked the number of fallen that nobody counted. Leo's dull eyes were closed all but a slit. Dread had turned to apathy. He felt the chill of death grip his thighs and climb across his stomach, to his heart. One by one the lights in his brain were going out, only one distant voice still reverberated, "Don't give in. Don't give in." But Leo could feel the sweat of death breaking out on his mortal flesh. He could no longer speak, but just marched and marched. And so he reached Buchenwald. He could just make out the gloom of the block into which he was being thrust and the crazy look in the eyes of the *Älteste,* and then he threw out his arms and fainted on the threshold. He woke to find himself lying on a straw mattress and did not know if one night had passed or a day and a night. Some stranger was supporting his neck with one bony hand and feeding him thick soup with the other. He couldn't tell whether it was tasteless or revolting, but the heat of the liquid hit the pit of his stomach. Then they asked him his name.

He said, "Leo."

"Leo what?"

"Arendt."

One of the old-timers lit his face with a candle and said in surprise, "My son, you are lying on the mattress of Rudi Arendt."

"Rudi was here?" astonishment jolted Leo awake. He

had had a cousin in Berlin whose imprisonment for distributing revolutionary propaganda in the pre-Nazi German army had once shocked the family, making the house rock. Leo remembered Rudi's last visit, before going off on a Lag B'Omer⁺ outing. Leo was five years old at the time, very envious of his cousin with his hobnailed boots and a real backpack, going off to the hills. Little Leo also wanted very much to be a member of the Kameraden.⁺ When Herr Arendt was informed that his son was a Communist and had been taken to the Moabit⁺ jail, he said, "*Also,*⁺ he is not my son any more." On January 25, 1933, five days before von Hindenburg installed Hitler as ruler of Germany, Rudi was released from prison.

He saw his mother, his sister, and one of his cousins, a third-year law student, waiting on the other side of the road, between the poplar and the telegraph pole (a thought entered his head: did they arrest Willi?). His father and the rest of the family had gone to Bordeaux in France, and his mother and elder sister had waited for Rudi to be released, when they would all follow them.

"Father has forgiven you; he will be happy to see you in safety," his mother said. While she was still holding him in her arms, Rudi told her he was staying.

That same evening he was with Willi and the other five members of the cell, almost all from the same neighborhood, all Jews, folding anti-Nazi leaflets that Willi had composed in the name of "sane Germans."

Rudi was one of the first prisoners of the Third Reich. From that moment on he made the rounds of suffering from camp to camp. Brandenburg-Dachau-Sachsenhausen-Buchenwald. Inside the barbed wire of the concentration camps in Germany his name was well known, and outside the walls it had been expunged from the land of the living.

In Buchenwald the Germans set up a special quarter for the Jews and made Rudi the *kapo* responsible for them. At first there were Jews from Berlin and Austria; later the quarter filled up with Jews from Poland. The Germans intended to let the Jews from Poland die of starvation. It was Rudi—two of the old-timers in Block 22 told Leo the story now—who had thwarted the plans of the SS.

Rudi filched food from the special stores in the camp headquarters, and drugs from the dispensary. At first he did it alone. Then he organized groups he could trust from among the political prisoners. His faithful followers worked with devotion. Rudi handed out the drugs to those Jews who needed them most, the sick, and those whose frailty was a cause for concern. Many of the recent arrivals among the Jews showed a lack of resourcefulness. Some of his comrades demanded that he give preference to the younger men, the members of the Communist cell, to strengthen those who would be "active in the future," but Rudi was not to be deterred from following his conscience: first the most needy, even in Buchenwald.

"Tell the lad," Hertz Fischel from Hamburg was speaking, whose front teeth had all been pulled out during interrogation, so that his lips moved in a ghastly smile, "about Rudi's quartet, tell him."

And Leo heard a strange story. His cousin Rudi, the Communist, was able to appeal to the heart of the Jews from Poland, whose language he could not speak and only barely understand, and kept their spirits up with the very same words that Nathan Cassuto, the rabbi from Florence, had used in Auschwitz: Don't give in. Jews must not give in to evil. In the end there would be victory—words that in those days in Buchenwald were worth any number of doctor's pills. Rudi had the nerve secretly to organize a string quartet among the prisoners and with the help of bribes got hold of instruments from the piles of property in the storerooms. The quartet brought Mozart, Haydn, and Beethoven to Buchenwald. And then their lords and masters lost patience. On the morning of the third of May—the date was fixed in his memory—Rudi was summoned to report to the gate of the camp. Ironically, the *Obersturmbannführer's*⁺ name was Schubert. The camp guards were drawn up in two files and at their head stood the commandant, Schubert. As Rudi in his uniform of stripes drew near the opening between the columns, which were drawn up like a guard of honor, Schubert shrieked, "To the King of the Jews, present—arms!" Schubert the SS man gave a second command and the soldiers obeyed, turning to meet the man striding toward them. The prisoners followed this frightening, incredible spectacle from a distance.

LAG B'OMER (Hebrew): The thirty-third day of the counting of the '*Omer* between Passover and Pentecost; a Jewish festival commemorating the revolt of the students of Rabbi Akiva against the Romans, traditionally celebrated by excursions to the countryside.

KAMERADEN (German): Literally, friends, but here referring to a Socialist Jewish youth movement in Germany before the Nazis.

MOABIT: The central prison in Berlin.

"ALSO . . ." (German): In that case.

OBERSTURMBANNFÜHRER: A senior rank in the SS, equivalent to colonel.

They held their breaths as they saw Rudi at first step back in confusion from the two files, probably thinking it was the *Obersturmbannführer* who would inspect the guard of honor, but when he was prodded forward by a bayonet in the back, he realized what was expected of him. They saw him hold himself erect, his long thin neck projecting from his striped shirt,[*] and march with head held high past the infamous "guard of honor." They said he marched as though on a ceremonial parade. No truncheons were brandished. Rudi was not beaten. At the foot of the hill, from the edge of the parade ground, a winding path led to the quarry behind the camp. Within a few minutes a volley of shots rang out from the quarry to which Rudi had been taken. At dusk representatives of the other blocks secretly made their way to Hut Number 22 to hold a memorial service. Even the veterans among the *Ka-Tzetniks*[*] could not remember an occasion when they had eulogized and mourned a single individual. At the end of the four eulogies they all got down from their bunks, stood together and sang the *Rotfront*.[*] Then the leader of the cell, a man named Emil who had been a friend of Ernst Toller, asked if there was anyone who could say *Kaddish*. There was one young man, a member of He-Ḥalutz Ha-Loḥem, the "fighting pioneers" from Krakow, who said yes he could, he was an orphan.

Outside the storm has abated. The grunts of the sleepers have died away. At the end of the long winding corridor a shadow suddenly became visible—of a head with a tefillin and a raised arm, also wrapped by a tefillin, swaying in front of a window and on the verge of falling. We hurried toward the man (Leo had woken) and the two of us lent him support. Leo took one side and I took the other and we held him in the draft of cold air after opening the window. "Do you need any help, Mr. Teleks?" I asked.

Teleks had been a well-known merchant in Lithuania, the representative of the JNF[*] in his town. The war caught him in Holland and for three years he was imprisoned in Wester-broek. When Canadian soldiers liberated the camp, he was the first *musulman* they saw. Today, one year later, you wouldn't recognize him—outwardly, I mean—there's no trace of the suffering, apart from his hair, which is prematurely white.

I was afraid he was having a heart attack. His face, which had suddenly grown old, was a wrinkled mask with glassy eyes. His mouth twisted in a grimace of anguish.

"What can we do to help you?" I asked again.

For a long while he stared at me emptily. I could barely catch what he was saying. "Do?" he marveled at my question. "You cannot dream my dreams for me, my son. Following my wife and children among the waves. Every night on my bed. Sometimes there are waves and trains, sometimes there are waves and mad dogs. The sea is here. With a thousand arms. When are we leaving this accursed continent?" His body began to shudder and he collapsed into our arms.

October 25

Let's get out of here! Out of here!

October 26

The British army used gas against the "illegal immigrants" on board the *Knesset Yisra'el,* for heaven's sake![*] How could they dare do such a thing as use gas, and against whom! Even if it was only tear gas. Only tear gas! God Almighty!! They haven't yet stopped wiping their eyes. What kind of a liberated world is this we've come to?[*]

October 27

Ruth, there's a girl on the deck of the *Knesset Yisra'el* that I want you to get in contact with at the very first opportunity. It's a matter of life and death.

STRIPED SHIRT: The literal translation of a Hebrew expression used in Genesis for the garment Jacob gives to Joseph, the "coat of many colors." An untranslatable irony.

KA-TZETNIKS: Prisoners in the concentration camps. "*Ka-Tzet*" is the German abbreviation for *Konzentration.*

ROTFRONT (German): Red front. The German Communists, especially the members of the militant units, used to greet each other with the words "red front."

JNF: The Jewish National Fund, which raised money for the Zionist enterprise both in Palestine and throughout the Diaspora.

The publication on May 17, 1939, of the "White Paper" by the British government closed the gates of the Land of Israel to Jewish refugees. It dashed the hopes of many people that humanitarian principles would outweigh narrow political considerations. Great Britain did not even allow the rescue of hundreds of thousands of children for whose lives the Jewish Agency was pleading.

"A letter to the children of the Land of Israel: Though I have not yet succeeded in actually playing in the lap of our Mother, Israel, I have a great longing for her, as my deeds can prove: After much suffering in the camp in Germany, which there is no need to spell out in detail, and after having been several times closer to death than life; after lying three months in a hospital for the sick, for which a more apt name would be a hospital for the dead—finally I was released and spent three weeks making my way home. But all my effort was in vain. When I got home, there was not a single member of the household there, not a single member of my family to be seen. I might have been born from the rock."

—MORDECHAI STERN (aged 15),
from a home for child survivors, in the
village of Salvino, northern Italy, 1946

October 28

The girl, Lena Feinstein (sixteen), has been listed in the group destined for our kibbutz. She was fourteen when the Germans entered Hungary. The whole family, ten of them, entered Auschwitz and she is the only one left alive. Near the end of the war she was still with her mother. In one of the camps her mother stole two carrots from the Germans' provision store. They led her to the scaffold in the sight of her daughter, but at the last moment her sentence was commuted to a whipping. Bruised and aching, the mother and her daughter supported each other on the death march until one day a German gave them a kick and sent them rolling down a muddy embankment like a bundle of old clothes. Lena found herself at the bottom of a pigsty, smothered by a pile of dying women (actually twenty-four out of two hundred), some squirming and screaming for help, some lying quietly indifferent to death. She had no idea how long she had been lying there, beset by cold, hunger, and rats. When she regained consciousness she saw Russian soldiers looking down at her and crying. She heard the word "hospital" and shrieked, "No, no, no hospital!"

The army doctor couldn't understand why the word "hospital" should fill her with such dread. They left her with a German family in the vicinity and ordered them to look after her. But Lena refused to eat, refused to live. She found out that her mother's dead body had been taken out of the pigsty. When I think about a tear gas grenade being thrown at Lena, near the gates of Israel, I could lose my mind. Ruth dear, "be a mother and sister to her."✢

October 30

Write this down! Write it all down! Cry aloud! Cry aloud! Let people know what happened. What can still happen.

In the small hours of the night, on the shore of the Mediterranean, opposite the Land of Israel, suddenly I began to understand that writing—perhaps only writing—is the way to achieve identity. To preserve us from alienation and to rescue them from the dark islands of memory.

November 1

For several days now I have been aware that what I am writing is not a letter. But what is it?

If this cry, like all the other cries, becomes paper, a book, another book, will anyone read it or not?

November 2

Leo is back from Dessau.✢ What was Leo Arendt doing in Dessau? His grandfather is buried there. He brought back a document. I saw the list; it's amazing. His grandfather, and six generations before him, apparently, were rabbis and religious dignitaries. His father was the first to break away. There was one old man there in the deserted community building. Leo told him who he was. The survivor told him that if he got to Breslau✢ and not everything had been burned, he would find records of twelve generations of his family. Leo heard from the old man that he was related to the author of *Two Tablets of Stone*.✢ He was astonished—to my shame, so was I—that only twelve generations separated him from the prophet Moses, the author of the two tablets of stone.

That's what Leo was doing in Dessau.

November 3

The mysterious impulse that drove Leo to go searching for his roots almost brought him absentmindedly to getting off the train at the station that led to the crematorium. No, he didn't enter the camp, just stopped in the village by the house that stood opposite the camp. It was an ordinary, red-bricked family house with a garden with a wicket gate. The ground floor windows were shuttered. Upstairs were a lace valance and a pleated muslin curtain. It was from that upstairs window that the crematorium chimney was directly visible. From that window they could see the

Child: **Did all this really happen,** Father, or was it likely to happen?
Father: It's true. It happened, my son, and it is still likely to happen.

"BE A MOTHER AND A SISTER TO HER":
Spread your wing to be my shelter,
Be my mother, sister, all.
Let my head nest in your bosom
And my prayers that vainly call.

—CHAIM NACHMAN BIALIK
(translated by Dom Moraes)

DESSAU: A town in Germany, southwest of Berlin.

BRESLAU: A town, also known as Wroclaw, now in southwestern Poland.

THE AUTHOR OF TWO TABLETS OF STONE: The reference is to Rabbi Isaiah bar Abraham Halevi Horowitz, who was born in Prague in 1565 and died in Tiberias in 1630. Horowitz immigrated to Israel in 1621 and was the rabbi of the Ashkenazic community in Jerusalem. His principal work, the *Two Tablets of Stone,* was first published posthumously in Amsterdam in 1649. It is a blend of doctrine, allegory, Kabbalah, and ethical teaching. Generations of Jews in central and Eastern Europe were educated in accordance with this book, which also had some influence on Hasidism.

If their blood is not avenged— what is justice and what accounting is there in this world? During World War II there were 500 concentration camps, and more than 1,000 ghettos and places of slaughter. In each of these places there were German generals, officers, sergeants, and rank and file soldiers and their collaborators who were actively involved in murder. Everywhere there were those who sat behind desks and planned the murders, who were involved in deporting and transporting the victims, who gave the commands to open fire, and who did the killing. Many of these murderers remain unknown because there were no survivors.

For example, in the area of Lublin in Poland 40,000 Jews fled to the forests. Murder squads of Germans and their henchmen went into the forests and slaughtered the Jews and the partisans. Who were the Germans who pressed the triggers? They are walking the streets of Germany and Austria to this day and no one knows their identities. And another example: On January 31, 1945, one of the many death marches made its way down to the beach of the northern Baltic Sea. Six thousand Jewish women and 100 men, survivors of 12 years of Nazi rule, moved like a giant shadow, straggling, bent. They were on their way to Stutthof, a camp near the quiet village of Flaminken, and their escort of German soldiers decided to let them rest. At the end of their rest period, the soldiers drove all the Jewish men and women into the raging sea, cutting them down with machine gun fire and Schmeissers. And the inhabitants of Flaminken on the beach saw what happened. And all was silent. And then, far, far away on the edge of the horizon, a colored rocket suddenly exploded and on all the wireless receivers flashed the news that World War II had come to an end.

How is it possible to understand? To fathom? To sing? To show friendship?

TZIVIA (1914–1978): One of the leading fighters and heroines of the uprising in the Warsaw ghetto. Tzivia Lubetkin was born in the small town of Biten near Slonim. She studied Judaism at a Polish school and from a private teacher, called "Berl *der Melamed.*" At an early age Lubetkin joined a Zionist youth movement. In 1939, she was a delegate to the Zionist Congress at Basel, but returned to Poland shortly before the outbreak of war, where she eventually served as one of the junior commanders of the uprising and as commander of the units of the Jewish National Organization. Her husband, Yitzhak Zuckerman (Antek), was second-in-command to Mordechai Anielewicz during the Warsaw ghetto uprising. Lubetkin succeeded in escaping from the central bunker, through the sewers and out of the ghetto. In August 1943, she and Antek sent a report to the embassy of the Polish National Assembly in London about what was happening in Warsaw and throughout Poland. Lubetkin sent an appeal for help and warned of what was to come. She joined the underground in Warsaw and took part in the Polish Uprising in October 1943. After the occupation of Warsaw by the Red Army in 1944, Lubetkin reached Palestine. She took part in the establishment of the Kibbutz Loḥamei Ha-Get-

flames. Day and night. I asked him if he went inside. Leo shook his head. "No, I was afraid I would lose control."

"Why did you go there?" I asked him, "to cause yourself pain?"

And Leo said, "Hezi, without that house outside, we shall never understand what went on in the camp inside."⁺ I wonder whether I fully understood what he meant. There are many things that are still obscure to us.

November 4

We met one of the survivors of the Warsaw ghetto uprising. He was the one who helped Tzivia⁺ escape through the sewers. It was hard to get him to talk. I told him of the grief on the kibbutz when the news arrived that Toussia⁺ had fallen. He was moved and said, "Really?" and then, "Yes, Toussia was burned." I asked him if it was true that Mordechai A.⁺ and all his staff had committed suicide

taot (Ghetto Fighters' Kibbutz) and was active on her kibbutz for many years. She died of an illness in 1978.

TOUSSIA (1918–1943): Toussia Altman was born in Wolotzelbek to a wealthy family. She studied in a Hebrew high school and joined Ha-Shomer Ha-Tza'ir at the age of 11. A talented speaker with an attractive personality, she was, by 1934, a youth leader in her branch, at camps and on trips. From 1937, Altman was a member of the branch leadership. In 1938, she went on *hakhsharah* at Czestochowa and later was asked to join the movement headquarters in Warsaw and coordinate the educational work of the younger level known as Bnei Midbar (Children of the Wilderness). Before the outbreak of war she was chosen to be the coordinator of the "B" leadership, designed to act in an emergency. When the Germans occupied Warsaw at the beginning of September 1939, Altman went to Vilna. She was among the first to make the arduous, agonizing return to Warsaw (at the end of 1939). There she resumed her work in the central management of He-Ḥalutz and managed to visit most of the areas under German occupation, in conditions of constant danger. With the setting up of the Jewish Fighting Organization in Warsaw, she was sent out of the ghetto to organize the acquisition of arms and establish contact with the underground forces. On May 8, 1943, she was in the command post at Mila 18, together with Mordechai Anielewicz. Most of the fighters perished there. Altman was among the 14 who survived and got away. She perished in a fire that broke out in a factory attic in the suburb of Praga (May 25, 1943), where armed Jewish fighters were hiding.

"I stop my breath, lest I give vent to the accumulated bitterness I feel against you and your friends for forgetting us so innocently. But today I don't want to settle accounts. It is just the recognition of the fact, the certainty, that we shall never see each other again that has impelled me to write. My sickness and that of Israel—and you know how long we have been fighting it—has now been discovered to be definitely incurable, so say the doctors. We must gradually get used to the idea. It's terrible, though, that we don't have enough time for this. Pogromski and Slaughter are living with us. There was nothing we could do to prevent this. The effect on Israel's health is fatal, I see how it hastens the end. I do everything I can to prevent it, but unfortunately there are factors that would restrict even the strongest will. Israel is dying before my eyes, I wring my hands but there is nothing I can do to help. Have you ever tried to bang your head against the wall? I have only one desire: to tell the world how sick Israel is. This is my best friend. And though nothing will really help very much, nevertheless the feeling that someone is with us, not only in thought, in this path of suffering brings some consolation."

—An underground message written by TOUSSIA ALTMAN, one of the commanders of the Warsaw ghetto revolt, smuggled to her comrades in Palestine, May, 1943

MORDECHAI A. (1919-1943): Commander of the Jewish Fighting Organization in the Warsaw ghetto. Mordechai Anielewicz was born in Warsaw to a poor family, who ran a grocer's shop in the suburb of Proltri (Podowiszla). He studied at the Hebrew-Polish high school La'or and joined Ha-Shomer Ha-Tza'ir at the age of 14. In 1937, he was already a youth leader, head of a brigade, and member of the branch management, where he frequently demonstrated his strength of personality and the decisive nature of his outlook and his deeds. On the outbreak of war, he devoted himself to organizing the movement in the occupied territories. At the end of 1939, Anielewicz visited Vilna in the Soviet-controlled zone, but rather than join the Ha-Shomer leadership, he returned to Warsaw with his companion, Mira Fuchrer, out of a sense of obligation and personal mission. He also went to visit the towns of Silesia in order to check the rumors about deportations to Auschwitz. After the murder of two prominent members, Josef Kaplan and Samuel Breslau, in autumn 1942, he returned to Warsaw and began to organize the fighting units for self-defense and rebellion. In January 1943, he commanded the first action against the Germans. On April 23, 1943, he wrote to Yitzhak Zuckerman, the representative of the "Fighting Organization" beyond the ghetto walls: "The dream of my life has been realized. Jewish defense in the ghetto is a fact. Jewish armed resistance exists. I can bear witness to the supremely heroic fighting of the Jewish rebels." On the day of the decisive battle, May 8, 1943, he was in command in the central bunker at Mila 18. The Germans surrounded the post and threw in gas grenades. Some of the fighters succumbed to the gas, including the commander. A few committed suicide, including Arie Wilner and Mira Fuchrer. Mordechai Anielewicz turned from a reality into a legend and joined the ranks of outstanding figures in the history of the Jewish people.

RUSCHKA (1921-1988): Ruschka Korchak-Marle was born in Bjelsk, attended a Polish school, and later was sent to *heder* to study Judaism. From childhood she was aware of her vulnerability to anti-Semitism. Korchak-Marle joined the branch of Ha-Shomer Ha-Tza'ir in Plotsk and became active first as a youth leader and then as a member of the management committee. With the outbreak of war and the occupation of the town by the Germans, she found her way with the help of the underground to Vilna. During the time of the German occupation and the ghetto, she was very active in the Organization for Resistance and Rebellion (PPA), along with Abba Kovner and Vitke Kempner. In September 1943, she left for the forest of Rudniki with the last of the fighters and took part in the partisans' armed resistance. In July 1944, Korchak-Marle

at Mila 18, and whether he knew anything about the final moments in the bunker. He looked at me for a long while, his gaze focused far beyond me, and this is what he said, "Would to God I had the strength to contemplate what those men were feeling in their last moments." And said no more.

November 5

A group of partisans passed through our post. I remembered their comrade (Ruschka)* whom I had heard at a trade union conference. I told them about the *Palmaḥniks* in the hall who wept when she described how the leader of the underground went to his death.* They were not all from the same place (there was one who had been with Haviva* in the Slovakian revolt) but most of them had been active in the forests of Lithuania and Byelorussia. Among them was the second Leo, a boy who had been a companion of Leo Arendt in the Dinslaken orphanage. His name now is Lenz and it was no accident that the two recognized each other. From the moment they came together, they have been having a conversation that must be without parallel in this world. They have been sitting together for three days now and most of the night they tell each other everything they have been through. I just listen.

and her unit of partisans returned to liberated Vilna. That same year–in December–she reached Palestine and for the first time told her story at the Histadrut Congress (January 1945) and wrote her book, *Lahavot Ba-Efer* (Flames in the Ashes), which tells the story of the torment and the struggle of Jewish Vilna before its destruction. In 1946, with a group of fellow fighters, she joined the kibbutz Ein Ha-Ḥoresh. Korchak-Marle was very active in the Zionist movement and its educational institutions, on her own kibbutz, and through personal contact with hundreds of friends and fellow activists. She died of an illness in March, 1988.

. . . **HOW THE LEADER OF THE UNDERGROUND WENT TO HIS DEATH**: "The leader of the organization of Jewish fighters in the Vilna ghetto was Itzik Wittenberg. He was a member of the Communist Party, and maintained contact with members of the party beyond the ghetto walls. One of them was arrested by the Gestapo and betrayed Wittenberg. On July 15, 1943, the Germans came to the ghetto and arrested him. Members of the fighting organization released him by force and hid him within the ghetto. The Germans gave the ghetto an ultimatum, threatening to destroy it. The head of the *Judenrat* insisted that one man be handed over and 20,000 thereby be saved. The Jewish masses were incensed by the underground, and they were on the verge of fighting, Jew against Jew. In the end it was decided, largely by the Communist cell in the ghetto, that Wittenberg should turn himself in. He went to the gate, to death at the hands of the Gestapo. The hardest day for the ghetto was the day Wittenberg died." –RUSCHKA KORCHAK-MARLE, *Flames in the Ashes*

"**He walked erect, a free man.** Behind him, as though in shame, trailed a policeman; beside him strode one of his comrades. For the last time, with measured tread, he passed Oszmianska Lane, the site of his headquarters, where men paid him respect, and Rudnitzke Street, where yesterday the daring Jewish fighters had bravely set him free. He was a veteran member of the Communist Party, experienced in the struggle for freedom and socialism. Now his death resembled the holy martyrdom of his forefathers. Was this what he was thinking now, in his last moments among his fellow-Jews–deluded, overwrought, totally humiliated–and among his fellow-fighters?" –RUSCHKA KORCHAK-MARLE, *Flames in the Ashes*

HAVIVA (1914-1944): An exemplary figure among the parachutists from Palestine who worked behind the enemy lines in 1944. Haviva Reik was born in the village of Slowki, near the town of Banska-Bystrica, Slovakia, went to a Jewish school, and joined a Zionist youth group. In 1939, before the outbreak of war, she made *aliyah* and was among the founders of the kibbutz Ma'anit. During the war, Reik volunteered to parachute into her hometown. Her mission was to reach Bratislava and make contact with a certain underground group, but she arrived too late. A revolt against the Nazi occupation had broken out in Slovakia, with the participation of partisans trained by Soviet officers and units of the Slovakian army. The uprising lasted six weeks. The German army was called in to suppress it and succeeded in doing so. Reik fled to the hills with a group of Jewish fighters, but was caught, interrogated under torture, and executed on November 20, 1944.

FRUMKE PLOTNITZKA (1914-1943): Plotnitzka was born to a Hasidic family in a small town in the region of Pinsk. She joined the kibbutz Hakhsharah at Bialystok and took part in Zionist movement seminars. She visited *kibbutzim,* gave them encouragement, and provided assistance. She dreamed of *aliyah* and living on a kibbutz. With the outbreak of war, Plotnitzka became a central figure in the Polish underground movement. She traveled the length and breadth of the occupied country and was the first to bring news to Warsaw of the mass extermination. With the establishment of the Jewish Fighting Organization, she became a contact for non-Jews outside the ghetto (with Toussia Altman, Arie Wilner, and others) and organized resistance. She survived the crushing of the Warsaw ghetto uprising, but her sister and most of her comrades were among the fallen. Plotnitzka died in Bedzin in defense of the bunker she shared with members of the kibbutz Hakhsharah on August 3, 1943.

PULVERFABRIK (German): Gunpowder factory.

November 6

I didn't hear everything and I didn't understand everything that I did hear. I felt uncomfortable, as though I were looking through a keyhole. They can see me sitting at the table (they are at the end of the bed) but my presence doesn't bother them. It's as though during the time when they are communing in a kind of conspiracy of memories, no one else can penetrate their circle.

November 7

The two have renewed their friendship. Leo intends to come to Palestine and Lenz has his eyes on America.

November 8

Dvora knew Frumke[+] very well. She met her in Warsaw and Vilna. She told us of her final days: an emissary had been sent from Slovakia to rescue her. He succeeded in meeting her in the bunker at Bedzin, but Frumke refused to move. She told the emissary, "I lived among my people and I shall die among them."

November 9

From the same meeting with the partisans came this information about the Liberation Assembly in Minsk. That was the day when the partisan units from the forests in the area came together to the capital of Byelorussia for a victory parade. Men and women for whom this was the most important day in their lives hugged and kissed each other, drank and danced in the streets. Not one of the units pitched its camp in the devastated area of the ghetto.

The head of the high command spoke of the suffering of the nations and the heroism of those who fought behind the enemy lines. He mentioned all the peoples who had taken part in the partisan movement, enumerating them one by one. But not a single word about the Jewish partisans, who had been among the first to fall in battle. Not a mention of the hundred thousand slaughtered in the Minsk ghetto. "Believe me," Lenz told his friend, "I feel a lot of love and gratitude to the Russians, but when I slipped across the frontier at Graz, I instinctively turned around–and spat."

November 15

When I entered Trofaiach, I had to hold my breath. The sights, the smell, the sounds. I was standing in the middle of a petrified forest. All around there were snow-capped mountains and over the gate there was a sign, *"Pulverfabrik."*[+] Exposed watch towers. From the central hut of the erstwhile concentration camp, which had become a club, emerged the sound of singing and feet stamping in a wild *hora*. As soon as they recognized the uniforms of the Jewish Brigade, there was a sudden hush and all eyes turned on us as though on some prophetic revelation. There were fifteen hundred of them, from most of the countries of Europe. In summer clothing. With torn shoes. The daily ration of bread is four hundred grams!

"What's that stink?" I asked my escort.

"It's the crematorium." The fellow pointed to a path, which led to a clearing in the forest. My skin bristled. Judenburg. Graz. Villach. Innsbruck. Vols. Salzburg.

All week I've been on the road. Traveling continually northward, across the Alps, to the refugee camps scattered across Austria. Everywhere general meetings were held. Everywhere they waited to hear from me news of the end of their wanderings.

Tomorrow I'm leaving for Paris for a convention of leaders of the Briḥah.✝

November 17

They stayed in a small, flea-bitten hotel whose windows overlooked the Boulevard Montparnasse. S., the head of the Mossad,✝ and S. C., in charge of procurement, didn't change their clothing, they hardly had time to eat, and already they were behind locked doors for a marathon session. Having nothing to do, I went off to feast the eyes of a Sabra from Galilee on the lights of Paris and the loungers in the famous cafes of Montparnasse.

November 18

I didn't see much of the lights of the "*Cité des Lumières.*"✝ But I cannot put out of my mind what happened to me last night. There's a hotel here in the neighborhood called the Lutetia. Survivors of the camps and others who have returned from deportation come here to seek information about their relatives. I didn't know what kind of a place it was until I approached the people crowding in the entrance. Mostly women. Then I saw a boy running after a woman and calling, "Mommy! Mommy!" Wrapped in a heavy sweater that screened half her face, the woman was leaving the place as though fleeing the boy who came chasing after her. At the entrance to a bistro, the woman abruptly turned around and shouted with suppressed fury, "I'm not your mother!" and with a single gesture removed the sweater from her head. A mass of hair framed a pretty face, still young, and there was no pity in her voice, "Can't you see I'm not your mother?" and at once she was swallowed up in the haze of the bistro, while the boy remained standing on the edge of the sidewalk, gaping dumbstruck. He didn't cry. But a long time after, when I drew near, he recognized the Shield of David on my insignia. He asked if I was a Palestinian soldier. I invited him into the cafe. His name was Robert, and he was ten years old. His father, Dr. Sternheim, had been a well-known doctor in Paris. When the Germans occupied Paris, Robert had been with his mother in Nice.

His mother had been a member of the fashionable society in the artist's quarter, and was quite unconcerned about their fate. When the Jews were ordered to register, of her own free will she reported to the police station. The second-in-command of the Nice police, an albino, a lover of painting and an enthusiastic admirer of the moderns—"though most of them are Jews, the ones they call '*fauves*'"✝—was totally bewildered that morning. "Surely, Madame, there is a mistake. You?"

"I am Jewish, monsieur," she said without fear, without pride. In all innocence she had gone in and in all innocence she left. Three days later she was deported to the camp at Gurs. She decided to wear her fur ski jacket, though this was the end of the summer of 1942, hotter than usual, and into her square, velvet-lined handbag, next to her Chanel No. 5, her lipstick, and a brush for her eyelashes, she placed a packet of pastel crayons and a drawing pad. Her Italian chambermaid liked to tell how Madame was somewhat concerned about her high-heeled shoes. In the end she took one pair for special occasions, or as a lucky charm. Though unaware of what was in store, she asked the Italian girl if she knew what a sad joy was. When Mam'selle rolled her eyes in ignorance, Madame explained, "That Robert is not with me." She said this in the doorway and left.

THE BRIḤAH: An illegal organization for the transport of Jews from eastern to central Europe and Italy, and from there to Palestine. The initiative for the organization of the Briḥah came from Jewish partisans, ghetto fighters, and graduates of the youth movements who had spent the war as refugees in the Soviet Union, all of whom realized that there was no future for the Jews in their former countries. The organization continued from 1945 to 1948. The illegal transport of Jews worked in various ways: with the help of forged documents, bribery, and the exploitation of any opportunity to steal across the borders. Centers of the Briḥah and absorption camps were set up (supported and financed by the Joint Distribution Committee for refugees assistance). After the pogrom at Kielce in 1946, the flood of refugees from Poland increased. About 200,000 people passed through the Briḥah, approximately 80 percent of all the Jewish refugees who left Eastern Europe.

MOSSAD: Jewish secret intelligence unit.

"CITÉ DES LUMIÈRES" (French): City of lights, a term for Paris.

'FAUVES' (French): Literally, wild ones. The term refers to a movement of painters founded in France at the end of the nineteenth century.

✤ Chapter Fourteen: Crossing the Sea ✤

CLOCHARD (French): A homeless tramp, one of the poor wretches who frequented Paris and slept under the bridges or in stations of the Métro.

PONT NEUF: "New Bridge." The name of one of the bridges over the Seine River.

TELLMAN BRIGADE: A German military unit of the International Brigade, which fought for the Republican Government during the Spanish Civil War (1936-1939). The unit was named in honor of the leader of the German Communist Party, Ernst Tellman (1886-1944), who was imprisoned in 1933, tortured, and put to death by the Nazis in one of the concentration camps when the Soviet army was nearing the borders of Germany.

An incident in the history of the rescue of French Jewish children.

During the period between June 1940 and November 1942, all of southern France was under the control of a French government (the Vichy Government) and free of Germans. The Jewish organizations made great efforts to rescue people who were not French citizens, especially children, and who were awaiting deportation. As the economic situation grew worse in the summer of 1942 and the mass transport of Jews to the death camps began in the southern region, non-Jewish public figures also took up the struggle to rescue Jewish children. The priest Bagnère turned to Pierre Laval, head of the Vichy Government, with a demand for the release of 10,000 children from impending arrest:

Bagnère: "Do you realize that in this way we shall be saving the children from certain death?"

Laval: "Whatever happens, the children must remain with their parents."

Bagnère: "But you know very well they will be separated from their parents. . . ."

Laval: "I know nothing of the kind. . . ."

Bagnère: "I tell you they will!"

Laval: "What do you want done with the children?"

Bagnère: "At least let them be adopted by French families."

Laval: "No, I'm not prepared to do that. I don't want even one of them to remain in France."

GARE DE L'EST: The eastern railway station in Paris.

To Denmark—a debt of gratitude.

(Information found in Hezi's briefcase, which he did not manage to include in his letter to his wife Ruth. He took down the details from Leo Arendt, everything that he saw in Denmark and that happened to him crossing the borders).

There was a Dane whose name was Jurgen Holbergsen, a teacher and editor of a local newspaper, *The Christian.* The name of the place was Lingbi, north of

Robert was practicing the piano that day at the other end of the town. The lesson was about to end when the telephone rang and his teacher told him to carry on for another hour, since tomorrow he would have to travel to a village "where there won't be a piano."

In the last year of the war, Robert fled the home of his benefactors and made his way under his own steam to Paris. A one-armed *clochard** known as l'Espagnol found him swollen with hunger and cold and took him under his wing—under his bridge. Actually, the *clochard* moved from under the Pont Neuf,* for a rumor had spread that the Germans were about to blow up the bridges over the Seine, and took Robert to his niche in a tunnel of the Métro, the underground railway system, far from the bridges, near a station called Platieu. This was the base from which Robert searched for his father. By night l'Espagnol would tell him about Barcelona and the Ebro and the members of the Tellman Brigade* who became so immersed in war that they even fired in their sleep and died heroes' deaths. And the boy did not know if this was true or whether l'Espagnol was just trying to amuse him. He told him about the camp at Gurs, where they had taken his mother, where the members of the International Brigade who escaped from Spain had once been imprisoned, "though then they never sent anyone to Poland."

One day l'Espagnol disappeared, and the boy was taken in by a Jewish woman who was also living on the edge of society. She was the mother of the underground hero, Marcel Raimand.

At the Hotel Lutetia he heard that his father had died in Auschwitz and his brother had not succeeded in getting to Palestine and was last seen on a death march on German soil.

The three days I was in Paris I met Robert several times but failed to persuade him to come with me. His mother, his father, his brother, his grandfather and grandmother on his mother's side, and two cousins were all sent to Auschwitz and none returned. But Robert will keep coming back to the Hotel Lutetia.*

On the train

More about little Robert. He came to the station to say goodbye. The sun was hiding behind the Gare de l'Est* and left us to our thoughts. For a long while we stood there silent together, the boy and I.

"I'm afraid I'll forget what they look like," he said suddenly.

"You don't forget your parents," I had to say something.

"It's happened to me twice that I made a mistake. I don't have any pictures."

December 21

Time goes by so slowly here, if it weren't for Sabbaths and Jewish festivals we would be totally unaware of its passing. I must get Leo to tell me about the rescue of the Jews of Denmark. He was there. How is it that in tiny Denmark things were different?*

the capital city of Copenhagen. The persecution of the Jews had already begun. And Holbergsen went to Bodinge Lane to visit the house where his friend David was in hiding. And the rain increased in violence and the houses in Bodinge Lane grew cold and gloomy, and Jurgen Holbergsen never imagined that this dark October night would mark the dawn of a new era in his life. He was 40 years old, the author of articles and books on literature, art, and philosophy, and David was a young man of 20.

And the hunt for Jews began. When Jurgen came to the bedroom, which led to the secret room, and opened the inner door, his friend did not turn to greet him, for he was praying. It was the Eve of the New Year 5704 (1943), and Jurgen had never seen a Jew praying before, and David was wrapped in a prayer shawl. Holbergsen sensed that he should not interrupt, but he could not restrain himself and told him, his coat still dripping water, that his neighbors had managed to get to Sweden but had been compelled to leave their children behind in Copenhagen until there was a children's convoy. The neighbors were a husband and wife, refugees from Prague, and when their children were refused admission to the boat, they wanted to commit suicide, for this was their third flight and their ability to bear suffering was exhausted. Eva Lund took the children under her wing; she was also responsible for the underground organization of the children's convoy. At five o'clock that morning, Inspector Mordisen, the head of the police in Lingbi, informed them that large concentrations of Gestapo forces had been discovered in the next village and a fleet of black boats (like the color of the Gestapo uniform) had secretly sailed out from the bay. All the time he was telling him, David did not stop praying and did not budge from the wall that pointed toward Jerusalem. Only when he was told, "I came to ask you to join the convoy, since it's a rule of the underground not to send out children without a reliable adult to accompany them," did David turn toward him, and from the way he wrinkled his eyebrows under the prayer shawl that swathed his forehead, Jurgen understood that he wanted to know when. "Tomorrow," said Holbergsen. "I'm sorry it's a holy day for you." He expected to be asked why that day of all days had been chosen. David was not yet thinking of escape, for he had a sick mother in Lingbi. He nodded his head in agreement and turned once more toward Jerusalem. The murmur of the words in the ancient language sounded to Jurgen like the rustle of a small fjord, and David's body swayed and bowed as though moving toward the unseen Jerusalem. Jurgen Holbergsen thought of what he would put in the book he would one day write, and at that moment, "I felt in my heart all the profundity and tension of a Jewish spiritual life, and my soul was filled with a mysterious feeling of holiness and solemnity in the room . . . if Jesus could have come back to earth now, he would have felt more at home here than in most churches."

And the hunt began. But the German plan to round up the Jews of Denmark on the Eve of the New Year and send them in boats to the port

January 2, 1947

Today's topic of conversation: *Les Enfants du Paradis.* We got the film to celebrate the civil New Year. I saw tears in people's eyes.

January 5

Krisia has begun to speak! The miracle was brought about by Velvele. Velvele, the youngest of the partisans, fell sick with jaundice, and stayed with us to convalesce. Krisia nursed him and he told her his history. Once upon a time there was a boy, and after they took away his father and mother and killed his brothers and sisters and his grandmother, he was left alone and went off to the forest to seek his uncle, who was a partisan.

The boy found no partisans but he did find cows. He hired himself out to a cowherd who had lost a leg in the war. For some time he was the boy who took the village cows to pasture. It was a remote village where nobody knew him and he knew nobody. He had a trustworthy face

of Stettin, and from there to the death camps of Poland, was frustrated by the Danish people. The action that saved the 7,000 Jews of Denmark was led by the anti-Nazi underground movement, assisted by thousands of Danes who offered temporary shelter, medical teams, railway linesmen, guides, and brave fishermen who set off in rowing boats for Sweden. And one should not forget the German naval attaché at Copenhagen (Leo asked that his name not be mentioned, lest it cause him harm), who betrayed secret orders and provided the underground command with information on the timing of the deportation. All this was recounted in due course by Eva Lund, a Danish scientist, in those days a wireless operator for the underground, 18 years old and known by the sailors as "Little Red Riding Hood" because of her red beret that could be seen bobbing on the quayside before dawn.

Eva and Anna were traveling once in a subway train (Leo was also with them, making a face because they were talking aloud about the business of rescuing Jews). Suddenly one of the passengers rose from her seat, turned toward them and said, "Do you need a little money?" and without waiting for an answer removed Eva's red beret and poured into it the total contents of her purse, coins and bank notes, and resumed her seat. They didn't even ask her name. At that time there was also anonymous goodness.

A Homeland for Every Jew in the World
(a journey to the Pyrenean frontier)

When the Germans invaded Holland, they found there a Jewish community of 140,000 souls. A general strike called by the Dutch in protest against the first persecutions of their Jewish neighbors was put down with cruelty. Subsequently the Germans deported 106,000 Jews to the camps of Eastern Europe, of whom 5,000 survived. The underground succeeded in smuggling young people via Belgium-France-Spain to Palestine. The leaders of the underground—Shosho, that is, Yochanan Simon, and Joup Vestruyl, a non-Jew, headmaster of a Montessori school—were captured and executed by the Germans.

These are the words spoken by Joup Vestruyl in a windswept hillside chalet on the Pyrenean frontier as he parted from his Jewish comrades before they crossed the border: "In a few days time you will be free. Soon your feet will tread the soil of freedom and you will be able to fulfill your destiny of rebuilding Palestine, creating a homeland for every Jew in the world. I wish every one of you success in the completion of this mission. But don't forget your comrades, thanks to whom you are able to reach freedom, those who gave all their strength and those who gave their lives so that you could achieve your aim. Build your country, and continue to act in accordance with their spirit. Remember Shosho, and Hannemann, and all the others who sacrificed themselves on your behalf. Remember the great grief of the world and build Palestine so that there be no more wars, but work and bread for all. I wish you a safe passage to freedom, a life of liberty and happiness."

189

and he made up some story about his life and they believed him. He spent a summer and a winter with the cows; in the end he forgot where he came from or what his name was. One day when he returned from grazing he noticed people were giving him some strange looks. That night the *soltis,* the head man of the village, came to his hut, accompanied by a stranger who scratched his back against the door post. The eyes of the stranger flickered in narrow, dark chimneys like inverted gun sights and he was wearing breeches. He spat out the pit of some fruit he had been chewing and nodded to the *soltis.*

The village elder held the boy by the ear and said, "You lied to us. Your name is Velvele and you're the son of Chaim-Ozer."

Velvele kissed the hand of the old man and said imploringly, "I wanted to live, I'm an orphan. Have pity on me, sir."

The old man said, "I'll tell you what you can do. Go to town and ask them to shoot you. In any event, you won't survive till the end of the war, and you'll cause harm to others. You don't want to harm good people, do you?"

That's what the village elder said. When the stranger asked for Velvele to be bound and led to town like an animal, so that they could collect a ransom from the Germans, the *soltis* admonished him and said, "We'll leave him a few days till we find another boy to replace him. Then he can be on his way."

Maybe he left the boy an avenue of escape or maybe the old man meant what he said. The next morning Velvele took the cows out as usual to the pasture beyond the hill with the wild marguerites. He felt nauseated. The same cows that he had grown to like and called by name, which seemed so beautiful as they grazed quietly among the clover and the cornflowers, now filled him with loathing. He couldn't look at their udders, so disgustingly replete. When the time came for them to return, he led the cows down the slope of the hill toward the village and set off himself in the opposite direction. For hours Velvele raced along unfrequented paths without looking back. Suddenly he was aware of the oncoming darkness and very much afraid. Where was he running to, and which was the path to salvation? Ten kilometers distant from the point where he crossed the river there was a partisan campfire burning. But he didn't see its light, and the partisans sitting around the fire, his uncle Sha'ul at their head, didn't hear the boy breathing like a wild animal that has climbed out of a pit.

January 6

After three days a column of partisans came from the east, a Russian at their head. And they took the boy out of the pit[+] and gave him food and drink, and the commissar took him under his protection. And for three months the partisans encamped in a valley, which was bare of forest. At the end of the valley there was a stock of bombs that the Soviet Air Force had abandoned during the retreat but not destroyed. The commissar taught Velvele how to disarm the bombs and thus provide the partisans with more explosives for making mines and blowing up German trains. The commissar also said, "If you carry out your duty bravely, the time will come when you will be awarded a medal for gallantry, for your contribution to the Great Patriotic War."

And Velvele faithfully performed his task. He would sit crouched over the back of a huge bomb, leaning over the nose, and very cautiously do as instructed until the detonator budged slightly between his fingers. His hands did not tremble as he removed the fuse from the bomb and placed it on the grass.

Every morning the boy went down to the valley of the bombs and fulfilled his quota for the day and never asked why he was the one chosen for the job, though he saw the small red flags placed all around the site to warn the partisans not to approach the danger area; they might get hurt if the boy should blunder. (I heard all this from Krisia, for Velvele had already left for Landsberg.) Once when he was hitting the top of the screwdriver with a hammer, he heard clicks like the ticking of a clock. He was convinced that by mistake he had activated the detonator of the bomb. He thought his heart would burst, his feet turned to stone, and he closed his eyes in anticipation of death's fiery chariot. His eyes were still closed when he realized the dry clicks came from beyond the bomb and he saw the head of a bird in the undergrowth pecking at the bark of a tree. And then Krisia said, "That was your ram."

Velvele said, "That wasn't a ram, it was only a woodpecker."

Krisia said, "But it's just like the story of Isaac."[+]

And Velvele asked no questions, just kissed her on the

AND THEY TOOK THE BOY OUT OF THE PIT: When Midianite traders passed by, they pulled Joseph up out of the pit. They sold Joseph for twenty pieces of silver to the Ishmaelites, who brought Joseph to Egypt. —GENESIS 37:28

Then Isaac said to his father Abraham, "Father!" And he answered, "Yes, my son." And he said, "Here are the firestone and the wood: but where is the sheep for the burnt offering?" And Abraham said, "God will see to the sheep for His burnt offering, my son." And the two of them walked on together. And they arrived at the place of which God had told him.

They arrived at the place of which God had told him. Abraham built an altar there; he laid out the wood; he bound his son Isaac; he laid him on the altar, on top of the wood. And Abraham picked up the knife to slay his son. Then an angel of the Lord called to him from heaven, "Abraham! Abraham!" And he answered, "Here I am." And he said, "Do not raise your hand against the boy, or do anything to him. For now I know that you fear God, since you have not withheld your son, your favored one, from Me." When Abraham looked up, his eye fell upon a ram, caught in the thicket by its horns. And Abraham went and took the ram and offered it up as a burnt offering in place of his son.

—GENESIS 22: 7–13

CHAIM ARLOSOROFF: The *Chaim Arlosoroff* ran the British blockade. The captain ran the ship aground on a sand bank opposite Bat Galim, near Haifa. More than 1,300 illegal immigrants were taken by force to deportation vessels. About 30 of them were injured while fiercely resisting the deportation. This took place on February 27, 1947.

forehead, as though it was natural for Krisia to speak without sobbing. The next day I asked Krisia where she heard the story of the Binding of Isaac, and she gazed at me a long while, wondering and searching her mind, and said, "Once, once I was sitting on my grandfather's knees and I think I heard it from him."

January 18

Before Velvele left he taught Krisia the song the Jewish partisans used to sing.✦ Now the whole camp sings the song and many of them stand up as though they were singing "Ha-Tikvah."

February 14

Tomorrow we go on board. A large ship. More than thirteen hundred will go on board. It's called the *Chaim Arlosoroff.*✦ Ahrele, the captain, made a speech. He explained to them what it was all about. That there would be difficulties and there might be violent clashes. "If anyone is afraid and wants to wait for a legal boat"—he kept repeating—"this is the moment to decide." Leo was sitting next to me, biting his fingernails with growing irritation. I know him, which is why I hastened to ask him if anything had happened. Leo said, "Tell your friend he doesn't have to frighten us. We're Jews who are not afraid anymore. Tell him." He rose and went to the door of the hall and opened it. A chill, salt wind blew in through the wide open door. And people's heads turned toward the door. Leo was standing there with his eyes closed. His eyelids blinked as though affected by the regular cycle of the tides. At that moment a new moon was breaking through a desolate, muddy sky, like the smile in a child's drawing. From some secret source the rocky shore was suddenly flooded with wave upon wave of light.

July 3, 1985 · 14 Tammuz 5745
Ein Ha-Ḥoresh, Tel Aviv

Never say there's only death
for you
Though leaden clouds are hiding
skies of blue
Because the hour we hungered
for is near;
Beneath our tread earth
trembles: we are here!
From lands of palms to distant
wastes of snow
We're coming with our torment
and our woe,
And everywhere our blood has
stained the earth,
Our bravery, our vigor blossom
forth!
The morning sun shall set our
day aglow,
Our yesterdays shall vanish with
the foe,
And if time drags before the sun
appears,
This song shall be a signal
through the years.
We wrote this song with blood,
and not with lead;
It's not a song that birds sing
overhead.
It was a people at the barricades
Who sang this song with pistols
and grenades.
So never say there's only death
for you,
Though leaden clouds are hiding
skies of blue
Because the hour we hungered
for is near;
Beneath our tread earth
trembles: we are here!

—HIRSH GLICK, based on an
English version by Aron Cremer